CRITIQUE
OF
PRACTICAL REASON

Immanuel Kant

CRITIQUE
OF
PRACTICAL REASON

Translated by

Werner S. Pluhar

Introduction by

Stephen Engstrom

Hackett Publishing Company, Inc.
INDIANAPOLIS/CAMBRIDGE

Immanuel Kant: 1724–1804

The *Critique of Practical Reason* was originally published in 1788.

Copyright © 2002 by Hackett Publishing Company, Inc.

08 07 06 05 04 03 02   1 2 3 4 5 6 7

For further information, please address:

Hackett Publishing Company, Inc.
P.O. Box 44937
Indianapolis, IN 46244-0937

www.hackettpublishing.com

Cover design by Listenberger Design & Associates

Library of Congress Cataloging-in-Publication Data

Kant, Immanuel, 1724–1804.
    [Kritik der praktischen Vernunft. English]
    Critique of practical reason / Immanuel Kant; translated by Werner S.
Pluhar; introduction by Stephen Engstrom.
        p.   cm.
    Includes bibliographical references (p.) and index.
    ISBN 0-87220-618-1 (cloth) — ISBN 0-87220-617-3 (paper)
    1. Practical reason. I. Pluhar, Werner S., 1940– . II. Title.
B2773.E5P59   2002
170—dc21   2002024148

The paper used in this publication meets the minimum requirements of American National Standard for Information Sciences—Permanence of Paper for Printed Library Materials, ANSI Z39.48-1984. ∞

To Elissa,

Nina and Jarrett

CONTENTS

CRITIQUE OF
PRACTICAL REASON

TRANSLATOR'S PREFACE

Kant's second *Critique* is, for me as translator, the third; my first was the *Critique of Judgment*[1] (Kant's third), my second the *Critique of Pure Reason*.[2] This sequence is no accident. Kant's third *Critique* was generally agreed to be the one most in need of a new translation.[3] The first was, by comparison, in much better condition; of the available translations, that by Norman Kemp Smith,[4] although deficient in various respects, had served scholars well for decades—even though, during the same time period, there was a steadily and significantly increasing need by Kant scholars for greater accuracy. The *Critique of Practical Reason,* on the other hand, has fared best of all. Among the translations available until a few years ago, the most favored was that by Lewis White Beck;[5] his translation, apart from having profited from Beck's profound familiarity with Kant's moral theory, was

---

[1] With an introduction by Werner S. Pluhar and a preface by Mary J. Gregor. Indianapolis, Ind.: Hackett, 1987.

[2] With an introduction by Patricia Kitcher. Indianapolis, Ind.: Hackett, 1996. There is also an abridged version of this translation, with an introduction by Eric Watkins. Indianapolis, Ind.: Hackett, 1999.

[3] In the mid-seventies, at Grinnell College in Iowa, I was teaching a Kant course that included the third *Critique.* Finding myself frustrated by the seeming impenetrability of much of the material as I found it in the existing translations, I decided to delve into the German original— and found, to my amazement, that the original was, on the whole, vastly clearer than the translations. By a fortuitous coincidence, the illustrious Lewis White Beck was visiting my department just then, and I expressed to him my frustration with the translations. His reaction was quick and simple. "Why don't *you* translate the *Critique of Judgment?*" he replied. I was stunned; the idea had never occurred to me. But it took hold, and I soon embarked on my first major project of translating Kant.

[4] London: Macmillan; New York: St. Martin's, 1929. 2nd impression with corrections. London: Macmillan; New York: St. Martin's, 1933, 1989.

[5] *Critique of Practical Reason, and Other Writings in Moral Philosophy.* Translated and edited, with an introduction, by Lewis White Beck. Chicago: University of Chicago Press,

xi

praised for being extraordinarily easy to read. However, Beck had attained this high degree of readability in part by sacrificing terminological consistency—even for key terms in Kant's philosophy—and thus, in effect, accuracy. This defect was finally addressed, with tremendous skill, in the recent translation of the second *Critique* by another great expert in Kant's moral theory: Mary J. Gregor.[6] On close scrutiny of Gregor's excellent work, however, I became convinced that even it still suffered from significant problems that needed to be remedied.[7] This new translation seeks to eliminate, as much as possible, these remaining problems. In addition, its appearance will make the three *Critiques* available, for the first time, in uniform English terminology.

This translation, like my previous ones, has profited immensely from contributions made by two eminent Kant scholars: Professor James W. Ellington, whose skill and sensitivity as a Kant translator I greatly admire, and Professor Stephen Engstrom. Ellington's contributions are indicated below. Engstrom's contribution is his exceedingly fine Introduction to this volume.

This translation of Kant's *Critique of Practical Reason* is based on the standard edition of Kant's works, *Kants gesammelte Schriften*, Königlich Preußische Akademie der Wissenschaften (Berlin: G. Reimer; Berlin and New York: Walter de Gruyter & Co. and Predecessors, 1902–), vol. 5, edited, with introduction, variant readings, and factual elucidations, by Paul Natorp (1908).

Like my two previous translations, this one also is copiously annotated. Kant's own footnotes are distinguished from the translator's footnotes by their larger print, by bold footnote and reference numbers, and by the ab-

---

[1949]. The *Critique* by itself. 3rd ed., with notes. New York: Macmillan; Toronto: Maxwell Macmillan Canada; New York: Maxwell Macmillan International, 1993; Upper Saddle River, N.J.: Prentice Hall, 1993. For the other earlier translations of Kant's second *Critique*—those by Thomas Abbott and Heinrich Cassirer (the latter published only recently)—see the Selected Bibliography.

[6] *Critique of Practical Reason.* Translated and edited by Mary Gregor; with an introduction by Andrews Reath. Cambridge Texts in the History of Philosophy. Cambridge: Cambridge University Press, 1997.

[7] The defects, briefly, are the following. Gregor's appropriately heightened concern for accuracy has unfortunately resulted in a significant loss of readability: her grammar is often unclear because of excessively convoluted sentence structure. Moreover, she frequently uses English pronouns that, unlike their German originals, leave their referents ambiguous; and even she commits occasional important but unnecessary terminological inconsistencies. Finally, in some places Gregor simply misreads or misunderstands the German text.

sence of brackets. Translator's footnotes use smaller print, have no bold numbers, and are bracketed. When a Kantian footnote has a footnote in turn, this latter note is referenced by a lower-case letter, and its number is the same as that of the original note but is followed by the lower-case letter.

Of the translator's footnotes, many contain references to other relevant passages in the work and to other Kantian works; I owe most of these notes to Ellington's kind efforts and keen expertise. Others provide references to works by other authors, explanatory comments, variant readings, or translations (all of which are my own). Still other such notes concern terminology. Of these, some explain or defend my renderings of certain German terms, but most give the original German terms whenever an original term has been translated rather freely or is otherwise of special importance or interest; whenever terminological relationships between adjacent terms in the original have either been lost or (seemingly) been created in translation; or whenever either the same German term is translated by different English terms or different German terms are translated by the same English term in the same context. The German terms are usually given in such footnotes not as they appear in the original, but as they can be found—by interested readers—in a modern German dictionary: viz., in their modern spelling, and the verbs in the infinitive, the nouns in the nominative, etc.

References provided in this volume are given as follows. Page references in the table of contents are to the pagination of the present volume. In footnotes, references to the text of the work are given by the page numbers of the *Akademie* edition, which appear in the margins of this translation. Similarly, references to footnotes give the *Akademie* edition's page containing the footnote's reference number, and then the footnote's number (or number and lower-case letter) preceded either by 'n.' ('ns.' in the plural) or by 'br. n.' ('br. ns.' in the plural)—respectively, for notes containing Kantian materials, or bracketed notes provided by the translator. References to other works by Kant are also to the *Akademie* edition and are given as 'Ak.', followed by volume and page numbers and, as applicable, by 'n.' for a note, except that references to the *Critique of Pure Reason* follow the standard format for that work, by indicating 'A' and 'B' (for the first and second original editions) and then the page numbers in those editions.

At the end of this volume will be found a Selected Bibliography, a Glossary of the most important German terms in the work along with my translations of them, and an Index.

Acknowledgments: In the course of translating the second *Critique* I frequently checked the translation by Mary Gregor, and occasionally also that by Lewis White Beck. I am tremendously grateful to Professor James W. Ellington for the contributions already mentioned, but especially for his careful reading of the entire manuscript. Indeed, Ellington's contribution to my translation of all three *Critiques* as a whole has been immeasurable. I address sincerest thanks, once again, to the various members of Hackett Publishing Company for their superbly professional and exceedingly friendly collaboration at every stage of this project. My warmest and deepest gratitude is reserved for my wife, Dr. Elissa J. Hoffman, whose expertise as a psychiatrist and writer has allowed me to share with her many philosophical and linguistic queries and qualms, and whose empathy and kindness have been immensely supportive to my project.

WERNER SCHRUTKA PLUHAR

The Pennsylvania State University
Fayette Campus, Uniontown

INTRODUCTION*

The *Critique of Practical Reason* (1788) is the second of the famous three *Critiques* that together form the core of Immanuel Kant's philosophical writings. In these works, Kant assesses the cognitive powers of the human mind with the aim of expounding, justifying, and delimiting the use that can be made of them a priori, or without the aid of experience. Each *Critique* investigates these capacities as they are employed in a different domain of activity. The *Critique of Pure Reason* (1781) examines the theoretical use of reason in the natural sciences; the *Critique of Practical Reason* is concerned with the use of reason in action, and in particular with the rational principles of morality that govern human conduct; and the *Critique of Judgment* (1790) considers the power of judgment as it is employed in our assessments of the products of nature and of human art as beautiful or purposive.

The second *Critique* is largely a self-contained work, which may profitably be studied by readers who lack a detailed acquaintance with the other *Critiques*. But as Kant is a systematic philosopher par excellence, a full appreciation of this work requires an understanding of the place it occupies within his philosophical system. Of particular significance is the fact that the second *Critique* carries to completion the momentous project Kant initiated in the first *Critique* of rethinking speculative metaphysics as it had been practiced throughout the entire history of Western philosophy. Although the second *Critique* is of interest to many readers today mainly because of the light it throws on particular themes and issues within Kant's ethical theory, Kant is grappling in this work with the much larger question of how ethics and metaphysics themselves are related.

In addressing this larger issue, Kant is responding in part to a general problem that had become pressing in his day and that has remained with us to the present. Ever since the bloody religious conflicts of the Reformation and the emergence of science and secular society in the modern period, philosophers have looked for ways of providing a secure basis for morality that is independent of the specific religious creeds and traditions that have

XV

divided society and culture throughout the modern era. Others before Kant had also sought solutions. Gottfried Wilhelm von Leibniz and his followers, for example, endeavored to provide ethics with a rational metaphysical foundation, and David Hume attempted to trace moral principles to an empirically discoverable source in human nature. Similar concerns have moved others after Kant as well. Many philosophers have been drawn to more recently developed moral theories, such as the nineteenth-century utilitarianism of Jeremy Bentham, John Stuart Mill, and Henry Sidgwick, or the emotivist theories that were popular in the mid-twentieth century, because such theories seem well suited to a secular, scientific outlook.

In the second *Critique* Kant pursues this larger issue to its deepest level. In addition to asking whether the principle of morality, the most basic standard of right and wrong, has its basis in experience or a priori in reason, Kant takes on the question whether ethics depends on any antecedently accepted metaphysical view at all—be it a doctrine congenial to a traditional religious faith or a modern, secular outlook tied to a thoroughly empirical and scientific view of the world. In answer to these questions, Kant argues that the principle of morality is based in pure practical reason rather than experience, that it stands entirely on its own, independently of speculative metaphysical doctrines (even one so minimal as to assert nothing more than the freedom of the will), and further that this principle itself provides the basis for a rationally acceptable metaphysics.

As Kant's argument for these claims is intimately linked to the critical assessment of traditional speculative metaphysics carried out in the first *Critique,* the second *Critique* is written with the presumption that its readers will have at least some familiarity with that work. Indeed, there are many points in the second *Critique* at which Kant steps back from his discussion of practical reason to point out how it relates to issues treated in the first *Critique* or to draw parallels and contrasts between the arguments and the arrangements of topics contained in these two great books. It will be appropriate, therefore, to situate the second *Critique* in relation to the larger aims of Kant's critical philosophy before turning to the specific problems and issues it addresses.

1. THE PLACE OF THE *CRITIQUE OF PRACTICAL REASON* WITHIN KANT'S CRITICAL PHILOSOPHY

Reason, according to Kant, is the highest of our cognitive capacities; its function is to introduce unity and order into our knowledge (or "cognition").[1] In doing so, it is guided by the idea of a system, an idea of which it is itself the source. In the *Critique of Pure Reason,* Kant considers this cognitive capacity as it figures in theoretical knowledge—that is, the sort of cognition that we first acquire through ordinary experience and then seek to deepen and expand through the investigations we carry out in the natural sciences. The objects of such cognition exist independently of it and therefore can come to be known by us only through their somehow affecting us, by means of the senses. Although Kant does not attempt to explain how this affection takes place, he does argue that our capacity for sense perception is so constituted that the representations (or "presentations") of those objects provided by our senses are always subject to the conditions of space and time. In the pursuit of theoretical cognition, reason's idea of a system amounts to the general idea of nature, or a realm of objects, or substances, that exist independently of one another yet also causally interact according to a system of fixed laws and so depend on one another for their accidents, or nonessential features. The law-governed motion of the moon, for example, depends in part on the position and motion of the earth, and the earth's motion similarly depends on the position and motion of the moon, though the earth and the moon themselves do not depend on one another for the very existence of the permanent substantial material, whatever it may be, of which they are composed. As is apparent from this brief characterization, the general idea of nature itself comprises several interrelated component concepts. Kant calls these concepts categories, or pure concepts of understanding. Three of them are of particular importance for our purposes: substance, cause, and community (or causal interaction among substances).

Kant maintains, however, that, because our sense perception of the objects of theoretical cognition is subject to the conditions of time, temporal interpretations, or meanings, must be assigned to the categories in order for them to be used in theoretical cognition. The pure concept of cause, for example, which might figure in a philosopher's metaphysical doctrine of God's timeless creation of the world, needs to be given a temporal meaning

---

[1] In the present translation of the second *Critique,* 'cognition' and 'cognize' are used to render Kant's *Erkenntnis* and *erkennen.* This practice is generally followed in this Introduction, though on numerous occasions I use 'knowledge' and 'know' instead, with a view to capturing Kant's thought more easily in ordinary English, or when I am relying on the fact that (according to the primary sense in which Kant uses this term) *Erkenntnis* is true, or in agreement with its object. Except where otherwise indicated, both 'cognition' and 'knowledge' are used only for *Erkenntnis* in this Introduction. It should be noted, however, that in the translation 'knowledge' is generally reserved for *Wissen,* which implies objectively grounded certainty.

through the representation of a rule-governed temporal succession of events. Only then can this concept be used in theoretical cognition of objects of experience, where the production of effects is always by temporal processes. By interpreting the categories in accordance with the temporal conditions of experience, Kant is able to argue that these concepts, despite having their origin in reason, nevertheless apply necessarily to the objects of experience. He does this by presenting proofs for various principles, such as the principle of causality, which asserts that every event is determined by causes acting in the preceding time. These "principles of pure understanding" explicate more determinately the general conception of a natural order provided by the categories. Kant argues that we are justified in applying this general conception a priori to the objects of experience on the grounds that the application of these principles is a constitutive element of experience itself, on which all pursuit of scientific theoretical cognition of nature depends.

But Kant also maintains that, throughout the entire history of philosophy, from the days of the ancient Greek philosophers to the time of his own contemporaries, speculative metaphysicians have attempted to use the three principal concepts that figure in this general idea of nature to acquire knowledge of things of which we can have no experience whatsoever. In their pursuit of such knowledge, metaphysicians have stripped these concepts of the temporally restricted meanings that are requisite for their legitimate use in systematizing the theoretical cognition we gain through experience. Through the removal of these restrictions, (1) the concept of a substance existing permanently in time is transformed into the idea of a substance existing outside of time (immortality); (2) the concept of a cause, which when used in experience always applies to things whose productions of effects are themselves effects produced by further causes operating in the preceding time, is transformed into the idea of an uncaused cause (freedom); and, finally, (3) the concept of a community among the substances of nature that makes possible their simultaneous interaction is transformed into the idea of the ground of all reality and of nature itself (God). Misled by an illusion to which human reason is naturally subject, traditional speculative metaphysicians dogmatically sought to establish theoretical knowledge of objects represented through these ideas (the immortality of the soul, the freedom of the will, the existence of God), whereas other, more skeptical philosophers were continually challenging these claims to knowledge. It was a primary aim of the first *Critique* to put an end to these disputes once and for all by establishing that theoretical knowledge of the objects represented by such unrestricted ideas is in principle impossible. Kant argued that, by removing the temporal restrictions that rendered reason's a priori concepts suitable for use in systematizing theoretical cognition, speculative metaphysicians had framed ideas of objects that were in principle impossible to encounter in experience and that, for this reason, could not be objects of our theoretical knowledge; but he also argued that, for the same reason, skeptical denials of the propositions asserted by these metaphysicians were equally dogmatic and unfounded.

The agnostic conclusion of the first *Critique* does not, however, represent Kant's final judgment on the fate of metaphysics. In the *Critique of Practical Reason,* Kant shifts his attention from theoretical to practical knowledge to determine what reason is capable of knowing a priori in its practical use. Kant sometimes expresses the difference between these two sorts of cognition by saying that theoretical cognition is cognition of what is, and practical cognition is cognition of what ought to be. But he also sometimes describes the difference in the following more illuminating way: Theoretical cognition is cognition of objects that exist independently of it and that therefore must, in order to be known, or cognized, by us at all, be given to us in some way through sense-perception. Practical cognition, on the other hand, is cognition of objects that can be brought into existence by that cognition itself, or cognition that is at the same time a determination of the will to produce its object. Thus, although our theoretical knowledge that the moon orbits the earth does not bring it about that the moon orbits the earth, a person's knowledge that one ought to help others in need where one can is practical insofar as this very knowledge can move that individual to choose to help others in need and thus bring its object, the action of helping others, into existence. Since reason determines the will through such practical cognition, Kant also describes reason in its practical use as concerned with "the determining bases of the will" (15).[2]

The second *Critique* takes up the question whether *pure* reason can determine the will—that is, whether reason by itself, without reliance on empirical conditions lying in the senses and feeling, is the source of practical knowledge, or whether the practical knowledge reason can provide is always empirically conditioned. This question is addressed in Book I of Part

[2] References to the *Critique of Practical Reason* use the page numbers of the Akademie edition. Except for references to the *Critique of Pure Reason,* which use the pagination of the first (A) or second (B) edition, references to passages from Kant's other writings are by the volume and page numbers of the Akademie edition.

I of the second *Critique,* the Analytic of Pure Practical Reason. There Kant first undertakes to identify what the principle must be by which pure reason determines the will, if it can indeed do so. Once he has isolated this principle, he points out that it is nothing other than the very principle we recognize to be operative in our practical life as the moral law and draws the conclusion that pure reason is indeed practical, the source of practical knowledge. This conclusion, however, turns out to have important implications concerning the ideas of pure reason. Once we recognize that pure reason is practical, Kant argues, we are rationally compelled and thereby entitled to assume that we are free—that is, that pure reason's idea of freedom applies to our will insofar as the latter can be determined by pure reason. And in Book II, the Dialectic of Pure Practical Reason, Kant argues further that the practicality of pure reason has implications that involve the other two ideas of pure reason as well. Pure practical reason places us under an obligation to make the complete object of practical knowledge, the highest good, our end, and this obligation provides a practical-rational basis for belief, or faith, regarding the immortality of the soul and the existence of God.

Thus, the investigation into practical reason undertaken in the second *Critique* has the striking result that the very ideas of pure reason that Kant argued in the first *Critique* could not figure in any *theoretical* cognition turn out to play a legitimate role in certain beliefs that are sustained and justified by their relation to the *practical* use of pure reason, a relation that Kant expresses by calling them "postulates of pure practical reason." In the end, then, the critical examination of the faculty (or "power") of reason that is carried out in the second *Critique* does fill in, after a fashion, the agnostic gap left at the conclusion of the first *Critique,* in that the former does credit pure reason with the capacity to have a type of a priori cognition of the objects of pure reason. This cognition, however, is neither theoretical cognition (for its objects cannot be given through sense-perception) nor practical cognition (for it does not bring its objects into existence); it is rather practical-rational *belief.*

2. The Relation of the *Critique of Practical Reason* to Kant's Ethics

For many readers, the second *Critique* is of interest not so much because of its relation to the first *Critique* and to the larger aims of Kant's critical philosophy as on account of its relevance to his ethical writings, and in partic-

ular to the two principal texts in which he presents his system of moral philosophy, or what we might call his "normative ethics": the *Grounding for
the Metaphysics of Morals* (1785), in which he seeks to identify and establish the supreme principle of morality, and the *Metaphysics of Morals*
(1797), in which he elaborates the system of duties derivable from that principle.[3] How exactly the second *Critique* is related to Kant's ethical system
is a matter of some disagreement among scholars, but the importance of this
work for our understanding of his ethics is beyond dispute. For the purposes
of this Introduction, it will be convenient to distinguish two ways in which
the second *Critique* is relevant to Kant's ethical thought. One of these ways,
to which we shall turn in the next section, is through the distinctive manner
in which the second *Critique* contributes to the practical aim of Kant's
moral philosophy. Isolating this work's contribution to that aim will provide
a useful standpoint from which to survey its specific claims and arguments.
The other way, our concern in this section, is through the light its discus-
sions of particular topics throw on a variety of specific ideas, claims, and
themes that are integral to Kant's ethical theory.

Kant's principal writings in practical philosophy did not begin to appear
until he was in his sixties, after some thirty years of research and publication devoted almost exclusively to natural science and metaphysics. This is
not to say, however, that it was only late in his career that Kant turned his attention to practical philosophy. Both "the moral law within" and "the starry
sky above" (to borrow the famous words of the second *Critique*'s conclusion) were enduring objects of Kant's philosophical interest as well as his
admiration and reverence. When the *Grounding,* his first major work in
moral philosophy, appeared in 1785, Kant had already been lecturing regu-
larly on ethics for nearly thirty years at the University in Königsberg. Numerous clear indications of his interest in this subject can be found in his
writings from that period.

In his practical philosophy as in his theoretical philosophy, Kant endeavored to arrive at a satisfactory understanding of how both intellectual and
sensible capacities are at work in our cognition. In each of these parts of his
system, he tried to preserve the elements of truth that he found in the Leib-
nizian rationalist tradition prevalent in his native Prussia while also ac-

---

[3] It is worth noting that the expression "metaphysics of morals," which figures in the titles of
both works, does not signify any type of *speculative* metaphysics—the illegitimate theoretical
metaphysics Kant criticized in the first *Critique*. It refers rather to the a priori part of morality,
which Kant takes to consist in the practical knowledge of the system of duties that pertain to
human beings considered merely as such.

knowledging the insights of the empiricist tradition in Great Britain. But he also opposed the reductive tendencies that he saw in each of these schools of thought; the rationalists attempted to view sensations and feelings as confused workings of the intellect, whereas the empiricists sought to resolve the acts of the intellect into the refined workings of imagination and feeling. In contrast to both approaches, Kant maintained that our cognition comprises two distinct elements—form and matter—which differ in kind and therefore must arise from different sources within the mind: The form of cognition, which is spontaneous and universal, is due to the intellect, whereas its matter, which is passive and particular, is provided by the senses. Kant's form/matter analysis as it applies to *practical* cognition is nowhere more clearly and forcefully articulated than it is in the second *Critique*. As we shall see later, Kant locates the form of practical knowledge in the idea of a practical law (or what he calls "the mere form of a universal legislation"), and he identifies the matter with the objects to be produced through that knowledge, such as the objects of sensible desire, the things we find pleasing, or agreeable. This form/matter analysis provides the key enabling Kant to formulate the supreme principle of morality.

As he sought to negotiate a path between the extremes of rationalism and empiricism, Kant also raised a variety of more specific criticisms against these two approaches. On the side of the rationalists, the two figures with whom he was most immediately engaged were Christian Wolff and his disciple Alexander Baumgarten. Following Leibniz, and to some extent the ancient Stoics, these thinkers based their ethical doctrines on a metaphysical system in which reality is identified with perfection. While only God, the being of highest reality, possesses perfection absolutely, all beings naturally seek perfection as their end, striving to imitate the divine, and share in it to the extent that circumstances and the natural limits on their powers allow. Against this metaphysical backdrop, the rationalists expounded an ethics of perfectionism. From their ideal of perfection they derived such principles as "Seek perfection," "Do good," and "Love the best"; and since the pursuit of perfection was, according to their metaphysics, something to which nature itself in any case directs us, they also endorsed the Stoics' principle "Live according to nature." Although Kant's earliest thinking about ethics grew out of this tradition, he soon began to raise objections to it, two of which are particularly worth noting. First, the general criticism that Kant directed in the first *Critique* against all traditional speculative metaphysics—that its claims pertaining to God and reality in general outstrip the reach of our capacity for theoretical cognition—meant that he could not accept the rationalists' metaphysical doctrines nor indeed any attempt to provide a meta-physical foundation for ethics. Second, he criticized the rationalists' attempts to derive moral principles from the concept of perfection as our natural end. Such attempts, he held, are vitiated not because this concept must lead us astray, but because it is empty and indeterminate and therefore throws no light on the question of what morality's principle is. The principle "Do good," for example, is an empty tautology, for it is implicit in the very idea of a prac-tical principle of reason that the action it prescribes is good.

On the other side were the British moral sense philosophers—the Earl of Shaftesbury, Francis Hutcheson, David Hume, and Adam Smith. From early on, Kant was much impressed by the writings of these thinkers, who sought to account for our approval of virtuous action by appealing to a moral sense woven into the fabric of human nature. Hutcheson saw this sense as originally expressed in our responses to benevolent action, and Hume, by developing an elaborate theory of the workings of the imagina-tion and our natural feeling of sympathy, ingeniously extended the idea to account for our approval of a wide range of virtuous action, including acts of justice. Aided by his study of these philosophers, Kant gained an appre-ciation of the indispensable role that moral feeling must play in any account of how a moral judgment can move us to act—an appreciation that in-formed all of his subsequent thinking on ethical topics. He did not, how-ever, accept their attempt to use feeling or sentiment as the standard by which actions are judged to be right or wrong. He argued, to the contrary, that if the standard were traceable to a moral sentiment, we would have to allow that it might be reasonably rejected by a rational being to whose nat-ural constitution this sentiment did not belong. Yet the characteristic univer-sal and necessary validity of our moral judgments reveals that the principle on which they depend applies not just to members of the human race, but to all rational beings, and hence that the standard must be known by reason. As a result, he also did not accept the moral sense philosophers' accounts of moral motivation. These accounts, he held, mistook the motive of virtuous action—a feeling of respect based in a rational recognition of the moral law—for an immediate inclination (or sensible desire) to perform the ac-tion. In keeping with his form/matter analysis of practical cognition, Kant held that there is a difference in kind between the motive expressed in morally worthy action and all other motives. The moral motive must ulti-mately have its source in reason, whereas other motives, because they arise from empirical sources, are all kindred to one another and belong to a per-son's general interest in personal happiness.

In the end, then, Kant could no more follow the moral sense philosophers than he could the Stoical rationalists. Moral principles can be derived neither from the transcendent heights of metaphysical speculation nor from the empirically discovered sentiments of human nature. As he later observed in the *Grounding,* moral philosophy's position "is supposed to be firm even though there is nothing in heaven nor on earth from which it depends or on which it is based" (IV, 425).

While his thinking was significantly advanced by his critical engagement with these two schools, it was not by drawing on these sources alone that Kant moved beyond them and worked out his most important positive ethical doctrines. It was rather his reading of the brilliant Swiss social and political philosopher Jean-Jacques Rousseau and an apparently momentous encounter with Plato in the 1760s that turned Kant onto the path that led to his formulation of the principle of morality and the mature moral philosophy expounded in the great works he published in the 1780s and 1790s. Although comparatively little is known about the development of Kant's ethical views during this early period, it seems likely that it was in connection with his study of these two philosophers that he developed some of his most important ideas, now familiar to us from the *Grounding*. His conception of the good will as the only thing that is good without qualification, for example, seems to have been inspired by an argument that Plato gave to show that practical wisdom is the only thing good by itself alone. And his attempt to formulate the principle of morality—conceived as the principle governing a good will—by developing the idea that such a will must be autonomous, or self-legislating, and therein free, can be seen as an elaboration, at a deeper level, of ideas that figure in Rousseau's account in the *Social Contract* of the general will as the basis of civic freedom.

Although the fundamental ideas of his ethical theory were all in place by the time he wrote the *Grounding,* Kant had not yet quite hit upon the idea of a critique of practical reason, at least not in the form in which it eventually appeared. In the *Grounding*'s Preface, he did briefly contrast the project he was undertaking in that work with a critique of *pure* practical reason, describing the latter as something that would both (1) provide the true "foundation" for a metaphysics of morals and also (2) show the unity of practical and theoretical reason (IV, 391); and he did, in the final chapter of the *Grounding,* claim to make a transition to the critique of pure practical reason. But when the *Critique of Practical Reason* was finally published three years later, Kant began the work by pointedly explaining why it was *not* titled Critique of *Pure* Practical Reason, observing that if there is such a thing as pure practical reason, no critique of it is needed, since pure reason itself furnishes the standard by which any critique of its employment is carried out (3, 15–16). What is needed instead, Kant claimed, is a critical examination of the entire practical use of reason, so that, once it has been shown that there is pure practical reason, empirically conditioned reason can be prevented from presuming that it is the sole determining basis of the will. This broader investigation, dealing with practical reason in its entirety, is what the second *Critique* undertakes to provide.

How significant a change in view is reflected in the omission of the word "pure" in Kant's title is a question on which scholarly opinion divides. It seems clear that Kant does attempt in the second *Critique* to deal, up to a point at least, with the question of the unity of practical and theoretical reason.[4] Whether he aims to provide the true "foundation" for a metaphysics of morals—the foundation that he said in the *Grounding* would be furnished by a critique of *pure* practical reason—is less clear. But it seems at the very least correct to say that Kant changes his thinking on the question whether it is possible and necessary to provide a "deduction," or justification, of the moral law. In the final chapter of the *Grounding,* the chapter in which a transition is made to a critique of *pure* practical reason, he actually presents what he there calls a "deduction" of the "supreme principle of morality" (IV, 453–54, 463), in which he relies on the claim that freedom can ("in a practical respect") be attributed to rational beings *independently* of their consciousness of the moral law and merely in virtue of their having a will. In the second *Critique,* on the other hand, he maintains that we can be conscious of ourselves as free *only* through our consciousness of the moral law and explicitly denies that a deduction of the moral principle can be provided, offering in its place his doctrine of the "fact of reason" and a "credential" for the moral law deriving from considerations bearing on the relation between practical and theoretical reason (46–48).

Although the *Critique of Practical Reason* provides no deduction of the supreme principle of morality, it illuminates Kant's ethical theory in a number of important respects. By carrying out a full examination of the practical use of reason, it furnishes Kant's clearest and most comprehensive argument to show that the principle identified in the *Grounding* as the supreme principle of morality is based solely in pure reason. In addition,

---

[4] See in particular the sections On the Deduction of the Principles of Pure Practical Reason (42ff.), Critical Examination of the Analytic of Pure Practical Reason (89ff.), and On the Primacy of Pure Practical Reason in Its Linkage with Speculative Reason (119ff.).

the second *Critique* contributes to our understanding of Kant's ethical views through its examination of a variety of related topics that are also of considerable interest in their own right. These include the idea of a practical principle and the distinction between maxims and practical laws, the relation between morality and freedom, the "justification" of morality, the meaning of 'good,' and the nature of moral motivation (see §§4–6).

Through its treatment of these topics, the second *Critique* brings into sharp relief the features of Kant's ethical theory that have chiefly contributed to his reputation as the preeminent exponent of modern ethical thought and the cosmopolitan ethics of the Enlightenment in particular, an ethics centered around the ideals of rationality, freedom, and equality. Here, as in the *Grounding,* we find Kant maintaining that genuine moral principles are based in reason rather than in human nature, social custom, or religious creed, and that they therefore hold not merely for the members of a particular race, tribe, or sect, but universally, enjoining all persons to act out of a regard for themselves and others as free and equal rational beings. We also find a characteristically modern emphasis on the idea of law and the representation of moral conduct as a matter of acting on principle rather than from inclination or with a view to the good. Indeed, the opposition between duty and inclination so emphatically asserted in the *Grounding* is echoed and amplified in the second *Critique* through its prominent depiction of a fundamental opposition between the principle of morality and that of personal happiness, and through Kant's claim that the concept of the good is not to be defined independently of the moral law, but rather in accordance with it.

Because of the great stress Kant lays on these and other similar claims, his ethics is sometimes thought to stand in stark opposition to the ethical thought of the ancient Greeks, who saw ethical conduct as lying in the pursuit of a good and happy life, and who conceived of ethical virtue as an essential element in such a life, rather than as something opposed to happiness. The second *Critique* is of particular interest in this regard because in it Kant completes his critical assessment of practical reason with a detailed examination of the central problem of ancient ethics: What does the *summum bonum,* or highest good, consist in, and what does its pursuit involve? Kant's discussion of this topic reveals that, however dedicated he may be to Enlightenment ideals, his ethical views are in important respects closely related to those of the ancients. Despite certain criticisms he raises against them, Kant agrees with the ancients that, in the highest good, virtue and happiness, far from being opposed, are rather necessarily united. It is a noteworthy fact that the only competing ethical theories receiving any detailed discussion at all in the second *Critique* are those of the Stoics and the Epicureans. Kant's extensive critical commentary on these schools of antiquity throws light back on his own position, showing that he regards his doctrine of the highest good as preserving the elements of truth in the opposing Stoic and Epicurean accounts.

Finally, as noted earlier, the second *Critique* contains an extensive treatment of the three "postulates of pure practical reason"—the freedom of the will, the immortality of the soul, and the existence of God. By expounding these postulates as presuppositions of the moral law and of the pursuit of the highest good, Kant completes his philosophical project of reconceiving the basis of metaphysics by replacing the traditional speculative arguments he criticized in the first *Critique* with supports that are derived from practical sources and furnish a moral basis for religious faith. In doing so, he provides his clearest statement of his distinctive account of the relationship between morality and religious faith, according to which morality leads to religion, though it cannot be founded on it.

3. THE PRACTICAL PURPOSE OF THE *CRITIQUE OF PRACTICAL REASON*

Through its contribution to Kant's aim of reconstituting traditional metaphysics by overthrowing its speculative arguments and replacing them with an ethical basis, the *Critique of Practical Reason* serves a further purpose, which is purely practical and moral in character. Kant holds that because the dogmatic metaphysical claims that the will is free, that God exists, and that the soul is immortal are theoretically insupportable, they lead in the end to skepticism about these propositions. He thus regards the dogmatism inherent in traditional metaphysics as "the true source of all the unbelief that conflicts with morality" and sets out to reconceive traditional metaphysics with a view to protecting morality from this threat.[5] But as we shall see, the second *Critique* serves to protect morality from other skeptical threats as well. Specifying more precisely this antiskeptical purpose and tracing its connection to the overall practical aim of Kant's moral philosophy will

---

[5] *Critique of Pure Reason* B xxx. The quotation is from the sentence containing Kant's famous remark that he found it necessary to overturn the dogmatic claims to theoretical knowledge (*Wissen*) in order to make room for practically based rational belief, or faith (*Glauben*).

put us in a good position to survey the claims and arguments presented in this work.

Kant emphasizes repeatedly that ordinary human beings already have an understanding of the moral law and of what it requires of them. This means that the moral-practical purpose of moral philosophy cannot be to discover anything we do not already at least implicitly know. It cannot be the business of the moral philosopher to presume to instruct the rest of the world as to what the moral law asserts. The proper moral contribution of moral philosophy must lie rather in helping to secure "acceptance and durability" for the moral law as an efficacious motive in conduct.[6]

There are, of course, a variety of ways in which the efficacy of the moral law is fostered. Parents contribute by providing their children with a good upbringing, the state contributes through its laws and the sanctions it attaches to them, and society contributes through the opinions, favorable or otherwise, that persons form of one another through their social interactions. But the distinctive way in which philosophy can further this end is by making our ordinary understanding of morality clearer and more secure. This is accomplished in part by clarifying the content of morality, by identifying its principle and expounding the system of duties derivable from it. This task is carried out in Kant's system of ethics proper, in the *Grounding* and in the *Metaphysics of Morals*. In addition to promoting the moral motive in this direct way, philosophy can also contribute indirectly by countering obstacles and threats to our naturally sound understanding of the moral law that arise from thought and reflection and that are themselves at least incipiently philosophical or theoretical in nature. It is here, in the domain of philosophical criticism, that the *Critique of Practical Reason* makes its distinctive practical contribution, removing and forestalling the confusions and misunderstandings from which certain doubts that can impede the moral law's acceptance might otherwise arise.

As Kant argues in the *Grounding*, the chief doubts concerning morality arise in large part from the fact that it has its origin in pure reason. Although obscurely present in ordinary moral thought, the idea that reason by itself can move us to act is so singular, so different from what we know about all

---

[6] See *Grounding* IV, 404–5. This broad practical aim is reflected in Kant's division of the second *Critique* into two parts—a Doctrine of Elements and a Doctrine of Method. After completing the critique proper, which is carried out in the first of these parts, Kant proceeds in the second part to describe, in general outline and in the light of the conclusions reached in the first part, the method to be followed in cultivating morality, whereby the laws of pure practical reason gain "*acceptance* in the human mind and *influence* on its maxims" (151).

other types of motivation familiar to us, that it can easily strike us as utterly strange and suspect. Thus, Epicurus and many other philosophers after him have concluded that the sole practical function of reason is to minister to the inclinations, and Hume famously proclaimed that "Reason is, and ought only to be the slave of the passions."[7] Those who would grant that morality must have its source in pure reason if it is possible at all may therefore be prompted to suppose, nihilistically, that it is simply a figment of our minds, without any genuine reality or capacity to move us to act. Others may rather doubt that morality has such an origin at all, and seek to understand it in some other way, by tracing it to self-interest, for example, as Epicurus did, or, like Hume, by deriving it from a feeling such as sympathy.

Such doubts can also arise or receive further support from two additional sources, one motivational and the other theoretical. On the one hand, these doubts can result from the fact that the needs and inclinations of an individual human being can come into conflict with what the moral law requires. Kant notes that because the demands of self-interest tend to seem reasonable to us even when the action that would be required to satisfy them is contrary to duty, they can awaken a certain propensity within us to quibble with the moral law and to raise doubts about its validity, or at least its strictness and purity. Under such circumstances, we may concoct specious grounds for qualifying this law and allowing exceptions to it to accommodate our wishes and inclinations. This source of doubt, however, at least when taken by itself, is more a matter of deficiency of motive and character than a matter of philosophical or theoretical confusion or misconception. It is therefore more properly countered directly, by clarifying the content of morality and by the other means of fostering the moral motive mentioned earlier, than by undertaking a critique of practical reason.

It is the other source of doubts about the rational basis of morality, the theoretical source, that is of primary significance for Kant's purposes in the second *Critique*. We have already noted that Kant undertakes his project of criticizing traditional speculative metaphysics with a view to protecting morality from the unbelief to which theoretically insupportable metaphysical claims regarding the freedom of the will, the existence of God, and so on can lead. But Kant recognizes that skeptical doubts can also arise more or less directly from experience and reflection on the character of empirical cognition. If reason by itself is practical, then it must be possible for us to choose and act directly from principles of reason without being determined

---

[7] *A Treatise of Human Nature* II.iii.3.

by anything outside of ourselves. But the empirical theoretical sciences seem to imply that our choices and even our moral judgments and convictions do not lie in the free exercise of our reason, but instead are determined, in accordance with empirical laws, by factors external to our understanding and our will. Biologists point to our genetic makeup and explain how it has arisen through natural selection; psychologists appeal to the drives, instincts, and other psychic mechanisms that are operative in mental processes; and social scientists, impressed by the diversity of custom and opinion prevalent in different societies and historical periods, treat morality as a social artifact, seeking to explain how particular moral codes arise and are sustained within their economic, social, and cultural settings.

This apparent conflict between the type of explanation of human choice that the theoretical sciences demand and the freedom of choice that morality presupposes does not arise by accident. As we noted earlier, Kant himself offers a general argument in the first *Critique* for the principle of causality, which is meant to demonstrate that every occurrence, every happening in time, is determined by antecedent causal conditions. Accordingly, he maintains that every particular act of choice, simply in virtue of being an occurrence, is necessarily the effect of some antecedent determining basis, which provides the impulse required to determine the will. The theoretical doubts about the rational basis of morality are thus decidedly philosophical in character, being at bottom inseparable from the problem of freedom and the related question whether practical and theoretical reason are compatible.

In order to indicate properly the scope of Kant's project in the second *Critique,* however, it is not enough to identify the theoretical source of doubt; it is also necessary to describe briefly the alternative conception of practical reason that accompanies these doubts and the role that reason, according to this conception, would play in moral thinking. The denial that there is pure practical reason is equivalent to the presumption that the practical employment of reason is always empirically conditioned. It is equivalent, that is, to the supposition that in prescribing a practical rule, or perhaps a virtuous trait of character, reason always depends on a theoretical judgment that the action or trait specified will contribute to the attainment of some object we have come to desire through experience—that is, through our discovery that its existence is something we find pleasing or agreeable. On this conception, then, the practical employment of reason presupposes materials provided by the concepts of such empirically discovered agreeable objects; and it is confined to the business of fashioning from them a determinate conception of an achievable end and specifying the means of attaining it. Accordingly, when philosophers develop theories of morality in the shadow of the theoretical doubt that reason by itself can be practical, they always follow the same path in their attempt to describe the role that practical reason plays in morality. They inevitably begin by looking among the things whose existence we know from experience to be pleasing or satisfying in the hope of finding in one or a few of them—or perhaps in their sum total (under the name of happiness)—an object that is such that, in the rules and the traits of character reason directs us to adopt in order to attain it, we can recover the familiar duties and virtues of morality. Thus, a theory developed in this way starts with an experience, some pleasing or agreeable feeling, which provides the basis for identifying an object to be pursued (usually happiness); this object, in turn, is the basis for deriving practical principles or conclusions regarding character and virtue.

The *Critique of Practical Reason* is a direct response to the theoretical doubts just described and to the associated presumption that the practical employment of reason, even in morality, is always empirically conditioned. To address these doubts, the *Critique* has "to show," as Kant announces at the beginning of the Preface, "that there is pure practical reason." Whereas empirical practical reason is just practical reason in respect of its capacity to produce rules or principles for the will on the basis of experience (of some agreeable object, or material), pure practical reason would be just practical reason in respect of its capacity to produce a principle for the will that can be known a priori, or independently of experience. Accordingly, to show that there is pure practical reason it is first necessary to expound completely a priori the idea of a principle of pure practical reason, deriving from this idea a formulation of what the principle would assert, and making clear that, being purely formal in character, it is different in kind from all material principles, which can be subsumed under the principle of personal happiness. It will then be necessary to show that the principle thus expounded and formulated is in fact operative in our practical life, which Kant does (in part) by identifying this principle as the basis of morality. It will also be necessary to address a concern regarding our right, or entitlement, to attribute to ourselves the freedom of the will that morality presupposes in virtue of having its origin in pure reason, given that all occurrences in nature are subject to theoretical reason's a priori principle of universal determinism. And to counter the presumption that the practical employment of reason, even in morality, is always empirically conditioned, it will be necessary to spell out (in an order that reverses the sequence followed in moral theories based on that presumption) an account of how pure reason can first immediately determine the will and thereby, through the application of its formal principle through which this determination takes place, subsequently provide for itself an object to be pursued and finally produce an effect on our feeling through which it can move us to act.

These tasks are addressed, in the order just presented, in the three chapters that make up the Analytic of Pure Practical Reason (Book I of the Doctrine of the Elements). The first chapter, On the Principles of Pure Practical Reason, endeavors to show that pure reason is practical by expounding the idea of a practical law, identifying this idea itself as the fundamental law of morality, and securing the presupposition of freedom that is revealed through our awareness of this law. After completing this argument, Kant appends two further sections to this chapter (42–57), in which he takes up questions of justification—that is, questions concerning the possibility of giving a "deduction" in his special sense of that term—that arise concerning this principle and the associated concept of freedom. The second chapter, On the Concept of an Object of Pure Practical Reason, then provides an account of the object of pure practical reason (the good), and the third chapter, On the Incentives of Pure Practical Reason, describes how the moral law functions as a motive or spring of action through producing effects on feeling. Having now surveyed the main tasks to be addressed in the Analytic, we are ready to look more closely at the argument.

4. Showing the Practicality of Pure Reason

A. The Idea of a Principle of Practical Reason (§1)

Reason, according to Kant, is the faculty of knowledge from principles, or our capacity to know the particular from the universal. In other words, it is the capacity to reach knowledge about particular things from universal knowledge that we already have. Thus, if we know that all hurricanes in the Northern Hemisphere rotate in a counterclockwise direction, we do not need to rely on observation to know that the next hurricane to hit Florida will rotate in that direction; we know this through reason, by applying the universal knowledge we have to the case in question. But the principles relied on in such knowledge of the particular from the universal are, in many cases if not all, not themselves known through reason. Our knowledge of the principle just mentioned, for example, depends on, among other things, our knowledge of the direction of the earth's rotation, which we have acquired from experience. The question thus arises whether there is any principle, or universal knowledge, that we already have in an *absolute* sense— that is, whether *pure* reason, or reason by itself, is a source of principles of knowledge, or whether the principles on which we rely in the use of our reason must always be borrowed from elsewhere—from experience itself or its sensible conditions. Principles that have their source in reason itself would have to be absolutely universal, pertaining not merely to all objects of a specific kind (for example, all hurricanes), but to all possible objects of rational knowledge, or to the fundamental material of which they are all composed. All more specific rational knowledge would therefore necessarily be in conformity with these principles, just as all more specific knowledge about hurricanes in the Northern Hemisphere is necessarily in conformity with the knowledge that they rotate in a counterclockwise direction. In the first *Critique,* Kant argues that, as far as theoretical knowledge is concerned, pure reason is not itself a source of principles.

In the second *Critique,* however, Kant raises a parallel question about reason in its practical employment and argues for a very different conclusion. Since practical knowledge is knowledge about how to act that can itself move the subject possessing it to act accordingly, the principles of practical knowledge are principles of action: They are universal cognitions from which efficacious knowledge about how one should act in particular circumstances can be derived. Thus, if the prudent shopkeeper Kant describes in his famous example in the *Grounding* knows that where there is much trade, one should not overcharge, but keep a fixed general price for everyone, then he can know through reason that he should not overcharge when, in such conditions, an inexperienced customer enters his shop. By applying this universal principle of action to the case at hand, the shopkeeper can know by reason what he should do, and insofar as the principle is practical, or capable of determining his will, this knowledge can move him to act accordingly. But though the shopkeeper's principle is universal in that it is conceived as equally applicable to any other merchant who aims to be successful in business (and, in a hypothetical way, even to all other human persons), it is nevertheless based on experience (whether the shopkeeper's own or that of others), from which the shopkeeper has learned that this policy works to one's advantage. Kant raises the question whether all such principles, on which our knowledge of what we are to do or of how we are to act is based, are similarly dependent on experience or whether pure reason is itself a source of practical principles. In the latter case, there would be universal practical knowledge that we already have in an absolute sense. Such knowledge would have absolute universality, and all more specific practical knowledge would necessarily be in conformity with it. If reason by itself is a source of such universal knowledge, universal knowledge that can move us to act, then pure reason is practical.

The question whether pure reason is practical, then, is a question about practical principles. Accordingly, Kant makes such principles his subject of investigation in the first chapter of the Analytic of Pure Practical Reason. In the introductory definition (Explication), practical principles are said to be propositions that contain a universal determination of the will. This characterization is clearly fixed by the points about practical principles just noted: In order to be the source of knowledge of the particular from the universal, they must themselves be universal, and being practical, they must determine the will.

This initial definition is too general, however, to isolate the specific sort of practical principle that will be operative in practical thought if pure reason is practical. Thus, Kant proceeds immediately to introduce the idea of a practical principle that is *objective,* or a *practical law* (rather than merely subjective, or a maxim). Such a principle, Kant states, is one in which the "condition" to which the determination of the will is subject is cognized as valid for the will of every rational being. No immediate clarification is provided of what such a "condition" of the will's determination might be, but an understanding of what Kant has in mind can be gained by returning to the idea of a principle of practical knowledge.

To the extent that a practical principle is a source of knowledge of the particular from the universal, there is another sense, in addition to the one indicated earlier, in which it can be said to be universal. All cognition, Kant holds, be it theoretical or practical, has what he calls *subjective* universal validity: If a particular judgment counts as knowledge, then it must be valid for every knowing subject, so that all such subjects could agree in the matter and share the same judgment. Thus, a principle of reason, being itself a cognition, is universally valid in two respects: In addition to being valid *of* all the objects that fall under its subject concept (objective universal validity), it is valid *for* every subject capable of rational cognition (subjective universal validity). This is true of both theoretical and practical principles of cognition. However, unlike theoretical cognition, which is of objects that are distinct from the cognizing subject and given to it from elsewhere by means of the senses, practical cognition is essentially knowledge subjects have that they themselves should act in a certain way, and as such it is always cognition of the very subjects who have such cognition. Therefore, in the case of a principle of practical cognition, the two sorts of universal validity coincide in the sense that the principle is valid *for* the very subjects *of* which it is valid: The principle applies to the will of every rational being, and every such being can recognize this universal applicability. This is as much as to say that principles of practical cognition are necessarily such that every subject can agree to every subject's acting on them, as would actually happen if all subjects were jointly to legislate this principle for themselves. Kant thus gives expression to this necessary feature of all principles of practical knowledge by speaking of "the mere *form* of a universal legislation" (27). Such universal legislation must therefore be possible if, for example, the shopkeeper can rightly be said to have practical knowledge that, where there is much trade, one should keep a fixed general price for everyone.

Because consideration of the bare idea of a principle of practical cognition reveals that this "mere form of a universal legislation" necessarily belongs to any such principle, this form is just the form of a principle of practical cognition. Thus, diverse principles of practical cognition will all alike share the common form of a universal legislation merely in virtue of being principles of practical cognition. All differences among them must accordingly lie in differences in their matter—that is, differences among the objects they represent, objects that are to be realized through the actions that spring from these principles as general determinations of the will.

This distinction between the form and the matter of a principle of practical knowledge can be drawn a priori, and, as soon as we draw it, we are in a position to see that *if* pure reason can determine the will—if, that is, reason by itself can be the source of practical principles—then the "form of a universal legislation" will necessarily be the "condition" to which its determination of the will is subject (that is, the condition that makes the determination possible), so that any principle that has its source in reason will necessarily have this form. Pure reason's determination of the will would have to be subject to this condition because principles that arise from a faculty of practical cognition from the universal must *necessarily* have the form of universal practical cognition. Because this "condition" is the a priori form of universal practical cognition, it is itself recognizable by every rational being as a condition of cognition that is valid for the will of every rational being, inasmuch as all rational beings, as such, share this same faculty of cognition from the universal. The principles Kant characterizes as *objective* principles and as *practical laws* are precisely those in which the determination of the will is subject to this universally valid condition.

As Kant points out in his Comment in §1, in some rational beings (human rational beings, for example), the will is "pathologically affected." By this Kant means not that such a will is in any way diseased, but that it is by its very nature related to sensible desires (for shelter, food, sex, and so on) in such a way that the latter can play a causal role in the will's determination. In a rational being whose will is of such a nature, it is possible for the will to contain practical principles that have as their conditions the pleasure a subject takes in the existence of the objects of sensible desires rather than the condition described earlier (the mere form of a universal legislation) and that are therefore not practical laws, or principles of practical cognition. Such principles would be merely *maxims*.[8]

B. Theorems about Practical Principles (§§2–4)

After presenting the initial definition in §1, Kant proceeds to deduce several theorems by drawing on the concepts introduced in the definition.[9] The task of §2 is to establish Theorem I, which concerns a certain type of practical principle, what Kant calls a "material practical principle." This theorem states, roughly, that if the determining basis of a practical principle lies in its matter—that is, in the object to be realized through acting on the principle—then the possibility of the will's determination is subject to a condition that is not valid for all rational beings, and the principle therefore cannot be a practical law. The argument for this proposition is striking in its simplicity and generality. Any such object, Kant maintains, can be a basis of the will's determination only under the condition that the object stands in a relation to the subject that consists in a feeling of pleasure in the existence of the object. This relation can be known only by experience, never a priori,

---

[8] It is worth noting here that, although it may appear that in the definition at the beginning of §1 Kant defines maxims in such a way as to preclude the possibility that one and the same practical principle could be both a maxim and a practical law, this is not a possibility he wishes to close off (see Theorem III in §4). If we follow Kant's characterizations of maxims in the *Grounding* (IV, 420n), according to which a maxim is a "subjective" principle in that it is one on which the *subject acts* (an objective principle being one on which the subject *ought* to act), we can then understand him to be saying in the opening definition in §1 that if a practical principle has a condition that is regarded by the subject as valid *only* for that subject's own will, then it is a maxim and nothing more—that is, not also a practical law.

[9] This is not to say that the definitions of practical principle, maxim, and practical law are the only ones on which Kant relies in his arguments for the theorems. He acknowledges in the Preface that he also makes use of certain other concepts not specific to practical philosophy, mentioning in particular that he can reasonably presuppose, as obtainable from psychology, definitions of the concepts of the power of desire and of the feeling of pleasure (9n).

and therefore cannot furnish a condition that is recognized to be valid for the will of every rational being. It is a relation of causal affection, in which the representation of an object's existence—for example, the visual impression of a sunset, or the sensations of taste and smell that accompany the eating of an apple—produces a feeling of pleasure in the mind; this connection, however, like any other specific causal connection, can be known only by experience. From the mere representation, independently of the actual feeling of pleasure it produces, it is thus impossible to know even in one's own case—to say nothing of that of others—that it has such an effect. Likewise, it is impossible to infer from the actual effect produced in oneself that the same effect would be produced in all other rational beings.

The examples just mentioned might suggest that this argument applies well enough to material principles that depend on what are sometimes called "the pleasures of the senses," but that it does not touch material principles whose objects lie in the exercise of our active and rational powers—objects that we could place under such headings as "the pleasures of the mind" (invention, discovery, learning, and the like) and "the pleasures of society" (friendship, conversation, competition, and so on). But it is clear from Kant's later discussion in §3 that even principles whose determining bases are objects of this latter sort are meant to be covered by his conclusion. As an example, we might consider a case in which the object is the action of helping others in need. The sympathetic man Kant describes in the *Grounding* delights in helping others out of an immediate inclination to help. This man, however, can hardly know a priori that every rational being will in every case find a similar delight in such action, and even in his own case occasions can arise in which, his mind being overclouded by his own grief, the delight he customarily takes in helping others dissolves (*Grounding* IV, 398). Moreover, for reasons that will emerge shortly when we consider Kant's discussion of the material principle of personal happiness, even if we could know that every rational being did delight in the action of helping others, this would not be enough to show that a principle of helping others that had this basis would be a practical law. The condition of the possibility of a practical principle whose determining basis lies in the object to be produced thus cannot be known to be valid for all rational beings, and therefore a principle with such a determining basis cannot be a practical law.

In §3 Kant argues for Theorem II, which asserts that all material practical principles belong under the general principle of self-love or personal happiness, a principle whose object is identified as the consciousness of the agreeableness of life uninterruptedly accompanying one's whole existence.

This principle too is a material principle, but one whose object is indeterminate, being specified simply in terms of the agreeable effect it produces in the subject. Kant claims that happiness is an end that every rational being has necessarily, by nature. This claim prompts the question whether, contrary to what was claimed in §2, this principle provides an example of a material practical principle that can be a practical law. Kant, however, denies that this is so. It is true that, if personal happiness is indeed an end every finite rational being has by nature, then there is a sense in which the principle of personal happiness can be said to have a condition that is recognized to be "valid for the will of every rational being"; but this is not the sense Kant has in view in his definition of a practical law. As he points out, personal happiness does not really supply a single determining basis, or condition, that is valid for all rational beings: In your case, the determining basis is *your* happiness; in my case, the determining basis is *my* happiness. So, strictly speaking, there is no common determining basis here that is valid for the will of every rational being, nor, therefore, are persons who act on the principle of personal happiness, strictly speaking, acting on the same practical principle. Where there is a single determining basis and a single principle that different persons share, there is no possibility of conflict among their wills (except incidentally, as when they disagree about the best means to a given end because they have different theoretical opinions about which course of action would be most effective). But nothing is more common than for the wills of persons who are pursuing the "same" end of personal happiness to come into conflict.

Having argued that practical principles whose condition lies in their matter cannot be practical laws, Kant has laid the ground for Theorem III (§4), which states that in order for a subjective practical principle, or maxim, to be a practical law, its determining basis, or the condition of its possibility, must lie in the principle's having the form of a universal legislation. The considerations on which Kant relies in making this linkage of practical laws to the form of a universal legislation have already been sketched in our foregoing discussion of the idea of a practical law. We observed that the universal validity of the "condition," or determining basis, of such a law is due to this condition's being the a priori cognizable form of a principle of practical cognition—a form that amounts to the form of a universal legislation. But in view of the highly abstract terms in which this important theorem is stated, it will be helpful to consider an example Kant provides a few pages later—in Comment I to Theorem IV (§8)—to illustrate how the form of a universal legislation can function as the determining basis of a practical principle. Noting that all finite rational beings necessarily have their own happiness as an end, Kant observes that such a being can pursue this object in accordance with a principle that is a practical law only by subjecting the end to the restricting condition that is provided by the form of a universal legislation—the condition that it be possible for every rational being to agree to every rational being's pursuing the end in question. Since all such beings necessarily have their own happiness as an end, the happiness of one rational being is not something other rational beings can agree to make their end unless their own happiness is also included. Therefore, subjecting the end of one's own happiness to this condition is a matter of including others' happiness along with one's own in the object, which yields an end that all can share. Insofar as the practical principle in accordance with which one pursues one's own happiness is adopted only subject to this condition, it is a practical law.[10]

C. Practical Laws and Freedom (§§5–6)

Having reached the conclusion that the determining basis of a practical law can lie nowhere but in the form of a universal legislation, Kant is in a position to argue, in his solutions to Problems I and II (§§5–6), that a will that can be determined only by this form (that is, a will whose practical principles can be practical laws) is a free will, and, conversely, that a free will is a will whose practical principles can be determined only by the form of a universal legislation. Indeed, the distinction Kant has already drawn between the form and the matter of practical principles enables him to present very succinct arguments for these claims.

In the first argument, Kant relies on a premise for which he argued in the first *Critique:* If a thing is determined in accordance with laws of nature and hence subject to natural necessity, its determining basis must lie among the appearances—that is, among things representable by means of the senses,

---

[10] Specifically, it is the law that underlies the duty of beneficence (cf. *Metaphysics of Morals* VI, 393). While there is not space here to discuss this principle in detail, it is worth mentioning that although it may at first sight appear to be similar to John Stuart Mill's principle of utility, according to which the object on which the standard of right conduct is based is the greatest happiness of the greatest number, it differs from the latter not only in respect of its determining basis but also in what it prescribes, which is not that one act in a way that maximizes happiness in general, but (roughly) that one limit the pursuit of one's own happiness by a readiness to give such assistance to others as one can when circumstances arise in which they are in need of help.

as existing in time. Drawing on the argument developed in the preceding sections (§§1–4), he adds to this the claim that a practical principle can have an appearance as its determining basis only insofar as the latter lies in the principle's matter rather than its form, since the form of a universal legislation is not representable by means of the senses at all. From these premises it follows that a will that is determinable only by the form of a universal legislation is not determinable in accordance with laws of nature and is therefore free.

Kant's argument in the reverse direction relies on the thought that, if a will is free, or not determinable in accordance with laws of nature, then the determining bases of the acts of self-determination in which its principles consist must lie, not in appearances, but rather in what the subject can think entirely a priori, through reason. As Kant argued in §2, however, the determining basis of a material practical principle lies in a feeling of pleasure resulting from the empirical awareness of the existence of some object. Such a determining basis therefore belongs among the appearances. On the other hand, the form of a universal legislation, as the a priori form of a principle of practical cognition, can be thought a priori by reason alone and is not the representation of any appearance at all. Thus, the determining basis of the principles of a free will must lie in this form.

As Kant well knows, to show that these reciprocal entailments hold is not to show that the two propositions are themselves true. By introducing the concept of freedom into his analysis, however, the arguments prepare the way for further important conclusions that Kant will soon be in a position to draw.

D. The Basic Law of Pure Practical Reason (§7)

Besides enabling him to introduce the concept of freedom, Kant's arrival at the conclusion stated in Theorem III puts him in a position to state the "basic law of pure practical reason." We have already noted that if pure reason is itself practical, then it must have its own a priori principle, to which all practical knowledge necessarily conforms. But since only practical laws have the form of practical knowledge (the form of a universal legislation), and since, as Theorem III states, the determining basis of all such practical laws lies in this very form, the a priori principle of pure practical reason with which these laws necessarily conform can be nothing other than this form of universal legislation itself. In Kant's statement of it, however, this a priori principle is couched in terms that capture not only this form, but also the specific way it manifests itself in the consciousness of a finite rational being. Because the will of such a being is pathologically affected, the principles actually adopted may lack the form of practical knowledge and so be maxims that are not also practical laws. For this reason, the basic law of pure practical reason is represented by such a being as an unconditional command, or imperative, of pure practical reason, which Kant states as follows: "So act that the maxim of your will could always hold at the same time as a principle of a universal legislation" (30).

There are several points to be noted here concerning Kant's presentation of this basic law of pure practical reason and the comment he offers regarding it. First, in contrast to the three theorems that preceded it, the basic law is not a proposition for which any proof is offered. One reason for this difference is that, as a *basic* law, it is not derivable from any more fundamental proposition and is, therefore, not any sort of theorem at all. But another reason can be found in the second point to be noted here—that, again in contrast to what precedes it, this basic law is a *practical* proposition. As the first principle of all practical cognition, this basic law lays down what *ought* to be, or how one *ought* to act, and it is therefore not entailed by the propositions preceding it. As theorems about practical principles reached by reflection on the concepts of such principles introduced in the opening definition (in §1), those propositions merely concern what necessarily *is* the case (provided that there are indeed practical principles). Kant's argument, up to this point, can establish no more than that *if* pure reason is practical, *then* its principle must be the one he identifies as the basic law of pure practical reason. This conclusion, however, is not the same as the imperative itself; it identifies what the basic law is and thus enables Kant to *display* it, but it does not *assert* it. On the one hand, then, this basic law is valid for all rational beings in the sense that all such beings should be able, by following the argument, to agree that if pure reason is practical, then its principle must be the one Kant states. Yet, on the other hand, the possibility has not thereby been excluded that pure reason is nevertheless not practical in some of these beings, or perhaps indeed not in any of them.

It is clear, moreover, that Kant does not intend to achieve his aim of showing that there is pure practical reason by reasoning from a priori concepts and definitions. As he remarks at the beginning of the Preface, if pure reason is practical, "it proves its reality and that of its concepts through the deed" (3). This somewhat cryptic statement anticipates the point Kant elaborates in the Comment that follows his statement of the basic law in §7, where he indicates that this law is produced or generated a priori as the fundamental *act,* or *deed,* of pure practical reason itself. To capture this idea of something reason *does,* Kant describes the basic law and the consciousness of it as a "fact of reason" (*Faktum der Vernunft*), employing a transliteration of the Latin term *factum,* which signifies a deed or action.[11] Thus, perhaps somewhat surprisingly, given our usual understanding of 'fact' today, Kant uses the expression "fact of reason" precisely to indicate that the basic law is neither given to us from without, as it would be if it were an empirical fact given to us through the senses, nor reached as a conclusion from any "antecedent data of reason," such as the antecedent consciousness of our freedom—something Kant denies we have, as it would require an intellectual intuition, a mode of cognition that, if possible at all, would be available only to an infinite rational being.

Unlike the familiar deeds that human beings perform in practical life, which are occurrences that take place in time, a deed of *pure* reason is not an action undertaken in response to any specific empirical conditions and cannot be assigned to any particular position in time; it is rather the activity of reason itself, manifest in practical life as a fundamental law, something unchangingly operative at all times and in all conditions, even if its effects may vary owing to differences in the conditions and circumstances in which it is operative. And in having this unchanging standing in practical thinking, the deed of pure reason has an independence from all particular acts of practical thinking that enables Kant also to characterize it as given, though of course not in the way that an empirical fact is given, but rather as a fact of reason. That is to say, it is not given *to* us, from some external source, but rather given *in* us, by our own reason.

If the basic law of pure practical reason is a fact in the sense just indicated, then showing that pure reason is practical must be a matter of drawing attention to this law, of directing thought to it in a way that clearly reveals its basis in reason and thereby puts us in a position to achieve a reflective (philosophical) recognition of it as given in us by reason. Kant does this in two ways. The first is through the argument of §§1–6, which, though it does not have the assertion of this fundamental law as its logical conclusion, does identify what the law is and show that it originates solely in reason. The argument thus directs our attention to the idea of such a law and puts us

---

[11] See *Metaphysics of Morals* VI, 227. Because the basic law of pure practical reason is a practical law, the law and the consciousness of it are ultimately the same, for practical laws differ from laws of theoretical cognition precisely in that they depend for their very reality on the at least implicit awareness of them by the beings who are subject to them.

in a position to be conscious of the practicality of pure reason in ourselves through our own awareness of the actuality of this law in our own practical thinking. Kant is thus in a position to state, as he does in the Corollary (31), that pure reason is indeed practical. To come to this awareness of pure reason's practicality in ourselves simply by working through the argument of §§1–6 is no easy feat, of course, owing at least in part to the necessarily highly abstract character of the philosophical considerations contained within it. The achievement of this recognition is aided, however, by the second way in which Kant draws our attention to the basic law, through his observation in the Corollary that this law is nothing other than what we have known all along under another name, as the moral law.[12] Recognizing the basic law as identical with the moral law enables us to appreciate its actuality in our practical thinking, and recognizing, in accordance with the argument of §§1–6, that this law originates solely in reason, enables us to see that the actuality of this law in our practical thinking is the actuality of pure reason itself.

E. Autonomy and Freedom (§8)

Kant is now finally in a position from which he can derive a positive conclusion regarding freedom. This conclusion, which he presents as Theorem IV, states that the autonomy, or freedom, of the will is the source of the moral law. Having established, in his solutions to Problems I and II (§§5–6), that a relation of mutual entailment holds between the concept of a will determinable only by the basic law of pure practical reason (now identified with the moral law) and the concept of a free will, Kant can now, by appealing to the actuality of that law, which is given in the fact of reason, infer the actuality of freedom as well and positively characterize this freedom in terms of that law as the will's autonomy, or self-legislation.

The fact that this proposition is placed under the heading "Theorem IV" should not prevent us from appreciating that its status is fundamentally dif-

---

[12] Kant does not present here any detailed argument in support of this identification of the basic law of pure practical reason with the moral law, presumably for the reason that he assumes a familiarity on the part of his readers with the first two chapters of the *Grounding,* where, in seeking to identify the principle that lies at the basis of morality, he eventually reached a formulation of it in terms of the idea of universal legislation (IV, 431–33). As Kant says in the Preface, the *Critique of Practical Reason* does presuppose the "preliminary acquaintance with the principle of duty" and an indication and justification of "a determinate formula of duty," which are provided in the *Grounding* (8).

ferent from that of the three theorems that precede it. This difference in status stems directly from the fact that Theorem IV is the only theorem whose derivation depends on the basic law of pure practical reason. Kant points out in his Comment on the basic law that, although not itself a postulate, this law can be compared to the postulates used in geometry insofar as it is a *practical* proposition. And just as geometers use their postulates to derive further theorems, so Kant uses this law as a basis for establishing Theorem IV. Thus, despite the fact that Theorem IV is like the three preceding theorems in that it is a theoretical proposition—a proposition about what is, rather than what ought to be—it is unlike the other three in that its proof depends on a practical proposition. To mark this difference in standing, Kant employs the phrase "postulate of pure practical reason," which, as he later tells us, signifies "a *theoretical* proposition, though one not provable as such [i.e., not provable by a purely theoretical argument, which relies on no practical propositions], insofar as it attaches inseparably to a *practical* law that holds a priori [and] unconditionally" (122).[13] Thus, we have reached here in Theorem IV the first of the three postulates of pure practical reason expounded in the second *Critique,* in which the ideas of pure reason, though declared in the first *Critique* to be unsuited for use in theoretical cognition, receive a practically justified application.

5. CAN THE HIGHEST PRINCIPLE OF PRACTICAL REASON BE JUSTIFIED?

The exposition of the fundamental principle of practical reason is followed by a section titled Of the Deduction of the Principles of Pure Practical Reason. Despite what this title might lead us to expect, Kant argues here that a deduction of the fundamental principle—that is, a justification of its objective and universal validity and of insight into its possibility—is neither possible nor needed. In the first *Critique,* Kant provided such justification of the a priori principles of theoretical cognition (for example, the principle that everything that happens has a cause) by relating them to the possibility of experience: To provide insight into how we are able to have such a priori theoretical cognition of the objects of experience, Kant sought to show that it is only by presupposing these principles that it is possible to have experi-

---

[13] As Kant points out in the Preface, in this use 'postulate' has a sense quite different from the one it has in mathematics (see 11n).

ence of those objects at all. The fundamental principle of pure practical reason, however, does not stand in any such relation to the possibility of experience. Nor, Kant points out, is it possible to supply in place of a deduction any proof from experience, given that the principle is formal rather than material.

Kant does present, in lieu of a deduction, a "credential" for the moral law, or what amounts to a philosophical confirmation of our awareness, through the fact of reason, of this law's actuality. A satisfactory elucidation of this credential would require an examination of doctrines in the first *Critique* that lie beyond the scope of this Introduction. In brief, Kant suggests that the credential is furnished by the fact that the moral law is itself the source of a deduction of the idea of freedom (as we noted, the proof of Theorem IV, in which the idea of freedom is applied to the will, depends on the moral law). The moral law thus provides an application for an idea that would otherwise have a merely problematic standing in the eyes of reason. According to Kant's argument in the Third Antinomy of the first *Critique,* theoretical reason cannot apply the idea of a freely acting cause to any object yet must regard this type of causality as somehow compatible with its principle of natural necessity, which states that everything that happens in nature is determined by the operation of causes in the time that precedes it. The compatibility of these two sorts of causality—that of freedom and that of natural necessity—depends, Kant argues, on a distinction between things as they appear to us and are knowable by means of the senses, through which they are represented according to the condition of time, and things as they are in themselves, as conceived by reason, without reference to that condition. With this distinction in place, it becomes possible to see that theoretical reason's principle that all occurrences in nature are determined by natural necessity applies only to things as appearances, and that the possibility is therefore left open that the actions of things in themselves may nevertheless be free, even though the latter cannot be known by theoretical reason. In the case of human beings, this possibility can be described more definitely by saying that, although the actions whereby the exercise of a human being's will appears and is knowable by means of the senses are all occurrences in time subject to natural necessity, the will itself, conceived solely by reason as the causality of the human subject as it is in itself, may nevertheless be free. The acts in which the will's exercise consists are not themselves occurrences in time appearing to us by means of the senses, but rather the very practical principles, or maxims, in which the will's self-determination consists and in accordance with which the temporally determined actions that appear to the senses occur. By providing a determinate conception of the law by which a free cause determines itself and a practically justified use for the concept of freedom, the moral law fills a gap that theoretical cognition by itself is unable to close. This harmonious way in which practical reason complements theoretical reason provides a confirmation of the fact of reason, or a credential for the moral law.

6. THE EFFECTS OF PURE PRACTICAL REASON

Having completed his argument that there is pure practical reason and having secured the concept of freedom for use in a practical connection, Kant is in a position to finish his task in the Analytic of countering the presumption that the practical employment of reason, even in morality, is always empirically conditioned. As noted earlier, this is to be accomplished by spelling out an account of how pure reason, by applying its formal practical principle, can provide for itself an object to be pursued and finally produce an effect on our feeling through which it can move us to act. Thus, Chapter II deals with the *objective effect* of the moral law—that is, the effect that is to be produced through action in accordance with pure practical reason's concept of that effect—and Chapter III concerns the *subjective effect* of this law—that is, its effect on feeling in the mind of the subject.

A. Defining the Concept of an Object of Practical Reason

We have noted that the basic law of pure practical reason requires that practical principles, or the will's general acts of self-determination, be in accordance with the mere form of a universal legislation, and that this form is just the form of a principle of practical knowledge. It follows that all practical principles that are in accordance with this basic law are principles of such knowledge. Thus, insofar as the will is determined by the basic law, the object, or the matter represented in its principle, is an object of practical knowledge. Accordingly, the task of Chapter II—to specify the object of a will determined by this law—amounts to the task of specifying the object of the will insofar as it is an object of practical knowledge. Pointing to certain features of our understanding of the concept of the good that mark it out as a concept that we employ in cognitive claims about objects, namely, that in calling something good we take it to be a *necessary* object of desire and suppose that rational beings should *universally* agree with our judgment

(59), Kant identifies the good as the object of practical knowledge. And relying on his argument in Chapter I that there is pure practical reason, which asserts its moral law a priori, independently of all experience, as the condition of all practical knowledge, Kant can now say of the good, identified as the object of such knowledge, that the determination, or specification, of what it consists in must be carried out in accordance with the moral law.

Kant acknowledges that many will find this claim paradoxical. The widespread assumption that the practical employment of reason is always empirically conditioned has led moral philosophers to suppose that the rational determination of the will must start with the identification of an object for the will (often under the heading of the agreeable, or happiness) and then proceed, with the aid of theoretical reason, to the specification of practical principles that have this object as their matter. On the strength of his demonstration that there is pure practical reason, Kant maintains to the contrary that the object of the will, thought under the concept of the good, must be determined only after and by means of the moral law (62–63). Readers familiar with the first *Critique* will recognize that this "paradox of method" parallels the approach Kant follows in that work with regard to theoretical cognition, wherein he abandons the assumption prevalent among traditional metaphysicians that "all our cognition must conform to the objects" and proclaims, to the contrary, that "the objects must conform to our cognition" (*Critique of Pure Reason* B xvi).

One important implication of this way of proceeding—given the cognitive character of the concept of the good and given Kant's argument in Chapter I that a practical principle whose determining basis lies in its matter cannot be practical knowledge—is that it makes it possible to call things good without thereby meaning merely that they are good *for something* (that is, as a means for attaining some object). If it is assumed that the practical employment of reason is always empirically conditioned, then the cognitive character of the concept of the good restricts the application of it to means, or to what is useful. On this assumption, the prudent shopkeeper could say that it is good to keep a fixed general price, but not that the aim of personal advantage or prosperity for the sake of which he follows that practice is likewise good, for the latter is not pursued for the sake of anything further. If, on the other hand, pure reason is practical, then the concept of the good can also be applied to ends to the extent that these are objects of practical laws and thus objects of practical knowledge. This enables Kant to go so far as to say that the concept of the good itself, where this is understood not as the mere relativized concept *good-for-something* but as a concept that is applicable to ends, is *made possible* by the moral law (64). And it will also enable him, in the Dialectic, to provide an account of the complete ultimate end as the highest good, to the pursuit of which all persons are enjoined by the moral law.

B. The Subjective Effects of Pure Practical Reason

In the third and concluding chapter of the Analytic, Kant provides an account of how the moral law can be an "incentive,"[14] or *subjective* determining basis of the will, an account in which, starting with the fact of reason, he indicates a priori what effects the moral law must produce in the mind of a rational being in whom the will is affected by sensible impulses. Kant has already argued, in Chapter I, that *objectively,* or in the a priori and ideal representation of reason, the moral law is the determining basis of a free will. But in the case of a rational being such as the human being, in whom the will is by its nature pathologically affected, the exercise of the will is liable to be influenced by subjective factors—that is, by feelings and the inclinations associated with them—and hence such a will is not necessarily, by its very nature, in conformity with the moral law. Therefore, if the moral law is to determine the will of such beings, it must do so not only objectively, in the judgment of reason, but also subjectively, through producing effects on feeling that both prevent sensible impulses from influencing the will's exercise and also, positively, provide a basis for our taking an interest in morally good action.

In this chapter, as in the preceding one, Kant develops his account in opposition to the presumption that the practical employment of reason is always empirically conditioned. With regard to the will's subjective determining bases, this presumption amounts to the thought that the only such determining bases are the feelings of pleasure or displeasure, agreeableness or disagreeableness, that attend the representation of the existence of some object. This presumption cannot accommodate the fact of reason, for the representation that figures in the will's determination by pure reason—the

---

[14] It has become the almost universal practice of English language translators of Kant's ethics to render the German term *Triebfeder* as 'incentive.' It is important, however, not to be misled by this practice into thinking that Kant has in mind some circumstance or prospect that incites or tends to incite a person to action—the sort of thing we mean when we speak, for example, of the bonuses or rebates a company may offer as providing prospective customers with an incentive to do business with it. Kant is rather thinking of a "spring" or source of action lying in the subject.

bare idea of practical law, or the mere form of a universal legislation—is not, and cannot be, the representation of the *existence* of anything at all. As the fact, or deed, of reason, this idea is itself actual, but it is not a representation of anything actual; it says nothing about how the will *is* determined but is rather a law that sets forth a priori how the will is *to be* determined.

Accordingly, the account Kant is to provide of how this law can produce a positive effect in feeling must accommodate the fact that, as a purely intellectual representation, it cannot itself be anything we find agreeable. Kant accomplishes this by identifying an *indirect* effect that the moral law has on feeling in a rational being in which, as in the human case, there is a sensible nature that, in addition to being the source of inclinations, also contains a certain propensity, under the name of self-love, to regard oneself as an objective determining basis of the will in general—a propensity that can be called self-conceit to the extent that one comes to regard oneself as an unconditional practical principle. This indirect effect arises through the moral law's striking down the presumptuous claims of self-conceit, which produces a painful feeling of humiliation. This feeling of humiliation, however, is, at the same time, a feeling of respect for the moral law, a feeling that can come to have a positive aspect to the extent that we recognize that it is in the judgment of *our own* reason that our self-conceit has been struck down. Through this recognition, the feeling of respect takes on a certain elevating and ennobling character, insofar as its object is recognized to be a law that has its source in our own rational nature. As a result, the feeling of respect can have a positive influence on the exercise of the will, providing us with an interest in acting according to this law and thereby a basis on which morally worthy maxims of action can be founded. To this feeling of respect for the moral law and for persons as subjects of the moral law Kant gives the name *moral feeling*. As the subjective effect the moral law produces on the human mind, this feeling is nothing other than the moral law's own operation as a *subjective* determining basis of the will.

7. THE HIGHEST GOOD AND THE ANTINOMY OF PRACTICAL REASON

As mentioned earlier, Kant argues in Chapter II that the moral law makes possible a concept of the good that is applicable to ends. This concept is taken up again in the Dialectic of Pure Practical Reason, which begins with an exposition of the idea of the totality of the good, under the name of the highest good, an idea that pure practical reason frames simply in virtue of its cognitive function of introducing unity and order into our practical cognition. Corresponding to the distinction drawn in the Analytic between the form and the matter of practical knowledge, two specifically different elements—virtue and happiness—are identified as constituents of the highest good. That virtue should be counted as something good comes as no surprise, of course, for virtue is just the will's perfection in determining itself in accordance with the moral law, or in making the form of a universal legislation the determining basis of one's maxims. But many readers are surprised to find Kant now claiming that, in the judgment of pure practical reason, the happiness of a virtuous person is also something good. Interpreters have often questioned whether this claim is consistent with Kant's earlier denial (§§3–4) that the principle of personal happiness can be a practical law, or with the many passages in which happiness is linked with the agreeable, which Kant sharply contrasts with the good. Yet the grounds for this claim can be found in the conclusions that have already been reached in the Analytic. As we have seen, a finite rational being's necessary end of happiness can be pursued in accordance with a maxim that has the form of a universal legislation if others' happiness is also included along with it, and we have also noted that this form is just the form of a principle of practical knowledge. Since the maxim in accordance with which a virtuous person pursues this necessary end has this form as its determining basis, it is a principle of practical knowledge. And since practical knowledge has the good as its object, the object of this virtuous maxim is good. Given, then, that the highest good includes all ends that are good, it must be conceived as a condition in which all persons are not only virtuous, but also happy.

To achieve an adequate conception of the highest good, however, it is not enough simply to identify virtue and happiness as its ingredients. In conceiving of the totality of the good, pure practical reason represents it as systematically unified. Hence it conceives of the highest good not as a mere aggregate of virtue and happiness, but as a whole in which these two elements are necessarily connected. Kant observes that both the Stoics and the Epicureans appreciated that, in the highest good, virtue and happiness are to be found united, but he argues that these two schools of antiquity erred in their understanding of how the elements are related. Each of these schools attempted, as best it could, to define the elements in such a way that the presence of one entailed the presence of the other. The Epicureans endeavored to reduce virtue to a maxim of prudence grounded in the secure cognizance that it leads to happiness, and the Stoics sought to reduce happiness to the satisfaction that comes from being conscious of one's virtue. Kant argues that in attempting such reductive definitions both schools overlooked the fundamental difference brought to light in the Analytic between the principle of morality and the principle of happiness. Since the former is a principle by which the will can immediately determine itself a priori, whereas happiness includes agreeable states of mind that depend on external conditions (health, material goods, and so forth), the attainment of happiness depends on further conditions beyond those on which the attainment of virtue depends. Neither virtue nor happiness, then, can be reduced or assimilated to the other through such definitions. Instead, Kant says, virtue and happiness must be regarded as connected within the highest good simply as cause and effect, so that in the achievement of the highest good, persons would be, through their virtuous conduct, the authors of their own happiness.

Once this proper understanding of the relation between these elements has been reached, however, a difficulty immediately arises, which lies at the heart of what Kant calls the Antinomy of Practical Reason. As in the case of the concept of freedom, the difficulty here concerns whether the ideas on which pure reason relies in its practical use are compatible with the principles of theoretical reason. Whereas the achievement of the highest good would require virtue and happiness to be so related that happiness follows as a necessary effect of virtue, the conception of nature on which theoretical reason relies seems to rule out the possibility of any such connection. How, after all, could virtue protect us from disease and other natural calamities? And even where we do succeed in making one thing serve as means for achieving another, we do so by ingenuity and skill, forms of intelligence quite different from the practical knowledge that lies at the basis of virtue. Because this antinomy seems to entail that the highest good is impossible, it threatens the validity of the moral law itself, insofar as the highest good is something the moral law unconditionally commands us to pursue.

We noted earlier that Kant's distinction between appearances and things in themselves makes it possible to understand how the concept of freedom is compatible with the principle of natural necessity. This compatibility, together with the connection between the moral law and freedom, enables Kant to find a credential for the moral law in lieu of a deduction. In the Dialectic, Kant again appeals to his distinction between appearances and things in themselves, this time to remove the antinomy concerning the concept of the highest good. By appealing to this distinction, Kant is able to introduce the other two ideas of pure reason as representations figuring in two further postulates of pure practical reason—namely, the immortality of the soul and the existence of God—which together express necessary and sufficient conditions under which the highest good is achievable. Despite the fact that the ideas of God and immortality are not concepts that can enter into our theoretical cognition of objects, Kant argues that, on account of the unconditionality of the moral law's command, pure practical reason has a primacy over theoretical reason that justifies us in using them for practical purposes.

Linking the two postulates just mentioned with the highest good's two elements, virtue and happiness, Kant first argues that the immortality of the soul must be postulated in order to conceive of the full attainment of virtue as possible. Since the human will is by its nature pathologically affected, complete adequacy to the moral law does not belong to it simply by nature, but rather must be attained, through the will's exercise; and, for the same reason, this attainment of complete adequacy to the moral law is not possible in a finite period of time. So in order to conceive of the attainment of such adequacy as possible, we must assume the possibility of an unending progress toward it. Conceiving of an unending progress enables us to conceive of the human will as *in itself* completely adequate to the moral law, for we can regard unending progress as the way in which, in a finite being, the complete adequacy that belongs to the exercise of its pathologically affected will in itself appears in time.

With regard to the other element of the highest good, Kant argues that the existence of God must be postulated in order to conceive of happiness as an effect that follows necessarily from virtue. We can think of virtue and happiness as necessarily connected in this way only by supposing that nature itself, which contains the external conditions on which virtuous action depends for its attainment of the happiness included in its end, depends in turn on a supreme moral being—that is, a being of infinite wisdom and power whose ultimate purpose in creating the world lies in the highest good. Although it is not explicitly asserted as part of his argument, we might reasonably surmise that, just as Kant sees the adequacy of a finite being's will in itself to the moral law as something that appears in time as unending progress toward perfect virtue, so he sees the happiness that follows as virtue's necessary effect in the highest good as something that gradually and proportionately increases in time as the human being—in the species as well as in the individual—makes progress in virtue.

These two postulates differ from the postulate of freedom in that they are necessarily required to conceive of the possibility of the *object* of the moral law, whereas the idea of freedom is immediately connected with the representation of the moral law itself. Yet all three postulates are alike insofar as they are theoretical propositions that, because they concern objects that cannot be given in experience, cannot be supported by theoretical reason, and so cannot contribute to our theoretical cognition of the world, yet are rationally justified for practical purposes merely through the relation they bear to the unconditional requirements of pure practical reason. In this regard, they have a unique standing within Kant's philosophy.

8. CONCLUSION

Having completed our outline of Kant's argument in the second *Critique,* we may now cast our glance back over the whole in a concluding observation. We noted earlier that, for Kant, the practical aim of moral philosophy is to remove and to forestall the confusions and misunderstandings from which certain doubts that can impede the moral law's acceptance might otherwise arise, especially the theoretically engendered doubts concerning the concept of freedom and the related presumption that the practical employment of reason is always, even in morality, empirically conditioned. Having traced Kant's attempt to remove these sources of doubt through his arguments in the Analytic and the Dialectic, we are now in a position to see that the philosophical understanding of morality expressed in these arguments also helps, in a direct and positive way, to secure "acceptance and durability" for the moral law in two quite distinct yet complementary ways. The first emerges in the Analytic, the second in the Dialectic.

In the Analytic, Kant carries out an analysis of the faculty of reason in its practical employment, in which the a priori and empirical sources of its principles and of the motives for acting on them are distinguished. Kant himself calls attention to this procedure of separating the pure from the empirical and explicitly likens it to a chemist's analysis. Indeed, it is difficult to overstate the great emphasis he places on the importance of clearly distinguishing the formal principle of pure practical reason from the principle of personal happiness, under which he places all empirical sources of motivation. And the reason for this emphasis is not difficult to see. In addition to enabling Kant to identify the source of morality in the autonomy of the will, this separation of the moral law from all other practical principles enables him to argue in Chapter III that in virtue of its origin in pure practical reason, the moral law can both inspire respect for itself and for ourselves as subjects who share this reason and also thereby be the source of a heightened consciousness of our freedom and autonomy, thus effecting an elevated and ennobled frame of mind that does much, Kant thinks, to strengthen the moral motive.

Yet this analysis, if taken by itself, can easily give the impression that the two elements it separates—morality and happiness—have no relation to one another. It may leave us with the image of a fragmented practical life, in which these two principles work within us in an altogether unrelated way. If not dispelled, such an image can itself easily become the source of doubts about morality that can weaken the moral motive, or (what is perhaps more likely) it can become the source of doubts about Kant's own analysis— doubts that have been raised by many critics of his moral philosophy.

Given this concern, the Dialectic takes on an additional importance, for it is here that Kant offers the means of removing it. Once the a priori and the empirical elements have been clearly separated through the analysis carried out in the Analytic and understood in their difference from one another, Kant is able in the Dialectic to show how these elements are necessarily combined in the highest good and to remove obstacles that may impede understanding of this object as something that is possible. In working out his doctrine of the highest good, Kant identifies the relation the moral law bears to the totality of the good, and the relation in which, within that good, virtue stands to happiness. By explaining these connections, he provides the outlines of a systematically unified conception of practical life, to which both virtue and happiness are integral, and in this way too helps to secure "acceptance and durability" for the moral law. Thus, through appreciating both parts of Kant's work—both the analysis with which it begins and the synthesis with which it is completed—it is possible, if Kant's argument is successful, both to find the moral law, taken just by itself, as based in the autonomy of the will, to be an ennobling and inspiring source of motivation, and also to find a source of further support for this motivation by comprehending how it is possible for the virtuous action that issues from it to contribute to the totality of the good and, therewith, to human happiness as well.[15]

STEPHEN ENGSTROM
UNIVERSITY OF PITTSBURGH

[15] I wish to thank Professors Werner Pluhar and Jerome Schneewind for a number of very helpful suggestions.

Critik

der

practischen Vernunft

von

Immanuel Kant

Riga,
bey Johann Friedrich Hartknoch
1788.

Critique

of

Practical Reason

by

Immanuel Kant

Riga
Johann Friedrich Hartknoch
1788

CRITIQUE

OF

PRACTICAL REASON

BY

IMMANUEL KANT

PREFACE

Why this *Critique*[1] is titled a critique not of *pure* practical reason but simply[2] of practical reason as such,[3] although its parallelism with the critique of speculative reason[4] seems to require the former—on this the treatise provides sufficient information. This *Critique* is to establish merely[5] *that there is pure practical reason,* and with this aim it critiques[6] reason's entire *practical power.*[7] If it succeeds in this [aim], then it does not need to critique (as does happen with speculative reason)[8] the *pure power itself* in order to see

[1] [*Kritik.* Here Kant uses the term to refer to the work rather than, as he does most often, to the activity of critique.]

[2] [*schlechthin,* used informally here; usually Kant employs this term (synonymously with *schlechterdings*) more formally, to mean 'absolutely.']

[3] [*überhaupt.* I render this term—except where doing so would be misleading—by 'as such' rather than by 'generally' (or 'in general') because the latter can too often be misread as an adverb modifying some nearby verb. In the few cases where 'as such' is used to translate *als solch-,* this use is readily identifiable by the expression's placement or by its being set off by commas.]

[4] [I.e., the critique of speculative *pure* reason—the subject of the *Critique of Pure Reason.* According to Kant's own definition of the term, 'speculative' means the same as 'theoretical' (compare the etymology of the two terms) except for being confined to objects beyond any possible experience: see the *Critique of Pure Reason,* A 634–35 = B 662–63, and cf. below, Ak. V, 47. However, Kant often uses the term more broadly, as pertaining not only to such objects but also to objects of possible experience.]

[5] [*soll bloß dartun,* which could also mean 'is merely to establish.' The rendering adopted here looks ahead to 'in order to see [i.e., establish]' in the next sentence.]

[6] [I.e., examines the scope and limits of: *kritisiert.*]

[7] [Or 'practical ability': *praktisches Vermögen.* I avoid translating *Vermögen* as 'faculty,' because this term may wrongly suggest—in line with the traditional "faculty psychology"—that a *Vermögen* is some kind of psychological entity "in" the mind, rather than a mere power or ability.]

[8] [Although in the original the parenthesis, as is typical for Kant's writing, occurs at the end of

whether reason is not *overreaching* itself, by merely claiming such a power. For if as pure reason it is actually[9] practical, then it proves its reality[10] and that of its concepts through the deed,[11] and all subtle reasoning[12] against the possibility of its being practical is futile.

With this pure practical power of reason, transcendental *freedom* is now also established—taken, moreover, in that absolute signification in which speculative reason needed this freedom, when using the concept of causality, in order to rescue itself from the antinomy into which it unavoidably falls when it wants to think the *unconditioned* in the series[13] of causal linkage.[14] Speculative reason was able to put this concept[15] forth only problematically, as not impossible to think, without securing the concept's objective reality,[16] but only in order to keep an alleged impossibility of what speculative reason must surely accept[17] at least as thinkable from challenging speculative reason's essence and from plunging this power into an abyss of skepticism.[18]

Kant's sentence (just after 'not *overreaching* itself'), the present context—including, in particular, the next sentence—clearly suggests that Kant intends it to apply to 'does not need to critique.']

[9] [*Wirklich.* Unlike in contemporary German, this term never means 'real' in Kant (as *he* uses this latter term), and translating it so tends to distort what Kant is trying to say, especially in contexts—such as the present one—where reality in Kant's sense is likewise mentioned.]

[10] [I.e., its applicability to things (Latin *res,* from which 'reality' is derived).]

[11] [Or 'through action': *durch die Tat.* In the *Metaphysics of Morals,* Ak. VI, 22, Kant defines 'deed' as follows: A *deed* is what we call an action insofar as it falls under [more precisely, 'is subject to': *unter . . . steht*] laws of obligation, thus also insofar as the subject is regarded in it in terms of the freedom of his power of choice.' (Translation mine.)]

[12] [*alles Vernünfteln.*]

[13] [The term is singular here: *Reihe.*]

[14] [*-verbindung.* Whenever possible (exceptions are noted), I use 'linkage' and sometimes 'link' (or, where needed, 'combination') for *Verbindung,* and 'connection' for *Verknüpfung;* similarly for the verbs. This is especially appropriate where the two terms occur in the same context, as, e.g., at Ak. V, 51.]

[15] [The concept of *transcendental freedom* taken in the absolute signification.]

[16] [I.e., without securing (rendering secure) the reality that the concept does indeed have. More literally, Kant says 'without securing [*sichern*] for the concept its objective reality.']

[17] [*gelten lassen.*]

[18] [See, in the *Critique of Pure Reason,* the Third Antinomy of Pure Reason, A 444–51 = B 472–79, and cf. A 488/B 516, A 532–58 = B 560–86.]

Now the concept of freedom, insofar as its reality is proved by an apodeictic law of practical reason, forms the *keystone* of the whole edifice of a system of pure reason, even of speculative reason.[19] All other concepts (those of God and immortality) that, as mere ideas, remain unsupported in speculative reason now attach themselves to the concept of freedom and acquire, with it and through it, stability and objective reality.[20] I.e., their *possibility*[21] is *proved* by freedom's being actual,[22] for this idea reveals itself through the moral law.

But freedom, among all the ideas of speculative reason, is also the only one whose possibility we *know*[23] a priori—though without having insight into it[24]—because it is the condition[25] of the moral law, which we do know.[26] The ideas of *God* and *immortality,* on the other hand, are not conditions of

4

---

[19] [See below, Ak. V, 28–57.]

[20] [See below, Ak. V, 119–34.]

[21] [Their real, not just logical, possibility.]

[22] [*wirklich.* Here again, translating this term as 'real' distorts what Kant is saying, especially since here too *reality* in Kant's sense has just been mentioned.]

[23] [*wissen.*]

[24] [*sie . . . einzusehen.* Insight (*Einsicht*), in Kant, is theoretical (rather than practical) cognition; cf. the etymology of 'theoretical.']

[25] Lest anyone surmise that he encounters *inconsistencies* here if I now call freedom the condition of the moral law and afterwards, in the treatise, maintain[a] that the moral law is the condition under which we can first of all *become aware*[b] of freedom, I wish only to point out[c] that whereas freedom is indeed the *ratio essendi* of the moral law, the moral law is the *ratio cognoscendi*[d] of freedom. For if the moral law were not *previously* thought distinctly in our reason, we would never consider ourselves entitled to *assume* such a thing[e] as freedom (even though freedom is not self-contradictory). But if there were no freedom, then the moral law *could not be encountered*[f] in us at all.
   [a] [*behaupten.*]
   [b] [Or '*conscious*': *bewußt.*]
   [c] [*erinnern.*]
   [d] [Respectively, 'reason for the being' and 'reason for the cognizing.']
   [e] [*so etwas.*]
   [f] [Literally, 'would not be [there] to be encountered': *würde . . . nicht anzutreffen sein.* This second case thus illustrates how freedom is the moral law's *ratio essendi,* whereas the preceding case illustrated how the moral law (as thought by us) is the *ratio cognoscendi* of freedom.]

[26] [See below, Ak. V, 27–33, 42–50.]

the moral law,[27] but conditions only of the necessary object[28] of a will determined by this law, i.e., conditions of the merely practical[29] use of our reason. Hence concerning those ideas we cannot claim[30] to *cognize*[31] and *have insight into*—I wish to say not merely their actuality, but even their possibility. But they are nonetheless conditions[32] for the application of the morally determined will to its object that is given to it a priori (the highest good).[33] Consequently their possibility can and must in this practical reference[34] be *assumed* even without our theoretically cognizing and having insight into them. For this latter demand [that we assume the possibility of these ideas] it suffices, for a practical aim,[35] that they contain no intrinsic impossibility (contradiction). Here there is, then, a basis of assent[36]— merely *subjective* in comparison to speculative reason, yet valid *objectively* for an equally pure but practical reason—whereby the ideas of God and immortality are provided, by means of the concept of freedom, with objective

---

[27] [*des moralischen Gesetzes.*]

[28] [Viz., the highest good. Cf. just below.]

[29] [Rather than theoretical.]

[30] [*behaupten.*]

[31] [Kant here means (cf. just below) *cognize theoretically: [theoretisch] erkennen;* on Kant's view we do have *practical* cognition of God and (our soul's) immortality—not, however, theoretical cognition and hence insight. It is essential, moreover, that *erkennen* (similarly for the noun, *Erkenntnis*) be translated throughout *not* as 'to know,' but as 'to cognize,' precisely because on Kant's view—as this passage begins to indicate—our practical cognitions (*Erkenntnisse*) of God and immortality are *not* instances of knowledge (*Wissen*) but of rational (moral) faith. See below, Ak. V, 122–48, esp. 132–38 and 144–46, cf. 57. See also the *Critique of Pure Reason,* B xxi and the famous passage at B xxx, as well as A 633–34 = B 661–62 and A 828–29 = B 856–57; and cf. the *Critique of Judgment,* Ak. V, 467, 469–70, 472, and 475.]

[32] [Reading *sind sie Bedingungen* for *sind die Bedingungen.* Karl Vorländer instead reads *sind sie die Bedingungen,* i.e., 'they are . . . the conditions.' The reading adopted here fits best with what Kant has just said.]

[33] [On the highest good, see below, Ak. V, 107–19.]

[34] [*Beziehung.*]

[35] [*in praktischer Absicht.*]

[36] [Literally, 'basis of considering-true': *Grund des Fürwahrhaltens.* With a few exceptions, I translate *Grund* as 'basis' rather than 'ground.' One advantage of this rendering is that the corresponding 'based on' is rather less awkward than 'grounded in.' But the main advantage is that whereas the 'ground' terminology tends to suggest a logical relation, the 'basis' terminology is much broader—almost always appropriately so. E.g., a *Bestimmungsgrund,* i.e., a basis determining something, can be all sorts of things.]

reality and with an authority,[37] indeed a subjective necessity (a need of pure reason), to assume them. This,[38] however, does not expand reason in its theoretical cognition, but only gives us the possibility[39] [of God and immortality], which previously was only a *problem* and here becomes an *assertion*,[40] and thus connects[41] the practical use of reason with the elements of the theoretical use. And this need [of pure reason] is by no means a hypothetical one for a *discretionary*[42] aim of speculation, where one must assume something if one *wants* to ascend to the completion[43] of reason's use in speculation; rather, it is a *legal* need[44] to assume something without which what one *ought* to set irremissibly as the aim of one's doing and refraining[45] cannot be done.[46]

It would indeed be more satisfying for our speculative reason to solve those problems[47] on its own, without this detour, and to preserve them as insight for practical use; but it so happens that our power of speculation is not so well off. Those who boast of such lofty cognitions should not keep them back but should exhibit them publicly to be tested and highly esteemed. They wish[48] to *prove;* very well, let them prove, and the critique[49] will lay all its weaponry at their feet, [acknowledging them] as victors. *Quid statis? Nolint. Atqui licet esse beatis.*[50] Since, then, they are in fact not

5

---

[37] [*Befugnis.*]

[38] [I.e., the providing of the ideas of God and immortality with objective reality and with an authority and subjective necessity to assume them.]

[39] [The real, not just logical, possibility.]

[40] [*Assertion.*]

[41] [*verknüpfen.*]

[42] [Or 'optional': *beliebig.*]

[43] [Or 'perfection': *Vollendung.*]

[44] [I.e., a need arising from the (moral) law: *ein gesetzliches.* I have deleted the emphasis on *ein* ('a').]

[45] [*seines Tuns und Lassens.*]

[46] [*geschehen.*]

[47] [Of God and immortality: *Aufgaben.*]

[48] [*wollen.*]

[49] [The (activity of) critique in general. Likewise at the beginning of the next paragraph.]

[50] [The quote is from Horace's *Satires,* I, i, 19. A god (who turns out to be Jupiter), having offered to people unhappy with their lives the opportunity to change places with others, yet find-

willing,[51] presumably because they are unable, we must only take up that weaponry again in order to seek the concepts of *God, freedom,* and *immortality*—for the *possibility*[52] of which speculation does not find sufficient warrant—in a moral use of reason, and to base them on this use.[53]

Here the critique's puzzle as to how one can *deny* objective *reality* to the suprasensible[54] *use of the categories* and yet *grant* them[55] this *reality* in regard to the objects of pure practical reason is also for the first time explained. For beforehand, as long as such a practical use is familiar[56] only by name, this must necessarily look *inconsistent.* But now one becomes aware, by a complete dissection of reason's practical use,[57] that here the reality at issue does not aim at any *determination of the categories* and expansion of cognition to the suprasensible, but that what is meant by this reality is only that in this [practical] reference *an object* belongs to them at all, because they are either contained in the necessary a priori determination of the will or inseparably linked with the object of this determination. Hence that inconsistency vanishes, because a different use is being made of those concepts[58] from the use that speculative reason requires. On the contrary, there now discloses itself a very satisfying confirmation, hardly to be expected before, of the speculative critique's *consistent way of thinking.* For while that critique urged us to allow objects of experience taken as such[59]—

---

ing them reluctant, says to them, "What are you waiting for?" (literally, "Why are you standing still?"), and then comments, "They are not willing; yet they could be happy." All translations given in footnotes are my own, though I do not say so on each occasion. As regards this particular translation, however, I am indebted to Garrett G. Fagan for his valuable and insightful assistance concerning both a grammatical subtlety in the passage (viz., the role of the dative in *beatis*) and Horace's most likely intended meaning.]

[51] [*nicht wollen.*]

[52] [I.e., again, real possibility.]

[53] [See below, Ak. V, 119–21, 134–41.]

[54] [*übersinnlich.*]

[55] [*ihnen.* Erdmann instead reads *ihm,* i.e., 'it,' which then refers not to the categories but to their suprasensible *use.*]

[56] [*man . . . kennt.* See below, Ak. V, 35 br. n. 120.]

[57] [Reading, with Erich Adickes and with Paul Natorp in the *Akademie* edition, *des letzteren* for *der letzteren,* which would refer (implicitly) to practical *reason.*]

[58] [I.e., the categories.]

[59] [I.e., taken *as* objects of experience, not as the things that these objects are in themselves. For Kant's view that the things that appear are things in themselves (although we can have the-

including even our own subject[60]—to hold only as *appearances,* but yet to base them on things in themselves, and therefore not to regard everything suprasensible as invention and the concept of the suprasensible as empty of content, [practical reason now yields confirmation]: practical reason, on its own and without having made an agreement with speculative reason, now provides a suprasensible object of the category of causality, namely *freedom,* with reality (although—since this [freedom] is a practical concept—it also does so only for practical use); thus it confirms by a fact[61] what in the speculative critique could only be *thought.*[62] With this, at the same time, the strange though indisputable assertion of the speculative critique, that **in inner intuition** even *the thinking subject is merely an appearance to himself,*[63] now also receives in the critique of practical reason its full confirmation—and is here confirmed so well that one must arrive at it even if the former critique had not proved this proposition at all.**[64]**

---

oretical cognition of them only as appearances), see the *Critique of Pure Reason,* B xxvi–xxvii, 56, 59, 305n, 333.]

[60] [I.e., ourselves as subjects.]

[61] [*Faktum.* On the fact of reason, see below, Ak. V, 31 incl. br. n. 75.]

[62] [See below, Ak. V, 27–33, 42–50.]

[63] [See the Paralogisms of Pure Reason in the *Critique of Pure Reason,* A 341–405/ B 399–428, esp. B 406–13.]

[64] The reconciliation[a] of causality as freedom with causality as natural mechanism—the first of which is established[b] through the moral law,[c] the second through the law of nature, and indeed in one and the same subject, the human being—is impossible without presenting[d] the human being in reference to the first as a being in itself but in reference to the second as an appearance, the former in *pure* and the latter in *empirical* consciousness. Otherwise the contradiction of reason with itself is unavoidable.

  [a] [*Vereinigung.*]
  [b] [*feststehen.*]
  [c] [*Sittengesetz.*]
  [d] [*vorstellen,* traditionally translated as 'to represent'; the noun, *Vorstellung,* is similarly translated here as 'presentation' rather than as 'representation.' (In contexts where 'to present' and 'presentation' might sound misleading and the original terms are applied narrowly, I use 'to conceive' and 'conception' instead.) Presentations, as the term is here used, are such objects of our direct awareness as sensations, intuitions, perceptions, concepts, cognitions, ideas, and schemata; see the *Critique of Pure Reason,* A 320/B 376–77 and A 140/B 179. I have abandoned the traditional rendering of *Vorstellung* (similarly for the verb) because it suggests that Kant's theory of sensation, perception, cognition, etc., is representational, which it is not. For one thing, *vorstellen,* in the Kantian use of the term that is relevant here, is not—as the 'representation' terminology tends to suggest—something that *Vorstellungen* do; it is some-

Through this [explanation] I also understand why the most significant objections against the *Critique [of Pure Reason]* that I have so far encountered revolve precisely about these two points: viz., *on the one hand*, an objective reality of the categories [as] applied to noumena that is denied in theoretical and asserted in practical cognition; *on the other hand*, the paradoxical demand to make oneself, as subject of freedom, a noumenon, but simultaneously also, with regard to nature, a phenomenon in one's own empirical consciousness. For, as long as people had not yet framed any determinate concepts of morality and freedom, they could not divine, on the one hand, on what, as noumenon, they were to base the alleged appearance, and, on the other hand, whether indeed framing a concept of this noumenon was still possible at all, if all the concepts of pure understanding in its theoretical use had already been dedicated beforehand exclusively to mere appearances. Only a comprehensive *Critique of Practical Reason* can remove all this misinterpretation and put the consistent way of thinking, which indeed amounts to its greatest merit, in a clear light.[65]

So much by way of justification as to why the concepts and principles[66] of pure speculative reason, which, after all, have already undergone their special critique, are in this work now and then subjected to examination

---

thing that *we* do. Above all, however, *vorstellen* as so used never means anything like 'to represent' in the sense of 'to stand for.' Even an empirical intuition, e.g., does not stand for—does *not* represent—an object of experience (let alone a thing in itself), but rather enters into the experience which that object of experience is. This already serious problem with the 'representation' terminology has traditionally been aggravated further by the fact that another Kantian term, *Darstellung* (similarly for the verb), has simultaneously been translated most commonly as 'presentation' (less often, but appropriately, as 'exhibition'), which suggests an incorrect and very misleading relation between *Vorstellung* and *Darstellung*. The traditional rendering of *Vorstellung* as 'representation' seems to have been prompted by Kant's own linking of *Vorstellung* to the Latin *repraesentatio*. However, this Latin term actually means no more than a 'making present to oneself'—cf. German *Vergegenwärtigung*—and thus, like Kant's *Vorstellung*, carries no implication whatsoever that perception, cognition, etc., are *representational*. Latin *praesentatio*, on the other hand, means only a 'handing over' (of something); and although Kant *could* have attached a new meaning to *praesentatio*—as I have done with 'presentation'—he had no need to, since *repraesentatio*, unlike 'representation,' already fit his meaning of *Vorstellung*. The terminological adjustments that I have here described are not new; I already made them in my translations of Kant's *Critique of Judgment* and *Critique of Pure Reason* (both listed in the Selected Bibliography).]

[65] [See below, Ak. V, 42–57.]

[66] [*Grundsätze*. In this *Critique*, as in the other two, I render both *Grundsatz* and *Prinzip* as 'principle,' since Kant does seem to use the two terms interchangeably. Cf. Kant's *Logic*, Ak. IX, 110, where this interchangeability is made explicit.]

once more. Ordinarily[67] this is not very fitting for the systematic progression of a science that is to be built (since matters that have been adjudicated must properly only be cited and not be raised again). Yet *here* it was permitted—indeed, necessary. For reason, with those concepts, is being considered in transition to a use of them that is entirely different from the use that it made of them *there*. Such a transition, however, makes it necessary to compare the older with the newer use, in order to distinguish carefully the new track from the previous one and to draw attention simultaneously to their coherence.[68] Hence considerations of this kind, including the consideration that has once more been directed—but in pure reason's practical use—to the concept of freedom, should not be regarded as interpolations that might serve only to fill gaps in the critical system of speculative reason (for this system is complete in its aim) and to be supplemented,[69] as tends to come about when a building is rushed, by props and buttresses attached afterwards. They should be regarded, rather, as true members that make discernible the coherence of the system, so that concepts that could there be presented[70] only problematically are now made accessible to insight[71] in their real exhibition.[72] This reminder concerns above all the concept of freedom. One cannot help noting with astonishment that so many people still boast of being capable of ready insight into this concept and of explaining the possibility of freedom.[73] They boast of these abilities because they consider the concept merely in psychological reference, whereas if they had previously examined it in transcendental reference they would have had to cognize[74] its *indispensability* as a problematic concept in a complete use of

---

[67] [*sonst.*]

[68] [*Zusammenhang.* Cf. 'coherence of the system,' below.]

[69] [*noch.*]

[70] [*vorgestellt.*]

[71] [*jetzt . . . einsehen zu lassen.*]

[72] [*Darstellung.*]

[73] [I follow the *Akademie* edition in reading *derselben,* in accordance with the first edition (of 1788). The second edition (of 1792) has *desselben,* which makes the possibility be that of the *concept* of freedom. It should be noted that the second edition does not seem to have been edited by Kant himself. See Paul Natorp's introduction to the *Akademie* edition of the work, Ak. V, 498, and Karl Vorländer's introduction to the *Philosophische Bibliothek* edition, v. 38, xlv–xlvi.]

[74] [Or 'recognize': *erkennen.*]

speculative reason as well as its utter *incomprehensibility;*[75] and if thereafter they had proceeded with it to the practical use, they would have had to arrive on their own at exactly the same determination of it in regard to its principles, which they are ordinarily so reluctant to accept.[76] The concept of freedom is the stumbling block for all *empiricists,* but also the key to the most sublime practical principles for *critical* moralists, who thereby gain the insight that they must necessarily proceed *rationally.* I therefore beseech the reader not to survey with merely a cursory glance what is said about this concept at the conclusion of the Analytic.[77]

I must leave it to the experts in this sort of work to judge[78] whether such a system of pure practical reason as is here being developed from the critique of this power[79] has made it a matter of much or little trouble not to miss, above all, the right viewpoint from which the whole of this power can be traced out correctly. The system[80] does presuppose the *Grounding for the Metaphysics of Morals,*[81] but only insofar as that work provides[82] a preliminary acquaintance with the principle of duty and indicates as well as justifies a determinate formula of duty;**[83]** otherwise it subsists on its own.

---

[75] [*Unbegreiflichkeit.*]

[76] [*sich zu . . . verstehen.*]

[77] [See below, Ak. V, 89–106.]

[78] [*beurteilen.* In most Kantian texts and in German generally, this is simply the transitive analogue of *urteilen*—cf. English 'bemoan' and 'moan.' By the same token, the corresponding nouns are likewise synonymous, except that *Beurteilung* means 'judgment' only in the sense of *(act of) judging* whereas *Urteil* means 'judgment' in this sense *or* in the sense of *proposition.*]

[79] [Of practical reason (as such; cf. the beginning of this Preface): *der letzteren.*]

[80] [The system of the critique, not of the science (cf. below): *Es.*]

[81] [Kant's *Grundlegung zur Metaphysik der Sitten* of 1785.]

[82] [Literally, 'makes': *macht.*]

[83] A reviewer[a] who wanted to say something to censure that work hit the mark better than he himself may have intended when he said that no new principle of morality[b] has been put forth in it[c] but only a *new formula.* But who indeed could[d] introduce a principle of all morality[e] and, as it were, first invent morality—just as if before him the world had been in ignorance or in thoroughgoing error concerning what [one's] duty is[f]? But whoever knows what a *formula* means to a mathematician, a formula that determines quite precisely and keeps one from missing what is to be done in order to comply with an assignment,[g] will not consider a formula that does this with regard to all duty as such to be something insignificant and dispensable.

[a] [Although there has been some disagreement on this point, it does seem clear that Kant is

That the *division* of all practical sciences to the point of *completeness,* such as the critique of speculative reason accomplished, has not been added—for this too a valid basis can be found in the constitution[84] of this practical power of reason. For, the particular determination of duties as human duties, which is needed in order to divide them, is possible only if the subject

referring to Gottlob August Tittel (1739–1816), ecclesiastical counselor at Karlsruhe, and his *Über Herrn Kant's Moralreform*—i.e., *On Mr. Kant's Moral Reform*—(Frankfurt and Leipzig: Gebrüder Pfähler, 1786; reprinted, Brussels: Culture et civilisation, 1969). In that work, Tittel speaks (ibid., 55) of Kant's "alleged *new principle* of the doctrine of morals" and asks (ibid., 35), "Is the entire Kantian moral reform indeed to limit itself just to a *new formula?*" See Paul Natorp's comments on the *Akademie* edition of this *Critique,* Ak. V, 506–07 (cf. 497), and Karl Vorländer's introduction to the *Philosophische Bibliothek* edition of the same work, vol. 38, xvi–xvii. Both Natorp and Vorländer (loc. cit.) do also mention another reviewer of the *Grounding for the Metaphysics of Morals,* viz., Johann Friedrich Flatt (1759–1821), a theologian and philosopher at Tübingen who was the regular philosophical reviewer for the *Tübingische gelehrte Anzeigen* (Vorländer modernizes *Tübingische* to *Tübinger*), i.e., *Tübingen Scholarly Announcements.* The review by Flatt (who was later ennobled to *von* Flatt) appeared there on February 16, 1786 (item 14, 105–12). However, both Natorp and Vorländer (loc. cit.) expressly link Tittel, not Flatt, to *this location* in Kant's Preface, presumably because the cited passages from Tittel fit the present context so perfectly. It is true that when Natorp, in his comments on Kant's *Metaphysics of Morals* of 1797 (Ak. VI, 521, cf. V, 497, 506–07), points out that Kant's reference in that work (at Ak. VI, 207) to "a Tübingen reviewer" is to Flatt, he adds that this "is in all probability the same reviewer whom Kant already had to fend off in the Preface to the *Critique of Practical Reason.*" But although Kant does in this Preface respond (without giving a name) to some of Flatt's charges (several of which, including that of "inconsistency," can also be found in Tittel's book), this comment by Natorp is entirely consistent with those cited above, since it does not imply that the reviewer alluded to *at this location* of the Preface is Flatt rather than Tittel.]

    b [*Prinzip der Moralität.*]

    c [See the *Grounding for the Metaphysics of Morals,* Ak. IV, 403–04.]

    d [*wollte,* in one of its less common senses.]

    e [*Grundsatz aller Sittlichkeit.*]

    f [*was Pflicht sei,* which can refer either to duty *per se* or to the actions that are one's duty. The reading adopted here fits the continuation of Kant's note. See also Kant's characterization of duty below, Ak. V, 80.]

    g [*Aufgabe.*]

84 [*Beschaffenheit.* In my translations of the first and third *Critiques* I have, wherever possible, translated this term—in the sense in which it occurs here—as 'character' (and *beschaffen sein* similarly as 'to be of [this or that] character' rather than 'to be constituted [in this or that way]'), in order to keep this term from being linked erroneously with Kant's technical term 'constitutive' as distinguished from 'regulative.' In this *Critique,* on the other hand, the paramount concern must be to keep the term *Beschaffenheit*—when used in this sense—from being confused with *Charakter* ('character') in the sense that is central to morality. However, *Beschaffenheit* has also another sense—in which things can be said to have *eine Beschaffenheit*—and when it occurs in that other sense I translate it, as I did in the other two *Critiques,* as 'characteristic.']

of this determination (the human being) has previously been cognized in terms of[85] the constitution with which he is actual, although only to the extent necessary in reference to duty as such.[86] This constitution,[87] however, does not belong in a critique of practical reason as such; such a critique is to indicate completely only the principles of this power's possibility, of its range and bounds, without particular reference to human nature. Here, therefore, the division belongs to the system of the science, not to the system of the critique.

A certain reviewer[88] of that *Grounding for the Metaphysics of Morals*— truth-loving and acute, therefore always still worthy of respect—raised the objection *that the concept of the good was not there established* (as, in his opinion, would have been necessary) *before the moral principle;* I have, I hope, dealt adequately with this objection in the second chapter[89] of the Analytic.[90] I have also taken into account—and I shall continue to do so—

---

[85] [*nach.*]

[86] [On human duties, cf. the *Metaphysics of Morals,* Ak. VI, 216–17, 394–95.]

[87] [The human being's actual constitution, i.e., his nature (cf. below), which thus *includes* the particular: *diese.*]

[88] [The reviewer was Hermann Andreas Pistorius (1730–98). The review, which appeared in *Allgemeine deutsche Bibliothek* (vol. 66, part II, 447–63), was anonymous. However, Daniel Jenisch (1762–1804), in a letter to Kant dated May 14, 1787 (Ak. X, 486 [second edition, published in 1922, of Kant's *Correspondence;* in the first edition, published in 1900, the page is 463]), says that the reviewer in question "is supposed to be [*soll . . . seyn*] Provost Pistorius on [the Baltic island of] Fehmarn, the translator of [David] Hartley [1705–57]," which identifies him as the Pistorius named above.]

[89] [See below, Ak. V, 57–71.]

[90] A further objection could be raised against me, viz., why I also did not explicate[a] beforehand the concept of our *power of desire,* or of the *feeling of pleasure*—although this reproach would be improper, because one should properly be able to presuppose this explication as given in psychology. However, in psychology the definition might indeed be so framed that the feeling of pleasure would (as is actually commonly done) be laid at the basis of the determination of our power of desire; but thus the supreme principle of practical philosophy would necessarily have to turn out to be *empirical*—which surely must first of all be established, and is utterly refuted in this *Critique.* Here, therefore, I want to give the explication as it must be [given] in order to leave this disputed point undecided at the beginning, as is proper. — **Life**[b] is a being's power[c] to act according to laws of the power of desire. The **power of desire**[d] is the being's *power to be, through its presentations, [the] cause of the actuality of the objects of these presentations.* **Pleasure**[e] is the *presentation of the agreement*[f] *of the object or of the action*[g] *with the* **subjective** *conditions of life,*

many other objections that have reached me from men who reveal by their will[power] that they have at heart the discovery of truth (for, those who have only their old system before their eyes and for whom it is already settled beforehand what is to be approved or disapproved are not about to demand a discussion that might stand in the way of their private aim).

When one is concerned to determine a particular power of the human soul in terms of its sources, contents, and bounds, then indeed, by the nature of human cognition, one cannot start except from the soul's *parts,* their exact and (as far as is possible according to the current situation of what elements of the soul we have already acquired) complete exhibition. But there is also a second attentiveness that is more philosophical and *architectonic:* viz., to

10

---

i.e., with the power [consisting] of the *causality of a presentation in regard to the actuality of its object* (or [in regard to] the determination of the subject's forces[h] to action in order to produce the object). I need [say] no more on behalf of a critique of concepts borrowed from psychology; the rest is accomplished by the *Critique* itself. This explication [of those concepts], one readily becomes aware, leaves undecided the question as to whether pleasure must always be laid at the basis of the power of desire, or whether under certain conditions it only follows upon that power's determination; for this explication is composed of none but characteristics[i] of pure understanding, i.e., categories, which contain nothing empirical. Such caution—viz., not to anticipate one's judgments by a risky definition before the concept has been dissected completely, which often is not achieved until very late—is very commendable in all of philosophy, and yet is often neglected. Indeed, it will be noticed in the entire course of the critique (of theoretical as well as practical reason) that one finds in this course ample[j] occasion to compensate for many deficiencies in the old dogmatic progression of philosophy, and to correct[k] mistakes that remain unnoticed until a use of reason is made of concepts[l] *that aims at the whole of reason.*

    a [*erklären.*]
    b [Cf. the *Metaphysics of Morals,* Ak. VI, 211–14.]
    c [Or 'ability': *Vermögen.*]
    d [Cf. the *Critique of Judgment,* Ak. V, 177n, and Kant's First Introduction to that work, Ak. XX, 230n.]
    e [Cf. (and contrast) the *Critique of Judgment,* Ak. V, 204, 220, 222, and the First Introduction thereto, Ak. XX, 230–31, also 206.]
    f [*Übereinstimmung.*]
    g [*Handlung.*]
    h [Or 'powers': *Kräfte.*]
    i [*Merkmalen.*]
    j [*mannigfaltig.*]
    k [Literally, 'alter': *abändern.*]
    l [*von Begriffen einen Gebrauch der Vernunft macht.* Natorp wonders if we should read, instead, *von Begriffen der Vernunft einen Gebrauch macht,* i.e., 'a use is made of concepts of reason.']

grasp correctly the *idea of the whole* and, on the basis of this idea and in a pure power of reason, to fix one's eyes upon all those parts in their recipro-cal reference to one another by means of their derivation from the concept of that whole. This examination and warrant is possible only through the most intimate acquaintance with the system. Those who were irked by the first investigation and hence did not consider acquiring that acquaintance worth the trouble do not reach the second level, viz., that of the overview, which is a synthetic return to what had previously been given analytically; and it is no wonder if they find inconsistencies everywhere even though the gaps that suggest these inconsistencies are to be encountered not in the sys-tem itself but merely in their own incoherent progression of thought.

I am not worried at all, in regard to this treatise, about the reproach that I want to introduce a *new language*,[91] because here the kind of cognition is one that by itself approaches popularity. Even in regard to the first *Critique* this reproach could not have occurred to anyone who had thought it through rather than merely leafed through it. To contrive new words where the lan-guage already has no lack of expressions for given concepts is a childish en-deavor to distinguish oneself from the crowd, if not by new and true thoughts then at least by new patches on the old garment. If, therefore, the readers of that work know of more popular expressions that are yet just as adequate to the thought as mine seemed to me, or if perhaps they would venture to establish the nullity of these thoughts themselves and thus simul-taneously of any expressions designating them, then by the first they would greatly oblige me, for I want only to be understood, but for the second they would deserve well of philosophy. However, as long as those thoughts con-tinue to stand, I very much doubt that expressions adequate to them and nonetheless more prevalent are likely[92] to be found for them.[93]

11

---

[91] [Kant's retort is directed mainly against Gottlob August Tittel (see above, Ak. V, 8 br. n. 83a), who in his book had chastised Kant for his "overly frequent use of abstract terminolo-gies" (op. cit., 4), and for "promulgating long since familiar things *as new* in an inarticulate language" (ibid., 25).]

[92] [*dürften.*]

[93] Here I am worried more (than about not being understood) about being now and then misinterpreted with regard to some expressions that I selected with the greatest care in order to keep them from missing the concept[s] to which they point. Thus in the table of categories of *practical* reason,[a] under the heading of modality, the *per-mitted* and *not permitted* (practically objectively possible and impossible) have almost the same sense in the ordinary use of language[b] as do the immediately fol-lowing categories *duty* and *contrary to duty.* Here, however, the *first* [pair] is to

In this way, then, it would seem that the a priori principles of two pow-   12
ers of the mind, the power of cognition and that of desire, have now

mean what is in agreement or conflict with a merely *possible* practical precept (as, say, the solution of all problems of geometry and mechanics), but the *second,* what stands in such a relation^c to a law *actually* residing in reason as such; and this distinction in meaning, although somewhat unusual, is not entirely foreign even to the ordinary use of language. Thus, e.g., to an orator, as such, it is *not permitted* to coin new words or constructions; to a poet this is to some extent *permitted.* In neither of these two [cases] is one thinking of duty. For if someone wants to forfeit his reputation as an orator, no one can bar him from doing it. The concern here is only with the distinction of *imperatives* in terms of^d a *problematic, assertoric,* and *apodeictic* determining basis.^e Similarly, in the note where I contrasted the moral ideas of practical perfection in different philosophical schools,^f I distinguished the idea of *wisdom* from that of *holiness,* although I myself have declared them to be^g basically and objectively one and the same.^h In that note, however, I mean by wisdom only that wisdom to which the human being (the Stoic) lays claim, hence wisdom attributed to the human being *subjectively* [and] fictitiouslyⁱ as a property. (Perhaps the expression *virtue,* [a property] which the Stoic also paraded, might designate better what is characteristic of his school.) But most of all the expression, *postulate* of pure practical reason,^j was capable of occasioning misinterpretation, if confused with the meaning that postulates of pure mathematics have, which carry with them apodeictic certainty. However, the latter postulate the *possibility of an action* whose object has previously with complete certainty been cognized theoretically a priori as *possible.* The postulate of pure practical reason, on the other hand, postulates the possibility of an *object* itself (God and the immortality of the soul) from apodeictic *practical* laws, and therefore only on behalf of a practical reason. This certainty of the postulated possibility is thus not at all theoretical, hence also not apodeictic, i.e., a necessity cognized with regard to the object, but is, rather, an assumption necessary, with regard to the subject, for complying with practical reason's objective but practical laws, hence merely a necessary hypothesis. I could not find a better expression^k for this subjective but nonetheless unconditioned necessity.

^a [See below, Ak. V, 65–67.]

^b [Kant's point here, at least in part, is that in ordinary German *unerlaubt*—just like 'not permitted' in ordinary English—means not merely 'permission has not been given' but, in effect, 'forbidden' or 'prohibited.' By the same token, *translating* the German term as either of these latter terms would obscure Kant's point. For the table that Kant has just mentioned, see below, Ak. V, 66.]

^c [*Beziehung.*]

^d [*unter.*]

^e [*Bestimmungsgrund.*]

^f [See below, Ak. V, 127 n. 151.]

^g [*erklären . . . für.*]

^h [The reference is probably to Ak. V, 130–31 incl. n. 178.]

ⁱ ['attributed fictitiously' translates *angedichtet.*]

been[94] ascertained and determined as to the conditions, range, and bounds of their use, and that a secure basis has been laid for a systematic theoretical as well as practical philosophy as science.

However, presumably nothing worse could befall these endeavors than that someone should make the unexpected discovery that there is and can be no a priori cognition at all.[95] But there is no danger of this. It would be tantamount to someone's wishing to prove by reason that there is no reason. For we say that we cognize something by reason only when we are conscious that we could have known it even if we had not encountered it thus in experience; hence reason's cognition and a priori cognition are one and the same. It is a direct contradiction to try to squeeze necessity out of an experiential[96] proposition (*ex pumice aquam*),[97] and to try to impart to a judgment, along with this necessity, also true universality (without which no inference of reason [is possible], and hence also no inference by analogy,

---

ʲ [See below, Ak. V, 122–33.]

ᵏ [Than *postulate*.]

[94] ['it would seem that . . . have now been' renders *wären . . . nunmehr*.]

[95] [Kant is referring to Johann Georg Heinrich Feder (1740–1821), the author of *Über Raum und Caussalität, zur Prüfung der Kantischen Philosophie* (Göttingen: Johann Christian Dieterich, 1787; reprinted, Brussels: Culture et Civilisation, 1968). In a letter to Christian Gottfried Schütz (1747–1832) dated June 25, 1787 (Ak. X, 490 [second edition of Kant's *Correspondence;* in the first edition the page is 467]), Kant says, "Better than any controversies with Feder and Abel [Jacob Friedrich von Abel (1751–1829), another critic of Kant] (the former of whom maintains that there is no a priori cognition at all . . .), this *Critique* will prove and make graspable that pure practical reason is possible, and that it compensates for what I denied to speculative reason . . . ." Feder is also the editor who wrote a notorious revision of an already shoddy review by Christian Garve (1742–98) of Kant's first *Critique* and published it in the supplement (*Zugaben*) to the *Göttingische gelehrte Anzeigen*, i.e., *Göttingen Scholarly Announcements*, on January 19, 1782 (item 3, 40–48; reprinted as Attachment [*Beilage*] II in the *Philosophische Bibliothek* edition of Kant's *Prolegomena to Any Future Metaphysics* (vol. 40, 167–74). Kant's reply to that review is contained in the Appendix (*Anhang*) to the *Prolegomena*, Ak. IV, 371–83.]

[96] [*Erfahrungs-*. In Kant, 'experiential' is not synonymous with 'empirical.' Whereas experience is indeed empirical (insofar as it includes sensation), *perception* (which includes sensation) is empirical (viz., empirical intuition) without as yet being experience. In order for perception to become experience, it must be given the synthetic unity provided by the understanding's categories. See the *Critique of Pure Reason*, B 422n, A 183/B 226 (cf. B vii, 12, 161), and the *Prolegomena*, Ak. IV, 297–98.]

[97] ['Water from a pumice stone.' The quote—more fully, *aquam a pumice nunc postulas*, i.e., 'you now demand water from a pumice stone [namely, money from a pauper]'—is from *Persa (The Persian)*, I, i, 41, by Titus Maccius Plautus (c. 250–184 B.C.), Roman comic dramatist.]

which is an at least presumed universality and objective necessity and therefore does always presuppose it[98]). To substitute subjective necessity— i.e., habit[99]—for objective[100] necessity, which occurs only in a priori judgments, is to deny to reason the ability to make a judgment about the object,[101] i.e., to cognize it and what belongs to it. For example, it is to say, concerning what repeatedly and always follows upon a certain prior state, not that one can *infer* it from that state (for this would mean objective necessity and the concept of an a priori linkage), but only that one may (in a way similar to animals) expect similar cases; i.e., it is to repudiate the concept of cause basically as false and a mere deception of thought.[102] As for trying to remedy this lack of objective and therefore universal validity by saying that, after all, one sees no basis for attributing to other rational beings a different way of presenting,[103] if that attempt yielded a valid inference, then our ignorance would render us greater services for expanding our cognition than any meditation. For merely because we are not familiar with[104] rational beings other than the human being, we would have a right to assume them to be constituted just as we cognize ourselves to be,[105] i.e., we actually would be familiar with them. I am not even mentioning here that universality of assent[106] does not prove a judgment's objective validity (i.e., its validity as cognition). I am saying, rather, that even if that universal assent[107] were contingently correct, this could still not yield a proof of [its] agreement[108] with the object, but that, on the contrary, objective validity alone amounts to the basis of a necessary universal agreement.

13

---

[98] [I.e., does always presuppose (true) universality and (thus) objective necessity: *diese.*]

[99] [Or 'custom': *Gewohnheit.*]

[100] [*objektiv.*]

[101] [*Gegenstand,* which Kant uses interchangeably with *Objekt.*]

[102] [See below, Ak. V, 50–57.]

[103] [Or 'kind of presentation': *Vorstellungsart.*]

[104] [*kennen.* See below, Ak. V, 35 br. n. 120.]

[105] [Cf. the *Critique of Judgment,* Ak. V, 290n.]

[106] [Literally, 'of considering-true': *des Fürwahrhaltens.*]

[107] [*jene,* which strictly speaking refers to 'universality of assent.']

[108] [*Übereinstimmung* here, *Einstimmung* below.]

Hume[109] also would be quite comfortable with this system of the *universal empiricism* concerning principles. For, as is familiar, he demanded nothing more than that, instead of any objective meaning of necessity in the concept of cause, a merely subjective meaning be assumed, viz., habit, in order to deny to reason any judgment about God, freedom, and immortality; and, provided that the principles were granted to him, he certainly knew very well how to draw inferences from them with all logical cogency.[110] But even Hume did not make empiricism so universal as to include in it mathematics also. He considered the propositions[111] of mathematics to be analytic; and if this were correct, they would indeed also be apodeictic, yet no inference could be drawn from this to an ability[112] of reason to make apodeictic judgments in philosophy as well, viz., such as would be synthetic (as [e.g.] the principle[113] of causality). However, if the empiricism concerning principles were assumed [as] *universal,* then mathematics too would be implicated in it.[114]

---

[109] [David Hume (1711–76), Scottish empiricist philosopher, historian, economist, essayist, and author of numerous works. Hume's empiricism is one of the two major philosophical traditions to which Kant's philosophy responds—the other being the rationalism of Leibniz, especially as developed by Christian Wolff. (Kant credits Hume with having awakened him from his "dogmatic slumber," which had been induced by that rationalism.) Hume's most important philosophical works are *A Treatise of Human Nature* (London: J. Noon, 1739–40); contemporary edition: edited, with an analytical index, by L.A. Selby–Bigge; 2nd ed. with text rev. and variant readings by P. H. Nidditch (Oxford: Clarendon Press; New York: Oxford University Press, 1978); and the *Philosophical Essays Concerning Human Understanding* (later renamed to *An Enquiry Concerning Human Understanding*) (London: A. Millar, 1748); contemporary edition: *An Enquiry Concerning Human Understanding; A Letter from a Gentleman to His Friend in Edinburgh; An Abstract of a Treatise of Human Nature;* edited and introduced by Eric Steinberg; 2nd ed. (Indianapolis, Ind.: Hackett, 1993).]

[110] [Cf. the *Critique of Pure Reason,* A 760–69 = B 788–97.]

[111] [*Sätze.* Sometimes *Satz* means 'principle' instead; see below.]

[112] [Or 'power': *Vermögen.*]

[113] [*Satz.*]

[114] [On this whole paragraph, cf. below, Ak. V, 50–57. As regards Hume's views on the propositions of mathematics, in *An Enquiry Concerning Human Understanding* (Sect. IV, Pt. I), he does indeed hold that the propositions of geometry, algebra, and arithmetic express "relations of ideas," i.e., to use Kant's term, they are analytic. In *A Treatise of Human Nature,* Hume had considered (Bk. I, Pt. III, Sect. I) the propositions of *geometry,* though not those of algebra and arithmetic, to be empirical and thus, to use Kant's term, synthetic. However, Kant became familiar with the *Treatise* (it is not known when) only indirectly, through citations (translated into German) from James Beattie's *Essay on the Nature and Immutability of Truth, in Opposi-*

Now if mathematics comes into conflict with that reason which admits only empirical principles,[115] as is unavoidable in the antinomy where mathematics proves incontestably the infinite divisibility of space but empiricism cannot permit this infinite divisibility,[116] then the greatest possible evidence of demonstration is in manifest contradiction with the alleged inferences from experiential principles;[117] and now one cannot help asking, like Cheselden's blind man, Which deceives me, sight or touch [feeling]?[118] (For empiricism is based on a *felt* necessity, but rationalism on a necessity into which one has *insight*.) And thus universal empiricism reveals itself as genuine *skepticism*, which has falsely been ascribed to Hume in such an unlimited meaning;[119] for, with mathematics, he left us at least one secure touchstone of experience, whereas genuine skepticism permits absolutely[120] no such touchstone (which can never be encountered except in a priori principles) even though experience consists indeed not of mere feelings, but also of judgments.

14

---

tion to Sophistry and Scepticism (Edinburgh: A. Kincaid & J. Bell, 1770; reprinted, New York: Garland Pub., 1983).]

[115] [*empirische Grundsätze.*]

[116] [See, in the *Critique of Pure Reason*, the Second Antinomy of Pure Reason, A 434–43 = B 462–71, and cf. A 487–88/B 515–16, A 523–27 = B 551–55. Cf. also the *Metaphysical Foundations of Natural Science*, Ak. IV, 503–08.]

[117] [*Erfahrungsprinzipien.*]

[118] [William Cheselden (1688–1752), an English anatomist and surgeon who succeeded in curing certain forms of blindness, reported the reaction of one of his patients in *Philosophical Transactions*, XXXV (1728), 447. Kant's source for this report probably was a work on optics by Robert Smith (1689–1768), *A Compleat System of Opticks* (Cambridge: Printed for the author, sold by Cornelius Crownfield, 1738), as translated and adapted by Abraham Gotthelf Kästner (1719–1800) as *Vollständiger Lehrbegriff der Optik* (Altenburg: Richterische Buchhandlung, 1755).]

[119] Names designating the adherents of a sect have at all times carried with them much perversion of justice, roughly as if someone said, *N* is an *idealist*. For although he definitely not only concedes but insists that for our presentations of external things there are corresponding actual objects as external things,[a] he nonetheless wants the forms of intuition of these [objects] to attach not to them but only to the human mind.[b]

    [a] [Literally, Kant says 'actual objects of external things': *wirkliche Gegenstände äußerer Dinge.*]

    [b] [On this entire note, which is probably directed against the mentioned Feder-Garve review of the first *Critique*, cf. the *Prolegomena*, Ak. IV, 375n and 376n.]

[120] [*schlechterdings.*]

Since, however, in this philosophical and critical age such an empiricism can scarcely be taken seriously, and is presumably being put forth only as an exercise for judgment and in order to put the necessity of rational a priori principles in a clearer light by contrast, one may still be grateful to those who want to take the trouble to do this otherwise indeed uninstructive work.

On the Idea of a
Critique of Practical Reason

The theoretical use of reason dealt with objects of the cognitive power alone, and a critique of reason with regard to this use concerned in fact only the *pure* cognitive power, because this power raised the suspicion—which was indeed confirmed thereafter—that it might easily stray beyond its bounds, losing itself among unattainable objects or even among concepts conflicting with one another. With the practical use of reason the situation is indeed different. In this use, reason deals with determining bases[121] of the will, which is a power either to produce objects corresponding to one's presentations, or, at any rate, to determine itself to bring about these objects (whether or not one's physical power is sufficient), i.e., to determine its causality. For there reason can at least succeed in determining the will and, insofar as volition[122] alone is at issue, always has objective reality. Here, therefore, the first question is whether pure reason is sufficient by itself alone to determine the will, or whether reason[123] can be a determining basis of the will[124] only as empirically conditioned. Now at this point there enters a concept of causality justified by the *Critique of Pure Reason* although incapable of being exhibited empirically, viz., the concept of *freedom;* and if we can now discover grounds for proving that this property does in fact be-

---

[121] [*Bestimmungsgründe.*]

[122] [Literally, 'the willing': *das Wollen.*]

[123] [Kant actually says *sie,* which strictly grammatically—but incorrectly—refers back to *pure* reason.]

[124] [Reading, with Gustav Hartenstein, *desselben* for *derselben.*]

long to the human will (and thus also to the will of all rational beings), then this establishes not only that pure reason can be practical, but that it alone, and not the empirically limited reason, is unconditionally practical.[125] Consequently we shall have to work on a critique not of *pure practical,* but only of *practical* reason as such. For pure [practical][126] reason, once one has established that there is such a reason, needs no critique. It itself is what contains the standard for the critique of all its use. Hence the critique of practical reason as such has the obligation[127] to keep the empirically conditioned reason from presuming to seek to provide, alone and exclusively, the determining basis of the will.[128] The use of pure [practical] reason, if one has established that there is such a reason, is alone immanent;[129] the empirically conditioned use [of practical reason] that presumes to be sole ruler is, on the contrary, transcendent and expresses itself in demands[130] and in commands that go entirely beyond that reason's domain—which is exactly the inverse relation of the one that we were able to state concerning pure reason in its speculative use.[131]

However, since it is still pure reason whose cognition here lies at the basis of reason's practical use, the division of a critique of practical reason will nonetheless have to be arranged, in its general outline, in conformity with that of the critique of speculative reason. Hence we shall have to have in this critique a *Doctrine of Elements* and a *Doctrine of Method;* and within the former an *Analytic,* as rule of truth, as the first part, and a *Dialectic* as exhibition and resolution of the illusion[132] in judgments of practical reason. Only the order in the subdivision of the Analytic will once again be the inverse of that in the critique of pure speculative reason.[133] For in the present critique we shall, starting from *principles,* proceed to *concepts* and

---

[125] [See below, Ak. V, 42–57.]

[126] [Cf. the first paragraph of Kant's Preface, Ak. V, 3.]

[127] [*Obliegenheit,* which is a synonym of *Verbindlichkeit.*]

[128] [See below, Ak. V, 22–26.]

[129] [I.e., keeps within the limits of possible experience. For the distinction between 'immanent' and 'transcendent' (below), see the *Critique of Pure Reason,* A 295–96/B 352–53, cf. A 326/B 383, A 643 = B 671, A 799 = B 827.]

[130] [*Zumutungen.*]

[131] [See below, Ak. V, 89–106.]

[132] [*des Scheins.*]

[133] [Cf. below, Ak. V, 90.]

only then, if possible, from these to the senses, whereas in the case of speculative reason we started from the senses and had to end with the principles. Now, the basis for this lies again in this: that we are now concerned with a will and have to examine reason not in relation to objects but in relation to this will and its causality; and thus the principles of the empirically unconditioned causality must come at the beginning,[134] and only thereafter can the attempt be made to establish our concepts of the determining basis of such a will, of their application to objects[135] and finally to the subject and his sensibility.[136] The law of the causality from freedom, i.e., some pure practical principle, here unavoidably comes at the beginning and determines the objects to which alone it can be referred.

[134] [See Chapter I below, Ak. V, 19–57.]

[135] [See Chapter II below, Ak. V, 57–71.]

[136] [See Chapter III below, Ak. V, 71–106.]

CRITIQUE OF PRACTICAL REASON

PART I

DOCTRINE OF THE ELEMENTS

OF

PURE PRACTICAL REASON

BOOK I

19

ANALYTIC OF
PURE PRACTICAL REASON

Chapter I
On the Principles of
Pure Practical Reason

§ 1
EXPLICATION[1]

Practical *principles*[2] are propositions that contain a general[3] determination
of the will, having under it several practical rules. They are subjective, or
maxims, if the condition [under which they apply] is regarded by the subject
as valid only for his will; but they are objective, or practical *laws,* if the condition is cognized as objective, i.e., as valid for the will of every rational
being.

Comment

If one assumes that *pure* reason can contain within itself a basis that is sufficient practically, i.e., sufficient to determine the will, then there are practical laws; but if not,[4] then all practical principles will be mere maxims. In a

---

[1] [*Erklärung.* This term has a variety of different meanings; see the *Critique of Pure Reason,*
A 730 = B 758. Sometimes, including here, it could legitimately be rendered as 'definition' instead of as 'explication,' but I prefer to reserve 'definition' for the German term *Definition* in
order to enable the reader to identify Kant's uses of this latter term.]

[2] [*Grundsätze,* the literal meaning of which is 'basic propositions.']

[3] [*allgemein,* which can also mean 'universal.']

[4] [I.e., if (*wo*) one does not make that assumption.]

pathologically affected will[5] of a rational being one can find a conflict of maxims with the practical laws cognized by that being himself.[6] For example, someone can make it his maxim to endure no affront unavenged and yet at the same time see[7] that this is not a practical law but only his maxim, and that, on the contrary, as a rule for the will of every rational being it could not—in one and the same maxim—harmonize[8] with itself.

In the cognition of nature the principles of what occurs (e.g., the principle of the equality of action and reaction[9] in the communication of motion) are at the same time laws of nature;[10] for there the use of reason is theoretical and determined by the constitution of the object. In practical cognition—i.e., cognition that deals merely with determining bases of the will—principles that one makes for oneself are not yet, on that account, laws by which one is unavoidably bound,[11] because in the practical [sphere] reason deals with the subject, namely with his power of desire,[12] to whose particular constitution the rule can multifariously conform. A practical rule is always a product of reason, because it prescribes[13] action[14] as a means to an effect that is the aim.[15] However, for a being in whom reason is not the sole determining basis of the will, this rule is an *imperative*, i.e., a rule which is designated by an *ought*,[16] expressing the ob-

20

---

[5] [I.e., in a will affected by motivating causes of sensibility (see the *Critique of Pure Reason,* A 534 = B 562, cf. A 802 = B 830, as well as below, Ak. V, 80, 120), which as such are subjective (Ak. V, 79, 32) and physical (Ak. V, 44).

[6] [Following Kant, I use 'it' with 'being' and 'creature,' but 'he' with 'human being' and 'subject,' despite the neuter gender of the German expressions. But unlike Kant, I also use—to preserve clarity—'he' when the being or creature in question is said or implied to be rational.]

[7] [Literally, 'have insight': *einsehen.*]

[8] [*zusammenstimmen.*]

[9] [*Gleichheit der Wirkung und Gegenwirkung.*]

[10] [Cf. the *Metaphysical Foundations of Natural Science,* Ak. IV, 544–51.]

[11] [More literally, 'laws to which one is unavoidably subject': *darunter man unvermeidlich steht.*]

[12] [*Begehrungsvermögen.*]

[13] [*vorschreiben*—the corresponding noun being *Vorschrift.*]

[14] [*Handlung.*]

[15] [*Absicht.*]

[16] [Emphasis added.]

jective necessitation[17] of the action, and which signifies that if reason entirely determined the will then the action would unfailingly occur in accordance with this rule. Hence imperatives hold objectively and are entirely distinct from maxims, which are subjective principles.[18] Imperatives, however, either determine the conditions of the causality of a rational being—as an efficient cause—merely in regard to the effect and the [causality's] adequacy to it; or they determine only the will, whether or not it is sufficient for the effect. The first would be hypothetical imperatives and would contain mere precepts[19] of skill; the second, on the contrary, would be categorical and would alone be practical laws.[20] Hence maxims are indeed *principles,* but not *imperatives.* Imperatives themselves, however, when they are conditional—i.e., when they determine the will not absolutely[21] as will but only in regard to a desired effect, i.e., when they are hypothetical imperatives— are indeed practical *precepts,* but not *laws.*[22] Laws must sufficiently determine the will as will even before I ask whether I do perhaps have the ability required for a desired effect, or what I am to do in order to produce it. Hence they must be categorical; otherwise they are not laws, for they lack the necessity which, if it is to be practical, must be independent of conditions that are pathological and that hence adhere to the will contingently. Tell someone, for example, that he must work and save in his youth in order not to want in his old age. This is a correct and at the same time important practical precept of the will. We readily see, however, that the will is here being directed to something *else* that one is presupposing to be desired by it; and this desire must be left to him, the agent himself, whether he foresees further resources apart from the assets acquired by himself, or whether perhaps he does not hope to grow old, or thinks that in case of future need he can manage [by living] plainly. Reason, from which alone can arise any rule that is to contain necessity, does indeed put necessity also into this its precept (for without it the precept would not be an imperative), but this neces-

---

[17] [*Nötigung.* The corresponding verb is *nötigen,* which Kant himself equates with *necessitieren* (*Metaphysics of Morals,* Ak. VI, 222). However, since the English 'to necessitate' is unsuitable (very awkward, at best) in most contexts, I use 'to compel' instead.]

[18] [Cf. the *Grounding for the Metaphysics of Morals,* Ak. IV, 420–21n.]

[19] [*Vorschriften.*]

[20] [Cf. the *Grounding for the Metaphysics of Morals,* Ak. IV, 414–16.]

[21] [*schlechthin.*]

[22] [*Gesetze.*]

sity is conditioned only subjectively and cannot be presupposed to the same degree in all subjects. For reason's legislation,[23] however, it is requisite that reason need presuppose merely *itself*, because the rule [it gives] is objectively and universally valid only when it holds without contingent, subjective conditions, which distinguish one rational being from another. Now tell someone that he ought never to make a lying promise. This is a rule that pertains merely to his will, whether or not the aims that the human being may have can be achieved by this will. The mere volition is what is to be determined by this rule completely a priori. If, now, it is found that this rule is practically correct, then it is a law, because it is a categorical imperative. Therefore practical laws refer solely to the will, without regard to what is accomplished through its causality, and one can abstract from this causality (as belonging to the world of sense) in order to have them pure.

§ 2
THEOREM I

All practical principles that presuppose an *object*[24] (matter) of the power of desire as determining basis of the will[25] are, one and all, empirical and cannot provide any practical laws.

By the matter of the power of desire I mean an object whose actuality is desired. Now if the desire for this object precedes the practical rule and is the condition for making the rule one's principle, then, I say (*first*), the principle is always empirical. For the determining basis of the power of choice[26] is then the presentation[27] of an object and [also] that relation of the presentation to the subject by which the power of desire is determined to

---

[23] [I.e., lawgiving (not the product thereof): *Gesetzgebung*. I am refraining from translating this term as 'lawgiving' because this rendering does not work in all contexts, and because it would also obscure the link between the German noun and *gesetzgebend*, for which (likewise) no term but 'legislative' works consistently.]

[24] [*Objekt* here, *Gegenstand* below. Kant uses the two terms interchangeably.]

[25] [*Wille*.]

[26] [*Willkür*, the root meaning of which is 'will-choice.' On *Wille* and *Willkür*, cf. the *Metaphysics of Morals*, Ak. VI, 213–14, 226, and the *Critique of Judgment*, Ak. V, 172. On the power of choice, see also the *Critique of Pure Reason*, A 534 = B 562, A 549–50 = B 577–78, A 552–53 = B 580–81, A 800 = B 828, A 802 = B 830.]

[27] [*Vorstellung*.]

make the object actual. Such a relation to the subject, however, is called *pleasure* in the actuality of an object.[28] Therefore this pleasure would have to be presupposed as condition for the possibility of the determination of the power of choice. However, one cannot cognize a priori concerning any presentation of some object, whatever the presentation may be, whether it will be linked with *pleasure* or *displeasure* or be *indifferent.* Therefore in such a case the determining basis of the power of choice must always be empirical, and hence so must be the practical material principle that presupposed it as a condition.

Now (*second*), a principle that is based only on the subjective condition of receptivity to a pleasure or displeasure ([a receptivity] which can always be cognized only empirically and cannot be valid in the same way for all rational beings) can indeed serve the subject—who possesses this receptivity—as his *maxim,* but it cannot serve even the subject himself[29] as a *law* (because it is lacking in objective necessity, which must be cognized a priori); and hence such a principle can never provide a practical law.

§ 3
THEOREM II

All material principles—as such—are, one and all, of one and the same kind and belong under the general principle of self-love or one's own happiness.

Pleasure from the existence[30] of a thing, insofar as it is to be a determining basis of desire for this thing, is based on the *receptivity* of the subject, because it *depends* on the existence of an object; hence it belongs to sense (feeling) and not to understanding, [a term] which expresses a referring of a presentation *to an object* according to concepts, but not to the subject according to feelings. Therefore pleasure is practical only insofar as the sensation[31] of agreeableness that the subject expects from the object's actuality

22

---

[28] [Cf. the *Metaphysics of Morals,* Ak. VI, 211–12.]

[29] [Reading, with Emil Wille, *seiner . . . dieses* for *ihrer . . . diese.*]

[30] [*Existenz* here, *Dasein* below.]

[31] [*Empfindung.* This term (similarly for *empfinden,* 'to sense,' near the end of the present paragraph), like its English equivalent, can refer either to a sensation involving one of the senses, or to a feeling (*Gefühl*). Kant sometimes attempts to restrict the term to the first of these meanings, most explicitly in the *Critique of Judgment,* Ak. V, 205–06, cf. 295; cf. also the *Metaphysics of Morals,* Ak. VI, 400, and the *Anthropology,* Ak. VII, 153. But he does not

determines his power of desire. However, a rational being's consciousness of the agreeableness of life as uninterruptedly accompanying his whole existence is *happiness,* and the principle whereby one makes happiness the highest determining basis of the power of choice is the principle of self-love.[32] Hence all material principles, which posit the determining basis of the power of choice in the pleasure or displeasure to be sensed from the actuality of some object, are entirely of *the same kind* insofar as they belong, one and all, to the principle of self-love or one's own happiness.

COROLLARY

All *material* practical rules posit the determining basis of the will in our *lower power of desire,* and if there were no *merely formal* laws of the will that sufficiently determined it, then one also could not admit *any higher power of desire.*

Comment I

It is surprising how otherwise acute men can believe that they find a distinction between the *lower* and the *higher power of desire* according to whether the **presentations** linked with the feeling of pleasure have their origin *in the senses* or in *understanding.* For if one inquires about the determining bases of desire and posits them in an agreeableness expected from something or other, then it does not matter at all where the *presentation* of this gratifying object comes from, but only how much the presentation *gratifies.* If a presentation, even though it may have its seat and origin in the understanding, can determine the power of choice only by presupposing a feeling of a pleasure in the subject, then its being a determining basis of the

23

---

consistently adhere to this restriction; apart from the present instance (cf. also Kant's use of 'sense' above), see, e.g., the *Critique of Pure Reason,* A 374, and cf. the *Grounding for the Metaphysics of Morals,* Ak. IV, 399. By the same token, Kant often distinguishes sensation in the first meaning by calling it *Sinnesempfindung,* which literally means 'sensation of sense.' On this expression and the issues involved in it, see my translation of the *Critique of Judgment,* Ak. V, 291 br. n. 19. Since the ambiguity between the two meanings is invariably resolved by the context, I have chosen in this translation (as I did in the previous two) to display Kant's terminological choices, rather than conceal them from the reader by translating not only *Gefühl* but also some occurrences of *Empfindung* as 'feeling.']

[32] [Cf. the *Grounding for the Metaphysics of Morals,* Ak. IV, 395–96.]

power of choice depends entirely on the constitution of inner sense, viz., [on the fact] that this sense can be affected with agreeableness by that presentation. However different in kind the presentations of objects may be—whether they be presentations of understanding or even of reason, in contrast to presentations of the senses—the feeling of pleasure by which alone they properly amount to the determining basis of the will (the agreeableness, the gratification that one expects from them and that impels the activity to produce the object) is nonetheless of the same kind.[33] It is so not only insofar as it can always be cognized merely empirically, but also insofar as it affects one and the same vital force manifesting itself in our power of desire, and in this regard can differ from any other determining basis in nothing but degree. How, otherwise, could one make a comparison in *magnitude* between two determining bases entirely different in terms of the kind of presentation [involved], in order to prefer the one that most affects one's power of desire? The same human being can return an instructive book, available to him only once, in order not to miss the hunt; he can leave in the middle of a beautiful speech in order not to be late for a meal; he can abandon an entertainment [marked] by rational conversations, which he otherwise greatly esteems, in order to sit down at the gambling table; he can even turn away a pauper to whom ordinarily[34] he is glad to be charitable, because he happens to have no more money in his pocket than he needs in order to pay for admission to the theater.[35] If the determination of the will rests on the feeling of agreeableness or disagreeableness that he expects from some cause, then it is all the same to him by what kind of presentation he is affected. All that concerns him, in order to decide on a choice,[36] is how intense, how long, how easily acquired, and how often repeated this agreeableness is. Just as, to someone who needs gold [coins] for his expenditure it is all the same whether the material therein, the gold, was dug from the mountains or washed from the sand, provided it is accepted everywhere at the same value, so no one asks, when he is concerned merely with the agreeableness of life, whether presentations of understanding or of sense [furnish him with gratification,] but only *how much and how great is the gratification* they furnish him for the longest time. Only those who would

---

[33] [Cf. the *Metaphysics of Morals,* Ak. VI, 377–78.]

[34] [*sonst.*]

[35] [*Komödie,* in an older and broader meaning of the term.]

[36] [*Wahl.*]

24

like to deny to pure reason the ability to determine the will without the presupposition of some feeling can stray so far—from their own explication—that what they have themselves previously brought under one and the same principle they nonetheless explicate thereafter as entirely different in kind. Thus we find, e.g., that one can find gratification also in the mere *application of strength,* in the consciousness of one's fortitude of soul in overcoming obstacles opposing one's project, in the cultivation of spiritual[37] talents, etc.; and we rightly call these the *more refined* joys and delights, because they are more under our control[38] than others, do not wear out, but rather fortify our feeling for still further enjoyment of them, and in delighting us they at the same time cultivate us. Yet to pass them off, on that account, as a way of determining the will different from that by mere sense, even though for the possibility of those gratifications they do presuppose in us, as the primary[39] condition of this liking,[40] a feeling aimed at them, [is a mistake]; it is just as when ignorant people who would like to dabble in metaphysics think of matter as so refined—so overrefined—that they could themselves get dizzy from it, and then believe that in this way they have devised a *spiritual* and yet extended being.[41] If in the case of virtue we rely, with *Epicurus,* on the will's being determined by the mere gratification that virtue promises, we cannot thereafter rebuke him for holding that this gratification is of entirely the same kind as those of the coarsest senses. For we have no basis at all for charging him with having assigned the presentations by which this feeling is aroused in us to the bodily senses only; as far as we can divine, he sought the source of many of these presentations just as much in the use of the higher cognitive power. But this did not and could not prevent him from holding, in accordance with the principle mentioned

---

[37] [Or 'intellectual': *Geistes-.*]

[38] [Or 'in our power': *in unserer Gewalt.*]

[39] [Or 'first': *erste.*]

[40] [*Wohlgefallen.*]

[41] [Kant may have in mind the English philosopher and poet Henry More (1614–87), a contemporary of Sir Isaac Newton who espoused the existence of effluences, which are spiritual substances that are extended in space (whereas most thinkers claimed that spiritual substances, e.g., God, angelic intellects, human souls, etc., do not occupy space at all). Some commentators on Newton suggest that he employed such effluences in his claim—which Kant never took seriously—that God (an unextended spiritual substance) is the ultimate cause of the gravitational attraction of all bodies for one another through the agency of effluences that are active in all the regions of space.]

above, that the gratification itself which those—even if intellectual—presentations afford us and by which alone they can be determining bases of the will is of entirely the same kind. To be *consistent* is the greatest obligation of a philosopher, and yet [consistency] is most rarely encountered. The ancient Greek schools give us more examples of it than we encounter in our *syncretistic* age, where a certain *coalition system* of contradictory principles is contrived—[a system] full of insincerity and shallowness—because it commends itself better to a public that is satisfied to know something of everything, and on the whole nothing, while yet being fit for anything. The principle of one's own happiness, however much understanding and reason may be used with this principle, would still comprise no determining bases for the will different from those that are appropriate to our *lower* power of desire; and thus either there is no higher[42] power of desire at all, or *pure reason* must be practical by itself alone, i.e., it must be able to determine the will by the mere form of the practical rule without the presupposition of any feeling, and hence without presentations of the agreeable or disagreeable as the matter of the power of desire, the matter which is always an empirical condition of principles. Only then, insofar as reason by itself determines the will (instead of being in the service of the inclinations), is reason a true *higher* power of desire, to which the pathologically determinable power of desire is subordinate, and only then is reason actually distinct—indeed, distinct in kind[43]—from the latter power, so that even the slightest admixture of the latter power's impulses impairs[44] reason's fortitude and superiority, just as the slightest empirical [component] as condition in a mathematical demonstration degrades and annihilates the demonstration's dignity and force.[45] In a practical law reason determines the will directly,[46] not by means of an intervening feeling of pleasure and displeasure, not even [one

25

---

[42] ['higher' (*oberes*) inserted by Kant in his working copy.]

[43] [*spezifisch unterschieden.*]

[44] [*Abbruch tut.* An appropriate alternative rendering for this expression would be 'infringes'; 'infringes upon,' on the other hand, is slightly weaker than what Kant has in mind, as is most evident in contexts in which *Abbruch tun* is paired with the comparably graphic *niederschlagen*, i.e., 'to strike down': see Ak. V, 73, also 78, and cf. 37–38; cf. also the *Critique of Pure Reason*, A 134/B 173, A 274/B 330, A 545 = B 573, A 570 = B 598, A 714 = B 742, A 776 = B 804, A 851 = B 879. Since 'to infringe' is now rarely used without 'upon,' it seems to me that 'to impair' is preferable.]

[45] [Cf. the *Metaphysics of Morals,* Ak. VI, 376–77.]

[46] [*unmittelbar.*]

taken] in this law, and only [the fact] that reason can be practical as pure reason makes it possible for it to be *legislative*.

Comment II

To be happy is necessarily the longing[47] of every rational but finite being, and hence is an unavoidable determining basis of its power of desire. For [the being's] satisfaction with its own existence is by no means an original possession and a bliss, a bliss that would presuppose [in the being] a consciousness of its independent self-sufficiency. Rather, this satisfaction is a problem[48] thrust upon the being by its finite nature itself; for the being is needy, and this need pertains to the matter of its power of desire, i.e., to something that refers to a subjectively underlying feeling of pleasure or displeasure which determines what the being needs in order to be satisfied with its [own] state. But precisely because this material determining basis can be cognized by the subject only empirically, this problem cannot possibly be regarded as a law, because a law, as objective, would have to contain *the same*[49] *determining basis* of the will in all cases and for all rational beings. For although the concept of happiness *everywhere* underlies the practical reference of *objects* to the power of desire, it is still only the general[50] heading for subjective determining bases and determines nothing specifically, even though this specific determination is the sole concern in this practical problem and without it the problem cannot be solved at all. For in what each [subject] has to posit his happiness hinges[51] on everyone's particular feeling of pleasure and displeasure and, even in one and the same subject, on the difference of the need according to the modifications of this feeling. Therefore a law that is *subjectively necessary* (as a law of nature) is *objectively* a very *contingent* practical principle that can and must be very different in different subjects. Hence it can never yield a [practical] law, because, in the desire for happiness, what counts is not the form of lawfulness

---

[47] [*Verlangen*, which can also mean 'demand.']

[48] [*Problem* here, *Aufgabe* in the next two sentences.]

[49] [*eben denselben.* Here—and in similar constructions elsewhere—Kant adds *eben* not in order to add force to 'the same' (as in 'the very same') but because in Kant's German *derselbe, dieselbe*, etc., are standardly used simply as pronouns referring back to some earlier noun (cf. the similar use of 'the same' in English legal jargon).]

[50] [*allgemein*, which most often—e.g., later in this paragraph—is translated as 'universal.']

[51] [*ankommen.*]

but solely the matter, viz., whether in complying with the law I am to expect gratification, and how much. Principles of self-love can indeed contain universal rules of skill (for discovering means to [one's] aims), but then they are merely theoretical principles[52] (e.g., how someone who would like to eat bread has to devise a mill). But practical precepts that are based on them can never be universal; for the determining basis of the power of desire is [then] based on the feeling of pleasure and displeasure, and this feeling can never be assumed to be directed universally to the same objects.

    26

But suppose that finite rational beings did think thoroughly alike also in regard to what they had to assume as objects of their feelings of gratification and pain, and likewise even in regard to the means they have to employ in order to attain the former objects and keep the others away. Even then they definitely could not pass off the *principle of self-love* as *a practical law,* because this agreement itself would still be only contingent. The determining basis would still be only subjectively valid and merely empirical and would not have that necessity which is thought in every law. I.e., it would not have the objective necessity from a priori bases, unless this necessity were passed off as not practical at all but as physical, viz., [by claiming] that the action is just as unfailingly forced from us by our inclination as is yawning when we see others yawn. One could sooner maintain that there are no practical laws at all but only *counsels* on behalf of our desires, than that merely subjective principles are being elevated to the rank of practical laws, which definitely must have objective and not merely subjective necessity and which must be cognized a priori by reason, not cognized by experience (however empirically universal this experience may be). Even the rules of accordant appearances are called laws of nature (e.g., the mechanical laws) only if either we actually cognize them a priori, or, at any rate (as with the chemical laws), we assume that we would cognize them a priori from objective bases if our insight went deeper.[53] But in the case of merely

---

[52] Propositions that are called *practical* in mathematics or natural science should properly be named *technical,* for these sciences[a] are not concerned with the determination of the will. These propositions indicate only the manifold—of the possible action—that is sufficient to produce a certain effect, and are therefore just as theoretical as are all propositions asserting the connection of the cause [at issue] with an effect. Thus whoever opts for the effect must also put up with being the cause.

    [a] [*Lehren;* similarly in 'natural science' above.]

[53] [Cf. the *Metaphysical Foundations of Natural Science,* Ak. IV, 468–69; also the *Metaphysics of Morals,* Ak. VI, 215.]

subjective practical principles it is expressly made a condition that they must be based not on objective but on subjective conditions of the power of choice, and hence that they must always be presented[54] only as mere maxims and never as practical laws. This latter comment[55] seems at first glance to be mere word-splitting; however, it defines the words for the most important distinction of all that can ever be considered in practical investigations.

27

§ 4
THEOREM III

If a rational being is to think of his maxims as practical universal laws, then he can think of them only as principles that contain the determining basis of the will not by their matter but merely by their form.

The matter of a practical principle is the object of the will. This object either is the determining basis of the will or it is not. If it [were to] be the will's determining basis, then the rule of the will would be subject to an empirical condition (viz., to the determining presentation's relation to the feeling of pleasure and displeasure), and consequently would not be a practical law. Now if from a law all the matter, i.e., every object of the will, is separated (as determining basis), nothing remains of the law but the mere *form* of a universal legislation.[56] Therefore a rational being either cannot think of *his* subjectively practical principles, i.e., maxims, at the same time as universal laws at all, or he must assume that the principles' mere form by itself alone, whereby they *are fitting for universal legislation,* makes them practical laws.

Comment

What form in a maxim is fitting for universal legislation, and what form is not, can be distinguished without instruction by the commonest understanding. I have, for example, made it my maxim to increase my assets by every safe means. Now I have a *deposit* in my hands, the owner of which is deceased and has left no record of it. Naturally, this is a case for my maxim.

---

[54] [*vorstellig gemacht.*]

[55] [I.e., Comment II.]

[56] [*Gesetzgebung.* See above, Ak. V, 20 br. n. 23.]

Now I want only to know whether that maxim can also hold as a universal practical law. I therefore apply the maxim to the present case and ask whether it could indeed take the form of a law and I could thus indeed, at the same time, give through my maxim such a law as this: that everyone may deny a deposit which no one can prove to him to have been made. I immediately become aware that such a principle, as a law, would annihilate itself, because it would bring it about that there would be no deposit[s] at all. A practical law that I cognize as such must qualify for universal legislation; this is an identical[57] proposition and therefore self-evident. Now if I say that my will is subject to a practical *law*, then I cannot cite my inclination (e.g., in the present case, my greed) as my will's determining basis fitting for a universal practical law; for this inclination, far from being suitable for a universal legislation, rather must, in the form of a universal law, erase itself.

28

Thus it is odd how it could have occurred to intelligent men, [merely] because the desire for happiness and hence also the *maxim* whereby everyone posits this happiness[58] as the determining basis of his will is universal, to therefore pass this [maxim][59] off as a universal *practical law*. For although ordinarily a universal law of nature makes everything accordant, here, if one wanted to give to the maxim the universality of a law, precisely the extreme opposite of accordance would result: the gravest conflict, and the utter annihilation of the maxim itself and of its aim. For then the will of all does not have one and the same object, but each person has his [own] object (viz., his own well-being[60]); and although contingently this object may indeed be compatible with the aims of other people as well, who likewise direct them at themselves, it is far from being sufficient for a law, because the exceptions that one is occasionally authorized to make are endless and cannot at all be encompassed determinately in a universal rule. In this way there results a harmony similar to that depicted by a certain satirical poem[61] on the concord of soul between a married couple who are [bent on] bringing themselves to ruin: *O marvelous harmony, what he wants she also wants,* etc.; or to what is reported about the pledge made by King Francis I against

[57] [I.e., analytic.]

[58] [*diese letztere.* Grammatically, this could refer back to 'desire' instead; however, see above, Ak. V, 22 (and cf. 23–25).]

[59] [Cf. the next sentence. Although Kant actually says *es* rather than *sie,* probably by anticipation of 'law' (*Gesetz*), he clearly does mean the maxim. Cf. above, Ak. V, 26.]

[60] [*Wohlbefinden,* which—like *Wohlsein*—is roughly synonymous with *Wohl.*]

[61] [I have not been able to identify this poem.]

Emperor Charles V:[62] What my brother Charles wants to have (Milan) I also want to have. Empirical determining bases are not suitable for any universal external legislation, but just as little also for an internal one; for each person lays at the basis of inclination his [own] subject, but another person another subject; and in each subject himself now this inclination and now another is superior in influence. Discovering a law that under this condition would govern them[63] all—viz., with accordance on all sides—is absolutely impossible.

§ 5
PROBLEM I

Supposing that the mere legislative form of maxims is alone the sufficient determining basis of a will: to find the constitution of that will which is determinable by this form alone.

Since the mere form of a law can be presented solely by reason and hence is not an object of the senses and thus also does not belong among appearances, the presentation of this form as determining basis of the will is distinct from all determining bases of events [occurring] in nature according to the law of causality, because in the case of these events the determining bases must themselves be appearances. But if, moreover, no determining basis of the will other than that universal legislative form can serve as a law for this will, then such a will must be thought as entirely independent of the natural law governing appearances in reference to one another, viz., the law of causality. Such independence, however, is called *freedom* in the strictest, i.e., the transcendental, meaning. Therefore a will which is such that the mere legislative form of a maxim can alone serve it as a law is a free will.

§ 6
PROBLEM II

Supposing that a will is free: to find the law that alone is suitable for determining it necessarily.

---

[62] [I have deleted the emphasis on *Franz* ('Francis') and on *Karl* ('Charles').]

[63] [I.e., the empirical determining bases.]

Since the matter of a practical law, i.e., the object of a maxim, can never be given except empirically, but a free will—as independent of empirical conditions (i.e., conditions belonging to the world of sense)—must nonetheless be determinable, a free will must, independently of the *matter* of the law, nonetheless find a determining basis in the law. But the law, apart from its matter, contains nothing more than the legislative form. Therefore solely the legislative form, insofar as it is contained in the maxim, can amount to a determining basis of the will.

Comment

Thus freedom and unconditional practical law reciprocally refer to each other.[64] Now, I do not ask here whether even in fact[65] they are different, or—rather—an unconditional law is merely the self-consciousness of a practical reason and this practical reason is entirely the same as the positive concept of freedom.[66] Instead I ask from what our *cognition* of the unconditionally practical *starts,* whether from freedom or from the practical law.[67] It cannot start from freedom, for we can neither become conscious of freedom directly, because the first concept of it is negative, nor infer it from experience, since experience allows us to cognize only the law of appearances and hence the mechanism of nature, the exact opposite of freedom. Therefore it is the *moral law* of which we become conscious directly (as soon as we draft maxims of the will for ourselves), which *first* offers itself to us, and which—inasmuch as reason exhibits it as a determining basis not to be outweighed by any sensible conditions and indeed entirely independent of them—leads straight to the concept of freedom. But how is even the consciousness of that moral law possible? We can become conscious of pure practical laws just as we are conscious of pure theoretical principles, by attending to the necessity with which reason prescribes them to us, and to the separating [from them] of all empirical conditions, to which that necessity points us. The concept of a pure will arises from the consciousness

30

---

[64] [I.e., they—more accurately, their concepts—are interchangeable: *weisen . . . wechselweise auf einander zurück.* Cf. the *Grounding for the Metaphysics of Morals,* Ak. IV, 450, where Kant says that "freedom and the will's own legislation are both autonomy and hence reciprocal concepts [or 'interchangeable concepts': *Wechselbegriffe*]." (Translation mine.)]

[65] [Rather than merely in relation to our cognition; see below.]

[66] [I.e., entirely the same as *freedom* under the positive concept.]

[67] [Cf. the *Grounding for the Metaphysics of Morals,* Ak. IV, 446–48.]

of pure practical laws, as the consciousness of a pure understanding arises from that of pure theoretical principles.[68] That this is the true subordination of our concepts and that morality first reveals the concept of freedom to us, and hence that *practical reason,* with this concept, first poses the most insoluble problem to speculative reason so as to put it in the greatest perplexity through that concept, is evident already from this: since nothing in appearances can be explained on the basis of the concept of freedom, but there the guide must always consist in the mechanism of nature; since, moreover, the antinomy of pure reason, when [reason] wants to ascend to the unconditioned in the series[69] of causes, gets [it] entangled in incomprehensibilities with the one as much as with the other, while yet the latter (mechanism) at least has its usefulness in the explanation of appearances, one would never have committed the daring deed of introducing freedom into science had not the moral law, and with it practical reason, come in and thrust this concept upon us. However, experience also confirms this order of concepts in us. Suppose someone alleges that his lustful inclination is quite irresistible to him when he encounters the favored object and the opportunity. [Ask him] whether, if in front of the house where he finds this opportunity a gallows were erected on which he would be strung up immediately after gratifying his lust, he would not then conquer his inclination. One does not have to guess long what he would reply. But ask him whether, if his prince demanded, on the threat of the same prompt penalty of death, that he give false testimony against an honest man whom the prince would like to ruin under specious pretenses, he might consider it possible to overcome his love of life, however great it may be. He will perhaps not venture to assure us whether or not he would overcome that love, but he must concede without hesitation that doing so would be possible for him. He judges, therefore, that he can do something because he is conscious that he ought to do it, and he cognizes freedom within himself—the freedom with which otherwise, without the moral law, he would have remained unacquainted.

---

[68] [Reading *dem ersteren . . . dem letzteren* for *den ersteren . . . dem letzteren,* inasmuch as the context is concerned with consciousness. Another, less plausible, alternative would be to read *den ersteren . . . den letzteren:* 'The concept of a pure will arises from pure practical laws, as the consciousness of a pure understanding arises from pure theoretical principles.']

[69] [Here again the term is singular: *Reihe.*]

§ 7
BASIC LAW OF PURE PRACTICAL REASON[70]

So act that the maxim of your will could always hold at the same time as a principle of a universal legislation.[71]

Comment

31

Pure geometry has postulates that are practical propositions, which, however, contain nothing more than the presupposition that one *can* do something if perhaps it were demanded that one should[72] do it; and these are the only propositions of pure geometry that concern an existence [of something]. They are therefore practical rules under a problematic condition of the will. Here, however, the rule says: one ought absolutely to proceed in a certain way. The practical rule is therefore unconditional,[73] and hence is conceived a priori as a categorical practical proposition by which the will is objectively determined absolutely and directly (by the practical rule itself, which therefore is here a law). For *pure* [*and*] *in itself practical reason* is here directly legislative. The will is thought as independent of empirical conditions and hence, *qua*[74] pure will, as determined *by the mere form of law,* and this determining basis is regarded as the supreme condition of all maxims. The thing is strange enough and has no equal in all the rest of practical cognition. For the a priori thought of a possible universal legislation, a thought which is therefore merely problematic, is commanded unconditionally as a law, without borrowing anything from experience or from any external will. On the other hand, this thought is not a precept according to which an action by which a desired effect is possible should be done (for then the rule would always be physically conditioned). Rather, it is a rule that determines the will a priori merely with regard to the form of its maxims; and thus there is at least no impossibility in thinking of a law that serves merely on behalf of the *subjective* form of principles as [yet being] a

---

[70] [The categorical imperative (moral law) is discussed extensively in Kant's earlier work, the *Grounding for the Metaphysics of Morals,* Ak. IV, 406–45.]

[71] [*Gesetzgebung.* See above, Ak. V, 20 br. n. 23.]

[72] [*solle,* rendered as 'ought' below.]

[73] [Or 'unconditioned': *unbedingt.*]

[74] [*als,* usually rendered as 'as'; see above and below.]

determining basis through the *objective* form of a law as such. The consciousness of this basic law may be called a fact of reason, because one cannot reason it out from antecedent data[75] of reason—e.g., from the consciousness of freedom (for this is not antecedently given to us)—and because, rather, it thrusts itself upon us on its own as a synthetic a priori proposition not based on any intuition, whether pure or empirical. This proposition would indeed be analytic if the freedom of the will were presupposed;[76] but for this, as a positive concept, an intellectual intuition would be required, which certainly cannot be assumed here at all.[77] However, in order to regard this law—without any misinterpretation—as *given,* one must note carefully that it is not an empirical fact but the sole fact of pure reason, which thereby announces itself as originally legislative (*sic volo, sic iubeo*).[78]

COROLLARY

Pure reason is practical by itself alone and gives (to the human being) a universal law, which we call the *moral law.*[79]

32   *Comment*

The previously mentioned fact is undeniable. One need only dissect the judgment which human beings make about the lawfulness of their actions:

---

[75] [I.e., from the Latin, *givens.* On the fact of reason, cf. below as well as Ak. V, 6, 32, 42, 43, 47, 55, 91, 104.]

[76] [Cf. the *Grounding for the Metaphysics of Morals,* Ak. IV, 446–47.]

[77] [On intellectual (original) intuition (and the intuitive understanding that would have it), see my translation of the *Critique of Pure Reason,* B 138–39, 145, A 166/B 207 incl. br. n. 67, A 249–52, B 307–09, A 256/B 311–12, and A 279–80 = B 335–36, and cf. B xl incl. br. n. 144g, B 68, 135, 149. See also the *Critique of Judgment,* Ak. 402–08, and cf. 418. For a discussion of how the concept of an intellectual intuition (and of an intuitive understanding) unites Kant's three *Critiques* in one system, see the Translator's Introduction to my translation of that work, lxxxvi–cii.]

[78] ['This I will, this I command.' The quote is from Juvenal, *Satires,* VI, 223, and is a Roman woman's retort to her husband, who has dared to object to her demand that an innocent slave be nailed to the cross. The actual text reads, *Hoc volo, sic iubeo, sit pro ratione voluntas;* i.e., 'That [is what] I will, this I command, instead of reasoning let there be the will.']

[79] [*Sittengesetz.*]

one will always find that, whatever [their] inclination may interject, their reason, incorruptible and self-constrained, nonetheless always holds the will's maxim in an action up to the pure will, i.e., to itself inasmuch as it regards itself as practical a priori. Now, this principle of morality, precisely on account of the universality of the legislation that makes it the formal supreme determining basis of the will regardless of all subjective differences of the will [among individuals], is declared by reason at the same time to be a law for all rational beings insofar as they have a will at all, i.e., a power[80] to determine their causality by the presentation of rules, hence insofar as they are capable of [performing] actions according to principles[81] and consequently also according to practical a priori principles (for these alone have that necessity which reason demands for a principle). Therefore this principle of morality does not restrict itself to human beings only, but applies to all finite beings having reason and will, and indeed includes even the infinite being as supreme intelligence.[82] In the case of those finite beings, however, the law has the form of an imperative, because in them, as rational beings, one can indeed presuppose a *pure* will, but, as beings affected by needs and sensible motivating causes,[83] not a *holy* will, i.e., a will that would not be capable of [drafting] any maxims conflicting with the moral law.[84] Hence in the case of those finite beings the moral law is an *imperative* that commands categorically because the law is unconditional.[85] The relation of such a will to this law is *dependence,* under the name of obligation, which [name] means a *necessitation,*[86] although only by reason and its objective law, to an action that is called *duty.* The action is called *duty* because a pathologically affected (although not thereby deter-

---

[80] [Or 'ability': *Vermögen.*]

[81] [*Grundsätze* here, *Prinzipien* below and similarly earlier in this paragraph. See above, Ak. V, 7 br. n. 66.]

[82] [Cf. the *Grounding for the Metaphysics of Morals,* Ak. IV, 412–14.]

[83] [I.e., motivating causes of sensibility. I render *Bewegursache* as 'motivating cause' rather than as 'motive' in order to preserve the reference to 'cause' (*Ursache*), which is especially important in contexts where causes are explicitly discussed, as indeed they are here.]

[84] [*moralisches Gesetz* here and below, *Sittengesetz* later in this paragraph and in the preceding Corollary. Kant uses the two expressions interchangeably.]

[85] [Cf. the *Grounding for the Metaphysics of Morals,* Ak. IV, 412–13.]

[86] [*Nötigung.* Cf. below, Ak. V, 81.]

mined, and hence always also free) power of choice[87] carries with it a wish that arises from *subjective* causes and that hence can often be opposed to the pure objective determining basis and therefore requires, as moral necessitation, a resistance of practical reason that may be called an inner but intellectual constraint. In the most sufficient intelligence of all, the power of choice is rightly presented as not capable of [drafting] any maxim that could not at the same time be objectively a law; and the concept of *holiness,* which on that account belongs to this power of choice, places it, not indeed beyond[88] all practical laws, but still beyond all practically restricting laws, and hence beyond obligation and duty. This holiness of will is nonetheless a practical idea that must necessarily serve as an *archetype,* which to approach *ad infinitum* is alone incumbent upon[89] all finite rational beings; and the pure moral law, which is itself called holy because of this, constantly and rightly holds this idea before their eyes. Being sure of this progression *ad infinitum* of one's maxims and sure of their immutability in [this] constant advance, i.e., virtue, is the highest [result] that finite practical reason can bring about.[90] Virtue itself, in turn, at least as a naturally acquired power,[91] can never be complete,[92] because the assurance in such a case never becomes apodeictic certainty and, as persuasion, is very dangerous.

§ 8
THEOREM IV

Autonomy of the will is the sole principle of all moral laws and of the duties conforming to them; any *heteronomy* of the power of choice, on the other hand, not only is no basis for any obligation at all but is, rather, opposed to the principle of obligation and to the morality of the will. For the sole principle of morality consists in the independence from all matter of the law (i.e., from a desired object) and yet, at the same time, the determination of

---

[87] [*Willkür.* See above, Ak. V, 21 br. n. 26. On 'pathologically affected,' see above, Ak. V, 19 br. n. 5.]

[88] [*über . . . weg.*]

[89] [*zusteht.*]

[90] [Cf. the *Metaphysics of Morals,* Ak. VI, 392–93, 446–47.]

[91] [Or 'ability': *Vermögen.*]

[92] [Or 'perfect': *vollendet.*]

the power of choice by the mere universal legislative form which a maxim must be capable of [having]. That *independence,* however, is freedom in the *negative* meaning, whereas this legislation—pure and, as such, practical reason's *own legislation*—is freedom in the *positive* meaning.[93] Therefore the moral law expresses nothing other than the *autonomy* of pure practical reason, i.e., freedom;[94] and this [autonomy] is itself the formal condition of all maxims, under which alone they can harmonize[95] with the supreme practical law. If, therefore, the matter of volition, which can be nothing other than the object of a desire that is being linked with the law, enters into the practical law **as the condition of its possibility**, then there results heteronomy of the power of choice, namely dependence on the natural law of following some impulse or inclination, and the will gives to itself not the law but only the precept for rational compliance with pathological laws. But the maxim, which in this way can never contain the universally legislative form within itself, not only brings about no obligation in this way, but is itself opposed to the principle of a *pure* practical reason and therefore also to the moral attitude,[96] even if the action arising from it were to be lawful.[97]

Comment I

34

Thus a practical precept that carries with it a material (hence empirical) condition must never be classed with the practical law. For the law of the pure will—which is free—places the will in a sphere entirely different from the empirical one, and the necessity expressed by the law, since it is not to be a natural necessity, can therefore consist only in formal conditions of the possibility of a law as such. Any matter of practical rules rests always on subjective conditions, which impart to them[98] no universality for rational

---

[93] [Cf. the *Grounding for the Metaphysics of Morals,* Ak. IV, 446–47, 452–53, 458–59, 461–62.]

[94] [Literally, 'of freedom': *der Freiheit.* Kant is using a limiting genitive (such as we find in 'the city *of* Berlin'). Cf. below, Ak. V, 87.]

[95] [*zusammenstimmen.*]

[96] [*Gesinnung.* I prefer 'attitude' to 'disposition' because, like the German term, it sounds somewhat more occurrent than dispositional.]

[97] [I.e., law-conforming: *gesetzmäßig.* I render this term as 'lawful' throughout the *Critique,* similarly for the noun.]

[98] [Reading *ihnen* for *ihr* ('it'—i.e., here, the matter), as suggested by Natorp.]

beings except merely the conditional one (in case I *desire* this or that, what I must then do in order to make it actual), and they all revolve about the principle *of one's own happiness.* Now, it is indeed undeniable that any volition must also have an object and hence a matter. But the matter is not, ·just because of this, the determining basis and condition of the maxim. For if it is, then the maxim cannot be exhibited in universally legislative form, since then the expectation of the object's existence would be the determining cause of the power of choice,[99] and the dependence of the power of desire[100] on some thing's existence would have to be laid at the basis of volition—a dependence which can always be sought only in empirical conditions and hence can never provide the basis for a necessary and universal rule. Thus presumably[101] the happiness of other[102] beings can be the object of a rational being's will.[103] But if it were the maxim's determining basis, then one would have to presuppose that we find not only a natural gratification in the well-being[104] of others but also a need, such as the sympathetic mentality[105] brings with it in human beings. But this need I cannot presuppose in every rational being (and in God not at all). Hence the matter of the maxim can indeed remain, but it must not be the maxim's condition, for otherwise the maxim would not be suitable for a law. Therefore the mere form of a law, which[106] restricts the matter, must at the same time be a basis for adding this matter to the will, but not for presupposing it. Let the matter be, for example, my own happiness. This happiness, if I attribute it to everyone (as in fact I may in the case of finite beings), can become an *objective* practical law only if I include in it also the happiness of others. Therefore the law to further the happiness of others arises not from the presupposition that this is an object for everyone's power of choice, but merely from [the fact] that the form of universality, which reason requires as condition for giving to a maxim of self-love the objective validity of a law, becomes the determining basis of the will. Hence not the object (the happiness of others)

---

[99] [*Willkür.*]

[100] [*Begehrungsvermögen.*]

[101] [*wird.*]

[102] [*fremder;* 'of others,' below, renders *anderer.*]

[103] [Cf. the *Metaphysics of Morals,* Ak. VI, 387–88, 393–94, 401–02.]

[104] [*Wohlsein,* which—like *Wohlbefinden*—is roughly synonymous with *Wohl.*]

[105] [*Sinnesart.*]

[106] [Reading *welche* for *welches,* as suggested by both Natorp and Vorländer.]

was the determining basis of the pure will, but this determining basis was solely the mere legal[107] form by which I restricted my maxim—which was based on inclination—in order to impart to the maxim the universality of a law and thus to make it adequate to pure practical reason. Solely this restriction, and not the addition of an external incentive,[108] could then give rise to the concept of the *obligation* to expand the maxim of my self-love to the happiness of others as well.

35

Comment II

The exact opposite of the principle of morality is [what results] when the principle of *one's own* happiness is made the determining basis of the will;[109] in this must be included, as I have shown above, any [theory] in general whereby the determining basis that is to serve as a law is posited in anything other than the legislative form of the maxim. This conflict, however, is not merely logical, as is that between empirically conditioned rules that one might nonetheless want to elevate to necessary principles of cognition. Rather, it is practical and would utterly destroy morality were not the voice of reason in reference to the will so distinct, so incapable of being shouted down, and even for the commonest human being so perceptible. As things are, however, this [theory][110] can continue to maintain itself only in the bewildering speculations of the schools, which are audacious enough to turn a deaf ear to that heavenly voice in order to uphold a theory that does not require them to rack their brains.

Suppose that a social friend,[111] whom you otherwise liked, sought to justify himself to you for having given false testimony by first pleading what he alleges to be the holy[112] duty of [furthering] one's own happiness, by then enumerating all the advantages he had gained by that [action], and by pointing to the prudence he is observing in order to be secure from any dis-

---

[107] [*gesetzlich.*]

[108] [*Triebfeder.* See below, Ak. V, 71–89, and cf. the *Grounding for the Metaphysics of Morals,* Ak. IV, 427.]

[109] [Cf. the *Grounding for the Metaphysics of Morals,* Ak. IV, 399, 442; also the *Metaphysics of Morals,* Ak. VI, 387–88, 493–94.]

[110] [The theory whereby the principle of one's own happiness is the determining basis of the will: *sie,* used apparently by anticipation of the rest of this sentence.]

[111] [*Umgangsfreund.*]

[112] [Or 'sacred': *heilig.*]

covery, even on the part of yourself, to whom he is revealing the secret solely inasmuch as[113] he can deny it at any time; but that he then alleged, in all seriousness, that he had performed a true human duty. You would either laugh straight in his face or recoil from it all[114] with loathing,[115] even though, if someone has geared his principles merely to advantages of his own, you would not have the slightest objection against these guidelines.[116] Or suppose that someone recommend[ed] to you[117] as a steward a man to whom you can blindly entrust all your concerns, and that, in order to instill trust in you, he extolled the man as a prudent human being with a masterly understanding of his own advantage and also as a tirelessly active[118] one who passes up no opportunity for [promoting] it; and that finally, lest any worries about a vulgar self-interest[119] in the man stand in the way, he extolled the man because he understands how to live with great refinement, seeks his gratification not in the accumulation of money or in brutish opulence but in the expansion of his knowledge,[120] in select and instrutive society, even in beneficence to the needy, while otherwise he is not scrupulous as to the means (which, after all, derive their worth or lack of worth only from the purpose[121]), and other people's money or property are as good for this [purpose] as his own, provided he knows that he can use it[122]

---

[113] [*damit.*]

[114] [*davon.*]

[115] [*Abscheu.* Cf. below, Ak. V, 58 incl. br. n. 247.]

[116] [*Maßregeln.*]

[117] [*euch.* Kant is now addressing his readers in the plural; in the previous example he had spoken to the individual reader in the singular.]

[118] [*wirksam.*]

[119] [*Eigennutz.*]

[120] [*Kenntnisse.* Wherever possible, I translate this term—similarly for the singular, *Kenntnis*—as 'acquaintance,' reserving 'knowledge' for *Wissen;* see above, Ak. V, 4 br. n. 31. The same applies to the verb, *kennen,* which I translate sometimes as 'to be acquainted with' but most often as 'to be familiar with' because the 'acquaintance' terminology is usually too awkward—as it does also with the participle *bekannt,* i.e., 'familiar.']

[121] [Or 'end': *Zweck.* I consistently translate this term as 'purpose' because 'end,' which also has a temporal meaning, frequently creates ambiguities, most devastatingly so in the *Critique of Judgment,* but in the present work as well. See my article on *Zweckmäßigkeit* ('purposiveness'): "How to Render *Zweckmäßigkeit* in Kant's Third Critique," in *Interpreting Kant,* ed. Moltke S. Gram, 85–98 (Iowa City, Ia.: University of Iowa Press, 1982).]

[122] [Literally, Kant just says 'do it': *es . . . tun.*]

without being discovered or thwarted. You would believe either that the rec-   36
ommending person is pulling your leg, or that he has lost his mind. So distinctly and sharply cut are the boundaries of morality and self-love that
even the commonest eye can in no way miss the distinction whether something belongs to the one or the other. The few comments that follow may
indeed, in the case of so obvious a truth, seem superfluous, but they
nonetheless serve at least to provide the judgment of common human reason with somewhat greater distinctness.

The principle of happiness can indeed yield maxims, but never maxims
that would be suitable for laws of the will, even if one made *universal*[123]
happiness one's object.[124] For since cognition of this [happiness] rests on
none but experiential data, because each judgment about it depends very
much on each person's opinion which is even itself very changeable, the
principle of happiness can indeed give *general* but never *universal*[125] rules;
i.e., it can give rules that on the average are most often correct but not rules
that must be valid[126] always and necessarily, and hence one cannot base on
it any practical *laws*. Precisely because an object of the power of choice is
here laid at the basis of this power's rule and hence must precede it, the rule
can be referred to and based on nothing other than what one approves,[127]
and hence referred to and based on experience, and thus the variety of judgment must be endless. This principle, therefore, does not prescribe to all
rational beings the same practical rules, even though they fall under a common heading, viz., that of happiness. The moral law, however, is thought as
objectively necessary only because it is to hold[128] for everyone having reason and will.

The maxim of self-love (prudence) merely *counsels;* the law of morality
commands.[129] But surely there is a great difference between what we are
counseled to do and what we are *obligated* to do.

---

[123] [*allgemein.*]

[124] [Cf. the *Grounding for the Metaphysics of Morals,* Ak. IV, 395–96, 399, 405, 415–16, 418–19.]

[125] [Respectively, *generell, universell.*]

[126] [*gültig.*]

[127] [*empfiehlt.* Hartenstein instead reads *empfindet* ('senses,' in the broad meaning of the term that includes feeling).]

[128] [*gelten soll.*]

[129] [Cf. the *Grounding for the Metaphysics of Morals,* Ak. IV, 414–21.]

On the principle of the autonomy of the power of choice, what is to be done can quite easily and without hesitation be seen[130] by the commonest understanding; under the presupposition of the heteronomy of the power of choice, what is to be done is difficult to see and requires acquaintance[131] with the world. I.e., what [one's] *duty* is[132] offers itself on its own to everyone; but what brings true, lasting advantage, if this advantage is to be extended to [one's] entire existence, is shrouded in impenetrable obscurity and requires much prudence in order that the practical rule attuned to that [aim can] be adapted even tolerably to life's purposes by means of suitable exceptions. Nonetheless, the moral law commands compliance, and indeed the most meticulous compliance, from everyone. Therefore, judging what according to it is to be done must not be so difficult that the commonest and most unpracticed understanding could not deal with this law, even without worldly prudence.

Satisfying the categorical command of morality is under everyone's control[133] at any time; satisfying the empirically conditioned precept of happiness is only rarely possible, and is far from being possible for everyone even just in regard to one single aim. This is so because in the case of the command of morality what counts is only the maxim, which must be genuine and pure, but in the case of the precept of happiness it is also one's powers and one's physical ability[134] to make a desired object actual. A command whereby everyone ought to seek to make himself happy would be foolish, for one never commands someone to do what already on his own he unfailingly wants to do; one would have to command him merely the guidelines[135] [for doing so], or rather offer them to him, because he is unable to do all that he wants[136] to do. But to command morality under the name of duty is entirely reasonable;[137] for, first, not everyone does willingly[138] obey

---

[130] [*einsehen.*]

[131] [Or 'familiarity': *-kenntnis.* See above, Ak. V, 35 br. n. 120, and 4 br. n. 31.]

[132] [*was Pflicht sei.* See Ak. V, 8 n. 83 incl. n. 83f.]

[133] [Or 'in everyone's power': *in jedes Gewalt.*]

[134] [*die Kräfte und das physische Vermögen.*]

[135] [*Maßregeln.*]

[136] [Or 'wills': *will;* likewise at the end of the sentence.]

[137] [*vernünftig,* which I usually translate as 'rational.']

[138] [*will . . . gerne.*]

its precept when it is in conflict with inclinations; and as for the guidelines as to how he can comply with this law, here these need not be taught, since what in this regard he wants to do he is also able to do.

Someone who has *lost* at play can indeed *be angry* at himself and his imprudence; but if he is conscious of having *cheated* at play (even though he has gained thereby), he must *despise*[139] himself as soon as he compares himself with the moral law. Hence this law must surely be something different from the principle of one's own happiness. For having to say to oneself, I am a *worthless person*[140] even though I have filled my purse, must surely have a different standard of judgment from applauding oneself and saying, I am a *prudent* human being, for I have enriched my coffer.

Finally, there is in the idea of our practical reason something else that accompanies the transgression of a moral law, viz., its *deserving punishment.*[141] Now, surely, coming to partake of happiness cannot be linked at all with the concept of a punishment, as such. For although the person who punishes can indeed at the same time have the benign intention of directing that punishment to this purpose as well, yet it must first be justified by itself as punishment,[142] i.e., as something merely bad,[143] so that the punished person, even if things stopped there and he looked to no indulgence hidden behind this harshness, must himself admit that he has been dealt with rightly and that his lot is perfectly appropriate to his conduct. In every punishment, as such, there must first be justice, and this amounts to what is essential in this concept.[144] Although benignity too can be linked with punishment, the person who deserves punishment has, according to his behavior,[145] not the slightest cause to count on it. Therefore punishment is something physically bad that, even if it were not linked with the morally evil[146] as a *natural* consequence [thereof], would still have to be linked [with it] as a conse-

---

[139] [*verachten.*]

[140] [*Nichtswürdiger.*]

[141] [*Strafwürdigkeit.*]

[142] [*Strafe.* This term means 'punishment' in the sense of what is inflicted—viz., something bad—on someone. The German term for 'punishment' in the sense of the *act* of inflicting something bad is *Bestrafung.*]

[143] [*als bloßes Übel.* On *Übel* and 'bad,' see below, Ak. V, 59 br. n. 259.]

[144] [Cf. the *Metaphysics of Morals,* Ak. VI, 227–28, 460–61.]

[145] [*Aufführung.*]

[146] [*dem moralisch Bösen.* See below, Ak. V, 59 br. n. 259.]

quence according to principles of a moral legislation. Now if all crime, even without taking account of the physical consequences regarding the agent, is by itself punishable—i.e., [involves] forfeiture of happiness (at least in part)—then it would obviously be absurd to say that the crime consisted precisely in the agent's having brought a punishment upon himself by impairing his own happiness (which according to the principle of self-love would have to be the proper concept of all crime). The punishment would in this way be the basis for calling something a crime, and justice would have to consist, rather, in omitting all punishment and preventing even natural punishment. For then there would no longer be any evil in the action, because the bad things[147] that ordinarily followed upon it and on account of which alone the action was called evil would now be kept away. But to regard all punishing and rewarding as being altogether only the machinery in the hands of a higher power,[148] a machinery that is to serve solely to thereby put rational beings into activity toward their final aim (happiness), is very manifestly a mechanism of their will that annuls all freedom, and thus we need not dwell upon it.

38

Even more refined, although just as untrue, is the allegation of those who assume a certain special moral sense[149] which, instead of reason, determines the moral law. According to this allegation, the consciousness of virtue would be linked directly with satisfaction and gratification, and the consciousness of vice with unease of soul and with pain. Thus these [philosophers] do, after all, stake everything on the longing[150] for one's own happiness. Without here drawing on what has been said above, I want only to note the delusion[151] that takes place in this. In order to conceive the vicious person as tormented with unease of mind by the consciousness of his offenses, they must conceive him already in advance as at least to some degree morally good in terms of the foremost foundation of his character, just as the person who is delighted by the consciousness of actions conforming to duty must be conceived by these [philosophers] already beforehand as virtuous. Therefore the concept of morality and duty surely had to precede any regard for this satisfaction and cannot at all be derived from it.

147 [die Übel.]

148 [Or 'might': Macht.]

149 [Cf. the Grounding for the Metaphysics of Morals, Ak. IV, 442–43.]

150 [Verlangen, which can also mean 'demand.']

151 [Täuschung.]

Now surely one must [already] beforehand esteem the importance of what we call duty, [and esteem] the authority[152] of the moral law and the direct worth that compliance with it gives a person in his own eyes, in order to feel this satisfaction in the consciousness of one's own adequacy to that law[153] and the bitter reprimand if one can reproach oneself with having transgressed it. Therefore one cannot feel this satisfaction or this unease of soul prior to the cognition of obligation and cannot make it the basis of obligation. One must be at least halfway an honest man already in order to be able even to frame a presentation of those sensations.[154] For the rest, I am in no way denying that, just as the human will by virtue of freedom is directly determinable by the moral law, so also can repeated performance in conformity with this determining basis ultimately bring about subjectively a feeling of satisfaction with oneself.[155] On the contrary, to establish and cultivate this feeling, which—properly—alone deserves[156] to be called moral feeling, itself belongs to duty.[157] But the concept of duty cannot be derived from it, for otherwise we would have to think of a feeling of a law *qua* law[158] and turn into an object of sensation what can only be thought by reason—which, if it is not to become a flat contradiction, would entirely annul any concept of duty and would put in its place merely a mechanical play of more refined inclinations sometimes falling into discord with the coarser.

If we now compare our *formal* supreme principle[159] of pure practical reason (as an autonomy of the will) with all hitherto [proposed] *material* principles of morality, we can present in a table all the[se] others as principles by which all possible other cases are actually at the same time exhausted except for a single[,] formal case, and can thus prove, as manifest to the eye, that it is futile to look around for any other principle than the one

39

---

[152] [*Ansehen.*]

[153] [Reading, with Vorländer, *desselben* for *derselben,* which would refer to duty here, even though below the original does have *desselben,* and thus does there refer to the moral law.]

[154] [In the broad meaning of the term that includes feelings: *Empfindungen.* See above, Ak. V, 22 br. n. 31.]

[155] [Cf. the *Metaphysics of Morals,* Ak. VI, 377–78.]

[156] [*verdienen.*]

[157] [Cf. the *Metaphysics of Morals,* Ak. VI, 399–400.]

[158] [*eines Gesetzes als eines solchen.*]

[159] [*Grundsatz* here, *Prinzipien* below. See above, Ak. V, 7 br. n. 66.]

set forth here. For, all possible determining bases of the will are either merely *subjective* and hence empirical, or else *objective* and rational; but both are either *external* or *internal*.

40

PRACTICAL MATERIAL DETERMINING BASES[160]
IN THE PRINCIPLE OF MORALITY ARE

Subjective		Objective	
external	*internal*	*internal*	*external*
Of *education* (according to *Montaigne*) Of the *civil constitution* (according to *Mandeville*)	Of *physical feeling* (according to *Epicurus*) Of *moral feeling* (according to *Hutcheson*)	Of *perfection* (according to *Wolff* and the *Stoics*)	Of the *will of God* (according to *Crusius* and other theological moralists)

[160] [Some information pertaining to the names that appear in Kant's table: Epicurus (341–270 B.C.), Greek philosopher and founder of the school known as Epicureanism; in this work, see Ak. V, 40–41, 88, 111, 115–16, 120, 126–27 incl. n. 151, 141; for an introduction to Epicurus, see *The Epicurus Reader: Selected Writings and Testimonia,* trans. Brad Inwood and Lloyd P. Gerson; introduction by D. S. Hutchinson (Indianapolis, Ind.: Hackett, 1994). The Stoics, members of the school known as Stoicism (which began in the third century B.C. and lasted for approximately 500 years); in this work, see Ak. V, 11 n. 93, 40, 60, 86, 111–12, 115, 126–27 incl. n. 151; for an introduction to Stoicism, see *The Stoics,* reprint of the Chatto and Windus edition of 1975 (Indianapolis, Ind.: Hackett, 1994; copublished in the U.K. by Gerald Duckworth and Company Ltd.). Michel Eyquem de Montaigne (1533–92), French writer (to whom we owe the term 'essay' in the literary sense) and philosopher; his philosophical skepticism is stated most fully in his "Apology" (i.e., "Defense"): "Apologie de Raymond Sebond," in the *Essais* (Bordeaux, France: S. Millanges, 1580); translation, *An Apology for Raymond Sebond,* translated and edited with introduction and notes by M. A. Screech (London: Penguin Books, 1993). Bernard Mandeville (1670–1733), Dutch physician who made his name in England as a satirist and philosopher; he is best known (cf. the work by Hutcheson, below) for his *The Fable of the Bees: or, Private Vices, Publick Benefits: Containing Several Discourses to Demonstrate That Human Frailties, During the Degeneracy of Mankind, May Be Turn'd to the Advantage of the Civil Society, and Made to Supply the Place of Moral Virtues* (London: J. Roberts, 1714); edited, with introduction, by E. J. Hundert (Indianapolis, Ind.: Hackett, 1997). Francis Hutcheson (1694–1746), British philosopher and proponent of the "moral sense" theory in ethics; he first introduced this theory in his *An Inquiry into the Original of Our Ideas of Beauty and Virtue; in Two Treatises, in Which the Principles of the Earl of Shaftesbury Are Explain'd and Defended Against the Author of The Fable of The Bees, and the Ideas of Moral Good and Evil are Establish'd According to the Sentiments of the Antient Moralists. With an*

The determining bases on the left side[161] are, one and all, empirical and are   41
obviously not suitable at all for [being] the universal principle of morality.
But those on the right side are based on reason (for perfection as a *characteristic* of things, and the highest perfection conceived in *substance,* i.e.,
God, can both be thought only through rational concepts). However, the
first concept [on the right side], viz., that of *perfection,* can be taken either
in a *theoretical* [or in a practical] signification. [In the former] it signifies
nothing but the completeness of each thing in its kind (transcendental perfection) or of a thing merely as thing as such[162] (metaphysical perfection),
and this cannot be the issue here. But the concept of perfection in the
practical signification is the suitability or adequacy of a thing to all sorts of
purposes.[163] This perfection, as a *characteristic* of the human being and
consequently as internal, is nothing other than *talent* and what strengthens
or complements it, *skill.* The highest perfection in *substance,* i.e., God, and
consequently as external, is (as considered for a practical aim)[164] the adequacy of this being to all purposes[165] as such. Suppose, then, that purposes
must be given to us beforehand, in reference to which alone the concept of
perfection (an internal perfection in ourselves[166] or an external one in
God[167]) can become a determining basis of the will; and that a purpose—as

---

Attempt to Introduce a Mathematical Calculation in Subjects of Morality (London: J. Darby,
1725); 4th, corrected, edition, (London: for D. Medwinter, 1738), reprinted (Westmead, Farnborough, Haunts, England: Gregg International, 1969). Baron Christian von Wolff
(1679–1754), German mathematician, natural scientist, and rationalist philosopher of the enlightenment; he is the author of numerous works. Christian August Crusius (1715–75), German theologian and philosopher, and critic of Wolffianism. His main works are *Entwurf der
nothwendigen Vernunft-Wahrheiten, wiefern sie den zufälligen entgegen gesetzet werden (Outline of Necessary Truths insofar as They Are Contrasted with Contingent Truths)* (Leipzig:
Gleditsch, 1745); reprinted (Hildesheim, Germany: G. Olms, 1964); and *Weg zur Gewissheit
und Zuverlässigkeit der menschlichen Erkenntniss (Path to Certainty and Reliability of Human
Cognition)* (Leipzig: Gleditsch, 1747); reprinted (Hildesheim, Germany: G. Olms, 1965).]

[161] [I.e., the *subjective* determining bases.]

[162] [*überhaupt.* See above, Ak. V, 3 br. n. 3.]

[163] [Or 'ends': *Zwecke.* See above, Ak. V, 35 br. n. 121.]

[164] [*in praktischer Absicht betrachtet.* On Vorländer's reading of the punctuation this parenthetical insertion occurs immediately after 'and consequently external' and hence is associated
with that clause.]

[165] [Or 'ends': *Zwecke.* See above, Ak. V, 35 br. n. 121.]

[166] [Cf. the *Metaphysics of Morals,* Ak. VI, 391–93, 446–47.]

[167] [Cf. ibid., Ak. VI, 487–89.]

an *object* that must precede the will's determination by a practical rule and contain the basis of the possibility of such a determination—and hence the *matter* of the will, taken as the will's determining basis, is always empirical and hence can serve as the *Epicurean* principle of the doctrine of happiness but never as the pure rational principle of the doctrine of morals and of duty. (For, indeed, talents and their furtherance can then become a motivating cause of the will only because they contribute to the advantages of life; or the will of God—if agreement with it has been taken as the will's object without an antecedent practical principle independent of the idea of God's will—can become such a motivating cause only through the *happiness* that we expect from it.) If we suppose this, it follows, *first,* that all the principles listed here are *material; second,* that they encompass all possible material principles; and, finally, the conclusion from this, that, since (as has been proved) material principles are entirely unsuitable for [being] the supreme moral law, the *formal practical principle* of pure reason—according to which the supreme and direct determining basis of the will must consist in the mere form of a universal legislation possible through our maxims—is the *only possible* principle that is suitable for categorical imperatives, i.e., practical laws (which make action duties), and in general for the principle of morality both in judging and in applying it to the human will in determining that will.

42

I
On the Deduction of the Principles of Pure Practical Reason

This Analytic establishes that pure reason can be practical, i.e., that it can on its own, independently of everything empirical, determine the will; specifically, it establishes this through a fact[168] wherein pure reason does indeed prove itself in us practically, viz., the autonomy in the principle of morality by which pure reason determines the will to the deed. At the same time the Analytic shows that this fact is inseparably linked with the consciousness of the freedom of the will—indeed, that it and this consciousness are one and the same. Through this consciousness of its freedom the

---

[168] [On the fact of reason, see above, Ak. V, 31 incl. br. n. 75.]

will of a rational being that, as belonging to the world of sense, cognizes itself as necessarily subject to the laws of causality like other efficient causes,
is yet in the practical [sphere] at the same time conscious—on another side,
viz., as a being in itself—of its existence [as] determinable in an intelligible
order of things. It is conscious of this not, indeed, in conformity with a special intuition[169] of itself, but in conformity with certain dynamical laws that
can determine its causality in the world of sense. For, [my assertion] that
freedom, if it is attributed to us, transfers us into an intelligible order of
things has been proved sufficiently elsewhere.[170]

　　Now if we compare with this Analytic the analytical part of the critique
of pure speculative reason,[171] we can see a noteworthy contrast between the
two. Not principles but pure sensible *intuition* (space and time) was there
the first datum that made a priori cognition possible, although only for objects of the senses. Synthetic principles [derived] from mere concepts without intuition were impossible; rather, these principles could occur only in
reference to intuition, which was sensible, and thus only in reference to objects of possible experience; for solely the concepts of understanding, combined[172] with this intuition, make possible that cognition which we call
experience. Beyond objects of experience, hence concerning things as
noumena, speculative reason was quite rightly denied anything positive [by
way] of *cognition.* Speculative reason did, however, accomplish this much:
it secured the concept of noumena—i.e., the possibility, indeed the necessity, of thinking such [things]—and, e.g., rescued from all objections the assumption of freedom, considered negatively, as entirely compatible with
those principles and restrictions of pure theoretical reason, yet without allowing us to cognize anything determinate and expansive,[173] since it rather   43
cut off any such prospect entirely.

　　On the other hand, although the moral law does not provide us with a
prospect, it nonetheless provides us with a fact that is absolutely inexplicable from any data of the world of sense and from the entire range of our theoretical use of reason—a fact that points to a pure world of understanding,

---

[169] [Viz., intellectual intuition (of a pure world of understanding, about to be mentioned in the
next paragraph). See above, Ak. V, 31 br. n. 77.]

[170] [*Grounding for the Metaphysics of Morals,* Section III: Ak. IV, 446–63.]

[171] [See the *Critique of Pure Reason,* A 19–292/B 33–349.]

[172] [Or 'linked': *verbunden.*]

[173] [I.e., anything that would expand (*erweitern*) cognition.]

and indeed even *positively determines* that world and allows us to cognize something of it, viz., a law.

This law is to furnish to the world of sense, as a *sensible nature,* the form (as far as rational beings are concerned)[174] of a world of understanding, i.e., a *suprasensible nature,* yet without impairing the mechanism of sensible nature. Now, nature in the most general meaning is the existence of things under laws. The sensible nature of rational beings in general is their existence under empirically conditioned laws, and hence is, for reason, *heteronomy.* The suprasensible nature of the same beings, on the other hand, is their existence according to laws that are independent of any empirical condition and that hence belong to the *autonomy* of pure reason. And since the laws according to which the existence[175] of things depends on cognition are practical, suprasensible nature, insofar as we can frame a concept of it, is nothing other than *a nature under the autonomy of pure practical reason.* The law of this autonomy, however, is the moral law, which is therefore the basic law of a suprasensible nature and of a pure world of understanding whose counterpart[176] ought to exist in the world of sense, yet without impairing that world's laws. The former nature could be called the *archetypal*[177] nature (*natura archetypa*), which we cognize merely in reason, whereas the latter—because it contains the possible effect of the idea of the former nature as determining basis of the will—could be called the ectypal[178] nature (*natura ectypa*). For in fact the moral law transfers us, in [our] idea, into a nature in which pure reason, if it were accompanied by the physical power adequate to it, would produce the highest good, and determines our will to confer the form [of a world of understanding] on the world of sense as a whole of rational beings.[179]

That this idea actually serves as the model for our determinations of the will—as a pattern, as it were—is confirmed by the commonest attentiveness to oneself.

---

[174] [On Vorländer's reading of the punctuation, this parenthetical insertion occurs immediately after 'as a *sensible nature*' and hence qualifies that clause.]

[175] [*Dasein* here, *Existenz* in all the preceding occurrences in this paragraph.]

[176] [Literally, 'counterimage': *Gegenbild.*]

[177] [*urbildlich,* from *Urbild* ('archetype'), literally 'original image.']

[178] [*nachgebildete,* i.e., roughly, 'reproduced' or 'copied.']

[179] [Cf. the *Critique of Pure Reason,* A 807–11 = B 835–39.]

When the maxim according to which I intend to give testimony is tested   44
by practical reason, I always consider how the maxim would be if it held as
a universal law of nature. Obviously, in this mode the [maxim as such a]
law would compel[180] everyone to be truthful. For to accept statements as
proof and yet as deliberately untrue is not consistent with the universality of
a law of nature. Similarly, the maxim that I adopt concerning the free disposition of my life is at once determined when I ask myself how this maxim
would have to be in order for a nature to maintain itself according to a law
based thereon.[181] Obviously, in such a nature no one could end his life *by
choice*,[182] for such a constitution[183] would not be an enduring order of nature. And thus in all other cases. However, in actual nature, as far as it is an
object of experience, the free will by itself is not determined to such maxims as could on their own establish a nature according to universal laws, or
as would by themselves even fit into a nature arranged according to such
laws; rather, its maxims are private inclinations that do indeed amount to a
whole of nature according to pathological (physical) laws, but not to a nature [of the sort] that would be possible only through our will according to
pure practical laws. Nonetheless, through reason we are conscious of a law
to which all our maxims are subject, as if through our will an order of nature must at the same time arise. Therefore this law must be the idea of a nature not given empirically and yet possible through freedom, hence of a
suprasensible nature to which, at least in a practical reference, we give objective reality,[184] since we regard it as an object of the will of ourselves as
pure rational beings.

Hence the difference between the laws of a nature to which *the will is
subject* and those of a *nature that is subject to a will*[185] (in regard to what
refers the will to its free actions) rests on this: that in the former nature the
objects must be causes of the presentations that determine the will, but in
the latter nature the will is to be the cause of the objects, so that the will's
causality has its determining basis solely in the pure power of reason, a
power that can therefore also be called a pure practical reason.

---

[180] [*nötigen.* See above, Ak. V, 20 br. n. 17.]

[181] [*nach einem Gesetze derselben.*]

[182] [*willkürlich.*]

[183] [I.e., of nature: *Verfassung.*]

[184] [I.e., applicability to things as objects.]

[185] [Emphasis expanded to include 'is subject,' to improve readability.]

There are, therefore, two very different problems: how, *on the one hand,* pure reason can a priori *cognize* objects; and how, *on the other hand,* it can be directly a determining basis of the will, i.e., of the rational being's causality regarding the actuality of objects (merely through the thought of the universal validity of its own maxims as law).

The first problem, as belonging to the critique of pure speculative reason, requires that we explain beforehand how intuitions, without which no object can be given to us and hence none can be cognized [by us] synthetically at all, are possible a priori; and its solution turns out to be that these intuitions are, one and all, only sensible and hence do not make possible any speculative cognition that would go further than possible experience extends, and that therefore all the principles of that pure speculative reason accomplish nothing more than making experience possible, either of given objects or of those that may be given *ad infinitum* but are never completely given.

The second problem, as belonging to the *critique*[186] of practical reason, requires no explanation as to how the objects of the power of desire are possible, for this, as a problem of the theoretical cognition of nature, is left to the critique of speculative reason, but only as to how reason can determine the will's maxim, whether this occurs only by means of empirical presentations as determining bases, or whether even pure reason would be practical and be a law of a possible order of nature not cognizable empirically at all. The possibility of such a suprasensible nature, the concept of which can at the same time be the basis of that nature's actuality through our free will, requires no a priori intuition (of an intelligible world), which in this case, as suprasensible,[187] would also have to be impossible for us. For what counts is only the determining basis of volition in the maxims thereof: whether this determining basis is empirical or a concept of pure reason (of its lawfulness as such), and how it can be the latter. Whether or not the causality of the will is sufficient for [bringing about] the actuality of the objects is left to reason's theoretical principles to judge; for this is an investigation of the possibility of the objects of volition, and hence in the practical problem the intuition of these objects does not at all amount to a moment[188] of the problem. What counts here is only the determination of the will and the determining basis of the maxim of this will as a free will, not the result. For

---

[186] [The aims of the *critique* of practical reason are limited; cf. the end of this paragraph.]

[187] [Viz., as intellectual intuition. Cf. above, Ak. V, 42 br. n. 169, and 31 br. n. 77.]

[188] [I.e., key element: (*das*) *Moment.*]

provided that the *will* is lawful for pure reason, then its *power* in carrying out [its aims] may be what it may, and a nature may or may not actually arise according to these maxims of the legislation of a possible nature, the   46
critique that investigates whether and how reason can be practical, i.e., can directly determine the will, does not worry about this at all.

In this task, therefore, the critique of practical reason can, without being censured, start from pure practical laws and their actuality, and must do so. But rather than on intuition, it bases these laws on the concept of their existence in the intelligible world, viz., the concept of freedom. For this concept signifies nothing else, and those laws are possible only in reference to freedom of the will; but on the presupposition of freedom they are necessary, or, conversely, freedom is necessary because those laws, as practical postulates, are necessary. How this consciousness of the moral law or, what is the same thing, the consciousness of freedom is possible cannot be further explained, but the admissibility of freedom can readily be defended in the theoretical critique.

The *exposition* of the supreme principle of practical reason is now done; i.e., we have shown, first, what the principle contains, that it subsists on its own entirely a priori and independently of empirical principles, and then what distinguishes it from all other practical principles. With the *deduction,* i.e., the justification of the principle's objective and universal validity and of insight into the possibility of such a synthetic a priori proposition, one cannot hope to get on so well as was feasible with the principles of pure theoretical understanding. For the latter principles referred to objects of possible experience, viz., appearances, and we were able to prove that these appearances can be *cognized* as objects of experience only by being brought under the categories in accordance with these laws, and that consequently all possible experience must be commensurate with these laws. Such a course, however, I cannot take in the deduction of the moral law. For this law pertains not to the cognition of the constitution of objects that may be given to reason from elsewhere by something or other, but to a cognition insofar as it can itself become the basis of the existence of objects and insofar as reason, through this cognition, has causality in a rational being, i.e., [as a] pure reason that can be regarded as a power directly determining the will.

However, all human insight is at an end as soon as we have arrived at basic powers or basic abilities;[189] for their possibility cannot be compre-   47

---

[189] [*Grundkräften oder Grundvermögen.*]

hended[190] through anything,[191] but neither must it be invented and assumed at one's discretion.[192] Hence in the theoretical use of reason only experience can entitle us to assume them. But this substitute, adducing empirical proofs in place of a deduction from a priori sources of cognition, is also denied us here with regard to the pure practical power of reason. For, whatever requires that the basis for proving its actuality be brought from experience must be dependent, as regards the bases of its possibility, on principles of experience; but pure and yet practical reason, by its very concept, cannot possibly be considered to be of that sort. Moreover, the moral law is given as a fact,[193] as it were, of pure reason of which we are conscious a priori and which is apodeictically certain, even supposing that in experience no example could be hunted up[194] where it is complied with exactly. Therefore the objective reality of the moral law cannot be proved through any deduction, through any endeavor of theoretical reason, speculative or empirically supported, and hence could not, even if one wanted to forgo apodeictic certainty, be confirmed through experience and thus proved a posteriori, and yet is—on its own—established.

However, something different and paradoxical [now] steps into the place of this vainly sought deduction of the moral principle, namely that, conversely, this principle itself serves as the principle of the deduction of an inscrutable power that no experience was able to prove but that speculative reason had to assume as at least possible (in order to find among its cosmological ideas what is unconditioned in terms of its causality, so as not to contradict itself): viz., the power of freedom, the freedom of which the moral law, which itself needs no justifying grounds, proves not only the possibility but the actuality in beings who cognize this law as obligating for them. The moral law is in fact a law of the causality through freedom and hence a law of the possibility of a suprasensible nature, just as the metaphysical law of the events in the world of sense was a law of the causality of

---

[190] [Or 'grasped': *begriffen*. Although in different contexts *begreifen* can also mean 'to comprise' and in that meaning is related to *Begriff*, i.e., 'concept,' it *never* means merely 'to conceive' (as this latter term is used in philosophy). Cf. my translation of the *Critique of Pure Reason*, A 792 = B 820 incl. br. n. 394.]

[191] [Cf. the *Critique of Pure Reason*, B 110, B 145–46, A 141/B 180–81; also the *Prolegomena*, Ak. IV, 318.]

[192] [Or 'optionally,' or perhaps 'arbitrarily': *beliebig*.]

[193] [On the fact of reason, see above, Ak. V, 31 incl. br. n. 75.]

[194] [*auftreiben*.]

sensible nature. Thus the moral law determines that which speculative philosophy had to leave undetermined, viz., the law for a causality the concept
of which was only negative in speculative philosophy; and it thus first provides this concept with objective reality.

This kind of credential of the moral law, where it is itself put forth as a   48
principle of the deduction of freedom as a causality of pure reason, is fully
sufficient in place of any a priori justification, since theoretical reason was
compelled to *assume* at least the possibility of [such] a freedom in order to
fill a need that it has. For the moral law satisfactorily proves its [own] reality, even for the critique of speculative reason, by supplementing a causality
thought merely negatively, the possibility of which was incomprehensible
to speculative reason but which it nonetheless needed to assume, by positive determination [of this causality], viz., the concept of a reason directly
determining the will (through the condition of a universal lawful form of
the will's maxims). Thus the moral law is able for the first time to give to
reason—which always became extravagant[195] when it wanted to proceed
speculatively with its ideas—objective although only practical reality, and
converts reason's *transcendent* use into an *immanent* use (wherein reason,
through ideas, is itself an efficient cause in the realm of experience).

The determination of the causality of beings in the world of sense, as
such a world, can never be unconditioned, and yet for every series of conditions there must necessarily be something unconditioned, and hence there
must also be a causality that determines itself entirely on its own. Therefore
the idea of freedom as a power of absolute spontaneity was not a require-
ment, but—*as far as its possibility is concerned*—an analytic principle, of
pure speculative reason. However, since it is absolutely impossible to give
an example in conformity with this idea in any experience, because no
determination of causality that would be absolutely unconditioned can be
encountered among the causes of things as appearances, we were able to
defend the *thought* of a freely acting cause, when we apply this thought to a
being in the world of sense, [on the one hand,] only insofar as this being is
also regarded as a noumenon, on the other hand. We defended this thought
by showing that there is no contradiction in regarding all actions of the
being as physically conditioned insofar as they are appearances, and yet at
the same time regarding their causality as physically unconditioned insofar
as the acting being is a being of the understanding, and in thus making the
concept of freedom a regulative principle of reason. Although through this

[195] [I.e., transcendent: *überschwenglich.*]

[principle] I do not at all cognize the object to which such a causality is attributed, as to what this object is, I nonetheless remove the obstacle inasmuch as on the one hand, in the explanation of events in the world and hence also of the actions of rational beings, I do justice to the mechanism of natural necessity by going back from the conditioned to the condition *ad infinitum,* while on the other hand I keep open for speculative reason the place that is vacant for it, namely the intelligible, in order to transfer the unconditioned there. However, I was not able to *realize* this *thought,* i.e., to convert it into *cognition* of a being acting in this way, not even as regards merely its possibility. Pure practical reason now fills this vacant place with a determinate law of causality in an intelligible world (causality through freedom), viz., the moral law. Although speculative reason does not gain anything through this as regards its insight, it does gain something as regards *securing* its problematic concept of freedom, which is here provided with *objective reality* that, although only practical, is yet indubitable. Even the concept of causality, which properly has application and hence also signification (as the *Critique of Pure Reason* proves) only in reference to appearances in order to connect them into experiences—even this concept reason does not expand in such a way as to extend its use beyond the mentioned boundaries. For if it sought to do this, it would have to try to show how the logical relation of basis[196] and consequence could be used synthetically with a kind of intuition different from the sensible,[197] i.e., how a *causa noumenon*[198] is possible. This it cannot accomplish at all; but as practical reason it is also in no way concerned with this, for it only posits the *determining basis* of the causality of the human being as a being of sense (a causality that is given) *in pure reason* (which is therefore called practical). Thus it needs the concept of the cause itself—from whose application to objects for the sake of theoretical cognition it can here abstract entirely (since this concept is always found a priori in the understanding, even independently of any intuition)—not in order to cognize objects but in order to determine the causality with regard to objects as such, and hence for none but a practical aim; and thus it can transfer the determining basis of the will into the intelligible order of things, inasmuch as it gladly[199] admits at the

[196] [Or 'ground': *Grund;* cf. above, Ak. V, 4 br. n. 36. Even here 'basis' is preferable, because the relation, although logical, is being taken beyond logic.]

[197] [I.e., an intellectual intuition. See above, Ak. V, 31 br. n. 77.]

[198] [Noumenal cause.]

[199] [*gerne.*]

same time that it does not understand at all what sort of determination the concept of cause may have [that would allow] for cognition of these things. Of course, causality with regard to actions of the will in the world of sense must be cognized by reason in a determinate way, for otherwise practical reason could not actually give rise to any deed. But as for the concept that it frames of its own causality as noumenon, this concept it need not determine theoretically for the sake of cognizing this causality's suprasensible exis-   50 tence, and thus it need not be able to give it signification to this extent. For this concept acquires signification anyway, even if only for practical use, viz., through the moral law. Even regarded theoretically it always remains a pure, a priori given concept of the understanding, which can be applied to objects whether these are given sensibly or not sensibly, although in the latter case the concept has no determinate theoretical signification and application but is merely the understanding's formal but nonetheless essential thought of an object as such. The signification that reason provides to this concept through the moral law is solely practical, inasmuch as the idea of the law of a causality (causality of the will) itself has causality, or is its determining basis.

II

On the Authority²⁰⁰ of Pure Reason in Its Practical Use to an Expansion That Is Not Possible for It in Its Speculative Use

In the moral principle we have put forth a law of causality which posits the determining basis of this causality beyond all conditions of the world of sense; and, as regards the will—as to how, as belonging to an intelligible world, it is determinable—and hence as regards the subject of this will, the human being,²⁰¹ we have not merely *thought* it (as could be done [even]

---

²⁰⁰ [*Befugnis.*]

²⁰¹ [I have removed the parentheses around 'the human being' (*den Menschen*) in order to allow *ihn* below—'it,' in '*determined* it'—to refer not only to the will but also to the human being, as I believe Kant (appropriately) intended, just as he did in the case of '*thought* it' (even though there the grammar of the original sentence happens to obviate the use of *ihn*).]

according to the critique of speculative reason) as belonging to a pure world of understanding though as unfamiliar[202] to us in this reference, but have also *determined* it, with regard to its causality, by means of a law that cannot be classed with any natural law of the world of sense; and thus we have *expanded* our cognition beyond the boundaries of that world—a claim that, after all, the *Critique of Pure Reason* declared void in all speculation. How, then, is the practical use of pure reason here to be reconciled[203] with that same pure reason's theoretical use as regards determining the boundaries of pure reason's power?

David Hume, who can be said to have in fact started all those challenges of the rights of a pure reason which made a complete investigation of these rights necessary,[204] inferred as follows. The concept of *cause* is a concept that contains the *necessity* of the connection[205] of the existence of what is different and, specifically, insofar as it is different—so that, if A is posited, I cognize that something entirely different from it, B, must necessarily also exist.[206] However, necessity can be attributed to a connection only insofar as the connection is cognized a priori; for experience would allow us to cognize concerning a linkage only that it is, but not that it is necessarily so. Now, it is impossible, he says, to cognize a priori and as necessary the connection between[207] one thing and *another* (or between one determination[208] and another entirely different from it), when [i.e.] they are not given in perception. Therefore the concept of a cause is itself fraudulent and deceptive. To talk about it in the mildest way: it is a delusion that can still be excused insofar as we have the *habit*[209] (a *subjective* necessity) of perceiving certain things or their determinations [seen] repeatedly alongside or after one another as associated with one another in their existence, and this habit is inadvertently taken for an *objective* necessity of positing such a connection in

51

---

[202] [*unbekannt.* See above, Ak. V, 35 br. n. 120.]

[203] [*zu vereinigen.* Cf. above, Ak. V, 6 n. 64 incl. br. n. 64a.]

[204] [Cf. the *Prolegomena,* Ak. III, 257–62, 310–13; also the *Critique of Pure Reason,* B 5, B 19–20, A 760 = B 788, A 764–67 = B 792–95.]

[205] [*Verknüpfung;* 'linkage,' below, renders *Verbindung.* See above, Ak. V, 3 br. n. 14.]

[206] [Cf. the *Critique of Pure Reason,* A 90/B 122.]

[207] [Reading, with Karl Rosenkranz, *die Verbindung zwischen* for *die Verbindung, die zwischen.*]

[208] [Or 'attribute': *Bestimmung.*]

[209] [Or '*custom*': *Gewohnheit.*]

the objects themselves. Thus the concept of cause is acquired surreptitiously and not legitimately; indeed, it can never be acquired [legitimately] or authenticated, because it demands a connection in itself void, chimerical, untenable before any reason, to which no object at all can ever correspond. Thus, with regard to all cognition that concerns the existence of things (hence mathematics still remained excepted), *empiricism* was first introduced as the sole source of principles,[210] but with it at the same time the toughest *skepticism* with regard even to the whole of natural science (as philosophy). For on such principles we can never *infer* a consequence from given determinations of things in terms of their existence (because for this the concept of a cause, which contains the necessity of such a connection, would be required), but can only expect, according to the rule of our power of imagination,[211] cases that are similar to what happens ordinarily; but this expectation is never secure, no matter how often it may have been fulfilled. Indeed, of no event could one say: something *must* have preceded it upon which it *necessarily* followed, i.e., it must have a *cause;* and hence, even if one were familiar with ever so frequent cases where such [an earlier event] preceded, so that a rule could be abstracted therefrom, one still could not, on that account, assume it as happening in this way always and necessarily. Thus one must also grant blind chance its right, and with blind chance all use of reason ceases; and this then firmly establishes, and makes irrefutable, skepticism regarding inferences ascending from effects to causes.

Mathematics had still come off well until then because Hume supposed that its propositions were all analytic, i.e., that they advanced from one determination to another on account of identity and hence according to the principle[212] of contradiction.[213] (However, this is false, for they are, rather, all synthetic;[214] and although geometry, e.g., deals not with the existence of things but only with their a priori determination in a possible intuition, it nonetheless passes—just as well as [we do] through causal concepts—from one determination, A, to an entirely different one, B, as nonetheless connected with the former necessarily.) But in the end that science, so highly praised for its apodeictic certainty, must also succumb to *empiricism in*

52

---

[210] [Cf. the *Critique of Pure Reason,* A 761–69 = B 789–797.]

[211] [*Einbildungskraft.*]

[212] [*Satz.* In most contexts, e.g., above, this term is translated as 'proposition.']

[213] [Cf. the *Prolegomena,* Ak. III, 272–73.]

[214] [Cf. the *Critique of Pure Reason,* B 14–17.]

principles on the same basis on which Hume posited habit in the place of objective necessity in the concept of cause. Regardless of all its pride, it must put up with toning down its bold claims commanding a priori assent, and must expect approbation for the universal validity of its propositions from the indulgence of the observers who, as witnesses, would surely not refuse to admit that what the geometrician sets forth as principles they too had always perceived [to be] thus, and would consequently grant that, even though it is indeed not necessary, one may yet continue to expect it to be thus. In this way Hume's empiricism in principles also leads unavoidably to skepticism even in regard to mathematics and consequently in every *scientific* theoretical use of reason (for this use belongs either to philosophy or to mathematics).[215] I will let each person judge on his own whether (in view of such a terrible overthrow as we see befalling the leaders[216] of cognition) the common use of reason will come through any better, and will not rather become entangled even more irretrievably in this same destruction of all science, and hence whether from the same principles a *universal* skepticism will not have to follow (although this skepticism would, to be sure, concern only scholars).

Now, as for my work in the *Critique of Pure Reason*—which was indeed prompted by that Humean skepticism[217] but yet went much further and encompassed the entire realm of pure theoretical reason in its synthetic use and hence also the realm of what is called metaphysics as such[218]—I proceeded as follows as regards the doubt of the Scottish philosopher concerning the concept of causality. When Hume, taking objects of experience to be *things in themselves* (as, indeed, is done almost everywhere), declared the concept of cause to be deceptive and a false illusion,[219] he acted quite rightly. For concerning things in themselves and the determinations that they have as such, one cannot have insight into why because something, A, is posited, something else, B, must necessarily also be posited; and thus he could in no way grant such an a priori cognition of things in themselves. Still less could this acute man permit an empirical origin of this concept, since this [empirical] concept straightforwardly contradicts the connec-

[215] [Cf. ibid., A 761–69 = B 789–797.]

[216] [Literally, 'heads': *Häupter.*]

[217] [*Zweifellehre* here, *Skeptizismus* elsewhere.]

[218] [Cf. the *Prolegomena*, Ak. III, 257–62.]

[219] [*Blendwerk.*]

tion's necessity which amounts to what is essential in the concept of causality. Hence the concept was proscribed, and into its place stepped habit in observing the course of perceptions.

From my investigations, however, it resulted that the objects with which we deal in experience are by no means things in themselves but merely appearances, and that, although with things in themselves one cannot at all tell[220] and indeed cannot possibly have insight into how, if A is posited, it is to be *contradictory* for B, which is entirely different from A, not to be posited (the necessity of the connection between A as cause and B as effect), yet one can readily think that as appearances they must necessarily be linked *in one experience* in a certain way (e.g., with regard to time relations) and cannot be separated without *contradicting* that linkage by means of which this experience, wherein they are objects and wherein alone they are cognizable by us, is possible. And this is indeed what was found; and thus I was able not only to prove the concept of cause as to its objective reality with regard to objects of experience, but also to *deduce* it as an a priori concept because of the connection's necessity that the concept carries with it, i.e., to establish its possibility from pure understanding without empirical sources.[221] And thus, after removing the empiricism concerning the concept's origin, I was able to uproot its inevitable consequence, namely skepticism, first regarding natural science and then also regarding mathematics because the skepticism there follows from quite completely the same bases—thus regarding both of the sciences that are referred to objects of possible experience—and thereby to uproot the total doubt of everything into which theoretical reason claims to have insight.

But what becomes of the application of this category of causality (and thus also of all the other categories, for without them no cognition of what exists can be brought about) to things that are not objects of possible experience but lie beyond the boundary of experience? For I was able to deduce the objective reality of these concepts only with regard to *objects of possible experience.* However, I have saved these concepts even in the mere case of my having shown that objects can at any rate be *thought* through them although not determined a priori; and it is precisely this that gives them a place in pure understanding, from which they are referred to objects as such

54

---

[220] [*absehen.*]

[221] [Cf., in the *Critique of Pure Reason,* the Second Analogy of Experience, A 189–211/ B 232–56, where Kant presents his own critical view regarding the necessary connection between cause and effect.]

(sensible or not sensible). If anything is still lacking, it is the condition for the *application* of these categories, and specifically that of causality, to objects. This condition is intuition, which, where it is not given, makes impossible the application of the categories for the *sake of theoretical cognition* of the object as noumenon. Hence such cognition, if anyone ventures upon it, is utterly blocked (as indeed happened in the *Critique of Pure Reason*), whereas the objective reality of the concept [of causality] nonetheless always remains and can be used even for noumena, but without our being able to determine the concept theoretically in the least and thereby bring about a cognition.[222] For that this concept, even in reference to an object, contains nothing impossible was proved by this: that its seat in pure understanding was secured in all application to objects of the senses; and even if perhaps thereafter, [as] referred to things in themselves (which cannot be objects of experience), it is not capable of being determined so that [one can] present *a determinate object* for the sake of a theoretical cognition, yet for the sake of something else (perhaps the practical) the concept could always still be capable of being determined for its application. This would not be so if, in accordance with Hume, this concept of causality contained something which it is not possible to think at all.

Now in order to discover this condition for the application of the mentioned concept to noumena we need only consider *why we are not satisfied with its application to objects of experience* but would like to use it also for things in themselves. For then we soon find that it is not a theoretical but a practical aim that makes this a necessity for us. Even if we were successful in this [application to noumena], for speculation we would still not be making any true acquisition in cognition of nature and, in general, with regard to objects that may perhaps be given to us. At most we would be taking a long step from the sensibly conditioned (as it is, we already have enough to do to stay with it and to wander diligently through the chain of causes) to the suprasensible, in order to complete[223] and to bound our cognition from the side of the bases—even though an infinite gulf between that boundary and what we are acquainted with[224] would always remain unfilled, and we would have listened more to an idle inquisitiveness than to a solid desire for knowledge.

55

---

[222] [Cf. the *Critique of Pure Reason*, A 235–60/B 294–315.]

[223] [Or 'to perfect': *vollenden*.]

[224] [*kennen*. See above, Ak. V, 35 br. n. 120.]

However, apart from the relation in which (in theoretical cognition) the *understanding* stands to objects, it also has one to the power of desire, which is therefore called the will and is called the pure will insofar as the pure understanding (which in that case is called reason) is practical through the mere presentation of a law. The objective reality of a pure will or—what is the same thing—of a pure practical reason is, in the moral law, given a priori through a fact,[225] as it were; for so we may call a determination of the will which is unavoidable, even though it does not rest on empirical principles. The concept of a will, however, already contains the concept of causality, and hence the concept of a pure will already contains the concept of a causality with freedom—i.e., a causality that is not determinable according to laws of nature and consequently not capable of any empirical intuition as proof of its reality, but that nonetheless completely[226] justifies its objective reality a priori in the pure practical law, though (as one can easily see[227]) for the sake not of the theoretical but merely of the practical use of reason. Now, the concept of a being that has free will is the concept of a *causa noumenon*;[228] and one is already assured that this concept does not contradict itself, because the concept of a cause, as having arisen entirely from pure understanding, as also—through the deduction—assured at the same time of its objective reality with regard to objects as such, while yet in its origin independent of all sensible conditions and therefore not by itself restricted to phenomena (unless one wanted to make a theoretical determinate use of it), can[229] indeed be applied to things as pure beings of the understanding.[230] But because one cannot base this application on any intuition, which always can only be sensible, *causa noumenon* is with regard to the theoretical use of reason indeed a possible, thinkable concept, but nonetheless an empty one. However, I also do not demand that through this concept I should *be theoretically acquainted with*[231] the constitution of a being *insofar as* it has a *pure* will; it is enough for me that through this concept I

56

---

[225] [On the fact of reason, see above, Ak. V, 31 incl. br. n. 75.]

[226] [Or 'perfectly': *vollkommen.*]

[227] [Literally, 'have insight into': *einsehen.*]

[228] [Noumenal cause.]

[229] [*könne.* Vorländer instead reads *könnte,* 'could.']

[230] [*reine Verstandeswesen.* Beings of the understanding are noumena; see the *Critique of Pure Reason,* B 306.]

[231] [*kennen.* See above, Ak. V, 35 br. n. 120.]

only designate it as such a being, and hence that I only link the concept of causality with that of freedom (and with what is inseparable from it, the moral law as determining basis of that [causality]).[232] The authority for this does indeed belong to me by virtue of the pure rather than empirical origin of the concept of cause, inasmuch as I consider myself authorized to make no other use of it than in reference to the moral law that determines its reality, i.e., only a practical use.

If, with Hume, I had removed the objective reality from the concept of causality in its theoretical[233] use not only with regard to things in themselves (the suprasensible) but also with regard to objects of the senses, then the concept would have lost all signification and, as a theoretically impossible concept, would have been declared entirely unusable; and since one also can make no use of nothing, the practical use of a *theoretically null* concept would have been entirely absurd. In fact,[234] however, the concept of an empirically unconditioned causality, although theoretically empty (without an intuition that fits it), is nonetheless always possible and refers to an undetermined[235] object; and in place of this [lacking signification] the concept is nonetheless given signification in[236] the moral law and consequently in a practical reference. Therefore the concept, even though I do not have an intuition that would determine its objective theoretical reality for it, does nonetheless have actual application that can be exhibited *in concreto* in attitudes or maxims, i.e., it has practical reality that can be indicated; and this is indeed sufficient to justify it even with regard to noumena.

But this objective reality of a pure concept of understanding in the realm of the suprasensible, once introduced, now gives objective reality to all the other categories as well—though always only insofar as they are linked *necessarily* with the determining basis of the will (the moral law)—except that this objective reality is one that has merely practical applicability, while having not the slightest influence on theoretical cognition of these objects, as insight into their nature by pure reason, so as to expand this cognition. As indeed we shall find later, these categories always have reference

---

[232] [Cf. the *Grounding for the Metaphysics of Morals,* Ak. IV, 450–63.]

[233] [Reading, with Otto Schöndörffer and with Paul Natorp in the *Akademie* edition, *theoretischen* for *praktischen.*]

[234] [*Nun.*]

[235] [Or 'indeterminate': *unbestimmt.*]

[236] [Or 'through': *an.*]

only to beings as *intelligences* and, in them, also only to the relation of *reason* to the *will* and consequently always only to the *practical,* and beyond this lay no claim to any cognition of these beings. But whatever further properties belonging to the theoretical way of presenting such suprasensible things may be brought forward in connection[237] with these categories, all of these are then classed not at all with knowledge, but only with the authority (however, for a practical aim, even with the necessity) to assume and presuppose them.[238] This holds even where one assumes[239] suprasensible beings (such as God) by an analogy, i.e., by the pure rational relation that we employ practically with regard to what is sensible. Thus by applying these categories to the suprasensible—but only for a practical aim—one does not give to pure theoretical reason the slightest encouragement to rove into the transcendent.

57

Analytic of Pure Practical Reason

Chapter II
On the Concept of an Object of Pure Practical Reason

By a concept of an object[240] of practical reason I mean the presentation of an object[241] as an effect possible through freedom. Therefore, to be an object of a practical cognition, as such, signifies only the reference of the will to the action through which the object or its opposite would be made actual;

---

[237] [*Verbindung.*]

[238] [Cf. the *Prolegomena*, Ak. III, 362–64.]

[239] [Inserting, with Hartenstein, *annimmt* after *bedienen* and the subsequent comma.]

[240] [Inserting *eines Gegenstandes* ('of an object'), as Natorp does in the *Akademie* edition and as is suggested also by Ernst von Aster, Otto Schöndörffer, and Karl Vorländer. I follow Vorländer in retaining *einem Begriffe* ('a concept') instead of reading *dem Begriffe* ('the concept'), as Paul Natorp does in the *Akademie* edition.]

[241] [*Objekt* here, *Gegenstand* above and below. In this entire paragraph, and in the work as a whole, Kant uses the two terms interchangeably.]

and to judge whether or not something is an object of *pure* practical reason is only to distinguish the possibility or impossibility of *willing* the action through which, if we had the ability[242] for this (and experience must judge that), a certain object would become actual. If the object is assumed as the determining basis of our power[243] of desire, then the object's *physical possibility* through the free use of our powers must precede the judgment[244] as to whether or not it is an object of practical reason. By contrast, if the a priori law can be regarded as the determining basis of the action and hence the action can be regarded as determined by pure practical reason, then the judgment as to whether or not something is an object of pure practical reason is entirely independent of that comparison with our physical ability, and the question is only whether we may *will* an action that is directed to the existence of an object if [making] this [object actual] were under our control;[245] hence the *moral possibility* of the action must precede [that judgment], for here the determining basis of the action is not the object but the law of the will.[246]

58

The sole objects of a practical reason are, therefore, those of the *good* and the *evil.* For by the first one means a necessary object of our power of desire, by the second, of our power of loathing,[247] but both according to a principle of reason.

If the concept of the good is not to be derived from an antecedent practical law but is rather to serve as its basis, then it can only be the concept of something whose existence promises pleasure and thus determines the causality of the subject to produce this something. Now, since it is impossible to have insight into which presentation is accompanied by *pleasure* and which, on the contrary, by *displeasure,* experience alone would count in deciding what is directly good or evil. The subject's property in reference to which alone he can engage in this experience is the *feeling* of pleasure and

---

[242] [*Vermögen.*]

[243] [*-vermögen.* Below, 'powers' translates *Kräfte;* above, as well as later in this paragraph, *Vermögen* is rendered as 'ability.']

[244] [*Beurteilung* here, *Urteil* below; similarly, for these nouns or for the corresponding verbs in this entire paragraph. See above, Ak. V, 8 br. n. 78.]

[245] [Or 'in our power': *in unserer Gewalt.*]

[246] [Cf. the *Grounding for the Metaphysics of Morals,* Ak. IV, 394–96.]

[247] [*Verabscheuungs-.* The term could also be rendered by 'detestation' or by 'abhorrence'; 'aversion,' on the other hand, seems rather too feeble; cf. Kant's example of 'loathing' (*Abscheu*) above, Ak. V, 35.]

displeasure, which is a receptivity[248] belonging to inner sense; thus the concept of what is directly good would apply only to that with which the sensation[249] of *gratification* is directly linked, and the concept of the absolutely[250] evil would have to be referred only to what directly gives rise to *pain*. However, this is contrary even to the use of language, which distinguishes the *agreeable* from the *good* and the *disagreeable* from the *evil* and which demands that good and evil always be judged by reason and hence through concepts, which can be communicated universally, rather than by mere sensation, which restricts itself to individual subjects and their receptivity. Moreover, pleasure and displeasure nonetheless cannot by themselves be linked a priori with any presentation of an object. Therefore a philosopher who believed himself compelled to base his practical judging on a feeling of pleasure would call *good* what is a *means* to the agreeable, and *evil* what is a cause of disagreeableness and of pain; for the judging of the relation of means to purposes[251] does indeed belong to reason. But although reason alone is capable of having insight into the connection of means with their aims (so that the will could also be defined as the power of purposes, inasmuch as these are always determining bases of the power of desire according to principles), yet the practical maxims that would follow from the above concept of the good as merely a means would never contain as the object of the will anything good by itself, but always only something good *for something or other;* the good would always be merely the useful, and that for which it is useful would always have to lie outside the will, in sensation. Now if the latter, as agreeable sensation, had to be distinguished from the concept of the good, then there would be nothing at all directly good, but the good would have be sought only in the means to something else, viz., in some agreeableness.[252]

59

There is an old formula of the schools:[253] *nihil appetimus, nisi sub ra-*

---

[248] [*Rezeptivität* here, *Empfänglichkeit* a few lines down.]

[249] [In the broad meaning of the term that includes feeling: *Empfindung;* likewise below, near the end of this paragraph. See above, Ak. V, 22 br. n. 31.]

[250] [*schlechthin.*]

[251] [Or 'ends': *Zwecke.* See above, Ak. V, 35 br. n. 121.]

[252] [Cf. the *Grounding for the Metaphysics of Morals,* Ak. IV, 414–20; also the *Metaphysics of Morals,* Ak. VI, 212–13.]

[253] [See Christian von Wolff (1679–1754), *Psychologia rationalis (Rational Psychology)* (Frankfurt: Renger, 1734) [cf. Kant's reference to this work in the *Grounding for the Metaphysics of Morals,* Ak. IV, 390]; contemporary edition: *Psychologia rationalis Christiani*

tione boni; nihil aversamur, nisi sub ratione mali.[254] This formula has a use that is often correct but also often very detrimental to philosophy, because the expressions *boni* and *mali* contain an ambiguity, owing to the limitation of the language, whereby they are capable of a double sense. Thus they unavoidably make practical laws equivocal,[255] and compel philosophy, which in using them can indeed become aware of the difference of concept[s] for the same word but still cannot find special expressions for them, to make subtle distinctions on which one cannot afterwards come to an agreement because one was unable to designate the difference[256] directly by any appropriate expression.[257]

The German language is fortunate to possess the expressions that keep this difference from being overlooked. It has two very different concepts and also equally different expressions for what the Latins designate by a single word, *bonum* [or *malum*]:[258] for *bonum* it has *das Gute* and *das Wohl;* for *malum* it has *das Böse* and *das Übel* (or *Weh*),[259] so that there are

---

Wolfii; critical edition with (French) introduction, notes, and index, by Jean École (New York: G. Olms, 1972); sections 880, 881, 892. And see Alexander Gottlieb Baumgarten (1714–62), *Metaphysica* (*Metaphysics*), (Magdeburg, Germany: Hemmerde, 1739); second reprint of the 7th edition of 1779 (New York: G. Olms, 1982); section 665.]

[254] ['We desire nothing except for (literally, 'under') the reason of [its being] good; we loathe nothing except for the reason of [its being] bad.' (Translation mine.)]

[255] [Literally, 'put practical laws on screw propellers': *die praktischen Gesetze . . . auf Schrauben stellen.*]

[256] [*Unterschied* here, *Verschiedenheit* just above and just below.]

[257] Moreover, the expression *sub ratione boni*[a] is also ambiguous. For it may be tantamount to saying this: we present something as good when and *because* we *desire* (will) it; but also this: we desire something *because* we *present* it *as good,* so that either the desire is the determining basis of the concept of the object as a good, or the concept of the good is the determining basis of the desire (the will). Thus, in the first case, *sub ratione boni* would mean that we will something *under the idea* of the good; in the second, that we will something *in consequence of this idea,* which must precede the volition as its determining basis.[b]
   [a] ['For the reason of [its being] good.']
   [b] [Cf., on this note, the *Metaphysics of Morals,* Ak. VI, 377–78.]

[258] [Respectively, 'good,' 'bad.']

[259] [Respectively, and with Kant's precise emphases restored: 'the *good*' and 'the *well-being*'; 'the *evil*' and 'the *bad*' (or '*woe*'). It is true that the meanings of several of the English terms, as these are used ordinarily, are not so clearly either *moral* or *nonmoral* as Kant here intends. Nor, however, are the German originals. Kant's explications should, rather, be taken as partly

two quite different judgments[260] according to whether in an action we take   60
into consideration its *good* and *evil* or our *well-being* and *woe* (bad). From
this it follows already that the above psychological proposition is at least
still very uncertain if translated thus: we desire nothing except on account
of our *well-being* or *woe;* whereas it is[261] indubitably certain and at the
same time quite clearly expressed if one renders it thus: according to reason's instruction we will nothing except insofar as we consider it to be good
or evil.

   Well-being or *bad* always signifies only a reference to our state of *agree-*
ableness or *disagreeableness*, of gratification or pain; and if we desire or
loathe an object on that account then we do so only insofar as it is referred
to our sensibility and the feeling of pleasure and displeasure that it brings
about. But *good* or *evil* always signifies a reference to the *will* insofar as the
will is determined by the *law of reason* to make something its object—as,
indeed, the will is never determined directly by the object and the presentation of it, but is a power to make a rule of reason the motivating cause of an
action (through which an object can become actual). Hence good or evil is
in fact referred to actions rather than to the person's state of sensation,[262]

---

prescriptive: e.g., as used ordinarily, the meaning of 'good' is not exclusively moral (but only
when the good "deserves this name absolutely": see below, Ak. V, 64), nor that of 'bad' exclusively nonmoral. The same applies to the German equivalents. (The standard contemporary
German equivalent of 'bad,' *schlecht,* rarely occurs in Kant; in this work, it occurs once, at Ak.
V, 78; in the *Critique of Pure Reason* it occurs once, at A 554 = B 582.) Thus Kant himself
(above, Ak. V, 38) refers to a person as *moralisch gut* ('morally good') without finding—as on
his explication of 'good' he should—the expression redundant. Likewise, the commonly used
expression *ein übler Mensch* clearly refers to a *morally* bad—hence evil—person. In fact,
'evil' is the English cognate of *übel* and shares this ambiguity: traditionally, the meaning of
this term has included both the moral and the nonmoral (as in the expression 'the problem of
evil'). Therefore, 'evil' is a legitimate rendering for *übel* in works that are not concerned to distinguish *übel* from *böse*. In this work, however, it is best to use 'evil' in its contemporary,
moral meaning, in which it is a legitimate rendering for *böse* with its predominantly moral
meaning. Even *böse*, however, *can* be used in a nonmoral sense: e.g., *eine böse Entzündung* is
a bad, not an "evil," inflammation; and this is why Kant (above, Ak. V, 37) can speak of *dem*
moralisch Bösen, i.e., 'the morally evil,' without finding that expression redundant. By the
same token, translating *böse* as (the somewhat quaint) 'wicked,' which already implies
'moral,' *would* make the same Kantian expression redundant. (As for quaintness: it is true that
'woe' is quaint; but so is the original *Weh.*)]

[260] [*Beurteilungen.* See above, Ak. V, 8 br. n. 78.]

[261] [Inserting *ist* ('is') after *ungezweifelt gewiß* ('indubitably certain').]

[262] [In the broad meaning of the term that includes feeling: *Empfindung.* See above, Ak. V, 22
br. n. 31.]

and if something is to be good or evil absolutely[263] (and in every respect and without any further condition), or to be considered so, then what could be so called would be only the way of acting, the maxim of the will, and hence the acting person himself as a good or evil human being, but not a thing.[264]

Thus however people may have laughed at the Stoic who in the most intense pains of gout exclaimed: Pain, however much you may torment me, I will still never admit that you are something evil (κακόν, *malum*)!; he was nonetheless right. It was something bad; this he felt, and this his outcry betrayed. But that an evil attached to him on that account, this he had no cause whatever to grant; for the pain does not in the least diminish the worth of his person but diminishes only the worth of his [own] state. A single lie of which he had been conscious would have had to strike down his mettle;[265] but the pain served only to prompt him to raise it, when he was conscious that he had not incurred the pain through any wrong action and thereby made himself deserving of punishment.

What we are to call good must in every reasonable human being's judgment be an object of the power of desire, and evil must in everyone's eyes be an object of loathing; hence in addition to sense this judgment[266] requires reason. This is the case with truthfulness as opposed to a lie, with justice as opposed to violence, etc. However, we can call something a bad thing[267] that everyone must yet at the same time declare to be good, sometimes indirectly[268] and sometimes even directly good. Someone who has a surgical operation performed on himself feels it without doubt as something bad; but through reason he and everyone declares it to be good. But if someone who likes to tease and agitate peace-loving people finally runs into trouble and is sent off with a sound thrashing, then this is indeed something bad, but everyone approves of it and considers it in itself to be good, even if nothing further were to issue from it; indeed, even the one who receives the thrashing must in his reason cognize[269] that he is being dealt with rightly,

[263] [*schlechthin.* See above, Ak. V, 3 br. n. 2.]

[264] [Cf. the *Grounding for the Metaphysics of Morals,* Ak. IV, 394–96.]

[265] [*Mut.*]

[266] [*Beurteilung* here, *Urteil* above.]

[267] [*ein Übel,* which I usually (e.g., twice below) render as 'something bad.']

[268] [Or 'mediately': *mittelbar;* 'directly,' below, renders *unmittelbar,* for which 'immediately' is in almost all cases a very misleading translation.]

[269] [Or 'recognize': *erkennen.*]

because he sees that the proportion between well-being and well-behaving,[270] which reason unavoidably holds before him, has here been carried out exactly.

Of course, in the judging of our practical reason *very much* indeed hinges on our well-being and woe, and, as far as our nature as sensible beings is concerned, *everything* hinges on our *happiness* if this is judged, as reason especially demands, not according to transitory sensation but according to the influence that this contingency has on our entire existence and our satisfaction with it; but, nonetheless, *everything as such* does not hinge on this. The human being insofar as he belongs to the world of sense is a needy being, and to this extent his reason does indeed have a mandate from the side of sensibility which he cannot reject, to attend to its interest and to frame practical maxims also with a view to happiness in this life and, if possible, in a future life as well. Yet he is not so entirely an animal as to be indifferent to all that reason says on its own, and so as to use reason merely as an instrument for satisfying his needs as a being of sense. For, that he has reason does not at all elevate him in worth above mere animality if reason is to serve him only for the sake of what instinct accomplishes in animals; reason would in that case be only a particular manner that nature had employed in order to equip the human being for the same purpose to which it has destined[271] animals, without destining him to a higher purpose. Hence he does indeed need reason, according to this arrangement that nature happens to have made for him, in order to take into consideration always his well-being and woe. But besides this he has it also for the sake of something higher, viz., in order not only to include in his deliberation what is in itself good or evil—about which solely pure and sensibly not at all interested reason can make a judgment—but to distinguish this judging entirely from the former[272] and to make it the supreme condition thereof.[273]

In this judging of what is in itself good and evil, as distinguished from what can be called so only in reference to well-being or bad, what counts are the following points. Either a principle of reason is thought as already in itself the determining basis of the will without regard to possible objects of

62

---

[270] [*Wohlbefinden und Wohlverhalten;* wherever feasible, I translate *Verhalten* as 'conduct,' and *Wohlverhalten* as 'good conduct.']

[271] [*bestimmen.*]

[272] [Cf. the *Grounding for the Metaphysics of Morals,* Ak. IV, 394–96.]

[273] [Reading, with Albert Nolte and with Paul Natorp in the *Akademie* edition, *der letzteren* for *des letzteren.*]

the power of desire (hence [as being this determining basis] merely through the legal form of the maxim); then that principle is a practical a priori law, and reason is assumed to be practical by itself. The law then determines the will *directly*, the action conforming to it is *in itself good*, and a will whose maxim always conforms to this law is *good absolutely, in every respect*, and is the *supreme condition of all good*.[274] Or else the maxim of the will is preceded by a determining basis of the power of desire which presupposes an object of pleasure or displeasure and hence something that *gratifies* or *pains*, and the maxim of reason to promote the former and avoid the latter determines the actions according as they are good in reference to our inclination and hence only indirectly (on account of a further purpose, as a means thereto); and these maxims can then never be called laws, but still rational practical precepts. The purpose itself, the gratification that we seek, is in the latter case not a *good* but a *well-being*, not a rational concept but an empirical concept of an object of sensation; however, the use of the means to it, i.e., the action, is nonetheless called good (because rational deliberation is required for it), yet good not absolutely but only in reference to our sensibility with regard to its feeling of pleasure and displeasure; but the will whose maxim is affected by this [feeling] is not a pure will, which is a will that aims only at that wherein pure reason can be practical by itself.[275]

Now, this is the place to explain the paradox of method in a critique of practical reason: viz., *that the concept of good and evil must be determined not prior to the moral law (it[276] would, so it seems, even have to be laid at the basis of this law) but only after it and by means of it (as is indeed being done here).* For even if we did not know that the principle of morality is a pure law determining the will a priori, yet—in order not to assume principles quite gratuitously[277] (gratis)—we would at least have to leave *unestablished* at first whether the will has only empirical determining bases or also pure a priori ones. For we go against all basic rules of philosophical procedure if already in advance we assume something as decided when we are yet to decide on it in the first place. Suppose, then, that we wanted to start from the concept of the good in order to derive from it the laws of the

63

---

[274] [Cf. the *Grounding for the Metaphysics of Morals*, Ak. IV, 408–09.]

[275] [Cf. ibid., Ak. IV, 414–21.]

[276] [Reading, with Hartenstein and with Natorp in the *Akademie* edition, *er* for *es;* the latter term would refer back not to 'concept' but to 'good and evil.']

[277] [*umsonst.*]

will; then this concept of an object (as a good object) would at the same time indicate it as the one determining basis of the will. Now, because this concept had no practical a priori law for its standard, the touchstone of good or evil could be posited in nothing other than the agreement of the object with our feeling of pleasure or displeasure, and the use of reason could consist only in determining partly this pleasure or displeasure in the[ir] entire coherence with all the sensations of my existence, and partly the means to provide myself with the object of this pleasure or displeasure. Now, since what conforms to the feeling of pleasure can be established only through experience, and since the practical law, by stipulation, is after all to be based on this as its condition, the possibility of practical a priori laws would straightforwardly be excluded—because it was deemed necessary to discover beforehand an object for the will, the concept of which object, as that of a good,[278] would have to constitute the universal though empirical determining basis of the will. In fact, however, it was necessary to investigate beforehand whether there is not also an a priori determining basis of the will (which would never have been found anywhere else than in a pure practical law, and, specifically, insofar as this law prescribes to maxims the mere legal form without regard to an object). But because an object, according to concepts of good and evil, was already being laid at the basis of any practical law, while this object—without an antecedent law—could be thought only according to empirical concepts, one had deprived oneself already in advance of the possibility of even thinking a pure practical law. By contrast, if one had beforehand investigated this law analytically, one would have found that, instead of the concept of the good as an object determining and making possible the moral law, it is, conversely, the moral law which first determines and makes possible the concept of the good insofar as it deserves this name absolutely.

64

This comment, which concerns merely the method of the supreme moral investigations, is important. It explains all at once the basis that occasions all the strayings of philosophers with regard to the supreme principle of morality. For these philosophers looked for an object of the will in order to turn it into the matter and basis of a law (this law was then to be the determining basis of the will not directly, but by means of that object applied to the feeling of pleasure or displeasure); instead they should have started by searching for a law that determined the will a priori and directly and that, in conformity with the will, first determined the object. Now, whether they

---

[278] [eines Guten. Vorländer instead reads eines guten, i.e., 'of a good object.']

posited this object of pleasure—which was to yield the supreme concept of the good—in happiness, in perfection, in moral feeling,[279] or in the will of God, their principle was always heteronomy and they had to come unavoidably upon empirical conditions for a moral law; for they could call their object—as direct determining basis of the will—good or evil only according to its direct relation to feeling, which is always empirical.[280] Only a formal law, i.e., one that prescribes to reason nothing more than the form of its universal legislation[281] as the supreme condition of maxims, can be a priori a determining basis of practical reason.[282] The ancients, however, betrayed this mistake openly by staking their moral investigation entirely on the determination of the concept of the *highest good,* hence the concept of an object that they meant afterwards to make the determining basis of the will in the moral law—an object that long thereafter, when the moral law has first been legitimated[283] on its own and justified as direct determining basis of the will—can be presented as object to the will that is now determined a priori in terms of its form; this we shall undertake in the Dialectic of Pure Practical Reason.[284] The moderns, among whom the question concerning the highest good has fallen out of use, or at least seems to have become a subordinate matter only, conceal the above mistake (as they do in many other cases) behind indeterminate words; but one can still see it peering forth from their systems, since it then betrays throughout heteronomy of practical reason, from which a moral law that a priori commands universally can never arise.

Now since the concepts of good and evil, as consequences of the a priori determination of the will, presuppose also a pure practical principle and hence a causality of pure reason, they do not (as, say, determinations of the synthetic unity of the manifold of given intuitions in one consciousness) refer originally to objects as do the pure concepts of understanding or categories of reason used theoretically,[285] but they rather presuppose these ob-

[279] [Reading, with Hartenstein and with Natorp in the *Akademie* edition, *Gefühle* for *Gesetze* ('law').]

[280] [Cf. the *Grounding for the Metaphysics of Morals,* Ak. IV, 441–44.]

[281] [*Gesetzgebung.* See above, Ak. V, 20 br. n. 23.]

[282] [Cf. the *Grounding for the Metaphysics of Morals,* Ak. IV, 444–45.]

[283] [Literally, 'verified': *bewährt.*]

[284] [See below, Ak. V, 107–48.]

[285] [Kant usually refers to the concepts of reason (used speculatively) as "ideas." See the *Critique of Pure Reason,* A 310–40/B 366–98, and cf. below, Ak. V, 69.]

jects as given. Instead they are, one and all, modes of a single category, viz., that of causality, insofar as the determining basis of causality consists in reason's presentation of a law of causality which, as law of freedom, reason gives to itself and thereby proves itself a priori to be practical. However, although the actions, *on the one hand,* [are] subject to a law that is not a natural law but a law of freedom, and consequently belong to the conduct of intelligible beings, yet, *on the other hand,* as events in the world of sense they also belong to appearances. Therefore the determinations of a practical reason will be able to take place only with reference to the world of sense and hence indeed in conformity with the categories of the understanding, not however with the aim of a theoretical use of the understanding in order to bring a priori the manifold of (sensible) *intuition* under one consciousness,[286] but only in order to subject a priori the manifold of *desires* to the unity of consciousness of a practical reason commanding in the moral law, or [i.e.] of a pure will.

These *categories of freedom*—for so we shall call them in contrast to those theoretical concepts that are categories of nature—have an obvious advantage over the latter. For the latter are only forms of thought which, by means of universal concepts, designate only indeterminately objects as such for every intuition possible for us. The categories of freedom, by contrast, aim at the determination of a *free power of choice.* (Although no intuition can be given as fully corresponding to this power, yet it—as does not happen with any concepts of the theoretical use of our cognitive power—is based a priori on a pure practical law.) Hence, as practical elementary concepts, instead of being based on the form of intuition (space and time) that does not lie in reason itself but must be taken from elsewhere, namely from sensibility, they are based on *the form of a pure will* as given in reason and thus in the power of thought itself. Through this, then, it happens that, since in all precepts of pure practical reason the concern is only with the *determination of the will,* not with the natural conditions (of the practical power) for *carrying out its aim,* the practical a priori concepts, in reference to the supreme principle of freedom, immediately become cognitions and do not need to wait for intuitions in order to acquire signification; specifically, this happens for the noteworthy reason[287] that they themselves give rise to the actuality of that to which they refer (the attitude of the will), which is not at

66

---

[286] [I.e., (the unity of) transcendental (original) apperception. See the *Critique of Pure Reason,* A 106–07, 117n, B 68, 131–32, 157.]

[287] [*Grund.*]

all the business of theoretical concepts. Now, it must be noted carefully that these categories concern only practical reason in general, and hence they proceed in their order from those that are morally still undetermined and sensibly conditioned to those that, being sensibly unconditioned, are determined only by the moral law.

TABLE
OF THE CATEGORIES OF FREEDOM IN REGARD TO
THE CONCEPTS OF GOOD AND EVIL

1
Of Quantity

Subjective, according to maxims (*intentions of the will*[288] of the individual)
Objective, according to principles (*precepts*)
A priori objective as well as subjective principles of freedom (*laws*)

2 **Of Quality**	3 **Of Relation**
Practical rules of *commission* (*praeceptivae*)[289]	To *personality*
	To the *state* of the person
Practical rules of *omission* (*prohibitivae*)	*Reciprocally,* of one person to the state of another
Practical rules of *exceptions* (*exceptivae*)	

4
Of Modality
The *permitted* and *not permitted*[290]
Duty and what is *contrary to duty*
Perfect and *imperfect duty*[291]

67   Here one soon becomes aware that in this table freedom is regarded as a kind of causality—which, however, is not subject to empirical determining

---

[288] [*Willensmeinungen.*]

[289] [I.e., *regulae* (rules) *praeceptivae;* similarly for the two categories below.]

[290] [Cf. above, Ak. V, 11 n. 93 incl. br. n. 93b.]

[291] [Cf. the *Metaphysics of Morals,* Ak. VI, 390–91; also the *Grounding for the Metaphysics of Morals,* Ak. IV, 421–23, esp. 421n.]

bases—with regard to the actions possible through it as appearances in the world of sense, and that freedom is consequently referred[292] to the categories of its[293] natural possibility, while yet each category is taken so universally that the determining basis of that causality can be assumed even outside the world of sense, viz., in freedom as a property of an intelligible being, until the categories of modality introduce, though only *problematically,* the transition from practical principles in general to those of morality, which afterwards can for the first time be exhibited *dogmatically* through the moral law.

I add nothing further here to elucidate the present table, because it is understandable enough on its own. This sort of division, drawn up according to principles, is very beneficial to any science on account of its thoroughness and understandability. Thus, e.g., from the above table and its first item one knows immediately from what one must start in practical considerations: from the maxims that each person bases on his inclination, the precepts that hold for a genus of rational beings insofar as these agree in certain inclinations, and finally the law that holds for all regardless of their inclinations, etc. In this way one surveys the entire plan of what one has to accomplish, even every question of practical philosophy that is to be answered and simultaneously the order that is to be followed.

On the Typic of the Pure Practical Power of Judgment[294]

The concepts of good and evil first determine an object for the will. They themselves, however, fall under a practical rule of reason which, if the rea-

---

[292] [Kant—possibly by conflating, as he frequently does, freedom and the concept of freedom— actually says 'refers': *sich . . . beziehe.*]

[293] [*ihre,* which I take to refer back to 'freedom,' not to 'actions.' First, by Kant's grammar it refers back to the original subject of the sentence, which is 'freedom'; to refer back to 'actions,' Kant would have used a phrase like *der letzteren,* 'the latter.' Second, the table lists categories not of action but of freedom: they determine freedom ("a free power of choice": above, Ak. V, 65); this they do *with regard to* the actions possible through freedom in nature; the natural possibility of freedom, I take it, simply is this determination. Third, the contrast ("while yet") implicit in the continuation of this very paragraph seems clearly to pertain to the causality, i.e., to freedom. Fourth, Kant is about to state expressly (below, Ak. V, 68) that the issue is *not* the possibility of the *action* as an event in the world of sense.]

[294] [*Urteilskraft.*]

son is pure,[295] determines the will a priori with regard to its object. Now whether an action possible for us in sensibility is or is not a case that falls under the rule requires practical power of judgment, by which what was said universally (*in abstracto*) in the rule is applied *in concreto* to an action. However, a practical rule of pure reason, *first*, as *practical,* concerns the existence[296] of an object, and *second,* as a *practical rule* of pure reason, carries with it necessity with regard to the existence of the action and hence is a practical law, and specifically not a law of nature [concerning action] through empirical determining bases but a law of freedom according to which the will is to be determinable independently of everything empirical (merely through the presentation of a law as such and of its form); yet all occurring cases of possible actions can only be empirical, i.e., can belong only to experience and nature. Therefore it seems paradoxical to want to find in the world of sense a case which, while to this extent it always falls only under the law of nature, nonetheless permits the application of a law of freedom to it, and to which the suprasensible idea of the morally good to be exhibited in that world *in concreto* can be applied. Hence the power of judgment of pure practical reason is subject to the same difficulties as that of pure theoretical reason, though the latter had a means available to get out of them: namely that, since what counted with regard to the theoretical use were intuitions to which pure concepts of understanding could be applied, such intuitions (though only of objects of the senses) could yet be given a priori, and hence, as far as the connection of the manifold in them is concerned, could be given (as *schemata*)[297] in a priori conformity with the pure concepts of understanding.[298] By contrast, the morally good is something that, in terms of the object, is suprasensible, so that nothing corresponding to it can be found in any sensible intuition; hence the power of judgment under laws of pure practical reason seems to be subject to special difficulties which are due to [the fact] that a law of freedom is to be applied to actions as events that occur in the world of sense and thus, to this extent, belong to nature.

68

---

[295] [Literally, Kant says 'if it is pure reason'—*wenn sie reine Vernunft ist*—which, contrary to Kant's focus in the sentence, would make not 'rule' but 'reason' the subject of the next clause.]

[296] [*Existenz* here, *Dasein* below.]

[297] [See below, Ak. V, 69.]

[298] [Or, possibly, 'given . . . in conformity with the pure a priori concepts of understanding': *den reinen Verstandesbegriffen a priori gemäß.*]

Yet here again an auspicious prospect opens up for the pure practical power of judgment. In the subsumption of an action possible for me in the world of sense under a *pure practical law* the concern is not with the possibility of the *action* as an event in the world of sense; for this possibility pertains to the judging of the theoretical use of reason according to the law of causality, a pure concept of understanding for which reason has a *schema* in sensible intuition. Physical causality, or the condition under which it takes place, belongs under the concepts of nature, and the schema of these concepts is drafted by the transcendental power of imagination.[299] Here, however, the concern is not with the schema of a case according to laws but with the schema (if this word is fitting here) of a law itself, because the *determination of the will* (not the action in reference to its result) through the law alone and without any other determining basis ties the concept of causality to conditions that are entirely different from those that amount to natural connection.

69

For a law of nature—as a law to which objects of sensible intuition, as such objects, are subject—there must be a corresponding schema, i.e., a universal procedure of the power of imagination (for exhibiting a priori to the senses the pure concept of understanding which the law determines).[300] But for the law of freedom (which is a causality not sensibly conditioned at all), and hence also for the concept of the unconditionally[301] good, there is no intuition and hence no schema that can be laid at its basis for the sake of its application *in concreto*. Consequently the moral law has no other cognitive power to mediate its application to objects of nature than the understanding (not the power of imagination). What the understanding can lay at the basis—as a law for the sake of the power of judgment—of the idea of reason is not a *schema* of sensibility but a law, but yet a law that can be exhibited *in concreto* in objects of the senses, and hence a law of nature, though only in terms of its form; therefore we can call this law the *type* of the moral law.

The rule of the power of judgment under laws of pure practical reason is this: Ask yourself whether, if the action you propose were to occur according to a law of the nature of which you yourself were a part, you could indeed regard it as possible through your will.[302] Everyone does in fact judge

---

[299] [*Einbildungskraft.*]

[300] [Cf. the *Critique of Pure Reason,* A 137–47/B 176–87.]

[301] [Or 'unconditioned': *unbedingt.*]

[302] [Cf. the *Grounding for the Metaphysics of Morals,* Ak. IV, 421.]

actions according to this rule as to whether they are morally good or evil. Thus one says, What if *everyone* permitted himself to deceive when he believed it to be to his advantage, or considered himself authorized to shorten his life as soon as he was beset by utter weariness of it, or viewed the plight of others with utter indifference, and if you too belonged to such an order of things, would you indeed be in it with the agreement of your will?[303] Now, everyone knows well that if he secretly permits himself to deceive, it does not follow that everyone else does it too, or that if—without being noticed—he is unloving, everyone would not immediately be so toward him as well; hence, by the same token, this comparison of the maxim of his actions with a universal law of nature is not the determining basis of his will. But this law is nonetheless a *type* for the judging of the maxim according to moral principles. If the maxim of the action is not so constituted as to stand the test against the form of a natural law in general, then it is morally impossible. Even the commonest understanding judges thus; for the law of nature lies at the basis of all its most common judgments, even those of experience. Thus it always has the law of nature available, except that in cases where causality from freedom is to be judged it makes that *law of nature* merely the type of a *law of freedom,* because, without having something available that it could make an example in a case of experience, it could not provide to the law of a pure practical reason its use in application.

Hence using the *nature of the world of sense* as the *type* of an *intelligible nature* is also permitted, so long as I do not transfer to the latter any intuitions and what depends on them, but refer to it merely the *form of lawfulness* as such (the concept of which occurs even in the commonest[304] understanding, though it cannot determinately be cognized a priori for any aim other than just the pure practical use of reason). For to this extent laws, as such, are the same, no matter from where they take their determining bases.

For the rest, [I shall offer one comment below.] Of all the intelligible absolutely nothing but freedom (by means of the moral law) has a reality for us except for the sake of this law and the use of pure practical reason, and even freedom has such reality only insofar as it is a presupposition inseparable from that law; and, furthermore, all intelligible objects in turn to which reason might perhaps still lead us under the guidance of that law have no reality other than this. However, reason is entitled and also required

70

---

[303] [Cf. ibid., Ak. IV, 422–23, 429–30.]

[304] [Reading, with Hartenstein and with Natorp in the *Akademie* edition, *gemeinsten* for *reinsten* ('purest').]

to use nature (in terms of nature's pure form of understanding) as the type of the power of judgment. Hence the present comment will serve to keep what belongs merely to the *typic* of concepts from being classed with the concepts themselves[:] This, then, as the typic of the power of judgment, guards against the *empiricism* concerning practical reason, which posits the practical concepts of good and evil merely in experiential consequences (so-called happiness);[305] and although happiness and the infinite useful consequences of a will determined by self-love, if this will at the same time turned itself into a universal law of nature, can indeed serve as an entirely adequate type for the morally good, it is still not identical therewith. The same typic guards also against the *mysticism* concerning practical reason, which turns what served only as a *symbol* into a *schema,* i.e., bases the application of moral concepts on actual and yet not sensible intuitions (of an invisible kingdom of God) and strays into the transcendent.[306] Only the *rationalism* concerning the power of judgment is adequate to the use of moral concepts; it takes from sensible nature nothing more than what pure reason can also think on its own, i.e., lawfulness, and carries into the suprasensible nothing but what can, conversely, be actually exhibited through actions in the world of sense according to the formal rule of a natural law in general. However, guarding against the *empiricism* concerning practical reason is much more important and advisable; for, the *mysticism* [concerning practical reason] is in fact still compatible with the purity and sublimity of the moral law, and, besides, stretching one's power of imagination all the way to suprasensible intuitions is not exactly natural and commensurate with the common way of thinking, so that on this side the danger is not so general. By contrast, the empiricism [concerning practical reason] eradicates by the root[307] the morality in attitudes (in which, after all, and not merely in actions, consists the high worth that humanity can and ought to procure for itself through morality), and substitutes for it something entirely different, namely in place of duty an empirical interest, with which inclinations as such traffic among themselves. Precisely because of this, moreover, empiricism—along with all inclinations which (no matter what style they are given) degrade humanity if they are elevated to the dignity of a supreme

71

---

[305] [Cf. the *Grounding for the Metaphysics of Morals,* Ak. IV, 442.]

[306] [Cf. ibid., Ak. IV, 443; also the *Metaphysics of Morals,* Ak. VI, 488–91.]

[307] [Although 'root' and 'eradicate' have the same origin, and 'eradicates by the root' may sound odd to an etymologically attuned ear, all of that applies to the respective German terms, *Wurzel* and *ausrotten.* Indeed, all four terms come from the same root!]

practical principle, and which[308] are nonetheless so indulgent to everyone's mentality[309]—is for this reason far more dangerous than any fanaticism,[310] which can never amount to a lasting state of many human beings.

[Analytic of Pure Practical Reason]

Chapter III
On the Incentives of Pure Practical Reason

What is essential in all moral worth[311] of actions is[312] that *the moral law must determine*[313] *the will directly.* If the determination of the will, although occurring *in conformity with* the moral law, does so only by means of a feeling—of whatever kind—that must be presupposed in order for that law to become a sufficient determining basis of the will, and hence does not occur *on account of the law,* then the action will indeed contain *legality,*[314] but not *morality.*[315] Now if by *incentive* (*elater animi*)[316] one means the subjective determining basis of the will of a being whose reason does not by its very nature necessarily conform to the objective law, then it will follow, first, that no incentives at all can be attributed to the divine will but that the [moral] incentive of the human will (and of the will of every created ra-

72

---

[308] [Reading *die* for *da sie,* as suggested by Natorp.]

[309] [*Sinnesart.*]

[310] [I.e., such as the mysticism concerning practical reason: *Schwärmerei.*]

[311] [Or 'value': *Wert.*]

[312] [Kant actually says (redundantly) 'hinges on': *kommt darauf an.*]

[313] [Here 'must determine' translates (the subjunctive) *bestimme.*]

[314] [*Legalität.*]

[315] [Cf. the *Grounding for the Metaphysics of Morals,* Ak. IV, 397–400; also the *Metaphysics of Morals,* Ak. VI, 219–20.]

[316] [Literally, 'driver of the soul.']

tional being) can never be anything other than the moral law;[317] [and, second,] that the objective determining basis must therefore always and quite alone be also the subjectively sufficient determining basis of the action if this action is not merely to fulfill the *letter* of the law without containing the law's *spirit*.[318]

Hence for the sake of the moral law and in order to provide it with influence on the will, one must not search for any further incentive in view of which the incentive of the moral law could be dispensed with, because this would bring about nothing but hypocrisy without stability; and it is *precarious* even to let some further incentives (such as that of advantage) so much as cooperate *alongside* the moral law. Thus nothing remains to be done except merely to determine carefully in what way the moral law becomes an incentive, and what, inasmuch as it is this incentive, happens to the human power of desire by way of an effect that this determining basis has on it. For how a law can by itself and directly be a determining basis of the will (this is, after all, what is essential in all morality) is an insoluble problem for human reason, and is one and the same problem as the one concerning how a free will is possible.[319] Therefore we shall have to indicate a priori not the basis on which the moral law intrinsically yields an incentive, but what, insofar it is an incentive, it brings about (or, to put it better, must bring about) in the mind.

What is essential in all determination of the will by the moral law is that, as a free will, and hence not merely without the cooperation of sensible impulses but even with rejection of all of them and with impairment of all inclinations insofar as they could be contrary to that law, it be determined merely by the law.[320] Thus to this extent the effect of the moral law as an incentive is only negative, and as such this incentive can be cognized a priori. For all inclination and every sensible impulse is based on feeling, and the negative effect on feeling (by the impairment done to the inclinations) is itself a feeling. Consequently we can see[321] a priori that the moral law as de-

73

---

[317] [Cf. the *Grounding for the Metaphysics of Morals,* Ak. IV, 412–14.]

318 Concerning every lawful action that is nonetheless not done on account of the law one can say that it is morally good merely according to the *letter* but not according to the *spirit* (the attitude).

[319] [Cf. the *Grounding for the Metaphysics of Morals,* Ak. IV, 456, 459, 461.]

[320] [Cf. the *Metaphysics of Morals,* Ak. VI, 391, 446–47.]

[321] [Literally, 'have insight into': *einsehen.*]

termining basis of the will, by infringing all our inclinations, must bring about a feeling that can be called pain; and here we have, then, the first and perhaps also the only case where we have been able to determine a priori from concepts[322] the relation of a cognition (here a cognition of a pure practical reason) to the feeling of pleasure or displeasure. All inclinations together (which presumably can also be brought into a tolerable system, and the satisfaction of which is then called one's own happiness) amount to *selfishness*[323] (*solipsismus*). This is either that of *self-love,*[324] a paramount *benevolence*[325] toward oneself (*philautia*), or that of *liking* for oneself (*arrogantia*). Specifically, the former is called *love for oneself,*[326] the latter *conceit for oneself.*[327] Pure practical reason merely *impairs*[328] love for oneself, inasmuch as it only restricts such love—as natural and as astir in us even prior to the moral law—to the condition of agreement[329] with this law, and this love is then called *rational self-love.* Self-conceit, however, pure practical reason *strikes down* altogether,[330] inasmuch as all claims of self-esteem that precede agreement with the moral law are null and without any authority,[331] since precisely the certainty of an attitude agreeing with this law is the primary condition of all worth of a person (we shall soon make this more distinct), and all presumption prior to this certainty is false and

---

[322] [*aus Begriffen a priori ... bestimmen.* Grammatically, this could also be taken to mean 'determine from a priori concepts.']

[323] [*Selbstsucht,* literally 'self-seekingness.' Below, the Latin term in parentheses, in the sense applicable here, could also be translated as 'self-indulgence.' See the *Metaphysics of Morals,* Ak. VI, 450.]

[324] [*Selbstliebe.* Below, 'love for oneself' translates *Eigenliebe.* Although *Eigen-,* unlike 'oneself,' is terminologically differentiated from *Selbst-* ('self-'), it still has the same meaning.]

[325] [*Wohlwollen.* Below, the Latin term (of Greek etymology) in parentheses means, literally, 'self-love' again; 'liking' translates *Wohlgefallen,* and the subsequent Latin term in parentheses means, literally, 'arrogance.']

[326] [Cf. the *Grounding for the Metaphysics of Morals,* Ak. IV, 406–07, 422, 432; also the *Metaphysics of Morals,* Ak. VI, 451–52, 462.]

[327] [*Eigendünkel,* translated hereafter simply as 'self-conceit.' See the *Metaphysics of Morals,* Ak. VI, 437, 462.]

[328] [*Abbruch tun.* See above, Ak. V, 25 br. n. 44.]

[329] [*Einstimmung* here, *Übereinstimmung* below; the terms are synonymous.]

[330] [Cf. the *Metaphysics of Morals,* Ak. VI, 437, 462.]

[331] [*Befugnis.* I also use 'authority' to translate *Ansehen.* See below, Ak. V, 76 br. n. 350.]

unlawful.[332] Now, the propensity to self-esteem, insofar as it rests merely on sensibility,[333] also belongs to the inclinations that the moral law impairs. Therefore the moral law strikes down self-conceit. But this law is, after all, something in itself positive, viz., the form of an intellectual causality, i.e., of freedom. Hence inasmuch as—in contrast to its subjective opposite, viz., the inclinations in us—it *weakens* self-conceit, the moral law is at the same time an object of *respect;* and inasmuch as it even *strikes down* self-conceit, i.e., humbles[334] it, the moral law is an object of the greatest *respect* and thus also the basis of a positive feeling that is not of empirical origin and is cognized a priori. Therefore respect for the moral law is a feeling that is brought about by an intellectual basis, and this feeling is the only one that we cognize completely a priori and the necessity of which we can have insight into.[335]

We saw in the preceding chapter that everything that offers itself as object of the will *prior to* the moral law is excluded from the determining bases of the will—the will under the name of the unconditionally good—by this law itself as the supreme condition of practical reason; and we saw that the mere practical form, which consists in the suitability of maxims for universal legislation, first determines what is good in itself and absolutely and is the basis for the maxim of a pure will, such a will alone being good in every respect. In fact, however, we find our nature as sensible beings to be so constituted that the matter of the power of desire (objects of inclination, whether of hope or fear) thrusts itself upon us first and that our pathologically determinable self,[336] even though by its maxims it is entirely unsuitable for universal legislation, nonetheless endeavors—just as if it amounted to our entire self—to validate[337] its claims beforehand and as primary and original. This propensity to make oneself, in terms of the subjective determining basis of one's power of choice, an objective determining basis of the will as such can be called *self-love,* which, when it makes itself legislative

74

---

[332] [Or 'contrary to the law': *gesetzwidrig.*]

[333] [Reading, with Albert Görland, A. Nolte, Erich Adickes, Emil Wille, and with Paul Natorp in the *Akademie* edition, *Sinnlichkeit* for *Sittlichkeit* ('morality').]

[334] [Or 'humiliates': *demütigen.*]

[335] [Cf. the *Grounding for the Metaphysics of Morals,* Ak. IV, 400, 401n, 403, 440; also the *Metaphysics of Morals,* Ak. VI, 402–03.]

[336] [Cf. the *Metaphysics of Morals,* Ak. VI, 376–77, 399–400.]

[337] [Or, less literally, 'to assert': *geltend machen.*]

and an unconditional practical principle, can be called *self-conceit.* Now, the moral law, which alone is truly objective (viz., objective in every respect), excludes entirely the influence of self-love on the supreme practical principle and infinitely impairs self-conceit,[338] which prescribes the subjective conditions of self-love as laws. Now, what in our own judgment impairs our self-conceit humbles us. Therefore the moral law unavoidably humbles every human being inasmuch as he compares with it the sensible propensity of his nature. If the presentation of something *as determining basis of our will* humbles us in our self-consciousness, then insofar as this something is positive and a determining basis it arouses *respect* for itself. Therefore the moral law is subjectively too a basis of respect. Now, everything found in self-love belongs to inclination, and all inclination rests on feelings; hence what in self-love impairs all of the inclinations has, precisely thereby, necessarily an influence on feeling. Thus we comprehend how it is possible to see[339] a priori that the moral law—inasmuch as it excludes the inclinations and the propensity to make them the supreme practical condition, i.e., self-love, from any participation[340] in the supreme legislation— can exert on feeling an effect that on the one hand is merely *negative* but on the other hand, specifically in regard to the restricting basis of pure practical reason, is *positive;* and for this no special kind of feeling need be assumed, under the name of a practical or moral feeling, as preceding the moral law and lying at its basis.

The negative effect on feeling (disagreeableness) is, like all influence on feeling and every feeling in general, *pathological.*[341] However, although as the effect of the consciousness of the moral law and consequently in reference to an intelligible cause—viz., the subject, of pure reason as supreme legislator—this feeling of a rational subject affected by inclinations is called humiliation (intellectual contempt), yet in reference to the positive basis of this humiliation,[342] the law, it is at the same time called respect for the law. No feeling for this law occurs at all; rather, inasmuch as the law moves the resistance out of the way, in the judgment of reason this removal of an obstacle is esteemed equal to a positive furtherance of its causality.

75

---

[338] [I.e., it strikes it down. See above, Ak. V, 73.]

[339] [Literally, 'have insight into': *einsehen.*]

[340] [*Beitritt.*]

[341] [See above, Ak. V, 19 incl. br. n. 5.]

[342] [Or perhaps 'of this effect': *derselben.*]

Because of this, this feeling can now also be called a feeling of respect for the moral law, while on both grounds together it can be called a *moral feeling*.[343]

Thus the moral law, just as through practical pure reason it is a formal determining basis of action, and just as it is indeed also a material but only objective[344] determining basis of the objects of the action under the name of good and evil, so it is also a subjective determining basis—i.e., an incentive—for this action, inasmuch as it has influence on the sensibility[345] of the subject and brings about a feeling that furthers the law's influence on the will. Here there is in the subject no *antecedent* feeling that would be attuned to morality, because this is impossible, since all feeling is sensible whereas the incentive of the moral attitude must be free from any sensible condition. Rather, sensible feeling, which underlies all our inclination, is indeed the condition of that sensation which we call respect. But the cause that determines this sensation[346] lies in pure practical reason, and hence this sensation, because of its origin, cannot be called *brought about pathologically*[347] but must be called *brought about practically*.[348] For, the presentation of the moral law deprives self-love of its influence and self-conceit of its delusion;[349] and thereby pure practical reason's obstacle is diminished and the presentation of the superiority of its objective law to the impulses of sensibility is produced, and hence—by the removal of the counterweight—so is, relatively, the law's weight (with regard to a will affected by sensibility) in the judgment of reason. And thus respect for the law is not an incentive to morality; rather, it is morality itself regarded subjectively as an incentive inasmuch as pure practical reason—by rejecting, in contrast to self-love, all of self-love's claims—imparts authority[350] to the law, which now alone has

76

---

[343] [Cf. the *Grounding for the Metaphysics of Morals,* Ak. IV, 442, 460; also the *Metaphysics of Morals,* Ak. VI, 387, 399–400, 464.]

[344] [*objektiv;* 'objects,' below, translates *Gegenstände.*]

[345] [Reading, with Nolte, Wille, and with Natorp in the *Akademie* edition, *Sinnlichkeit* for *Sittlichkeit* ('morality').]

[346] [Reading *derselben* for *desselben,* which would refer back not to *Empfindung* ('sensation') but to *Gefühl* ('feeling') and hence, in this sentence, to 'sensible feeling.']

[347] [Emphasis added.]

[348] [Cf. the *Metaphysics of Morals,* Ak. VI, 212–13, 377–78.]

[349] [*Wahn.*]

[350] [*Ansehen.* I also translate *Befugnis* as 'authority' because there is no consistently acceptable alternative term for either of the German originals. In particular, although *Ansehen* as used in contemporary German could be translated as 'prestige,' this term would make the

influence. Now, here it must be noted [first,] that, as far as respect is an effect on feeling and hence on the sensibility of a rational being, it[351] presupposes this sensibility and hence also the finitude of such beings on whom the moral law imposes respect; and [second,] that respect for the *law* cannot be attributed to a supreme being or even to a being free from all sensibility, for whom therefore sensibility also cannot be an obstacle to practical reason.[352]

This feeling (under the name of moral feeling) is thus brought about solely by reason. It does not serve for judging actions, let alone for being the basis of the objective moral law itself, but serves only as an incentive to make this law a maxim within oneself. But what name could more fittingly be assigned to this odd feeling which cannot be compared with any pathological feeling? It is of such a peculiar kind that it seems to be at the command solely of reason, specifically of practical pure reason.

Respect always applies only to persons,[353] never to things. Things can arouse in us *inclination* and, if they are animals (e.g., horses, dogs, etc.), even *love*—or else *fear*, like the sea, a volcano, a beast of prey—but never *respect*. Something that does approach this feeling is *admiration,* and this as an affect, amazement, can apply also to things,[354] e.g., sky-high mountains, the magnitude, multitude, and distance of the celestial bodies, the strength and swiftness of many animals, etc. But none of this is respect. A human being can also be for me an object of love, fear, or admiration even to the point of amazement, and yet not be for me therefore an object of respect. His jocular temper, his courage and strength, his power due to his rank among others, can instill such sensations in me, yet inner respect toward him [may] still be lacking. *Fontenelle*[355] says: *"Before a prominent*

Kantian *Ansehen* too relative to people's views; and although *Befugnis* could sometimes be rendered as 'warrant,' this term has epistemic connotations that would often make it misleading or even unintelligible: see, e.g., 'authority' and the closely related 'authorized' (*befugt*) at Ak. V, 56, and especially 'authorized' at Ak. V, 69. However, I believe that the meaning of the two German terms, as Kant uses these, is in fact just similar enough to make using the same English term acceptable.]

[351] [Reading, with Vorländer, *sie* for *es.*]

[352] [Cf. the *Grounding for the Metaphysics of Morals,* Ak. IV, 412–14.]

[353] [Cf. the *Metaphysics of Morals,* Ak. VI, 448–50, 462–64.]

[354] [Cf. the *Critique of Judgment,* Ak. V, 269, 272, 365.]

[355] [Bernard Le Bovier de Fontenelle (1657–1757), a man of letters, scientist, and popular philosopher. His most famous work is *Entretiens sur la pluralité des mondes* (*Conversations on the Plurality of Worlds*) (Paris: C. Blageart, 1686); contemporary critical edition with

man I bow, but my spirit does not bow." I can add this: Before a lowly, plain common man in whom I perceive righteousness of character in a certain 77 measure that I am not conscious of in myself *my spirit bows,* whether I want it or not and whether I hold my head ever so high to keep him from over-looking my preeminence. Why is this? His example holds before me a law that, when I compare it with my conduct, strikes down my self-conceit, and I see compliance with it—and hence the law's *practicability*—proved be-fore me through the deed. Now, I may even be conscious of an equal degree of righteousness in myself, and yet the respect remains. For since in human beings any good is always deficient, the law—made intuitive by an exam-ple—still always strikes down my pride. The standard for this is provided by the man whom I see before me; what impurity[356] may still attach to him is not so familiar to me as is my own, and he therefore appears to me in a purer light. *Respect* is a *tribute* that, whether we want to or not, we cannot refuse [to pay] to merit; we may perhaps hold it back outwardly, yet we cannot help feeling it inwardly.

So little is respect a feeling of *pleasure* that we give way to it only reluc-tantly in regard to a human being. We try to discover something [in him] that could lighten the burden of it for us, some blemish to compensate us for the humiliation that comes upon us through such an example. Even the de-ceased are not always safe from this [kind of] critique. Even the moral law itself in its *solemn majesty* is exposed to this endeavor to fend off respect for it. Does one suppose that our being so ready to degrade the moral law to [the level of] our familiar[357] inclinations can be ascribed to any other cause—or that everyone's taking such trouble to turn this law into the fa-vored precept of our well-understood advantage is due to any other causes—than that we wish to be rid of the intimidating respect that holds our own unworthiness[358] so sternly before us? On the other hand, there is nonetheless so *little displeasure* in respect that, once we have shed our self-conceit and have permitted that respect to have practical influence, we can in turn not take our eyes off the splendor of this law, and the soul believes

---

(French) introduction and notes, by Alexandre Calame (Paris: Nizet, 1984); translated by H. A. Hargreaves, with an introduction by Nina Rattner Gelbart (Berkeley: University of California Press, 1990).]

[356] [*Unlauterkeit.* Ordinarily, including below, I use 'purity' for *Reinigkeit.*]

[357] [*vertraulich.* Ordinarily I use 'familiar' to translate *bekannt.*]

[358] [*Unwürdigkeit.*]

78

that it elevates itself to the extent that it sees the holy law elevated[359] above itself and its frail nature. To be sure, great talents and an activity proportionate to them can also bring about respect or a feeling analogous thereto, and it is also entirely proper to devote this feeling to them; and it then seems as if admiration and this sensation are one and the same. But if one looks more closely one will notice that, because it always remains uncertain what share innate talent and what share cultivation through one's own diligence has in the skill [that we admire], reason presents the skill to us as presumably the fruit of cultivation and hence as merit; this noticeably tones down our self-conceit, and [reason] either reproaches us with it or enjoins us to follow such an example in the way that is appropriate to us. Hence this respect which we show to such a person (properly, to the law that his example holds before us) is not mere admiration, as is confirmed also by this: that when the common horde of [a man's] fanciers believes that it has from somewhere else discovered the bad[360] in the character of such a man (as, say, Voltaire), it abandons all respect toward him, whereas the true scholar continues to feel it at least from the viewpoint of the man's talents, because he is himself involved in a business and a calling that to a certain extent makes imitation of the man a law for him.

Respect for the moral law is therefore the *sole* and also indubitable[361] moral incentive, and this feeling is also directed to no object except on this basis alone. First the moral law determines the will objectively and directly in the judgment of reason; but freedom, the causality of which is determinable only through the law, consists precisely in this, that it restricts all inclinations, and hence the esteem of the person himself, to the condition of compliance with its pure law. This restriction now has an effect on feeling and brings about the sensation of displeasure which can be cognized a priori from the moral law. But this effect is to this extent merely a *negative* one that, as having arisen from the influence of a pure practical reason, above all impairs the subject's activity insofar as inclinations are his determining basis, and hence impairs[362] the opinion concerning his personal worth

---

[359] [Or 'exalted': *erhaben.*]

[360] [*das Schlechte.* On *schlecht,* see above, Ak. V, 59 br. n. 259.]

[361] [*unbezweifelt.* Literally, this term means 'undoubted,' but Kant uses it to mean 'indubitable'; see, e.g., the *Critique of Pure Reason,* B 275. The same holds for the synonymous *ungezweifelt;* see ibid., B 274, also A 46/B 63, A 184/B 227, and cf. A 48/B 66, A 374, A 498/B 526, A 634 = B 662.]

[362] [*Abbruch tun;* likewise above. See above, Ak. V, 25 br. n. 44.]

(which, if there is no agreement with the moral law, is downgraded to nothing); and thus the effect of this law on feeling is merely humiliation, into which we do therefore indeed have insight a priori, though we cannot cognize in it the force of the pure practical law as incentive but only the resistance against incentives of sensibility. However, the same law is yet objectively, i.e., in the presentation of pure reason, a direct determining basis of the will, and consequently this humiliation occurs only relatively to the purity of the law; and thus the downgrading of the claims of moral self-esteem, i.e., humiliation on the sensible side, is an elevation of the moral, i.e., practical, esteem for the law itself on the intellectual side—in a word, it is respect for the law, and thus also a feeling that is positive in terms of its intellectual cause and is cognized a priori. For, any diminution of obstacles[363] to an activity is a furtherance of this activity itself. However, acknowledgment of the moral law is the consciousness of an activity[364] of practical reason [engaged in] from objective bases, an activity that fails to express its effect in actions only because subjective (pathological) causes hinder it. Therefore respect for the moral law must be regarded as also a positive though indirect effect of the law on feeling insofar as the law weakens the hindering influence of the inclinations by humiliating [one's] self-conceit, and hence must be regarded as a subjective basis of activity, i.e., as an *incentive* to comply with the law, and as a basis for maxims of a way of life conforming to it. From the concept of an incentive arises that of an *interest*, which can never be attributed to a being unless the being has reason, and which signifies an *incentive* of the will insofar as it is *presented by reason*. Since in a morally good will the law itself must be the incentive, *moral interest* is a pure sense-free interest of practical reason alone. Moreover, on the concept of an interest is based that of a *maxim*. Hence a maxim is morally genuine only when it rests solely on the interest that one takes in complying with the law. All three concepts, however—those of an *incentive*, of an *interest*, and of a *maxim*—can be applied only to finite beings.[365] For they presuppose, one and all, a limitedness of the nature of a being inasmuch as the subjective constitution of the being's power of choice does not by itself agree with the objective law of a practical reason: viz., they presuppose a need to be impelled to activity by something or other because the

79

---

[363] [Or 'hindrances': *Hindernisse.*]

[364] [*Tätigkeit.* Below, 'action' translates *Handlung.*]

[365] [Cf. the *Grounding for the Metaphysics of Morals,* Ak. IV, 449–50, 459–60 incl. esp. 459n, 462; also the *Metaphysics of Morals,* Ak. VI, 212–13.]

activity is confronted by an internal obstacle. Hence they cannot be applied to the divine will.[366]

80

There is something so special in the boundless esteem[367] for the pure moral law stripped of all advantage—as this law is presented to us, for compliance, by practical reason, whose voice makes even the boldest offender tremble and compels him to hide from his [own] sight[368]—that one need not be surprised to find this influence of a merely intellectual idea on feeling unfathomable for speculative reason, and to have to settle for being capable nonetheless of this much insight a priori: that such a feeling is inseparably linked with the presentation of the moral law in every finite rational being. If this feeling of respect were pathological and hence a feeling of *pleasure*[369] based on inner *sense,* then [trying to] discover a priori a link of it to any idea would be futile. In fact, however, it is a feeling that applies only to the practical; moreover, it attaches to the presentation of a law merely in terms of the law's form and not on account of any object of the law; hence it cannot be classed either with gratification or with pain, and yet it produces an *interest* in compliance with the law which we call *moral* interest—as, indeed, the capacity to take such an interest in the law (or respect for the moral law itself) is, properly, *moral feeling.*[370]

Now, the consciousness of a *free* submission of the will to the law, yet as linked with an unavoidable constraint inflicted—but only by one's own reason—on all inclinations, is respect for the law. The law that demands and also inspires this respect is, as we see, none other than the moral law (for no other law excludes all inclinations from the directness of their influence on the will). An action that is objectively practical according to this law, with exclusion of all determining basis from inclination, is called *duty,*[371] which, because of this exclusion, contains in its concept practical *necessitation,* i.e., determination to actions however *reluctantly* they may be done. The feeling that arises from the consciousness of this necessitation is not possi-

---

[366] [Cf. the *Grounding for the Metaphysics of Morals,* Ak. IV, 413–14, 432.]

[367] [Literally, 'boundless high esteem': *grenzenlosen Hochschätzung.*]

[368] [*vor seinem Anblicke.* This could also mean 'from the law's sight,' but cf. Kant's description of someone who "does not have cause to be ashamed before himself and to dread the inner spectacle of self-examination" at Ak. V, 87.]

[369] [Emphasis added.]

[370] [Cf. the *Grounding for the Metaphysics of Morals,* Ak. IV, 442–43, 460; also the *Metaphysics of Morals,* Ak. VI, 399–400.]

[371] [*Pflicht.* On duty construed as an action, cf. above, Ak. V, 8 n. 83 incl. n. 83f.]

ble pathologically, as would be a feeling brought about by an object of the senses, but possible only practically,[372] i.e., through a preceding (objective) determination of the will and causality of reason. Hence, as *submission* to a law, i.e., as a command (proclaiming constraint for the sensibly affected subject), this feeling contains within itself no pleasure, but rather—to this extent—displeasure, in the action. But, on the other hand, since this constraint is exerted only by the legislation of one's *own* reason, it also contains an *elevation* [of oneself], and the subjective effect on feeling, insofar as the sole cause thereof is pure practical reason, can only be called *self-approval* with regard to this reason.[373] For one cognizes oneself as determined to this [effect on feeling] solely by the law and without any [sensible] interest, and now becomes conscious of an entirely different interest—produced subjectively by this [law]—which is purely practical and *free*. To take such an interest in an action conforming to duty is by no means counseled by an inclination; rather, reason through the practical law commands this absolutely and also actually produces this [interest], which therefore bears a name entirely peculiar to it, viz., respect.

81

Therefore the concept of duty demands *objectively*—in the action— agreement with the law, and *subjectively*[374]—in the maxim of the action— respect for the law, as the sole way of determining the will by the law. And thereon rests the distinction between the consciousness of having acted *in conformity with duty* and *from duty,* i.e., from respect for the law.[375] The first of these (legality) is possible even if only inclinations were to have been the determining bases of the will; but the second (*morality*), moral worth, must be posited solely in this, that the action is done from duty,[376] i.e., only on account of the law.[377]

---

[372] [I follow Natorp and the *Akademie* edition—rather than Vorländer and the *Philosophische Bibliothek* edition—in retaining the comma before *möglich* ('possible') at the end of Kant's sentence. Cf. the similar sentence near the end of Ak. V, 79, above.]

[373] [Or, possibly, 'with regard to this elevation' (in contrast to the submission): *in Ansehung der letzteren.*]

[374] [Emphasis added.]

[375] [Cf. the *Grounding for the Metaphysics of Morals,* Ak. IV, 390, 397–401, 406–07, 421–23, 439–440.]

[376] [Cf. the *Metaphysics of Morals,* Ak. VI, 219–220, 225–26, 392–93.]

[377] If one examines the concept of respect for persons exactly, as it has previously been set forth, one becomes aware that respect always rests on the consciousness of a duty held before us by an example, and hence that it can never have any basis other

It is of the greatest importance in all moral judgments[378] to attend with the utmost exactness to the subjective principle of all maxims, so that all the morality of actions is posited in their necessity *from duty* and from respect for the law, not [in their necessity] from love and fondness[379] for what the actions are to produce. For human beings and for all created rational beings moral necessity[380] is necessitation,[381] i.e., obligation, and every action based thereon is to be conceived as duty, not as a way of proceeding that by itself we already favor or might come to favor. As if we could ever bring it about that without respect for the law, which is linked with fear or at least worry about transgressing it, we on our own—like the deity exalted beyond all dependence—could ever come into possession of a *holiness* of will through a harmony of the will with the pure moral law—a harmony that had, as it were, become our nature and could never be dislodged.

82

In other words, for the will of a maximally perfect[382] being the moral law is a law of *holiness,* but for the will of every finite rational being it is a law of *duty,* of moral necessitation, and of the determination of his actions through *respect* for that law and from reverence for his duty. No other subjective principle must be assumed as incentive, for otherwise the action can indeed turn out as the law prescribes it, but since despite being in conformity with duty it is not done from duty, the attitude toward it is not moral; yet this attitude is, in fact, what counts in this legislation.

It is very beautiful to do good to human beings from love for them and from compassionate[383] benevolence, or to be just from love of order; but this is not yet our conduct's genuine moral maxim appropriate to our station

---

than a moral one; and that for knowledge[a] of human beings it is very good and, for a psychological aim, even very useful—wherever we use this expression—to attend to the secret and surprising while yet frequently encountered—regard that the human being in his judgments has for the moral law.

[a] [-*kenntnis.* In this context, my usual rendering of this term as 'acquaintance' or 'familiarity' might be misleading.]

[378] [*Beurteilungen;* likewise in Kant's note, above. See above, Ak. V, 8 br. n. 78.]

[379] [*Zuneigung.*]

[380] [*Notwendigkeit.* See above, Ak. V, 20 br. n. 17.]

[381] [*Nötigung.*]

[382] [*allervollkommenst.*]

[383] [*teilnehmend.*]

among rational beings *as human beings,* when with proud conceit[384] we presume—as volunteers, as it were—to brush aside the thought of duty and, as independent of command, to want to do merely from our own pleasure what we would need no command to do. We are subject to a *discipline* of reason, and in all our maxims must not forget to be submissive to it, not to detract from it in any way, and not to curtail in any way—through delusion based on self-love—the authority of the law (even though our own reason gives it) by positing the determining basis of our will, even if in conformity with the law, still in something other than the law itself and in respect for this law. Duty and obligation[385] are the only designations[386] that we must give to our relation to the moral law. We are indeed legislating[387] members of a kingdom of morals possible through freedom and presented to us by practical reason for our respect; but we are at the same time subjects of this kingdom, not its sovereign, and a failure to recognize[388] our low level as creatures—as well as self-conceit's [attitude of] refusal toward the authority of the holy law—is already a defection from the law in spirit, even if its letter were fulfilled.[389]

With this, however, the possibility of such a command[390] as *Love God above all and your neighbor as yourself*[391] agrees quite well. For as a command it does demand respect for a law that *orders love,* and does not leave it to one's discretionary[392] choice to make this love one's principle. But love for God as inclination (pathological love) is impossible; for he is not an

83

---

[384] [*Einbildung.*]

[385] [*Schuldigkeit* (a synonym of *Verbindlichkeit* and of *Obliegenheit*). The term is, of course, etymologically linked to *Schuld,* 'debt,' just as the English terms 'ought' (to which the noun 'obligation' corresponds in meaning) and 'duty' are so linked, respectively, to 'owed' and to 'due.']

[386] [*Benennungen.*]

[387] [Or 'legislative': *gesetzgebend.*]

[388] [*Verkennung.*]

[389] [Cf. the *Grounding for the Metaphysics of Morals,* Ak. IV, 433–37.]

[390] [Or 'commandment': *Gebot.* Similarly hereafter.]

[391] The principle[a] of one's own happiness, which some want to turn into the supreme principle of morality, gives rise to an odd contrast with this law; this principle would say: *Love yourself above all, but love God and your neighbor for your own sake.*
  [a] [*Prinzip* here, *Grundsatz* below.]

[392] [Or 'optional,' or perhaps 'arbitrary': *beliebig.*]

object of the senses. The same love toward human beings is indeed possible, but cannot be commanded; for no human being has it within his power to love someone merely on [someone's] order. Therefore it is only *practical love* which is understood in that kernel of all laws. To love God, in this signification, means to fulfill his commands *gladly;*[393] to love one's neighbor means to perform all duty toward him *gladly.* The command that makes this a rule, however, also cannot command one to *have* this attitude in actions conforming to duty, but only to *strive* for it. For, a command to do something gladly is intrinsically contradictory, because if we already know on our own what we are obligated to do, and if we were moreover conscious of being glad to do it, then there would be no need at all for a command concerning it; and if we did do it, yet not gladly but only from respect for the law, then a command that makes this very respect the incentive of the maxim would act precisely contrary to the commanded attitude. That law of all laws, therefore, like all moral precepts of the Gospel, exhibits the moral attitude in its entire perfection, in the way in which, as an ideal of holiness that is not attainable by any creature, it is yet the archetype that we ought to strive to approach and—in an uninterrupted but infinite progression—to become equal to.[394] For if a rational creature could ever get to the point of fulfilling all moral laws completely *gladly,* this would be tantamount to meaning that there would not be in him[395] even the possibility of a desire stimulating him to deviate from them; for, overcoming such a desire always costs the subject [some] sacrifice and hence requires self-constraint, i.e., inner necessitation to what one does not do entirely gladly. But to this level of the moral attitude no creature can ever attain. For, being a creature and hence always dependent with regard to what he requires for complete satisfaction with his state, he can never be entirely free from desires and inclinations. These, because they rest on physical causes, do not by themselves harmonize with the moral law, which has entirely different sources. Hence they always make it necessary [for the creature], on account of them, to base the attitude of his maxims on moral necessitation—[i.e.,] not on willing acquiescence but on respect, which *demands* compliance with the law even if this were done reluctantly[396]—rather than on love, which does not

84

---

[393] [*gerne,* also rendered as 'being glad to' below.]

[394] [Cf. the *Metaphysics of Morals,* Ak. VI, 446–47.]

[395] [See above, Ak. V, 19 br. n. 6.]

[396] [*ungerne.*]

worry about any inner refusal of the will toward the law. Yet [they also make it necessary for the creature] to make this love—viz., mere love for the law (since this law would then cease to be a *command,* and since morality, which would now subjectively pass over into holiness, would cease to be *virtue*)—the constant though unattainable goal of his endeavor. For in what we highly esteem but yet dread (because of the consciousness of our weaknesses), the greater ease in satisfying it results in the reverential dread's being transformed into fondness, and respect into love; at least this would be the perfection of an attitude devoted to the law, if it were ever possible for a creature to attain it.

This consideration is aimed not so much at bringing the just cited Gospel command to distinct concepts in order to restrain or, if possible, forestall *religious fanaticism* in regard to the love of God, but at accurately determining the moral attitude directly in regard to our duties toward human beings as well, and to restrain or, if possible, forestall a *merely moral* fanaticism that infects many minds. The moral level on which the human being stands (as does, according to all the insight we have, every rational creature as well) is respect for the moral law. The attitude that he is obligated to have in complying with this law is to do so from duty, not from voluntary[397] fondness or even perhaps from an endeavor that on his own he undertakes gladly, without having been ordered to do so; and the moral state in which he can be each time[398] is *virtue,*[399] i.e., the moral attitude in the *struggle,* and not *holiness* in the supposed *possession* of a complete *purity* of the will's attitudes. By exhortation to actions as noble, sublime, and magnanimous, minds are attuned to nothing but moral fanaticism and enhancement of self-conceit. For it leads them into the delusion [which makes it seem] as if it were not duty—i.e., respect for the law whose yoke (which is nonetheless gentle because reason itself imposes it on us) they *must* bear, even if reluctantly—which amounts to the determining basis of their actions, and which always still humbles them inasmuch as they comply with the law (*obey* it), but as if these actions were expected of them not from duty but as bare merit. For by imitating such deeds, viz., deeds performed from such a principle, not only have they not in the least satisfied the spirit of the law—which consists in the attitude that subjects itself to the law, not in the lawfulness of the action (whatever the principle may be)—and are positing the

85

---

[397] [*freiwillig.*]

[398] [Each time that he complies with the moral law: *jedesmal.*]

[399] [Cf. the *Metaphysics of Morals,* Ak. VI, 379–81, 383, 394–95, 405–09.]

incentive *pathologically* (in sympathy or even in self-love[400]) rather than morally (in the law), but they produce in this way a frivolous, overreaching, fantastic way of thinking. For they flatter themselves with a voluntary good nature[401] of their mind—a mind which requires neither spur nor bridle and for which not even a command is needed—and thereby forget their obligation, of which they should, after all, think sooner than of merit. Actions of others which have been done with great sacrifice and, moreover, solely on account of duty, may indeed be praised under the name of *noble* and *sublime* deeds, yet even this only insofar as there are indications suggesting that they were done entirely from respect for one's duty, not from bursts of emotions.[402] But if one wants to present these actions to someone as examples to be followed, then what one must use throughout as the incentive is respect for duty (the only genuine moral feeling): this serious, holy precept that does not leave it to our vain self-love to dally with pathological impulses (insofar as they are analogous to morality) and to credit ourselves with *meritorious* worth. If only we search carefully, then for all actions that are praiseworthy we shall surely find a law of duty which *commands* instead of leaving it to our discretion [to choose] what may be to our propensity's liking. This is the only way of exhibiting these actions that molds the soul morally, because it is the only one capable of firm and accurately determined principles.[403]

If *fanaticism*[404] in the most general meaning is an overstepping of the bounds of human reason undertaken according to principles, then *moral fanaticism* is[405] such an overstepping of the bounds that practical pure reason sets for humanity. Practical pure reason thereby forbids us to posit the subjective determining basis of actions conforming to duty—i.e., their moral incentive—in anything other than the law itself, and to posit the attitude that is thereby brought into the maxims anywhere else than in respect for this law; and it commands us to make the thought of duty—the thought which strikes down all *arrogance* as well as vain *self-love*[406]—the supreme *life-principle* of all morality in human beings.

86

---

[400] [*Philautie.*]

[401] [*freiwillige Gutartigkeit.*]

[402] [Literally, 'ebullitions of the heart': *Herzensaufwallungen.*]

[403] [Cf. the *Grounding for the Metaphysics of Morals,* Ak. IV, 406–12.]

[404] [*Schwärmerei.*]

[405] [I have deleted the emphasis on *so ist* ('then' and 'is').]

[406] [*Philautie* here, *Eigenliebe* in the next paragraph.]

If this is so, then not only novelists and sentimental educators (even if they are ever so zealously opposed to sentimentality) but sometimes even philosophers—indeed, the sternest among them all, the Stoics—have introduced *moral fanaticism* in place of sober but wise moral discipline,[407] though the fanaticism of the latter was more heroic while that of the former was of a more insipid and tender constitution. And one can, without being hypocritical, say quite truthfully about the moral teaching of the Gospel that, by the purity of its moral principle but at the same time by the appropriateness of this principle to the limits of finite beings, it first subjected all good conduct of human beings to the discipline of a duty laid before their eyes—which does not let them rove[408] among fancied moral perfections—and set limits of humility (i.e., of self-cognition) to self-conceit as well as to self-love, both of which readily fail to recognize their bounds.

Duty!—you sublime, grand name which encompasses nothing that is favored yet involves ingratiation, but which demands submission, yet also does not seek to move the will by threatening anything that would arouse natural aversion in the mind and terrify, but merely puts forth a law that on its own finds entry into the mind and yet gains grudging veneration (even if not always compliance), a law before which all inclinations fall silent even if they secretly work against it: what origin is worthy of you, and where does one find the root of your noble descent[409] that proudly rejects all kinship with inclinations, the root from which to be descended[410] is the irremissible condition of that worth which human beings alone can give themselves?

It can be nothing less than what elevates the human being above himself (as a part of the world of sense), what links him to an order of things that only the understanding can think and that at the same time has under it the entire world of sense and with it the human being's empirically determinable existence in time and the whole of all purposes[411] (which whole is alone appropriate to such unconditional practical laws as the moral law). It is nothing other than *personality*,[412] i.e., the freedom and independence from the mechanism of all of nature, yet regarded at the same time as a

87

---

[407] [*Disziplin* here, *Zucht* below.]

[408] [*schwärmen.*]

[409] [*Abkunft.*]

[410] [Literally, 'to stem': *abzustammen.*]

[411] [*Zwecke*. See above, Ak. V, 35 br. n. 121.]

[412] [I.e., personhood: *Persönlichkeit.*]

power of a being subject to pure practical laws that are peculiar to it, viz., are given by its own reason, so that the person as belonging to the world of sense is subject to his own personality insofar as he at the same time belongs to the intelligible world.[413] Thus it is not surprising if the human being,[414] as belonging to both worlds, must regard his own being in reference to this second and highest vocation[415] solely with veneration, and regard the laws of this vocation with the highest respect.

Now, this origin is the basis of many expressions that designate the worth of objects according to moral ideas. The moral law is *holy* (inviolable). The human being is indeed unholy enough, but the *humanity* in his person must be holy to him. In all of creation everything one wants and over which one has any power can also be used *merely as a means;* only the human being, and with him every rational creature, is a *purpose in itself.*[416] For by virtue of the autonomy of his freedom he is the subject of the moral law, which is holy. Precisely on account of this autonomy, every will, even every person's own will directed to himself, is restricted to the condition of harmony with the *autonomy* of a rational being, viz., the condition not to subject such a being to any aim that is not possible in accordance with a law that could arise from the will of the subject himself who undergoes [the action], thus never to use this subject merely as a means but [always] at the same time as himself a purpose. This condition is rightly attributed by us even to the divine will with regard to the rational beings in the world as its creatures, inasmuch as the condition rests on these beings' *personality,* by which alone they are purposes in themselves.

This idea of personality, which arouses respect and which the sublimity of our nature (as regards its vocation) puts before our eyes while at the same time drawing attention to the lack of our conduct's adequacy to this idea and thereby striking down self-conceit, is natural and easily discernible even to the commonest human reason. Has not every even moderately honest man sometimes found that he abstained from an otherwise harmless lie by which he could either have extricated himself from an irksome transaction or even procured a benefit for a beloved and deserving friend, merely in

88

---

[413] [Cf. the *Grounding for the Metaphysics of Morals,* Ak. IV, 450–55.]

[414] [*der Mensch;* 'being,' below, translates *Wesen.*]

[415] [*Bestimmung.*]

[416] [Cf. the *Grounding for the Metaphysics of Morals,* Ak. IV, 429–32, 437–440; also the *Metaphysics of Morals,* Ak. VI, 420, 450–51, 462–64. On my rendering of Zweck as 'purpose' rather than as 'end,' see above, Ak. V, 35 br. n. 121.]

order not to have to despise himself secretly in his own eyes?[417] When a righteous man is in the greatest misfortune, which he could have avoided if only he could have brushed duty aside, is he not still sustained by the consciousness that the humanity in his person has after all been maintained and honored by him in its dignity, that he does not have cause to be ashamed before himself and to dread the inner spectacle of self-examination? This comfort is not happiness, not even the smallest part thereof. For, no one will wish to have the occasion for it, perhaps not even a life in such circumstances. But he lives and cannot endure being, in his own eyes, unworthy of life. This inner tranquility is therefore merely negative in regard to everything that may make life agreeable; viz., it is the forestalling of the danger of sinking in personal worth after the worth of his [own] state has already been given up by him entirely. It is the effect of a respect for something entirely different from life, something in comparison and contrast to which life with all its agreeableness has, rather, no worth at all. He now lives only because it is his duty, not because he has the slightest taste for living.

This is how the genuine incentive of pure practical reason is constituted. This incentive is none other than the pure moral law itself insofar as this law allows us to discern the sublimity of our own supranatural existence[418] and subjectively brings about, in human beings, respect for their higher vocation: viz., in human beings who are conscious at the same time of their sensible existence and of the dependence, linked therewith, from their—to this extent—very pathologically affected nature. Now, so many charms and agreeablenesses in life can quite readily be linked with this incentive that even just on their account the most prudent choice of a reasonable *Epicurean*— meditating on the greatest well-being of life—would declare itself for morally good conduct. It may even be advisable to link this prospect of a cheerful enjoyment with that supreme motivating cause which is already sufficiently determining by itself—but only in order to maintain the counterweight to the enticements that vice does not fail to display on the opposite side, and not in order to posit in this prospect the proper motive force, not even in the slightest part, when duty is at issue. For this would be tantamount to trying to defile the moral attitude in its source. The venerability of duty is not concerned with the enjoyment of life; it has its own law, also its

89

---

[417] [Cf. the *Grounding for the Metaphysics of Morals,* Ak. IV, 402–03, 422, 429–30, 441; also the *Metaphysics of Morals,* Ak. VI, 429–31; also *On a Supposed Right to Lie Out of Love of Humankind* (*Über ein vermeintes Recht, aus Menschenliebe zu lügen*), Ak. VIII, 427–30.]

[418] [*Existenz* here, *Dasein* below.]

own tribunal, and however much one tried to shake them together in order to hand their mixture—as a medicine, as it were—to the sick soul, they yet promptly separate on their own; and if they do not, then the first [ingredient] is not effective at all, and even if physical life were to gain some force in this, yet the moral life would fade away irrecoverably.

Critical Examination of the Analytic of Pure Practical Reason

By the critical examination of a science, or of a section thereof that by itself amounts to a system, I mean the investigation and justification as to why it must have precisely this and no other systematic form when it is compared with another system that has a similar cognitive power as its basis. Now, practical reason has as its basis one and the same cognitive power as does speculative reason insofar as both are *pure reason.* Therefore the difference in the systematic form of the one from that of the other will have to be determined by a comparison of the two, and the basis of this [difference] will have to be indicated.

The Analytic of pure theoretical reason dealt with cognition of the objects that may be given to the understanding; it therefore had to start from *intuition* and hence (since intuition is always sensible) from sensibility;[419] only from there could it first advance to concepts (of this intuition's objects),[420] and only after preparing the way by means of both[421] was it allowed to end with *principles.*[422] Practical reason, by contrast, deals not with objects in order to *cognize* them but with its own power *to make them actual* (in conformity with the cognition of them), i.e., with a *will,* which is a causality insofar as reason contains the determining basis thereof; consequently it does not have to indicate an object of intuition, but (because the concept of causality always contains the reference to a law that determines the existence of the manifold [elements] in relation to one another) it has to indicate, as practical reason, *only a law* of objects.[423] Therefore a critique of

---

[419] [See the *Critique of Pure Reason,* A 19–49/B 33–73.]

[420] [See ibid., A 50–147/B 74–187.]

[421] [Literally, 'after sending both ahead': *nach beider Voranschickung.*]

[422] [See the *Critique of Pure Reason,* A 148–235/B 187–294.]

[423] [*derselben,* which I take to refer back not to *Anschauung* ('intuition') but to *Gegenständen* ('objects') as related, by contrast, to cognition rather than actualization.]

the analytic of reason insofar as it is to be a practical reason (which is the problem proper) must start from the *possibility of practical a priori principles*.[424] Only from there was it able to proceed to *concepts* of the objects of   90
a practical reason, viz., those of the absolutely good and evil, in order first to give them in conformity with those principles[425] (for, prior to these principles these concepts cannot possibly be given as good or evil by any cognitive power);[426] and only then could the last chapter, viz., that concerning the relation of pure practical reason to sensibility and concerning its [own] necessary and a priori cognizable influence on it, i.e., concerning *moral feeling*, conclude this part.[427] Thus the Analytic of practical pure reason divided the whole range of all conditions of its use quite analogously to that of theoretical pure reason, but in inverse order.[428] The Analytic of theoretical pure reason was divided into Transcendental Aesthetic and Transcendental Logic;[429] that of practical pure reason, inversely, into Logic and Aesthetic of pure practical reason (if I may here be allowed, merely on account of the analogy, to use these otherwise not at all appropriate designations). The Logic, in turn, was there divided into Analytic of Concepts and Analytic of Principles, but is here divided into the Analytic of principles and that of concepts. The Aesthetic there had two parts,[430] because of the two kinds[431] of sensible intuition;[432] here sensibility is regarded not at all as a capacity for intuition but merely as a feeling (which can be a subjective basis of desire), and with regard to it pure practical reason permits no further division.

   That this division into two parts with their subdivisions was not actually undertaken here (though the example of the former division might well have misled one initially into attempting it)—for this too the reason can

---

[424] [See above, Ak. V, 19–57.]

[425] [*Grundsätze* here, *Prinzipien* below. See above, Ak. V, 7 br. n. 66.]

[426] [See above, Ak. V, 57–71.]

[427] [See above, Ak. V, 71–89.]

[428] [Cf. above, Ak. V, 16.]

[429] [Actually, it was not the Analytic but the Doctrine of Elements that was thus divided; the Analytic, together with the Dialectic, constituted the (Transcendental) Logic. Moreover, it was the Analytic (not the Logic, as Kant goes on to say) that was divided into that of concepts and that of principles.]

[430] [Viz., Space and Time.]

[431] [Literally, 'the twofold kind': *der doppelten Art.*]

[432] [See the *Critique of Pure Reason,* where space is treated at A 22–30/B 37–45, time at A 30–41/B 46–58.]

quite readily be seen.[433] For since it is *pure reason* that is here considered in its practical use, and hence considered as commencing from a priori principles and not from empirical determining bases, the division of the Analytic of Pure Practical Reason will have to turn out similar to that of a syllogism:[434] viz., proceeding from the universal in the *major premise* (the moral principle), by a subsumption—undertaken in the *minor premise*—of possible actions (as good or evil ones) under the major premise, to the *conclusion,* viz., the subjective determination of the will (an interest in the practically possible good and the maxim based on this interest). For someone who has been able to convince himself of the propositions occurring in the Analytic, such comparisons will be gratifying; for they rightly prompt the expectation of perhaps being able some day to attain insight into the unity of the entire pure power of reason (theoretical as well as practical) and to derive everything from one principle—this being the unavoidable need of human reason, which finds full satisfaction only in a completely systematic unity of its cognitions.[435]

91

But if we now consider also the content of the cognition that we can have of a pure practical reason as well as through it, as that content is set forth by the Analytic of this reason, we find, despite a noteworthy analogy between this reason and the theoretical, differences that are no less noteworthy. With regard to theoretical pure reason, one was able to prove our *power of a pure a priori rational cognition* quite easily and evidently through examples from sciences.[436] (In sciences, since they put their principles to the test in such a variety of ways by methodical use, one does not so easily as in common cognition have to worry about a secret admixture of empirical bases of cognition.) But that pure reason without the admixture of any empirical determining basis is practical by itself alone, this [fact] one had to be able to establish from the *commonest practical use of reason,* by authenticating the supreme practical principle as a principle that every natural human reason cognizes—as completely a priori, dependent on no sensible data—as the supreme law of its[437] will. One first had to legitimate[438] and justify this

---

[433] [*einsehen.*]

[434] [Literally, 'inference of reason': *Vernunftschluß.*]

[435] [Cf. the *Critique of Pure Reason,* A 10–16/B 24–30.]

[436] [Cf. ibid., B x–xiv.]

[437] [Reading *ihres* for *seines;* Kant seems to have forgotten that the referent is *Menschenvernunft* ('human reason'), not *Mensch* ('human being').]

[438] [Literally, 'verified': *bewähren.*]

principle as to its origin even *in the judgment of this common reason,* before science could take it in hand in order to make use of it as a fact,[439] as it were, that precedes all subtle reasoning[440] about its possibility and all the inferences that could perhaps be made from it. But this circumstance too can quite readily be explained from what was briefly set forth just now: it is because practical pure reason must necessarily start from principles, which must therefore be laid at the basis of all science as the first data, and cannot first arise from science.[441] There is, however, another reason why[442] we were able, quite readily and with sufficient assurance, to conduct this justification of moral principles[443] as principles of a pure reason by merely appealing to the judgment of common human understanding: viz., because anything empirical that might slip into our maxims as a determining basis of the will *becomes recognizable*[444] at once through the feeling of gratification or pain that necessarily attaches to it insofar as it arouses desire, whereas pure practical reason straightforwardly *opposes* admitting this feeling into its principle as a condition.[445] This difference in kind between the determining bases (empirical and rational) is made recognizable through this resistance of a practically legislating reason against all interfering inclination [and specifically] through a peculiar kind of *sensation*[446]— which, however, does not precede practical reason's legislation but instead is brought about only by it, and, moreover, as a constraint. The difference in kind is made recognizable, viz., through the feeling of a respect such as no human being has for inclinations of whatever kind but [every human being] does have for the law; it is made so recognizable and so salient and prominent that no one, not even the commonest human understanding, could fail to become instantaneously aware, in an example put before him, that he can indeed be counseled by empirical bases of volition to follow their induce-

92

---

[439] [On the fact of reason, see above, Ak. V, 31 incl. br. n. 75.]

[440] [*vor allem Vernünfteln.*]

[441] [On all this, see above, Ak. V, 19–57.]

[442] [I take *darum* to refer forward to *weil* ('because,' below).]

[443] [*Prinzipien* here, *Grundsätze* below as well as above.]

[444] [*sich . . . kenntlich macht.* Below, 'is made recognizable' similarly renders *wird . . . kenntlich gemacht.*]

[445] [See above, Ak. V, 71–89.]

[446] [In the broad meaning of the term that includes feeling: *Empfindung.* See above, Ak. V, 22 br. n. 31.]

ments but that he can never be required[447] to *obey* any law other than the pure practical law of reason.

Now, the distinction of the *doctrine of happiness* from the *doctrine of morals,* in the first of which empirical principles amount to the whole foundation whereas in the second they amount not even to the slightest addition to it, is the first and most important enterprise incumbent upon the Analytic of Pure Practical Reason, in which the Analytic must proceed as *meticulously* and indeed, if called upon, as *painstakingly* as the geometrician ever does in his occupation. The philosopher has to struggle with greater difficulties here (as always in rational cognition through mere concepts without construction of them[448]), because he cannot lay any intuition at the basis (of a pure noumenon[449]). However, it also stands him in good stead that, almost like the chemist,[450] he can at any time perform an experiment with any human being's practical reason in order to distinguish the moral (pure) determining basis from the empirical—viz., when he adds the moral law (as determining basis) to the empirically affected will (e.g., of someone who would gladly lie because he can gain something thereby). It is as if the chemist adds alkali to a solution of calcareous earth[451] in muriatic acid:[452] the muriatic acid at once abandons the lime and unites with the alkali; and the lime is deposited at the bottom. In the same way, [take] a man who is otherwise honest (or who even just puts himself in thought in the place of an honest man this time) and hold before him the moral law by which he cognizes the worthlessness of a liar: his practical reason (in judging what ought to be done by him) at once abandons the advantage and unites with what maintains in him the respect for his own person (truthfulness); and now the advantage, after it has been separated and washed from any appendage of reason (which is wholly on the side of duty), is weighed by everyone, so that perhaps it [can] still enter into combination[453] with reason

93

---

447 [*zumuten.*]

448 [Cf. the *Critique of Pure Reason,* A 712–738/B 740–66.]

449 [Reading, with Vorländer, *einem reinen* for *reinem.*]

450 [Kant's term here is *Chemist* (in place of the contemporary *Chemiker*); below it is *Scheidekünstler,* literally, 'separation artist.']

451 [*Kalkerde.* Below, 'lime' translates *Kalk.*]

452 [I.e., hydrochloric acid.]

453 [Or 'linkage': *Verbindung.*]

in other cases, only not where the advantage could be opposed to the moral law, which reason never abandons but unites with most intimately.

But this *distinction* of the principle of happiness from that of morality is not therefore at once an *opposition* between the two, and pure practical reason does not want us to *give up* our claims to happiness, but wants only that as soon as duty is at issue we take *no account* of them at all. In a certain regard it can even be a duty to attend to one's happiness, partly because happiness (to which belong skill, health, wealth) contains means to the fulfillment of one's duty, partly because the lack of it (e.g., poverty) contains temptations to transgress one's duty. Only the furtherance of one's happiness can never directly be a duty, still less a principle of all duty. Now, since all determining bases of the will except for the single pure practical law of reason (the moral law) are one and all empirical and hence, as such, belong to the principle of happiness, they must one and all be separated from the supreme moral principle and never be incorporated in it, because this would annul all moral worth just as much as an empirical admixture to geometric principles would annul all mathematical [self-]evidence, which (in Plato's judgment) is the most excellent thing[454] that mathematics possesses, surpassing even all its utility.[455]

However, in place of [a] deduction[456] of the supreme principle of pure practical reason, i.e., explanation of the possibility of such an a priori cognition, we were able to adduce nothing more than this: that if one had insight into the possibility of the freedom of an efficient cause, then one would also have insight not merely into the possibility but even into the necessity of the moral law as the supreme practical law of rational beings, to whom one attributes freedom of the causality of their will. For, the two concepts are so inseparably linked that practical freedom could also be defined as[457] independence of the will from anything else except solely the moral law. However, one cannot in any way have insight into the freedom of an efficient cause, above all in the world of sense, as regards this freedom's possibility; fortunate we are!, if we can just be sufficiently assured that there is no proof of its impossibility, and are now—by the moral law, which postulates this freedom—compelled and precisely thereby also entitled to as-

94

---

[454] [*das Vortrefflichste.*]

[455] [Cf. Plato's *Republic,* 522–28.]

[456] [See above, Ak. V, 42–50, esp. 45–48.]

[457] [Kant actually says *durch* ('by'). He means, i.e., defined by 'independence of the will . . . .']

sume it. However, there are still many who continue to believe that they can explain this freedom in terms of empirical principles, like any other natural ability.[458] They regard it as a *psychological* property, the explanation of which hinges[459] solely on a more exact investigation into the *nature of the soul* and into [an] incentive of the will, and not as a *transcendental* predicate of the causality of a being that belongs to the world of sense (although this alone is actually at issue); and thus they annul the splendid disclosure that comes upon us through pure practical reason by means of the moral law, viz., the disclosure of an intelligible world through realization[460] of the otherwise transcendent concept of freedom, and with it they annul the moral law itself, which throughout assumes no empirical determining basis. Therefore it will be necessary to adduce here some further [considerations] in order to guard against this deception[461] and exhibit *empiricism* with its shallowness entirely laid bare.

The concept of causality as *natural necessity,* as distinguished from causality as *freedom,* concerns only the existence of things insofar as it is *determinable in time* and consequently [of things] as appearances, in contrast to their causality as things in themselves. Now if one takes the determinations of the existence of things in time to be determinations of things in themselves (which is the most ordinary way of conceiving[462] [them]), then the necessity in the causal relation can in no way be reconciled[463] with freedom; rather, they are contradictorily opposed to each other. For from that necessity it follows that every event, and consequently also every action that takes place at a point of time, is necessary under the condition of what was in the preceding time. Now, because past time is no longer under my control,[464] every action that I perform must be necessary because of determining bases *that are not under my control,* i.e., at the point of time in which I act I am never free. Indeed, even if I assumed my entire existence[465]

---

[458] [Or 'power': *Vermögen.*]

[459] [*ankommt,* also translated as 'is . . . at issue' below.]

[460] [I.e., providing with reality (applicability to objects).]

[461] [*Blendwerk.*]

[462] [Or 'presenting': *vorstellen.*]

[463] [*vereinigen.* Cf. above, Ak. V, 6 n. 64 incl. br. n. 64a.]

[464] [Or 'in my power': *in meiner Gewalt;* likewise just below and later in the paragraph.]

[465] [*Dasein* here, *Existenz* below.]

as [being] independent of any foreign[466] cause (e.g., God), so that the determining bases of my causality and even of my entire existence are not outside me at all, this would still not in the least convert that natural necessity into freedom. For at every point of time I am still always subject to the necessity of being determined to action by *what is not under my control,* and the series of events—which is infinite *a parte priori*[467] and which I can always continue only according to an already predetermined order—would nowhere start on its own [but] would be a steady chain of nature, and therefore my causality would never be freedom.

95

Hence if one wants to attribute freedom to a being whose existence is determined in time, then at least to this extent one cannot exempt this being from the law of the natural necessity of all events in its existence and hence also of all its actions; for, this would be tantamount to handing the being over to blind chance. However, this law unavoidably concerns all causality of things insofar as their *existence* is determinable *in time;* hence if this were the way in which one had to conceive also the *existence of these things in themselves,* then freedom would have to be repudiated as a null and impossible concept. Consequently, if one still wants to rescue it, no other path remains than to attribute the existence of a thing insofar as it is determinable in time, and hence also the [thing's] causality according to the law of *natural necessity, merely to appearance,* but to attribute *freedom to the same being as a thing in itself.* This is indeed unavoidable if one wants to maintain simultaneously both of these mutually repellent[468] concepts; in application, however, if one wants to explain them as reconciled in one and the same action and hence explain this reconciliation itself, great difficulties emerge that seem to make such a reconciliation unfeasible.

If concerning a human being who commits a theft I say that this deed is, according to the natural law of causality, a necessary result of the determining bases in the preceding time, then it was impossible that the deed could have been left undone. How, then, can the judging according to the moral law make a change in this and presuppose that the deed surely could have been omitted because the law says that it ought to have been omitted? That is, how can that person be called entirely free at the same point of time at which, and in regard to the same action regarding which, he is nonetheless

---

[466] [*fremd.*]

[467] [I.e., on the side of what is prior, or antecedent.]

[468] [*widerwärtig.*]

96

subject to an unavoidable necessity? It is a pitiful expedient to seek to escape from this by merely adapting the *kind* of determining bases of this causality according to natural law to a *comparative* concept of freedom. (According to this concept, now and then something is called free action[469] if its determining natural basis lies in the acting being *internally*. For example, [one says this of] what a projectile[470] performs when it is in free motion, because while it is in flight it is not impelled by anything outside it. Again, we also call the motion of a clock a free motion, because the clock itself moves its hand, which therefore does not need to be pushed externally. In the same way, a human being's actions, although they are necessary through their determining bases that precede in time, are nonetheless called by us free, because we are still dealing with[471] internal presentations produced by our own powers, desires generated thereby according to circumstances occasioning [them], and hence actions brought about at our own discretion.) Some still let themselves be put off with this expedient; and thus they suppose that with a little word-splitting they have found the solution to that difficult problem on which [for] millennia [people] have worked in vain and whose solution therefore is not likely to be found so utterly on the surface. For in the question concerning that freedom on which we must base all moral laws and the imputation conforming to them, it does not matter at all whether the causality determined according to a natural law is necessary through determining bases lying *within* the subject or *outside* him, or, in the first case, through instinct or through determining bases thought by means of reason. If, as these same men admit, these determining presentations themselves do have the basis of their existence in time and moreover in the *previous state,* and this state in turn in a preceding one, etc., then by all means let them—these determinations—be internal, let them have psychological rather than mechanical causality, i.e., produce action through presentations rather than through bodily motion: they are always *determining bases* of the causality of a being insofar as this being's existence is determinable in time and hence under necessitating conditions of past time. Thus these determinations, if the subject is to act, *are no longer*

---

[469] [*Wirkung* (which can also mean 'effect'). This is action in the sense applicable to things generally (cf. above, Ak. V, 19 incl. br. n. 9), as contrasted with *Handlung,* which is action in the sense applicable only to intelligent beings. Accordingly, 'actions,' below, translates *Handlungen.*]

[470] [Literally, 'thrown body': *geworfener Körper.*]

[471] [*weil es doch . . . sind.*]

under his control; hence they do carry with them psychological freedom (if indeed one wants to use this term for a concatenation of the soul's presentations that is merely internal) but nonetheless natural necessity. Therefore they leave no *transcendental freedom,* which must be thought as independence from everything empirical and thus from nature as such, whether this   97
nature is regarded as an object of inner sense merely in time, or also of outer sense in both space and time. Without this freedom (in the latter and proper signification), which alone is practical a priori, no moral law is possible and [also] no imputation according to it. Precisely because of this, all necessity of events in time according to the natural law of causality can also be called the *mechanism* of nature even though one does not mean by this that things that are subject to it must be actual material *machines.* One is here taking account only of the necessity of the connection of events in a time series as it develops according to natural law, whether the subject in whom this elapsing occurs is called *automaton materiale* inasmuch as the machinery is driven by matter, or, with Leibniz,[472] [*automaton*] *spirituale*[473] inasmuch as it is driven by presentations; and if the freedom of our will were none other than the latter [kind] (say, psychological and comparative freedom, not simultaneously transcendental, i.e., absolute, freedom), then it would basically be no better than the freedom of a turnspit, which, once it has been wound up, also performs its motions on its own.

Now in order to annul, in the case at hand, the seeming contradiction between the mechanism of nature and freedom in one and the same action, one must remember what was said in the *Critique of Pure Reason*[474] or follows therefrom: viz., that the natural necessity that is not consistent with[475] the subject's freedom attaches merely to the determinations of a thing

---

[472] [Baron Gottfried Wilhelm von Leibniz (1646–1716), a German philosopher, mathematician, and author of numerous works. The rationalism of Leibniz is one of the two major philosophical traditions (the other being empiricism) to which Kant's philosophy responds. Leibniz's most important philosophical work, called the *Monadology*, is *Principia philosophiae, more geometrico demonstrata* (*The Principles of Philosophy, Demonstrated in the Manner of Geometry*), 1714; contemporary edition: *Monadology, and Other Philosophical Essays;* translated by Paul Schrecker and Anne Martin Schrecker; with an Introduction and Notes by Paul Schrecker (Indianapolis, Ind.: Bobbs-Merrill, 1965).]

[473] [Respectively, 'material automaton' and 'spiritual automaton.']

[474] [Cf. the *Critique of Pure Reason,* A 444–51 = B 472–79, A 488/B 516, A 532–58 = B 560–86.]

[475] [Literally, 'cannot coexist with': *nicht zusammen bestehen kann.*]

which falls under[476] conditions of time and thus only to the determinations of the acting subject as appearance, and that therefore—to this extent—the determining bases of every action of the subject lie in what belongs to past time and *is no longer under his control* (in this must be included also his already committed[477] deeds and the character, thereby determinable for him, that he as phenomenon has in his own eyes). But the same subject, who on the other hand is also conscious of himself as a thing in itself, also considers his existence *insofar as it does not fall under conditions of time,* and considers himself as determinable only by laws that he on his own[478] gives to himself through reason; and in this existence of his there is for him nothing antecedent to the determination of his will, but every action—and in general every determination of his existence varying in conformity with inner sense, even the entire sequence of his existence[479] as a being of sense[480]—is in the consciousness of his intelligible existence nothing but a consequence, and is never to be viewed as a determining basis of his causality as a *noumenon.*[481] Now, in this regard the rational being can rightly say concerning every unlawful action which he commits that he could have omitted it, even though as appearance it is sufficiently determined in the past and is to this extent unfailingly necessary; for, this action, with everything past that determines it, belongs to a single phenomenon of his character—the character which he on his own imparts to himself and according to which he on his own imputes to himself, as a cause independent of all sensibility, the causality of those appearances.

The judicial pronouncements of that wondrous power in us that we call conscience are also in perfect agreement with this.[482] Let a human being use what art he wants in order to paint to himself a remembered unlawful behavior as an unintentional oversight—as a mere carelessness, which one can never avoid entirely, and thus as something in which he was carried away by the stream of natural necessity—and to declare himself innocent of it; he nonetheless finds that the lawyer who speaks in his favor can in no

[476] [I.e., is subject to: *unter . . . steht;* similarly a few lines down.]

[477] [*begangen,* from *begehen,* which has the same negative connotation as 'commit.']

[478] [*selbst.* Likewise twice near the end of this paragraph.]

[479] [*Existenz* here and below, *Dasein* (repeatedly) earlier in this paragraph.]

[480] [*Sinnenwesen.*]

[481] [Cf. the *Grounding for the Metaphysics of Morals,* Ak. IV, 450–63.]

[482] [Cf. the *Metaphysics of Morals,* Ak. VI, 400–01, 437–40.]

way silence the prosecutor in him, if only he is conscious that at the time when he committed the wrong he was in his senses, i.e., had the use of his freedom. He nonetheless *explains* his offense to himself [as arising] from a certain bad habit brought upon himself by a gradual neglect of attentiveness to himself, [and he does so] to such a degree that he can regard the offense as a natural consequence of this habit, even though this still cannot secure him against the self-censure and the reprimand that he casts upon himself. This is also the basis of the repentance for a deed committed long ago, at every recollection of it. Repentance is a painful sensation[483] which is brought about by a moral attitude and which, to the extent that it cannot serve to undo what has been done, is empty practically. Repentance would even be absurd (indeed, *Priestley*,[484] as a genuine *fatalist* who proceeds consistently, declares it to be absurd, and for this candor he deserves more applause than those who, while asserting the will's mechanism in the deed[485] but its freedom by means of words, still want to be considered as including repentance too in their syncretistic system, though without making the possibility of such an imputation comprehensible), but as pain it is nonetheless entirely legitimate, because reason, when the law of our intelli-   99
gible existence (the moral law) is at issue, acknowledges no distinction of time and asks only whether the event belongs to me as a deed, but then always connects the same sensation with it morally, whether the deed[486] is being done now or was done long ago. For, the *life of sense* has in regard to the *intelligible* consciousness of one's existence (the consciousness of freedom) [the] absolute unity of a phenomenon that, insofar as it contains merely appearances of the attitude which is of concern to the moral law (appearances of character), must be judged not according to the natural necessity which belongs to it as appearance but according to the absolute spontaneity of freedom. Hence one can grant that if it were possible for us to have so deep an insight into a human being's way of thinking—as this manifests itself through internal as well as external actions—that we would

---

[483] [In the broad meaning of the term that includes feelings: *Empfindung*. See above, Ak. V, 22 br. n. 31.]

[484] [See Joseph Priestley (1733–1804), *The Doctrine of Philosophical Necessity Illustrated* (London: J. Johnson, 1777); contemporary edition: *Disquisitions Relating to Matter and Spirit and The Doctrine of Philosophical Necessity Illustrated* (New York: Garland, 1976).]

[485] [*Tat*. Cf. Kant's definition of this term as given above, Ak. V, 3 br. n. 11.]

[486] [*sie*, which, at this point in the sentence, I take to refer not to *Begebenheit* ('event') but to *Tat*.]

become acquainted with every incentive to actions, even with the slightest, and likewise with all external promptings[487] affecting these incentives, then we could calculate a human being's conduct for the future with certainty, just like any lunar or solar eclipse, and could nonetheless also[488] assert that the human being is free. For if we were capable also of another view (a view which, to be sure, has not been bestowed upon us at all, but in place of which we have only the rational concept), viz., an intellectual intuition[489] of the same subject, then we would nonetheless[490] become aware that this entire chain of appearances depends, with regard to whatever can be of concern to the moral law, on the spontaneity of the subject as a thing in itself—a spontaneity for the determination of which no physical explanation can be given at all. In the absence of this intuition, the moral law assures us of this distinction of the reference that our actions as appearances have to our subject's sensible being[491] from that [reference of our actions] whereby this sensible being is itself referred to the intelligible substrate in us. From this point of view, which is natural though inexplicable to our reason, one can justify even judgments[492] which, though made in all conscientiousness, yet seem at first glance to conflict thoroughly with all equity. There are cases where human beings, even with the same upbringing that was simultaneously profitable for others, nevertheless show from childhood such early villainy[493] and increase[494] it so continuously into their years of manhood that they are considered to be born villains and entirely incapable of improvement as far as their way of thinking is concerned; yet they are just as much tried[495] for their doing and refraining,[496] just as much reprimanded as guilty of their crimes, and indeed they (the children) themselves find these reprimands [just] as well-based, as [would be the case] if regardless of the

100

---

[487] [Veranlassungen.]

[488] [dabei.]

[489] [See above, Ak. V, 31 br. n. 77.]

[490] [I.e., in spite of what was granted in the preceding sentence.]

[491] [Sinnenwesen.]

[492] [Beurteilungen. See above, Ak. V, 8 br. n. 78.]

[493] [Bosheit; 'villains,' below, similarly translates Bösewichter.]

[494] [Reading, with Vorländer, steigern for steigen.]

[495] [Figuratively speaking: richten.]

[496] [Tuns und Lassens.]

hopeless natural constitution of their minds which is attributed to them they remained just as responsible as any other human being. This could not occur if we did not presuppose that whatever arises from one's power of choice (as every deliberately performed action undoubtedly does) has as its basis a free causality, which from early youth expresses its character in its appearances (the actions). These actions, because of the uniformity of conduct, make recognizable[497] a natural connection;[498] this connection, however, does not render the malicious[499] constitution of the will necessary, but is rather the consequence of the voluntarily[500] assumed and immutable evil principles, which only make the will all the more reprehensible and deserving of punishment.

However, freedom still faces a difficulty insofar as it is to be reconciled with the mechanism of nature in a being that belongs to the world of sense, a difficulty which, even after all the foregoing has been consented to, nonetheless threatens freedom with its utter demise. But, in this danger, one circumstance nonetheless also gives us hope for an outcome still favorable to affirming[501] freedom, namely that the same difficulty weighs much more heavily (indeed, as we shall soon see, weighs only) upon the system in which the existence determinable in time and space is considered to be the existence of things in themselves; that the difficulty therefore does not compel us to give up[502] our foremost presupposition of the ideality of time as a mere form of sensible intuition and thus as merely a way of presenting which is peculiar to the subject as belonging to the world of sense; and that the difficulty therefore requires only that we reconcile this presupposition with the idea of freedom.

For even if it is conceded to us that the intelligible subject can still be free with regard to a given action even though, as a subject who also belongs to the world of sense, he is mechanically conditioned with regard to this action, it nonetheless seems that as soon as one assumes that *God* as universal original being is *the cause* also *of the existence of substance* (a proposition that can never be given up without simultaneously also giving

---

[497] [*kenntlich.*]

[498] [*Naturzusammenhang.*]

[499] [*arg.*]

[500] [*freiwillig.*]

[501] [*behaupten.*]

[502] [Reading, with Hartenstein, *aufzugeben* for *abzugehen.*]

up the concept of God as the being of all beings and therewith his all-sufficiency, on which everything in theology hinges), one must then also concede that a human being's actions have their determining basis in *what is entirely beyond his*[503] *control,* viz., in the causality of a supreme being which is distinct from him and on which the human being's existence and the entire determination of his causality depends utterly.[504] Indeed, if a human being's actions, as far as they belong to his determinations in time, were determinations of him not merely as appearance but as a thing in itself, then freedom could not be rescued. A human being would be a puppet,[505] or a Vaucansonian automaton[506] built and wound up by the supreme master of all artificial devices;[507] and although self-consciousness would turn the automaton into a thinking one, yet the automaton's consciousness of its spontaneity, if regarded as freedom, would be mere delusion, because this spontaneity deserves to be called freedom only comparatively. For although the proximate determining causes of the automaton's motion—and a long series of these [determining] causes [extending] upward to their [own] determining causes—are internal, the last and highest one is still found entirely in a foreign[508] hand. Therefore I do not see how those who persist in regarding time and space as determinations belonging to the existence of things in themselves are to avoid here the fatalism of actions. Or, if (like the otherwise acute *Mendelssohn*)[509] they straightforwardly admit

101

---

[503] [Reading *seiner* for *ihrer* ('their'). Kant seems to have thought that he had said 'human beings.']

[504] [*ganz und gar.*]

[505] [*Marionette,* in the older and broader sense still in use in French. Cf. below, Ak. V, 147.]

[506] [Jacques de Vaucanson (1709–82), a French engineer from Grenoble, completed his sophisticated and celebrated life-size automaton flute-player in 1736 (or, according to some sources, in 1737); it was followed by even more ingenious automata, including a tambourine-player and a duck that could imitate eating, drinking, and quacking. These automata were first exhibited in Paris in 1738. Some materialists pointed to them to support their view that human beings are machines.]

[507] [*Kunstwerke.*]

[508] [*fremd.*]

[509] [Moses Mendelssohn, *Morgenstunden, oder Vorlesungen über das Dasein Gottes* (*Morning Hours, or Lectures on the Existence of God*) (Berlin: C. F. Voss & Sohn, 1785); recent edition: including the *Briefwechsel (Correspondence) Mendelssohn–Kant,* edited by Dominique Bourel (Stuttgart: Reclam, 1979); Section 11. In the controversy over the Spinozism (see below, Ak. V, 102 incl. br. n. 512) of the German writer and dramatist Gotthold Ephraim Lessing (1729–81), Mendelssohn defended Lessing against the German philosopher Friedrich

time and space to be conditions necessarily belonging only to the existence[510] of finite and derivative beings but not to that of the infinite original being, I do not see how they are to justify whence they get this authority for making such a distinction. I do not even see how they are to evade the contradiction that they perpetrate when they regard existence in time as a determination attaching necessarily to finite things in themselves, while God is the cause of this existence: for he still cannot be the cause of time (or of space) itself (because time must be presupposed as a necessary a priori condition of the existence of things), and consequently his causality in regard to the existence of these things must itself be conditioned in terms of time; and thus[511] all the contradictions against the concepts of his infinity and independence must unavoidably arise. For us, on the other hand, it is quite easy to make the distinction between the determination of divine existence as independent of all conditions of time and [the determination of] the existence of a being of the world of sense, viz., as that between the *existence of a being in itself* and that of a *thing in appearance.* Hence if that ideality of space and time is not assumed, solely *Spinozism*[512] remains, in which space and time are essential determinations of the original being itself, while the things dependent upon it (hence also we ourselves) are not substances but merely accidents inhering in it; for if these things exist merely as its effects *in time,* which would be the condition of their existence in themselves, then the actions of these beings would also have to be merely his actions performed by him[513] somewhere and sometime.[514] Hence Spinozism, despite

102

Heinrich Jacobi (1743–1819), who found Spinoza's rationalism repellent. Kant, in suggesting that Mendelssohn's view on space and time is less than acute, may be implying that Mendelssohn's failure to espouse transcendental idealism commits him to Spinozism.]

[510] [*Existenz* here, *Dasein* above and below; similarly in the remainder of this paragraph.]

[511] [*wobei.*]

[512] [The view of Baruch (Benedict) Spinoza (1632–77), rationalist philosopher of Portuguese extraction who lived as a refugee in Holland. His most important work is *Ethica ordine geometrico demonstrata* (*Ethics Demonstrated in Geometric Order*), part of the *Opera posthuma* (*Posthumous Works*) (Amsterdam: Rievwertsz, 1677); contemporary edition of the *Ethica*: edited by J. van Vloten and J. P. N. Land (The Hague: Nijhoff, 1914); English translation: *The Ethics; Treatise on the Emendation of the Intellect; Selected Letters,* 2nd ed., translated by Samuel Shirley, edited, with an introduction, by Seymour Feldman (Indianapolis, Ind.: Hackett, 1992).]

[513] [*er;* Kant has just switched from the neuter gender appropriate for *Urwesen* ('original being') to the masculine gender appropriate for *Gott* ('God').]

[514] [*irgendwo und irgendwann.*]

the absurdity of its basic idea, does [thereafter] infer far more cogently than can be done on the creation theory when the *beings* assumed to be substances and in themselves *existing in time* are regarded as effects of a supreme cause and yet not also as belonging to him and his action but as substances by themselves.

The difficulty mentioned above is resolved briefly and plausibly in the following manner. If existence *in time* is merely a sensible way of presenting on the part of thinking beings in the world and consequently does not pertain to them as things in themselves, then the creation of these beings is a creation of things in themselves, because the concept of creation does not belong to the sensible way of presenting existence and to causality but can be referred only to noumena. Consequently, if I say concerning beings in the world of sense that they are created, then I regard them to that extent as noumena. Just as it would thus be a contradiction to say that God is a creator of appearances, so it is also a contradiction to say that as creator he is the cause of the actions in the world of sense and hence [of these actions] as appearances, even though he is the cause of the existence of the acting beings (as noumena). If, now, it is possible (provided only that we assume existence in time to be something that holds merely of appearances, not of things in themselves) to affirm freedom without detriment to the natural mechanism of actions as appearances, then [the fact] that the acting beings are creatures cannot make the slightest change in this, because creation concerns their intelligible but not their sensible existence and therefore cannot be regarded as determining basis of appearances; but this would turn out quite differently if the beings of the world existed as things in themselves *in time,* since the creator of substance would then also be the originator of the entire machinery[515] in this substance.

103

Of such great importance is the separation—performed in the critique of pure speculative reason—of time (as well as space) from the existence of things in themselves.[516]

But, it will be said, the difficulty's solution that has been set forth here does have much difficult [material] in it and is hardly susceptible of a clear exhibition. However, is any other solution that has been attempted, or that may be attempted, indeed easier and more graspable? One might rather say that the dogmatic teachers of metaphysics have shown more shrewdness on their part than sincerity in moving this difficult point as far as possible out

---

[515] [Or 'mechanism': *Maschinenwesen.*]

[516] [Cf. the *Critique of Pure Reason,* A 22–49/B 37–73.]

of sight, in the hope that if they did not speak of it at all then presumably no one would readily think of it either. If a science is to be promoted, all difficulties must be *uncovered,* and those that may still lie hidden in its way must even be *sought out;* for, every difficulty calls forth a remedy that cannot be found without providing the science with an increase either in range or in determinateness, and thus even obstacles become means for furthering the thoroughness of the science. By contrast, if the difficulties are intentionally covered up, or removed merely through palliatives, then sooner or later they break out in incurable bad [consequences] that bring the science to ruin in a complete skepticism.

Since it is, properly, the concept of freedom which, among all the ideas of pure speculative reason, alone provides such great expansion in the realm of the suprasensible, even if only in regard to practical cognition, I ask myself *whence such great fruitfulness has been imparted to it exclusively,* whereas the other ideas can indeed designate the empty place for possible pure beings of the understanding, but cannot determine the concept of them by anything. I soon comprehend that, since I cannot think anything without a category, I must also first seek out the category in reason's idea of freedom, with which I am now dealing, and here this is the category of *causality;* and I comprehend that, even though one cannot base the *rational concept* of freedom, which is a transcendent concept, on any corresponding intuition, nonetheless a sensible intuition must first be given to the *concept of understanding* (that of causality)—for the synthesis of which the *rational concept* of freedom demands the unconditioned—and thereby objective reality is first secured to the concept. Now, all the categories are divided into two classes: the *mathematical,* which aim merely at the unity of synthesis in the presentation of objects, and the *dynamical,* which aim at the unity of synthesis in the presentation of the existence of objects.[517] The former categories (those of magnitude[518] and quality) always contain a synthesis of the *homogeneous,* and in this synthesis the unconditioned for the conditioned in space and time given in intuition cannot be found at all, since it itself would in turn have to belong to space and time and thus would in turn always have to be conditioned. Hence, by the same token, in the dialectic of pure theoretical reason the two opposed ways of finding the un-

104

---

[517] [Cf. ibid., B 110, A 160–62/B 199–202, A 523–32 = B 551–60.]

[518] [I.e., quantity: *Größe.*]

conditioned and the totality of conditions for it were both false.[519] The categories of the second class (those of causality and of the necessity of a thing) did not at all require this homogeneity (of the conditioned and the conditioned in the synthesis), because here the intuition was to be presented not as it is assembled[520] from a manifold in it, but only [insofar] as the existence of the conditioned object corresponding to it is added to the existence of the condition (added, as connected with this existence, in the understanding); and there it was permitted to posit, for the thoroughly[521] determined in the world of sense, the unconditioned—although otherwise undetermined—in the intelligible world (in regard to the causality as well as the contingent existence[522] of the things themselves) and to make the synthesis transcendent. Hence, by the same token, in the dialectic of pure speculative reason it was indeed found that the two seemingly opposed ways of finding the unconditioned for the conditioned—e.g., in the synthesis of causality, to think, for the conditioned in the series[523] of causes and effects in the world of sense, of the causality that is not further sensibly conditioned—do not in fact contradict each other; and that the same action which, as belonging to the world of sense, is always sensibly conditioned— i.e., mechanically necessary—can yet at the same time, as [belonging] to the causality of the acting being insofar as this being belongs to the intelligible world, also be based on a sensibly unconditioned causality and therefore be thought as free.[524] The only issue now was to convert this *can* into an *is,* i.e., to be able to prove in an actual case—through a fact,[525] as it were—that certain actions presuppose such a causality (the intellectual, sensibly unconditioned causality), whether these actions are actual or, for that matter, only commanded, i.e., objectively practically necessary. In actions actually given in experience, which are events in the world of sense, we could not hope to encounter this connection, because the causality through freedom must always be sought outside the world of sense in the

[519] [Cf. the *Critique of Pure Reason,* A 531–32 = B 559–60.]

[520] [*zusammengesetzt.*]

[521] [*durchgängig.*]

[522] [*Dasein* here, *Existenz* repeatedly earlier in this paragraph.]

[523] [Here again the term is singular: *Reihe.*]

[524] [Cf. the *Critique of Pure Reason,* A 444–51 = B 472–79, A 488/B 516, A 532–58 = B 560–86.]

[525] [On the fact of reason, see above, Ak. V, 31 incl. br. n. 75.]

intelligible. However, other things apart from beings of sense are not given to us for perception and observation. Hence nothing remained but that there might be found an incontestable and, moreover, objective principle of causality that excludes from its determination any sensible condition, i.e., a principle in which reason does not further appeal to anything *else* as determining basis regarding causality but rather itself already contains this determining basis through that principle, and where it is therefore itself practical as *pure reason*. This principle, however, does not need to be searched for or invented; it has all along been in the reason of all human beings and incorporated in their essence,[526] and is the principle of *morality*. Therefore that unconditioned causality as well as [our] power thereof, freedom, and with it a being (I myself) that belongs to the world of sense, has not merely indeterminately and problematically been *thought* as nonetheless also belonging to the intelligible world (this even speculative reason was able to ascertain as feasible), but has *with regard to the law* of its causality even been *determinately* and assertorically *cognized* as also belonging to that world;[527] and thus the actuality of the intelligible world has been given to us, and given to us *determinately* in a practical respect,[528] and this determination, which for a theoretical aim would be *transcendent* (extravagant),[529] is for a practical aim *immanent*. Such a step, however, we were unable to take with regard to the second dynamical idea, viz., that of a *necessary being*.[530] We were unable, without the mediation of the first dynamical idea,[531] to ascend to it from the world of sense. For, had we wanted to attempt this, we would have had to venture a leap: we would have had to leave all that is given to us and soar to that of which again nothing is given to us whereby we could mediate the connection of such an intelligible being with the world of sense (because the necessary being was to be cognized as

---

[526] [Or 'in their being': *in ihrem Wesen*. This could also mean 'in its [i.e., reason's] essence,' in line with Kant's earlier statement (above, Ak. V, 32) that " . . . this principle of morality does not restrict itself to human beings only but applies to all finite beings having reason and will, ..." The present context, however, does suggest the reading adopted here.]

[527] [Cf. the *Grounding for the Metaphysics of Morals*, Ak. IV, 450–63.]

[528] [*Rücksicht.*]

[529] [*überschwenglich.*]

[530] [Cf. the *Critique of Pure Reason*, A 452–61 = B 480–89, A 488/B 516, A 559–65 = B 587–93.]

[531] [The idea of freedom.]

given *outside us*). By contrast, this [sort of mediation] is entirely possible, as is now obvious, with regard to *our own* subject insofar as *on the one hand* this subject through the moral law (by virtue of freedom) determines [and thus cognizes] himself as an intelligible being and *on the other hand* he cognizes himself as active in accordance with this determination in the world of sense. Solely the concept of freedom permits us to find the unconditioned and intelligible for the conditioned and sensible without needing to go outside ourselves. For it is our reason itself which cognizes itself through the supreme and unconditioned practical law and cognizes the being—the being which is conscious of this law (our own person)—as belonging to the pure world of understanding, and in so doing even determines the way in which, as such, this being can be active. Thus one can comprehend why in the entire power of reason it can be *only the practical* that helps us [proceed] beyond the world of sense and that provides us with cognitions of a suprasensible order and connection—cognitions, however, which precisely therefore can indeed only be extended just as far as is necessary for our pure practical aim.

106

 Permit me to take this opportunity to call attention to just one more thing, namely, that every step which one takes with pure reason, even in the practical realm, where subtle speculation is not taken into account at all, nonetheless meshes with all the moments[532] of the critique of theoretical reason so precisely, and indeed on its own, as if each step had been thought out with deliberate foresight merely in order to provide theoretical reason with confirmation. Such a precise concurrence—in no way sought but turning up on its own (as anyone can convince himself on his own if only he will pursue moral investigations up to their principles)—of the most important propositions of practical reason with the comments of the critique of speculative reason, which often seemed too subtle and unnecessary, occasions surprise and amazement and reinforces the maxim already cognized and praised by others, that in every scientific investigation one should with all possible exactness and frankness pursue one's course undisturbed, without being concerned about what the investigation might perhaps offend against outside its realm, carrying it out by itself truly and completely as much as one can. Repeated observation has convinced me that when this [kind of] business has been brought to an end, what halfway through it seemed to me at times very precarious in view of extraneous other doctrines

---

[532] [I.e., key elements: *Momente.*]

was, in the end, in an unexpected way perfectly harmonious with what, without the slightest regard for those doctrines and without any partiality and predilection for them, had turned up on its own—provided only that I left this precariousness out of sight and attended merely to my business until it was completed. Writers would save themselves many errors and much wasted effort (because it was aimed at illusion), if only they could resolve to go to work with somewhat more frankness.

107

BOOK II

DIALECTIC OF PURE PRACTICAL REASON

Chapter I
On a Dialectic of Pure Practical Reason as Such[1]

Pure reason, whether considered in its speculative or in its practical use, always has its dialectic;[2] for it demands the absolute totality of conditions for a given conditioned, and this totality absolutely[3] cannot be found except in things in themselves. However, all concepts of things must be referred to intuitions, which for us human beings can never be other than sensible[4] and which therefore allow us to cognize objects not as things in themselves but merely as appearances; and in the appearances' series[5] of the conditioned and the conditions [thereof] the unconditioned can never be found. Thus an unavoidable illusion[6] arises from the application of this rational idea of the totality of conditions (and hence rational idea of the unconditioned) to appearances as if they were things in themselves (for in the absence of a warning critique they are always considered to be that). But this illusion would never be noticed as deceptive if it did not betray itself on its own through a *conflict* that reason has with itself in applying to appear-

---

[1] [Or 'in general': *überhaupt.* See above, Ak. V, 3 br. n. 3.]

[2] [See the *Critique of Pure Reason,* A 293–341/B 349–99.]

[3] [Or 'simply': *schlechterdings.* Cf. above, Ak. V, 3 br. n. 2. Above, 'absolute' translates *absolut.*]

[4] [I.e., they cannot be intellectual and thus pertain to things in themselves. Cf. above, Ak. V, 45 incl. br. n. 187 and 31 br. n. 77.]

[5] [Here again the term is singular: *Reihe.*]

[6] [*Schein.*]

ances its principle of presupposing the unconditioned for everything conditioned. Through this [conflict], however, reason is compelled to explore this illusion—from what it arises and how it can be removed—and this cannot be done except through a complete critique of the entire pure power[7] of reason. Thus the antinomy of pure reason,[8] which becomes manifest in pure reason's dialectic, is in fact the most beneficial straying into which human reason could ever have fallen, because it ultimately impels us to seek the key to get out of this labyrinth—the key which, when found, also uncovers what one did not seek and yet requires, namely an outlook into a higher, unchangeable order of things; we already are in this order of things now, and from now on we can be instructed by determinate precepts to pursue[9] our

108   existence in it in conformity with the highest vocation[10] of reason.

How that natural dialectic is to be resolved and the error arising from an otherwise natural illusion is to be prevented in the speculative use of pure reason can be found in detail in the *Critique* of that power.[11] But reason in its practical use fares not a whit better. As pure practical reason it seeks for the practically conditioned (which rests on inclinations and natural need) likewise the unconditioned; moreover, it does not seek this unconditioned as determining basis of the will, but, even when this determining basis has been given (in the moral law), it seeks the unconditioned totality of the *object* of pure practical reason, under the name of the **highest good.**[12]

To determine this idea practically—i.e., sufficiently for the maxim of our rational conduct—is [the task of] the *doctrine of wisdom,*[13] and this in turn as *science* is *philosophy* in the meaning in which the word was understood by the ancients, for whom philosophy was an instruction [directed] to the concept wherein the highest good is to be posited and to the conduct whereby this good is to be acquired. We would do well to leave this word in its ancient meaning, as [signifying] a *doctrine of the highest good* insofar as reason endeavors therein to attain to *science.* For, on the one hand, the attached restricting condition would be appropriate to the Greek expression

---

[7] [-*vermögen.* See above, Ak. V, 3 br. n. 7.]

[8] [See the *Critique of Pure Reason,* A 405–567/B 432–595.]

[9] [Or 'continue': *fortsetzen.*]

[10] [-*bestimmung.*]

[11] [See the *Critique of Pure Reason,* A 293–704/B 349–732, esp. A 669–704/B 697–732.]

[12] [See above, Ak. V, 57–67.]

[13] [*Weisheitslehre.*]

(which means love of *wisdom*)[14] while yet at the same time sufficing to comprise under the name of philosophy also the love of *science* and thus of all of reason's speculative cognition insofar as it is useful to reason for that concept[15] as well as for the practical determining basis,[16] and would nonetheless keep us from losing sight of the main purpose on account of which alone it can be called doctrine of wisdom. On the other hand, it would also not be bad if, to deter the self-conceit of someone who ventured to lay claim to the title of philosopher, one held before him, through the very definition, the standard of self-estimation that would very much tone down his pretensions. For to be a *teacher of wisdom*[17] would surely mean something more than [to be] a pupil, who still has not got far enough to guide himself, and still less to guide others, with secure expectation of so high a purpose; it would mean a *master in acquaintance with wisdom,*[18] which says more than a modest man will himself claim. Philosophy would, like wisdom itself, still remain an ideal, which objectively is presented completely in reason alone, but subjectively, for the person, is only the goal of his unceasing endeavor; and no one would be entitled to profess to be in possession of it, under the claimed name of philosopher, unless he could also adduce its unfailing effects in his own person as an example (in self-control and the indubitable interest that he preeminently takes in the general good), which the ancients also demanded in order that [someone] could deserve that name of honor.

109

Just one further preliminary reminder is needed regarding pure practical reason's dialectic in point of the determination of the concept *of the highest good* (a dialectic which, if its resolution is successful, allows us to expect—like that of theoretical reason—the most beneficial effect, because the sincerely performed and unconcealed contradictions of pure practical reason with itself compel us to undertake a complete critique of that reason's own ability[19]).

---

[14] [I.e., reason's attempt to proceed scientifically is appropriate to philosophy as a *doctrine of the highest good.*]

[15] [The concept wherein the highest good is to be posited.]

[16] [Of the will.]

[17] [Or, 'doctor of wisdom,' in the original sense of 'doctor,' which goes with 'doctrine': *Weisheitslehrer.*]

[18] [*Meister in Kenntnis der Weisheit.*]

[19] [Or 'power': *Vermögen.*]

The moral law is the sole determining basis of the pure will. However, this law is merely formal (viz., it demands only the form of the maxim to be universally legislative), and thus as determining basis it abstracts from all matter and hence from any object of volition.[20] Hence although the highest good may indeed be the entire *object* of a pure practical reason, i.e., of a pure will, yet it is not on that account to be considered the *determining basis* of that will, and the moral law alone must be regarded as the basis for making the highest good and the effectuation or furtherance thereof one's object. This reminder, in so delicate a case as the determination of moral principles, where even the slightest misinterpretation corrupts attitudes, is of significance. For it will have been seen from the Analytic that if we [were to] assume, prior to the moral law, any object—under the name of a good— as determining basis of the will and then [to] derive the supreme practical principle from it, this would always bring about heteronomy and displace the moral principle.[21]

It goes without saying, however, that if in the concept of the highest good the moral law as supreme condition is already likewise included,[22] then not only is the highest good [the] *object* of the pure will, but the concept of this good and the presentation of its existence as possible through our practical reason are also at the same time the *determining basis* of the pure will; for then it is in fact the moral law, already included and likewise thought in this concept, and not any other object, which determines the will in accordance with the principle of autonomy. This order of concepts of the determination of the will must not be lost sight of; for otherwise we misunderstand ourselves and believe that we contradict ourselves even though everything stands side by side in the most perfect harmony.

110

---

[20] [See above, Ak. V, 19–57.]

[21] [Cf. the *Grounding for the Metaphysics of Morals,* Ak. IV, 396, 399, 444–58.]

[22] [*mit eingeschlossen.* Below, 'likewise thought' similarly translates *mitgedacht.*]

Chapter II
On a Dialectic of Pure Reason in Determining the Concept of the Highest Good

The concept of the *highest* already contains an ambiguity that, if one pays no attention to it, can occasion needless controversies. The highest can mean either the supreme[23] (*supremum*) or the complete[24] (*consummatum*).[25] The first is that condition which is itself unconditioned, i.e., not subordinate to any other condition (*originarium*);[26] the second is that whole which is not a part of a still greater whole of the same kind (*perfectissimum*).[27] [The fact] that virtue (as the worthiness to be happy) is the *supreme condition* of whatever may seem to us desirable, and hence also of all our pursuit of happiness, and that it is therefore the *supreme* good has been proved in the Analytic. But virtue is not yet, on that account, the whole and complete good as the object of the power of desire of rational finite beings. For, in order to be that, *happiness* too is required in addition [to virtue], and this not merely in the partial eyes of a person who makes himself a purpose[28] but even in the judgment of an impartial reason, which regards a person as such in the world as a purpose in itself. For, to be in need of happiness, and also worthy of it, but nonetheless not to partake of it is not at all consistent with[29] the perfect[30] volition of a rational being that also had all power,[31] even if we only think such a being by way of experiment. Now, inasmuch as virtue and happiness together amount to possession of the

23 [*das Oberste.*]

24 [*das Vollendete,* which can also mean 'the perfect' (cf. the etymology of 'perfect').]

25 ['The consummate.']

26 ['The original.']

27 ['The most perfect.']

28 [Or 'end': *Zweck.* See above, Ak. V, 35 br. n. 121.]

29 [Literally, 'cannot coexist with': *kann mit . . . nicht zusammen bestehen.* Cf. above, Ak. V, 97 incl. br. n. 475.]

30 [*vollkommen.*]

31 [*Gewalt.*]

highest good in a person, and thereby happiness distributed [to persons] quite exactly in proportion to [their] morality (as a person's worth and his worthiness to be happy) amounts also to the *highest good* of a possible world, the highest good means the whole, [i.e., it means] the complete good.[32] In this complete good, however, virtue as the condition is always the supreme good, because it has no further condition above it, whereas happiness is something that, although always agreeable to him who possesses it, is not by itself alone good absolutely and in every respect but always presupposes morally lawful conduct as [its] condition.[33]

Two determinations *necessarily* linked[34] in one concept must be connected as basis[35] and consequence, and so connected, moreover, that this *unity* is regarded either as *analytic* (logical connection) or as *synthetic* (real connection), the former according to the law of identity, the latter according to the law of causality. Therefore the connection of virtue with happiness can either be understood in such a way that the endeavor to be virtuous and the rational pursuit of happiness would be not two different but [instead] entirely identical actions, in which case one would not have to base the former [action] on any other maxim than the latter; or this connection is posited in such a way that virtue produces happiness as something distinct from the consciousness of virtue, as a cause produces an effect.

Of the ancient Greek schools there were in fact only two that [dealt with this issue]. In determining the concept of the highest good, they did indeed follow one and the same method insofar as they did not accept[36] virtue and happiness as two different elements of the highest good, and hence sought the unity of principle according to the rule of identity; but they separated, in turn, inasmuch as between the two [elements] they selected the basic concept differently. The *Epicurean* said, to be conscious of one's maxim leading to happiness—that is virtue; the *Stoic,* to be conscious of one's virtue is happiness. To the former, *prudence* was tantamount to morality; to the latter, who selected a higher designation for virtue, *morality* alone was true wisdom.

---

[32] [Cf. the *Critique of Pure Reason,* A 812–14 = B 840–42.]

[33] [Cf. the *Metaphysics of Morals,* Ak. VI, 377–78.]

[34] [Or 'combined': *verbunden.*]

[35] [Or 'ground': *Grund.* See above, Ak. V, 49 incl. br. n. 196, cf. 4 br. n. 36.]

[36] [*gelten lassen.*]

One must regret that the acuteness of these men (whom one must yet at the same time admire for having in such early times already tried all conceivable paths of philosophical conquest) was applied infelicitously in excogitating identity between extremely heterogeneous concepts, that of happiness and that of virtue. However, it was commensurate with the spirit of their times—and sometimes misleads subtle minds even now—to annul essential and utterly irreconcilable[37] differences in principle by trying to convert them into a dispute about words, and thus seemingly to contrive unity of the concept merely under different designations; and this commonly applies to cases where the unification[38] of heterogeneous bases lies so deep or so high, or would require so complete a transformation of the doctrines otherwise assumed in the philosophical system, that people dread to enter deeply into the real difference and prefer to treat it as a disunity in mere formalities.

112

While the two schools tried to excogitate the sameness of the practical principles of virtue and happiness, they did not on that account agree with each other as to how they were to force out this identity; rather, they separated to an infinite distance from each other inasmuch as the one posited the principle thereof on the aesthetic[39] side and the other on the logical side, the former in the consciousness of sensible need, the other in the independence of practical reason from all sensible determining bases. According to the *Epicurean,* the concept of virtue already resided in the maxim [whereby one is] to further one's own happiness; according to the *Stoic,* on the other hand, the feeling of happiness was already contained in the consciousness of one's virtue. What is contained in another concept, however, is indeed the same as a part of the containing [concept] but not the same as the whole; moreover, two wholes can be different from each other in kind even though they consist of the same material, viz., if the parts in each are being combined into a whole in an entirely different manner. The Stoic asserted that virtue is the *whole highest good* and happiness is only the consciousness of the possession of this virtue as belonging to the subject's state. The Epicurean asserted that happiness is the *whole highest good* and virtue is only

[37] [Literally, 'never to be united': *nie zu vereinigende.*]

[38] [*Vereinigung.*]

[39] [I.e., sensible. See the *Critique of Pure Reason,* A xvii–xviii (also A 21n/B 35n and A 57/B 81); the *Critique of Judgment,* Ak. V, 188–89 (also 226); the First Introduction to that work, Ak. XX, 221–22 (also 226n); and cf. the *Metaphysics of Morals,* Ak. VI, 399–400 (also 471).]

the form of the maxim [whereby one is] to pursue this happiness, [consisting,] viz., in the rational use of means to it.

However, it is clear from the Analytic that the maxims of virtue and those of one's own happiness are entirely heterogeneous with regard to their supreme practical principle,[40] and that, far from being accordant, even though they belong to a highest good, they very much restrict and impair[41] each other in the same subject in order to make this good possible. Hence the question, *How is the highest good practically possible?* still remains an unsolved problem, despite all *attempts at coalition* made thus far. But what makes this problem difficult to solve is given in the Analytic: viz., that happiness and morality are two *elements* of the highest good which are entirely *different* in kind, and that therefore one cannot cognize their linkage[42] *analytically* (that, say, someone who seeks his happiness will in this [very] conduct of his find himself virtuous by merely resolving his concepts; or that someone who follows virtue will in the very consciousness of such conduct *ipso facto* find himself happy); rather, this linkage is a *synthesis* of concepts. But because this linkage is cognized as a priori and hence as practically necessary, and consequently not as derived from experience, and because this possibility of the highest good therefore does not rest on any empirical principles, the *deduction* of this concept will have to be *transcendental*. It is a priori (morally) necessary *to produce the highest good through freedom of the will;* therefore the condition for the possibility of this good must also rest solely on a priori bases of cognition.

113

I
THE ANTINOMY OF PRACTICAL REASON

In the highest good that is practical for us, i.e., to be made actual through our will, virtue and happiness are thought as necessarily linked, so that the one cannot be assumed by pure practical reason without the other's belonging to it also. Now, this linkage (like any linkage as such) is either *analytic* or *synthetic*. But since, as has just previously been shown, the given linkage cannot be analytic, it must be thought synthetically and, specifically, as a

---

[40] [See above, Ak. V, 34–41.]

[41] [*Abbruch tun.* See above, Ak. V, 25 br. n. 44.]

[42] [Or 'combination': *Verbindung.*]

connection of the cause with the effect, because it concerns a practical good, i.e., one that is possible through action. Therefore either the desire for happiness must be the motivating cause for maxims of virtue, or the maxim of virtue must be the efficient cause of happiness. The first is impossible *absolutely,* because (as has been proved in the Analytic) maxims that posit the determining basis of the will in the longing for happiness are not moral at all and cannot be the basis of any virtue. But the second is *impossible also,* because any practical connection of causes and effects in the world, as a result of the determination of the will, conforms not to moral attitudes of the will but to acquaintance[43] with the laws of nature and to the physical ability to use them for one's aims, and because consequently no necessary connection, sufficient for the highest good, of happiness with virtue in the world can be expected [to come about] through the most meticulous observance of moral laws. Now, since the furtherance of the highest good, the good which contains this connection in its concept, is an a priori necessary object of our will and is inseparably linked with the moral law, the impossibility of the highest good must also prove the falsity of the moral law. If, therefore, the highest good is impossible according to practical rules, then the moral law which commands us to further this good must also be fantastic and aimed at empty imaginary purposes, and hence in itself false.

114

II
CRITICAL ANNULMENT OF THE ANTINOMY
OF PRACTICAL REASON

In the antinomy of pure speculative reason we find a similar conflict between natural necessity and freedom in the causality of events in the world.[44] It was annulled by proving that the conflict is not a true one if the events and even the world in which they occur are regarded (as indeed they ought to be) only as appearances. For, one and the same acting being *as appearance* (even to his own inner sense) has a causality in the world of sense which always conforms to the mechanism of nature; but, with regard to the same event, insofar as the acting person regards himself simultaneously as *noumenon* (as pure intelligence, in his existence that is not determinable in

---

[43] [Or 'familiarity': *Kenntnis.* See above, Ak. V, 35 br. n. 120, and 4 br. n. 31.]

[44] [See the *Critique of Pure Reason,* A 444–51 = B 472–79.]

terms of time), he can contain a determining basis—of that causality according to natural laws—which is itself free from any natural law.[45]

Now, the same applies to the antinomy of pure practical reason, which is at issue here. The first of the two propositions, that the striving for happiness produces a basis for a virtuous attitude, is *false absolutely;* but the second, that a virtuous attitude necessarily produces happiness, is false *not absolutely* but only insofar as this attitude is regarded as the form of causality in the world of sense, and hence only if I assume the existence in that world to be the only kind of existence[46] of a rational being, and therefore is false only *conditionally.* However, since I not only am authorized to think my existence also as [that of a] noumenon in a world of understanding but even have in the moral law a purely intellectual determining basis of my causality (in the world of sense), it is not impossible that the morality of [one's] attitude should have a connection, and moreover a necessary one, as cause with happiness as effect in the world of sense, if not a direct connection then still an indirect one (by means of an intelligible originator of nature), a linkage which in a nature that is merely an object of the senses can never take place except contingently and cannot be sufficient for the highest good.

Hence despite this seeming conflict of a practical reason with itself, the highest good is the necessary highest purpose of a morally determined will—a true object of practical reason;[47] for, this good is practically possible, and the maxims of such a will, which refer to this good in terms of their matter, have objective reality.[48] At first this objective reality was affected by that antinomy in linking morality with happiness according to a universal law, but only through a misunderstanding, because the relation among appearances was regarded as a relation of things in themselves to these appearances.

When we find ourselves compelled[49] to seek the possibility of the highest good—which reason marks out for all rational beings as the goal of all their moral wishes—at such distance, namely in the connection with an intelligible world, it must seem strange that philosophers of ancient as well as modern times could nonetheless have found—or have persuaded them-

---

[45] [See ibid., A 532–58 = B 560–86.]

[46] [*Existenz* here, *Dasein* above and below.]

[47] [*derselben.* Cf. above, Ak. V, 57 and 108–09.]

[48] [Cf. the *Critique of Pure Reason,* A 806–14 = B 834–42.]

[49] [*nötigen.* See above, Ak. V, 20 br. n. 17.]

selves of being conscious of—happiness in very fitting proportion to virtue already *in this life* (in the world of sense). For, the happiness that arises from the consciousness of virtue in life was elevated above everything by *Epicurus* as well as the *Stoics;* and Epicurus was not so low-minded in his practical precepts as one might infer from the principles of his theory, which he used for explanation and not for action, or as the precepts were interpreted by many who were misled by [his use of] the expression lust[50] for satisfaction.[51] Rather, he included the least self-interested[52] performance of the good among the ways of savoring[53] the most intimate joy,[54] and whatever tempering and restraining of the inclinations may be demanded by the strictest moral philosopher belonged likewise to his scheme of gratification[55] (by which he meant a constantly cheerful heart);[56] in this he deviated from the Stoics primarily only in positing the motive in this gratification, which the Stoics refused [to do], and rightly so. For, on the one hand, the virtuous Epicurus—like many men even now who are morally well-meaning,[57] although they do not meditate deeply enough on their principles—committed the mistake of already presupposing the virtuous *attitude* in the persons for whom he wanted first of all to indicate the incentive to virtue (and in fact a righteous person cannot think himself happy if he is not first conscious of his righteousness; for, with that [virtuous] attitude, the reprimands—which his own way of thinking would compel him to cast upon himself in the case of transgressions—and the moral self-condemnation would rob him of all enjoyment of the agreeableness that his state might otherwise contain). However, the question is, through what does such an attitude and way of thinking in estimating the worth of one's existence become possible in the first place, since before it no feeling at all for a moral worth as such would be found yet in the subject? To be sure, if a human being is virtuous he will indeed not find joy in life unless in every

116

---

[50] [I.e., carnal pleasure (*Fleischlust*); see the *Metaphysics of Morals,* Ak. VI, 424, and cf. above, Ak. V, 30.]

[51] [*Zufriedenheit.*]

[52] [*uneigennützigste.*]

[53] [Or 'ways of enjoying': *Genußarten.*]

[54] [*Freude.*]

[55] [*Vergnügen.*]

[56] [Cf. the *Metaphysics of Morals,* Ak. VI, 485.

[57] [*wohlgesinnt.*]

action he is conscious of his righteousness, however much fortune may favor him in the physical state of life; but in order to make him virtuous in the first place, and hence even before he assesses the moral worth of his existence [as being] so high, can one then indeed extol to him the tranquility of soul that will arise from the consciousness of a righteousness for which, after all, he has [as yet] no mind?

But, on the other hand, here the basis for an error of subreption[58] (*vitium subreptionis*)[59] and, as it were, for an optical illusion always lies in the self-consciousness of what one *does,* as distinguished from what one *senses,*[60] an illusion that even the most tested person cannot completely avoid. The moral attitude is linked necessarily with a consciousness of the will's being determined *directly by the law.* Now, the consciousness of a determination of our power of desire is always the basis of a liking[61] for the action produced by this [determination]. But this pleasure, this liking in itself, is not the determining basis of the action; rather, the will's being determined directly, by reason alone, is the basis of the feeling of pleasure, and this determination remains a purely practical, not aesthetic,[62] determination of the power of desire.[63] Now, since this determination has inwardly precisely the same effect—that of an impulse to activity—which a feeling of agreeableness expected from the desired action would have had, we easily look upon what we ourselves do as something that we merely passively feel, and take the moral incentive for a sensible impulse, just as always happens in the so-called illusion[64] of the senses (here, of the inner sense). It is something very sublime in human nature to be determined to actions directly by a pure law of reason, and so is even the illusion of regarding the subjective [element] of this intellectual determinability of the will as something aesthetic and as an effect of a special sensible feeling (for an intellectual feeling would be a contradiction). It is also of great importance to call

117

---

[58] [*Fehler des Erschleichens.*]

[59] [Fallacy of subreption.]

[60] [In the broad meaning of the term that includes feeling.]

[61] [*Wohlgefallen.*]

[62] [I.e., sensible; cf. Ak. V, 112 incl. br. n. 39.]

[63] [Cf. the *Metaphysics of Morals,* Ak. VI, 212–13.]

[64] [*Täuschung,* which in most contexts—but not here (likewise below)—is best translated as 'delusion.']

attention to this property of our personality[65] and to cultivate as best we can the effect of reason on this feeling. But one must also be on guard against degrading and disfiguring the proper and genuine incentive, the law itself, through spurious laudations of this moral determining basis as incentive, by founding it on feelings of special joys as its bases (although they are only consequences)—by means of a false foil, as it were. Respect, and not the gratification and enjoyment of happiness, as[66] something for which no *antecedent* feeling laid at the basis of reason is possible (because such a feeling would always be aesthetic and pathological), and as consciousness of the direct necessitation[67] of the will by the[68] law, is hardly an analogue of the feeling of pleasure, although in relation to the power of desire it does exactly the same, but from different sources.[69] Only through this way of conceiving [respect], however, can one attain what one seeks, viz., that actions be done not merely in conformity with duty (as a consequence of agreeable feelings) but from duty, which must be the true purpose of all moral molding.

But do we not have a word that, without designating an enjoyment, as the word happiness does, indicates nonetheless a liking for one's existence, an analogue of the happiness that must necessarily accompany the consciousness of virtue? Yes! This word is *self-satisfaction,*[70] which in its proper meaning always implies only a negative liking for one's existence, a liking in which one is conscious of needing nothing. Freedom, and the consciousness of it as a power to comply with the moral law with an overweighing attitude, is *independence from inclinations*—independence from them at least as motivating causes determining (even if not as *affecting*) our desire—and insofar as I am conscious of this freedom in complying with my moral maxims, it is the sole source of an unchangeable satisfaction linked necessarily with it and resting on no special feeling, and this satisfaction can be called intellectual. Aesthetic[71] satisfaction (improperly so   118

---

[65] [I.e., personhood: *Persönlichkeit.*]

[66] [I follow Natorp's suggestion to read *als* for *ist also.*]

[67] [*Nötigung.* See above, Ak. V, 20 br. n. 17.]

[68] [Reading, with Vorländer, *durchs* for *durch.*]

[69] [Cf. the *Critique of Pure Reason,* A 812–15 = B 840–42.]

[70] [*Selbstzufriedenheit.*]

[71] [I.e., sensible; cf. Ak. V, 112 incl. br. n. 39.]

called[72]), which rests on gratifying the inclinations, however delicately these may be excogitated, can never be adequate to what one thinks concerning it. For, the inclinations vary, grow with the indulgence that one allows them, and always leave behind an even greater void than one had meant to fill. Hence to a rational being they are always *burdensome*, and even if the being cannot easily shed them, they nonetheless force from him[73] the wish to be rid of them. Even an inclination to what conforms to duty (e.g., to beneficence) can indeed greatly facilitate the effectiveness of *moral* maxims, but it cannot produce any. For in such a maxim everything must be aimed at the conception of the law as determining basis, if the action is to contain not merely *legality* but also *morality*. Inclination, whether it be good-natured[74] or not, is blind and servile; and reason, where morality is at issue, must not merely represent the guardian of inclination but must, without taking account of inclination and as pure practical reason, attend all by itself to its own interest. Even that feeling of sympathy[75] and softhearted compassion,[76] if it precedes deliberation as to what [one's] duty is[77] and becomes a determining basis, is itself burdensome to right-minded[78] persons, brings their deliberate maxims into confusion, and gives rise to the wish to be rid of them and subject solely to legislative[79] reason.

From this one can understand how the consciousness of this power of a pure practical reason through [the] deed[80] (virtue[81]) can produce a con-

---

[72] [I.e., improperly called 'satisfaction.']

[73] [See above, Ak. V, 19 br. n. 6.]

[74] [*gutartig.*]

[75] [*Mitleid.*]

[76] [*Teilnehmung.*]

[77] [See above, Ak. V, 8 n. 83 incl. n. 83f.]

[78] [*wohldenkend.*]

[79] [Or 'legislating': *gesetzgebend.*]

[80] [*durch Tat.* See above, Ak. V, 3 br. n. 11.]

[81] [*die Tugend.* Kant here seems to equate virtue with the *consciousness* that the power of a pure practical reason has through the deed. This is compatible with his characterization of virtue as one's morality, moral attitude, or moral state (above, Ak. V, 84). It is also compatible with the fact that Kant often—in particular, at the start of this very discussion of self-satisfaction at Ak. V, 117—speaks of the consciousness *of virtue,* provided that we then construe the 'of' as a *limiting* genitive (see above, Ak. V, 33 br. n. 94). It is true that Kant sometimes calls virtue a *power* (*Vermögen*)—see, e.g., above, Ak. V, 33, and cf. the *Metaphysics of Morals,*

sciousness of supremacy over one's inclinations, and hence also from the dissatisfaction that always accompanies them, and therefore can produce a negative liking for one's state, i.e., *satisfaction,* which in its source is satisfaction with one's person. Freedom itself becomes in this way (viz., indirectly) capable of an enjoyment. This enjoyment cannot be called happiness, because it does not depend on the positive participation[82] of a feeling; nor, strictly speaking, *bliss,* because it does not contain complete independence from inclinations and needs. But it is still similar to bliss, viz., insofar as one's determination of the will can at least keep itself free from the influence of inclinations and needs and this enjoyment is thus analogous, at least in its origin, to the self-sufficiency that can be ascribed only to the supreme being.

From this resolution of the antinomy of practical pure reason it follows that in practical principles one can at least think as possible (although, to be sure, not yet therefore cognize and have insight into) a natural and necessary linkage between the consciousness of morality and, as a consequence of this morality, the expectation of a happiness proportionate to it; that, on the other hand, principles of the pursuit of happiness cannot possibly produce morality; and that, therefore, the *supreme* good (as the primary condition of the highest good) consists in morality, whereas happiness amounts indeed to the second element of the highest good, but in such a way that it is only the morally conditioned but yet necessary consequence of morality. Only in this subordination is the *highest good* the entire object of pure practical reason, which must necessarily present this good as possible, because to contribute everything possible to its production is a command of this reason.[83] However, the possibility of such a linkage of the conditioned with its condition belongs entirely to the suprasensible relation of things and cannot be given at all according to the laws of the world of sense, although the practical consequence of this idea, viz., the actions that aim at making the highest good actual, do belong to the world of sense. We shall, therefore,

119

Ak. VI, 394; but if he were doing so in the present context, he would say not *die Tugend* but *der Tugend,* to match the genitive in *dieses Vermögens.* Finally, Kant is surely *not* equating virtue with the *deed;* for not only would he then presumably say *durch Tugend,* but equating these two would create serious conflicts with many other contexts in this work and, especially, in the *Metaphysics of Morals.*]

[82] [*Beitritt.*]

[83] [Cf. the *Critique of Pure Reason,* A 806–14 = B 834–42.]

seek to exhibit the bases of that possibility, first[84] with regard to what is directly under our control,[85] and then, second,[86] in that which reason (necessarily, according to practical principles) offers us, to compensate[87] for our inability, for the possibility of the highest good and which is not under our control.

III
ON THE PRIMACY OF PURE PRACTICAL REASON
IN ITS LINKAGE WITH SPECULATIVE REASON[88]

By primacy among two or more things linked by reason I mean the preeminence of one thing [insofar as] it is the first determining basis of the linkage with all the rest. In a narrower, practical signification it signifies the preeminence of the interest of one thing insofar as to this [interest] (which cannot be put second[89] to any others) the interest of the others is subordinate. To every power of the mind[90] one can attribute an *interest,* i.e., a principle that contains the condition under which alone the power's exercise is furthered.[91] Reason, as the power of principles, determines the interest of all the mental powers,[92] but its own interest it determines for itself. The interest of its speculative use consists in the *cognition* of the object up to the highest a priori principles; that of its practical use, in the determination of the *will* with regard to the ultimate and complete purpose.[93] What is required

120

---

[84] [See below, Ak. V, 122–23.]

[85] [Or 'directly in our power': *unmittelbar in unserer Gewalt.*]

[86] [See below, Ak. V, 124–31.]

[87] [*als Ergänzung.*]

[88] [See above, Ak. V, 55–57; also below, Ak. V, 134–36.]

[89] [*nach-.*]

[90] [*Vermögen des Gemüts.* On *Vermögen,* see above, Ak. V, 3 br. n. 7.]

[91] [See above, Ak. V, 79–81; cf. also the *Grounding for the Metaphysics of Morals,* Ak. IV, 413n, 432, 448–50, 460n.]

[92] [*Gemütskräfte. Kraft,* in the sense applicable here, is synonymous with *Vermögen.*]

[93] [*des letzten und vollständigen Zwecks;* cf. below, Ak. V, 130. Above, at Ak. V, 115, Kant called it the *highest* purpose (*höchster Zweck*); below, at Ak. V, 129, he calls it the *final* purpose (*Endzweck*). In the *Critique of Judgment* (1790), where he calls it the *final* purpose, he *distinguishes* between this and the ultimate purpose, there characterized as the last *natural*

for the possibility of a use of reason as such,[94] viz., that its principles and assertions must not contradict one another, does not amount to a part of its interest but is the condition of having reason at all;[95] only reason's expansion, not its mere agreement with itself, is classed with its interest.

If practical reason may assume and think as given nothing further than what *speculative* reason by itself has been able to offer it from its [own] insight, then the latter has primacy. But supposing that practical reason on its own had original a priori principles with which certain theoretical positions were inseparably linked but which nonetheless eluded all possible insight of speculative reason (although they also must not contradict that insight), then the question is which interest is supreme (not which interest must yield, for one does not necessarily conflict with the other). [I.e., the question then is] whether speculative reason, which knows nothing of all that which practical reason offers to it [as something] to assume, must admit[96] these propositions and, although they are extravagant[97] for it, seek to reconcile[98] them with its concepts, as a foreign possession transferred to it; or whether speculative reason is entitled to follow obstinately its own separate interest and, in accordance with the canon of *Epicurus,* reject as empty subtle reasoning[99] everything that cannot authenticate its objective reality by obvious examples to be adduced in experience, however much it were interwoven with the interest of the practical (pure) use of reason, and were also not in itself contradictory to theoretical reason, merely because it actually impairs the interest of speculative[100] reason insofar as it annuls the bounds that the latter has set itself and surrenders it to every nonsense or madness[101] of the imagination.

---

member in the chain of purposes leading to the final purpose, which itself lies beyond nature; see Ak. V, 425–45. On my rendering of *Zweck* as 'purpose' rather than as 'end,' see above, Ak. V, 35 br. n. 121.]

[94] [Or 'in general': *überhaupt.* See above, Ak. V, 3 br. n. 3.]

[95] [*überhaupt.*]

[96] [*aufnehmen.*]

[97] [I.e., transcendent: *überschwenglich.*]

[98] [*vereinigen.* Cf. above, Ak. V, 6 n. 64 incl. br. n. 64a.]

[99] [*leere Vernünftelei.*]

[100] [On theoretical and speculative reason, see above, Ak. V, 3 br. n. 4.]

[101] [*Unsinn oder Wahnsinn.*]

In fact, in case practical reason were presupposed as pathologically conditioned, i.e., as merely administering the interest of the inclinations under
the sensible principle of happiness, this demand[102] could not be made on
speculative reason at all. *Mohammed's* paradise or the *theosophists'* and
mystics' fusion[103] with the deity, each [thinker] after his own mind, would
thrust their monstrosities upon reason, and it would be just as well to have
no reason at all as to surrender it in this way to all sorts of dreams.[104] But if
pure reason by itself can be practical and actually is, as is evinced by the
consciousness of the moral law, it is yet always only one and the same reason which, whether for a theoretical or a practical aim, judges according to
a priori principles. Thus it is clear that, even if for a theoretical aim reason's
ability is not sufficient to establish certain propositions affirmatively, while
indeed they also do not contradict reason, as soon as these same propositions belong *inseparably to the practical interest* of pure reason, it must
assume them—although as a foreign offering not grown on its soil but yet
sufficiently authenticated—and seek to compare and connect them with
everything that it has within its power[105] as speculative reason. It must be
content, however, that these are not its insights but are yet expansions of its
use for some other, namely a practical, aim—this being not at all contrary to
its interest, which consists in the restriction of speculative outrage.

Thus in the linkage of pure speculative with pure practical reason for a
cognition the latter has *primacy*—supposing, i.e., that this linkage is by no
means *contingent* and discretionary[106] but based a priori on reason itself
and hence *necessary*. For without this subordination a conflict of reason
with itself would arise, because if pure speculative and pure practical reason were merely adjoined (coordinate),[107] the former would by itself tightly
close up its boundary and admit nothing from the latter into its domain,
while pure practical reason would nonetheless extend its boundaries over
everything and, where its need requires, would seek to encompass pure
speculative reason too within them. But one cannot at all require pure practical reason to be subordinate to speculative reason and thus reverse the

---

[102] [To adopt the mentioned propositions and seek to reconcile them with its own concepts.]

[103] [Literally, 'melting union': *schmelzende Vereinigung*.]

[104] [*allen Träumereien*.]

[105] [*Macht*.]

[106] [Or 'optional': *beliebig*.]

[107] [*beigeordnet (koordiniert)*.]

121

order, because all interest is ultimately practical and even the interest of speculative reason is only conditional and is complete in practical use alone.

IV
THE IMMORTALITY OF THE SOUL,
AS A POSTULATE OF PURE PRACTICAL REASON

122

To bring about the highest good in the world is the necessary object of a will determinable by the moral law. In such a will, however, the *complete adequacy*[108] of attitudes to the moral law is the supreme condition of the highest good. This adequacy must therefore be just as possible as its object, because it is contained in the same command to further this object. Complete adequacy of the will to the moral law, however, is *holiness,*[109] a perfection of which no rational being in the world of sense is capable at any point of time in his existence.[110] Since this adequacy is nonetheless demanded as practically necessary, it can be encountered only in a progression[111] proceeding *ad infinitum* toward that complete adequacy; and according to principles of pure practical reason it is necessary to assume such a practical advance[112] as the real object of our will.

This infinite progression, however, is possible only on the presupposition of an *existence*[113] and personality—of the same rational being—continuing *ad infinitum* (which is called the immortality of the soul).[114] Therefore the highest good is practically possible only on the presupposition of the immortality of the soul, and hence this immortality, as linked inseparably with the moral law, is a **postulate** of pure practical reason (by which I mean a *theoretical* proposition, though one not provable as such,[115] insofar as it attaches inseparably to a *practical* law that holds a priori [and] unconditionally).

---

[108] [Or 'commensurateness': *Angemessenheit.*]

[109] [Cf. the *Grounding for the Metaphysics of Morals,* Ak. IV, 414.]

[110] [*Dasein.*]

[111] [*Progressus.*]

[112] [*Fortschreitung.*]

[113] [*Existenz.*]

[114] [Cf. the *Critique of Pure Reason,* A 810–11 = B 838–39.]

[115] [Cf. ibid., B 429–32, A 682–84 = B 710–12; also the *Prolegomena,* Ak. IV, 333–37.]

The proposition concerning the moral vocation of our nature, that we can reach complete adequacy to the moral law[116] solely in an advance proceeding *ad infinitum,* is of the greatest benefit, not merely on account of the present compensation for the inability of speculative reason, but also with regard to religion.[117] In the absence of it, one either degrades the moral law completely from its *holiness* by misconstruing[118] it to oneself as *forbearing* (indulgent) and thus adequate[119] to our comfortableness, or else one stretches one's calling as well as expectation to an unattainable vocation, viz., a hoped-for complete acquisition of holiness of will, and loses oneself in roving theosophical dreams that quite contradict self-cognition—both of which [consequences] only prevent the unceasing *striving* toward meticulous and thoroughgoing compliance with a strict and unforbearing but nonetheless true rather than ideal command of reason. For a rational but finite being only the progression *ad infinitum* from lower to the higher levels of moral perfection is possible. The *infinite one,*[120] to whom the time condition is nothing, sees in this series—which for us is endless—the whole of adequacy to the moral law; and the holiness, which his command unremittingly demands in order [for one] to conform to his justice in the share that he determines for each in the highest good, is to be found whole in a single intellectual intuition[121] of the existence of rational beings. All that can belong to a creature with regard to hope for this share would be the consciousness of his tested attitude, so that, on the basis of the progress that he has thus far made from the worse to the morally better, and of the immutable resolve which has thereby become familiar[122] to him, he [may] hope for a further uninterrupted continuation[123] of this progress, however far his existence[124] may extend, even beyond this life;[125] and thus he can

123

---

[116] [*Sittengesetz* here, *moralisches Gesetz* repeatedly above.]

[117] [Cf. the *Metaphysics of Morals,* Ak. VI, 486–91.]

[118] [*verkünsteln.*]

[119] [Or 'commensurate': *angemessen.*]

[120] [I.e., the infinite being: *der Unendliche.*]

[121] [See above, Ak. V, 31 br. n. 77.]

[122] [*bekannt.* See above, Ak. V, 35 br. n. 120.]

[123] [*Fortsetzung.*]

[124] [*Existenz* here, *Dasein* above and below.]

[125] *Conviction* of the immutability of his attitude in the progress toward the good seems, nonetheless, to be impossible for a creature [to attain] on its own. Because of

never hope to be fully adequate[126] to God's will (without forbearance or re-mission, which do not agree with justice) either here or at any foreseeable future point of time in his existence, but can hope to be so only in the infin-ity of his continuance[127] (which God alone can survey).

124

V
THE EXISTENCE OF GOD,
AS A POSTULATE OF PURE PRACTICAL REASON

The moral law led, in the preceding dissection, to a practical problem[128] prescribed by pure reason alone, without any participation[129] of sensible in-centives, viz., that of [bringing about] the necessary completeness of the first and foremost part of the highest good, **morality;** and since this prob-lem can be solved fully only in an eternity, it led to the postulate of *immor-*

---

this, moreoever, the Christian religious doctrine allows it to stem solely from the same spirit that brings about sanctification,[a] i.e., brings about this firm resolve and with it the consciousness of perseverance[b] in moral progress. But by nature, too, someone who is conscious of having for a long part of his life until its end persisted in progress for the better, and this moreover from genuine moral motives, may[c] in-deed have the comforting hope, although not the certainty, that he will persevere in these principles even in an existence continued beyond this life; and although in his own eyes he is never justified here—nor, [even] in view of the hoped-for future in-crease of his natural perfection but therewith also [the increase] of his duties, may ever hope for this [justification]—nonetheless in this progress which, while con-cerning a goal moved outward *ad infinitum,* yet counts for God as possession, he may have an outlook into a *blessed* future. For, this is the term that reason employs to designate a complete *well-being* independent of all contingent causes in the world, a well-being that, like *holiness,* is an idea that can be contained only in an in-finite progression and its totality and hence is never fully attained by the creature.

ᵃ [*Heiligung.*]
ᵇ [*Beharrlichkeit.*]
ᶜ [*dürfen.*]

126 [*adäquat.*]

127 [*Fortdauer.*]

128 [Or 'task': *Aufgabe;* likewise below and in the next paragraph. The adopted rendering agrees better with 'can be solved,' below (and cf. Ak. V, 112), and with most of Kant's uses of *Aufgabe.* See above, Ak. V, 5 and esp. 25 (cf. 126 below), where Kant even uses *Aufgabe* in-terchangeably with *Problem.*]

129 [*Beitritt.*]

tality. The same law must also lead to the possibility of the second element of the highest good, viz., to the **happiness** commensurate to that morality, and must do so with just as little self-interest[130] as before, solely from impartial reason. In other words, it must lead to the presupposition of the existence[131] of a cause adequate to this effect; i.e., it must postulate the *existence of God,* as belonging necessarily to the possibility of the highest good (the object of our will which is linked necessarily with the moral legislation of pure reason).[132] We shall exhibit this connection[133] convincingly.

Happiness is the state of a rational being in the world for whom in the whole of his existence *everything proceeds according to his wish and will;* it therefore rests on the harmony[134] of nature with his whole purpose[135] as well as with the essential determining basis of his will. Now, the moral law as a law of freedom commands through determining bases that are to[136] be wholly independent of nature and of its harmony with our power of desire (as incentives); but the acting rational being in the world is, after all, not also the cause of the world and of nature itself. Hence there is in the moral law not the slightest basis for a necessary connection between morality and the happiness, proportionate thereto, of a being belonging to the world as a part [thereof] and thus dependent on it, who precisely therefore cannot through his will be the cause of this nature and, as far as his happiness is concerned, cannot by his own powers make it harmonize[137] throughout with his practical principles. Nonetheless, in the practical problem[138] of pure reason, i.e., [that of] working necessarily for the highest good, such a connection is postulated as necessary: we *ought*[139] to seek to further the highest good (hence this good must, after all, be possible). Therefore the existence of a cause of nature as a whole, distinct from nature, which con-

125

---

130 [*ebenso uneigennützig.*]

131 [*Dasein* here and (twice) in the next paragraph; *Existenz* in the heading above, and below.]

132 [Cf. the *Critique of Pure Reason,* A 809–14 = B 837–42.]

133 [*Zusammenhang;* likewise in the next paragraph.]

134 [*Übereinstimmung.*]

135 [*Zweck.* See above, Ak. V, 35 br. n. 121.]

136 [Or 'ought to': *sollen.*]

137 [*einstimmig.*]

138 [Or 'task': *Aufgabe.*]

139 [*sollen.*]

tains the basis of this connection, namely the basis of the exact harmony of [one's] happiness with [one's] morality, is also *postulated*. This supreme cause, however, is to contain the basis of nature's harmony not merely with a law of the will of rational beings, but also with the presentation of this *law* insofar as they posit this law to themselves as the *supreme determining basis of the will*, and hence not merely with morals[140] according to their form but also with their morality as their motive, i.e., with their moral attitude. Therefore the highest good in the world is possible only insofar as one assumes a supreme cause of nature that has a causality conforming to the moral attitude. Now, a being capable of [performing] actions according to the presentation of laws is an *intelligence* (a rational being), and such a being's causality according to this presentation of laws is a *will* of this being. Therefore the supreme cause of nature, insofar as it must be presupposed for the highest good, is a being that is the cause of nature through *understanding* and *will* (and hence is its originator), i.e., **God**. Consequently the postulate of the possibility of the *highest derivative good* (the best world) is simultaneously the postulate of the actuality of a *highest original good*, viz., [the postulate] of the existence of God. Now, it was a duty for us to further the highest good; and hence [we have] not only the authority, but also the necessity linked as a need with duty, to presuppose the possibility of this highest good, which, since it has [its] place only under the condition of the existence of God, links the presupposition of God inseparably with duty; i.e., it is morally necessary to assume the existence of God.

Now, it must be noted carefully here that this moral necessity is *subjective*, i.e., a need, and not *objective*, i.e., itself a duty; for there can be no duty whatever to assume the existence[141] of a thing (because doing so concerns only the theoretical use of reason). I also do not mean by this that it is necessary to assume the existence of God *as a basis of all obligation as such* (for this basis rests, as has been proved sufficiently, solely on the autonomy of reason itself). What belongs to duty here is only this: to work for the production and furtherance of the highest good in the world; the possibility of this good can therefore be postulated.[142] Our reason, however, finds this possibility thinkable solely on the presupposition of a highest intelligence; to assume the existence of this intelligence is therefore linked with the con-

126

---

[140] [I.e., one's habitual ways of acting: *Sitten*. Cf. the *Metaphysics of Morals*, Ak. VI, 216.]

[141] [*Existenz* here, *Dasein* just below and later in the paragraph.]

[142] [Cf. the *Critique of Pure Reason*, A 814–19 = B 842–47.]

sciousness of our duty, although this assumption itself belongs to theoretical reason. In regard to theoretical reason alone, considered as a basis of explanation, it can be called a *hypothesis*. But in reference to the understandability of an object (the highest good) assigned[143] to us, after all, by the moral law, and hence of a need with a practical aim, it can be called *faith,*[144] specifically pure *rational faith,* because pure reason alone (in its theoretical as well as in its practical use) is the source from which it springs.

From this *deduction* it now becomes comprehensible why the *Greek* schools could never succeed in solving their problem of the practical possibility of the highest good. It was because they always made only the rule of the use that the human will makes of its freedom the sole and by itself sufficient basis of this possibility, without needing for this, as it seemed to them, the existence of God. They were indeed right in establishing the principle of morals by itself, independently of this postulate and solely from the relation of reason to the will, thus making it the *supreme* practical condition of the highest good; but this principle was not, on that account, the *entire* condition for the possibility of this good.[145] The *Epicureans* had, to be sure, assumed an entirely false principle of morals as the supreme one, namely that of happiness, and had substituted for a law a maxim of discretionary choice[146] according to the inclination of each. But they proceeded *consistently* enough inasmuch as they degraded their highest good in the same way, viz., in proportion to the lowliness of their principle, and expected no greater happiness than can be acquired through human prudence (to which temperance and moderation of the inclinations belong as well), which, as we know, must [be] paltry enough and turn out very differently according to circumstances, not even counting the exceptions that their maxims had to admit incessantly and that made them unsuitable for laws. The *Stoics,* by contrast, had chosen their supreme practical principle quite correctly, viz., virtue, as condition of the highest good. But inasmuch as they presented the degree of virtue that is required for its pure law as fully attainable in this life, they had not only stretched the moral ability of the *human being,* under the name of a *sage,* high above all the limits of his nature and assumed

127

[143] [As a problem (or task): *aufgegeben.*]

[144] [*Glaube.* On faith, see the *Critique of Pure Reason,* A 820–31 = B 848–59; and the *Critique of Judgment,* Ak. V, 471–72 incl. 471n, and cf. 475.]

[145] [See above, Ak. V, 39–41.]

[146] [Or 'optional choice': *beliebigen Wahl.*]

something that contradicts all [our] knowledge[147] of the human being, but above all they had also refused to accept[148] the second component belonging to the highest good, viz., happiness, as a special object of the human power of desire. Instead they had made their *sage*, like a deity in the consciousness of the excellence of his person, entirely independent of nature (with regard to his satisfaction), exposing him indeed to [the] bad things[149] of life but not subjecting him to them (simultaneously depicting[150] him as also free from evil). Thus they actually omitted the second element of the highest good, [one's] own happiness, by positing it merely in acting and in satisfaction with one's personal worth and thus including it too in the consciousness of one's moral way of thinking—though in this they could have been sufficiently refuted by the voice of their own nature.

The doctrine of Christianity,[151] even when not yet regarded as religious doctrine, provides on this point a concept of the highest good (the kingdom

---

[147] [-*kenntnis.*]

[148] [*gelten lassen.*]

[149] [*Übeln;* 'evil,' below, translates *Bösen.* See Ak. V, 59 br. n. 259.]

[150] [*darstellen.*]

[151] It is commonly supposed that the Christian precept of morals has no advantage, as regards its purity, over the moral concepts of the Stoics; but the difference between the two is nonetheless quite manifest.[a] The Stoic system made consciousness of fortitude of soul the pivot around which all moral attitudes were to turn; and although its adherents talked about duties and even determined them quite well, they nonetheless posited the incentive and proper determining basis of the will in an elevation of the way of thinking above the lowly incentives of the senses, which have power[b] only through weakness of soul. Hence virtue was for them a certain heroism of the *sage*[c] who, elevating[d] himself above the animal nature of the human being, is sufficient to himself, and although he propounds duties to others he is himself exalted[e] above them and not subject to any temptation to transgress the moral law. All this, however, they could not have done if they had conceived this law in the [same] purity and strictness as does the precept of the Gospel. If by an *idea* I mean a perfection to which nothing can be given adequately in experience, then the moral ideas are not therefore—like the ideas of speculative reason—something extravagant,[f] i.e., something of which we cannot even sufficiently determine the concept, or concerning which it is uncertain whether an object corresponds to it at all; rather, the moral ideas, as archetypes of practical perfection, serve as [the] indispensable guideline[g] of moral conduct and simultaneously as *standard*[h] *of comparison.* If I now consider *Christian morality*[i] from its philosophical side, then, compared with the ideas of the Greek schools, it would appear as follows: The ideas of the *Cynics,*

128   of God) which alone is adequate to the strictest demand of practical reason. The moral law is holy (unforbearing) and demands holiness of morals,[152] although any moral perfection that a human being can reach is always only virtue. Virtue is a lawful[153] attitude based on *respect* for the law, and hence is a consciousness of a continual propensity to transgression or at least to impurity,[154] i.e., to an admixture of many spurious (not moral) motives for complying with the law. Hence virtue is a self-esteem combined with humility. Therefore, with regard to the holiness that the Christian law demands, the moral law leaves the creature with nothing but progress *ad infinitum*, but precisely therefore also entitles the creature to hope for his continuance [as] proceeding *ad infinitum*. The *worth* of an attitude *fully* ad-

-----

the *Epicureans,* the *Stoics,* and the *Christians* are [respectively] *natural simplicity, prudence, wisdom,*[j] and *holiness.* With regard to the path for arriving at them, the Greek philosophers differed from one another inasmuch as the Cynics found the *common human understanding* sufficient for this, the others only the *path of science,* [but] thus both, after all, the mere *use of* [*our*] *natural powers.*[k] Christian morality, because it sets up its precept (as must indeed be done) [as] so pure and unforbearing, deprives the human being of the confidence of being fully adequate to it, at least here in life,[l] but yet also uplifts it again by [the prospect] that if we act as well as is within our *power,*[m] we can hope that what is not within our power will be accorded to us from elsewhere, whether or not we know in what way. *Aristotle* and *Plato* differed only with regard to the *origin* of our moral concepts.

    a [See above, Ak. V, 86.]
    b [*macht-.*]
    c [*der Weise.*]
    d [*erheben.*]
    e [*erhaben,* which also means 'sublime.' The first edition had *erhoben,* 'elevated.']
    f [I.e., transcendent: *überschwenglich.*]
    g [Or 'standard': *Richtschnur.*]
    h [*Maßstab.*]
    i [*Moral.* Likewise later in this note.]
    j [*Weisheit.*]
    k [*Kräfte.*]
    l [I follow Vorländer and the *Philosophische Bibliothek* edition in dropping the comma after *Leben.* With the comma present, the sentence reads, ' . . . deprives the human being of the confidence, at least here in life, of being fully adequate to it . . . .']
    m [Or 'ability': *Vermögen;* likewise below.]

152 [Cf. the *Metaphysics of Morals,* Ak. VI, 487; also the *Grounding for the Metaphysics of Morals,* Ak. IV, 408–09.]

153 [I.e., law-conforming: *gesetzmäßig.*]

154 [*Unlauterkeit.* Ordinarily, I use 'purity' for *Reinigkeit,* and 'pure' for *rein.*]

equate[155] to the moral law is infinite, because all possible happiness, in the judgment of a wise and all-powerful distributor of it, has no restriction other than the lack of adequacy of rational beings to their duty. Yet the moral law by itself does not *promise* any happiness; for happiness is not, according to concepts of a natural order as such, linked necessarily to compliance with that law. Now, Christian morality compensates for that lack (of the second indispensable component of the highest good) by depicting[156] the world in which rational beings dedicate themselves with their whole soul to the moral law as a *kingdom of God,* in which nature and morals come into a harmony, foreign to each by itself, through a holy originator who makes the derivative highest good[157] possible. The *holiness* of morals is assigned to rational beings as a standard already in this life; but the well-being proportionate to it, i.e., *bliss,* is conceived as attainable only in an eternity. For, the *former* must always be the archetype of their conduct in any station, and the advance toward it is possible and necessary already in this life; but the *latter,* under the name of happiness, cannot (insofar as our own ability is at issue) be attained in this life at all and hence is made solely an object of hope. In spite of this, the Christian principle of *morality*[158] is yet itself not theological (and hence heteronomy); rather, it is autonomy of pure practical reason by itself, because it makes the cognition of God and of his will the basis not of these laws but only of [one's] reaching the highest good under the condition of compliance with these laws, and because it posits even the proper *incentive* for compliance with them not in the wished-for consequences of this compliance but in the conception[159] of duty alone; [for,] the worthiness to acquire those consequences consists solely in the faithful[160] observance of duty.

129

In this way the moral law, through the concept of the highest good as the object and the final purpose[161] of pure practical reason, leads to *religion,*

---

[155] [Or 'commensurate': *angemessen.*]

[156] [*darstellen.*]

[157] [See above, Ak. V, 125.]

[158] [*Moral.*]

[159] [Or 'presentation': *Vorstellung.*]

[160] [*treu.*]

[161] [*Endzweck.* See above, Ak. V, 120 br. n. 93.]

i.e., to the cognition[162] *of all duties as divine commands,*[163] *not as sanctions—i.e., chosen*[164] *and by themselves contingent ordinances of another's*[165] *will*—but as essential *laws* of every free will by itself.[166] [Even as such,] these laws must nonetheless be regarded as commands of the supreme[167] being, because we can hope to reach the highest good, which the moral law makes it our duty to posit as the object of our endeavor, only through[168] a will that is morally perfect (holy and benign) and simultaneously also all-powerful, and thus through harmony with this will. Hence here, too, everything remains devoid of self-interest[169] and based only on duty, and does not have to[170] be based on fear or hope, which, when they become principles, annihilate the whole moral worth of actions. The moral law commands me to make the highest possible good in a world the ultimate object of all my conduct. But I cannot hope to bring this good about except through the harmony of my will with that of a holy and benign originator of the world; and although the concept of the highest good, as that of a whole in which the greatest happiness is presented as linked in the most exact proportion with the greatest degree of moral perfection (possible in creatures), includes also *my own happiness,* yet the determining basis of the will that is instructed to further the highest good is not this happiness but the moral law (which, on the contrary, severely[171] restricts my unbounded longing for happiness to conditions).

130

Hence, by the same token, morality is properly the doctrine not of how we are to *make* ourselves happy but of how we are to[172] become *worthy* of

[162] [Or 'recognition': *Erkenntnis.* See above, Ak. V, 4 br. n. 31.]

[163] [Cf. the *Critique of Judgment,* Ak. V, 481; the *Critique of Pure Reason,* A 818–19 = B 846–47; *Religion within the Bounds of Reason Alone,* Ak. VI, 153; and the *Dispute among the [University's] Schools [Fakultäten],* Ak. VII, 36.]

[164] [*willkürlich.*]

[165] [*fremd.*]

[166] [Cf. the *Metaphysics of Morals,* Ak. VI, 487.]

[167] [*höchst,* translated as 'highest' in other expressions.]

[168] [Kant actually says 'from' (*von*).]

[169] [*uneigennützig.*]

[170] [*nicht dürfen,* which in contemporary German—and sometimes already in Kant as well (see, e.g., Ak. V, 142 incl. br. n. 280)—means 'must not.' Cf. above, Ak. V, 30.]

[171] [Or 'strictly': *streng.*]

[172] [Or 'ought to': *sollen.*]

happiness. Only if religion is added to it does there also enter the hope of some day coming to partake of happiness to the degree to which we have taken care not to be unworthy of it.

Someone is *worthy* of possessing a thing or state when his being in this possession harmonizes with the highest good. One can readily see now that all worthiness hinges on moral conduct, because in the concept of the highest good this conduct amounts to the condition of the rest (which pertains to one's state), viz., one's share in happiness. Now, from this it follows that *morality*[173] in itself must never be treated as a *doctrine of happiness*, i.e., as an instruction for coming to partake of happiness; for it deals solely with the rational condition (*conditio sine qua non*)[174] of happiness and not with the means of acquiring it. But when morality (which merely imposes duties and does not provide us with guidelines for self-interested wishes), has been set forth completely, then—after the moral wish, based on a law, to further the highest good (to bring the kingdom of God to us), which could not previously have sprung up in any self-interested soul, has been awakened and for the sake of this wish the step to religion has been taken—then for the first time can this doctrine of morals[175] also be called a doctrine of happiness, because only with religion does the *hope* for happiness first arise.

One can also see from this that if one inquires about *God's ultimate purpose* in creating the world, one must mention not the *happiness* of rational beings in the world but *the highest good,* which adds to that wish of these beings a condition as well, namely the condition of being worthy of happiness, i.e., the *morality* of these same rational beings; [for] only this [condition] contains the standard by which alone they can hope to come to partake of happiness at the hand of a *wise* originator. For, since *wisdom* considered theoretically means *the cognition of the highest good,* and considered practically it means *the adequacy of the will to the highest good,* one cannot attribute to a highest self-dependent[176] wisdom a purpose that would be based merely on *benignity.*[177] For, one cannot think the effect of this benignity (with regard to the happiness of rational beings) as adequate to the highest original good except under the restricting conditions of harmony with the

131

---

[173] [*Moral;* likewise below.]

[174] [Indispensable (or necessary) condition.]

[175] [*Sittenlehre.*]

[176] [*selbständig.*]

[177] [*Gütigkeit.*]

holiness of his will.[178] Hence those who have posited the purpose of creation in the glory of God—supposing that this is not thought anthropomorphically, as inclination to be praised—may have found the best expression. For, nothing glorifies[179] God more than what is the most estimable thing[180] in the world, viz., respect for his command, observance of the holy[181] duty that his law imposes on us, when this is supplemented by his splendid provision to crown such a beautiful order with commensurate happiness. If the latter (to speak in the human manner) makes him worthy of love, then he is by the former an object of worship (adoration). Even human beings can through beneficence[182] indeed acquire love, but through it alone they can never acquire respect, so that the greatest beneficence does them honor[183] only by being exercised in accordance with worthiness.

[178] At this point, and in order to make recognizable what is peculiar to these concepts, I add only the following comment. Although one attributes to God various properties whose quality is found appropriate[a] also to creatures except that in God they are raised to the highest degree—e.g., might, knowledge, presence, benignity,[b] etc. under the designations of omnipotence, omniscience, omnipresence, omnibenevolence,[c] etc.—still there are three that are attributed to God exclusively, yet without the addition of magnitude,[d] and that are one and all moral: he is the *alone holy one*, the *alone blessed one*, the *alone wise one*, because these concepts already carry the unlimitedness with them. According to the order of these properties, he is thus also the *holy legislator*[e] (and creator), the *benign governor*[f] (and preserver), and the *just judge*—three properties that contain within themselves everything by which God becomes the object of religion, and commensurately with which the metaphysical perfections add themselves on their own in reason.

  [a] [*angemessen.*]

  [b] [Respectively, *Macht* (also translatable as 'power'), *Wissenschaft* (which also means 'science'), *Gegenwart*, *Güte* (which literally means 'goodness' but here connotes *moral* goodness and is being used synonymously with *Gütigkeit*).]

  [c] [Respectively, *Allmacht, Allwissenheit, Allgegenwart, Allgütigkeit* (literally, 'omnibenignity').]

  [d] [*Größe.*]

  [e] [Or 'lawgiver': Cf. above, Ak. V, 20 br. n. 23.]

  [f] [Or 'ruler': *Regierer.*]

[179] [Or 'honors': *ehren.* Similarly, 'glory,' above, also means 'honor.']

[180] [*das Schätzbarste.*]

[181] [Or 'sacred': *heilig.* Likewise in the next paragraph.]

[182] [*Wohltun* here, *Wohltätigkeit* below.]

[183] [*Ehre.*]

It now follows on its own that in the order of purposes the human being (and with him every rational being) is a *purpose in itself,*[184] i.e., he can never be used merely as a means by anyone (not even by God) without being in this at the same time a purpose himself, and that therefore the *humanity* in our person must be *holy* to ourselves. For he is the *subject*[185] *of the moral law* and hence of that which is holy in itself [and] on account of which and in agreement with which alone anything can indeed be called holy at all. For, this moral law is based on the autonomy of his will, as a free will which, according to its universal laws, must necessarily be able at the same time to *agree* with that to which it is to *subject*[186] itself.

132

VI
ON THE POSTULATES OF
PURE PRACTICAL REASON AS SUCH

All of these postulates commence from the principle of morality, which is not a postulate but a law[187] by which reason determines the will directly;[188] and this will, precisely by being so determined, as a pure will, demands[189] these necessary conditions[190] of observance of its precept. These postulates are not theoretical dogmas but *presuppositions* from a necessarily practical point of view; hence, although they do not expand theoretical cognition, they do give objective reality to the ideas of speculative reason *in general* (by means of their reference to the practical [sphere]) and entitle it to concepts of which it could not otherwise presume to assert even the possibility.[191]

---

[184] [Or 'end in itself': *Zweck an sich selbst.* For my rendering of *Zweck* as 'purpose,' see above, Ak. V, 35 br. n. 121.]

[185] [*Subjekt.*]

[186] [*unterwerfen.*]

[187] [See above, Ak. V, 31.]

[188] [*unmittelbar.*]

[189] [I.e., *postulates,* in the original sense of this term. See the *Critique of Judgment,* Ak. V, 468; and cf. the *Critique of Pure Reason,* A 220/B 267 and A 225/B 272.]

[190] [The three mentioned in the next paragraph.]

[191] [I.e., real, not merely logical, possibility. For this distinction, see the *Critique of Pure Reason,* B xxvi n., A 240–42 incl. 242n, A 596/B 624n.]

These postulates are those of *immortality,* of *freedom* considered positively (as the causality of a being insofar as this being belongs to the intelligible world),[192] and of the *existence of God.* The *first* flows from the practically necessary condition of adequacy of [one's] duration to the complete fulfillment of the moral law; the *second,* from the necessary presupposition of independence from the world of sense and of the ability to determine one's will according to the law of an intelligible world, i.e., the law of freedom;[193] the *third,* from the necessity of the condition for such an intelligible world, in order for it to be the highest good, through the presupposition of the highest self-dependent[194] good, i.e., the existence of God.

The aim at the highest good—an aim necessary because of respect for the moral law—along with the presupposition, flowing from it, of the objective reality of this good, thus leads through postulates of practical reason to concepts that speculative reason could indeed set forth as problems but that it could not solve. Thus, first,[195] it leads to the problem in the solution of which speculative reason could do nothing but commit *paralogisms*[196] (viz., the problem of immortality), because it lacked the characteristic of permanence by which to supplement the psychological concept of an ultimate subject—a concept that is necessarily ascribed to the soul in self-consciousness—to [yield] a real presentation of a substance. Practical reason accomplishes this [supplementation] by the postulate of [the] duration required for adequacy to the moral law, [this adequacy being one element] in the highest good as the whole purpose of practical reason. Second, it[197] leads to something of which speculative reason contained nothing but [an] *antinomy*[198]—whose resolution it could base only on a concept that, although problematically thinkable, was for it not provable and determinable

133

---

[192] [On freedom in the negative and positive meanings, see Ak. V, 33, cf. 29, 31, 42–43, 47–48, 133. See also the *Critique of Pure Reason,* A 553–44, B 581–82; the *Grounding for the Metaphysics of Morals,* Ak. IV, 446–47, 452–53, 454–55, 457–58; and the *Metaphysics of Morals,* Ak. VI, 213–14, 221, 226.]

[193] [See above, Ak. V, 29–30.]

[194] [*selbständig.*]

[195] [*1.,* i.e., literally, '1st.' Similarly for 'Second' and 'Third,' below.]

[196] [See the Paralogisms of Pure Reason, *Critique of Pure Reason,* A 341–405/B 399–432.]

[197] [I.e., the aim at the highest good: *sie.*]

[198] [See the Antinomy of Pure Reason, *Critique of Pure Reason,* A 405–567/B 432–595.]

as regards its objective reality[199]—viz., [to] the *cosmological* idea of an intelligible world and the consciousness of our existence therein. It leads to this by means of the postulate of freedom (the reality of which it[200] displays[201] through the moral law, and with this law also the law of an intelligible world, [a world] to which speculative reason could only point but the concept of which it could not determine). Third, it provides with signification what speculative reason could indeed think but had to leave undetermined as a mere transcendental *ideal*,[202] viz. the *theological* concept of the original being. It provides this concept with signification (for a practical aim, i.e., as a condition for the possibility of the object of a will determined by that law) as the supreme principle of the highest good in an intelligible world through authoritative[203] moral legislation[204] therein.

However, is our cognition actually expanded in this way by pure practical reason, and is that which was *transcendent* for speculative reason *immanent* in practical reason? Of course, but *only for a practical aim*.[205] For, indeed, we thereby cognize neither the nature of our soul, nor the intelligible world, nor the supreme[206] being as to what they are in themselves, but have only united the concepts of them in the *practical* concept *of the highest good* as the object of our will; and we have done so completely a priori through pure reason, but only by means of the moral law and also merely in reference to it, with regard to the object it commands. But how freedom is even possible and how we are to present this kind of causality theoretically and positively—into this we do not thereby have insight; rather, that there is such freedom[207] is only being postulated through the moral law and for its sake.[208] The situation is the same with the other ideas: no human under-

---

[199] [I.e., the applicability of the concept to objects.]

[200] [*sie.* Although grammatically this still refers to *the aim at the highest good,* Kant may actually be thinking of practical reason itself. Similarly for the 'it' in the sentence beginning 'Third,' below.]

[201] [*darlegen.*]

[202] [See the Ideal of Pure Reason, *Critique of Pure Reason,* A 567–642/B 595–670.]

[203] [Literally, 'power-having': *gewalthabend.*]

[204] [Or 'lawgiving': *Gesetzgebung.* Cf. above, Ak. V, 20 br. n. 23.]

[205] [*nur in praktischer Absicht.*]

[206] [*höchst,* translated as 'highest' in other expressions.]

[207] [Or perhaps 'such a causality': *eine solche.*]

[208] [See the *Grounding for the Metaphysics of Morals,* Ak. IV, 446–53.]

standing will ever fathom them as regards their possibility; nor, however, will any sophistry ever wrest from the conviction of even the commonest human being that they are not true concepts.

134

VII
HOW IT IS POSSIBLE TO THINK AN EXPANSION OF PURE REASON FOR A PRACTICAL AIM WITHOUT THEREBY ALSO EXPANDING ITS COGNITION AS SPECULATIVE[209]

In order not to get too abstract, we shall answer this question at once as it applies to the case before us. In order to expand a pure cognition *practically*, an *aim*[210] must be given a priori, i.e., a purpose[211] as an object (of the will) that, independently of all theoretical principles, is presented as practically necessary through an imperative determining the will directly[212] (a categorical imperative); and here this is the *highest good*. This [good], however, is not possible unless three theoretical concepts are presupposed (for which, because they are mere[ly] pure rational concepts, no corresponding intuition can be found, and hence, by the theoretical path, no objective reality): viz., freedom, immortality, and God. Hence through the practical law, which commands the existence of the highest good possible in a world, the possibility[213] of those objects of pure speculative reason—the objective reality[214] which speculative reason could not secure to them—is postulated. By this, then, the theoretical cognition of pure reason does of course acquire an increase, which however consists merely in this: that those concepts, which are otherwise problematic (merely thinkable), are now assertorically declared[215] to be concepts to which objects actually belong, because practical reason unavoidably requires the existence of these for the

[209] [See above, Ak. V, 55–57 and 119–21.]

[210] [Or 'intention': *Absicht.*]

[211] [*Zweck.* See above, Ak. V, 35 br. n. 121.]

[212] [*unmittelbar.*]

[213] [The real, not just logical, possibility. Cf. above, Ak. V, 132 br. n. 191.]

[214] [Of the three concepts.]

[215] [*erklären,* which can also mean 'to explicate.']

possibility of its object, the highest good, which moreover is absolutely necessary practically, and theoretical reason is thereby entitled to presuppose them. However, this expansion of theoretical reason is not an expansion of speculation, i.e., no positive use can now be made of it for a *theoretical aim*. For since nothing more has been accomplished in this by practical reason than that those concepts are real and [thus] actually have their (possible) objects, but nothing is thereby given to us by way of intuition of them (nor, indeed, can be demanded), no synthetic proposition is possible through this granted reality. Consequently this disclosure does not help us in the least to expand this cognition of ours for a speculative aim, but it does indeed do so with regard to the practical use of pure reason.[216]   135
The above three ideas of speculative reason are in themselves not yet cognitions; nonetheless, they are (transcendent) *thoughts* in which there is nothing impossible. Now, through an apodeictic practical law, as necessary conditions of the possibility of what this law commands one *to make one's object*,[217] they acquire objective reality; i.e., we are instructed by this law that *they have objects*, yet without being able to indicate how their concept[218] refers to an object. By the same token, this is not yet cognition *of these objects;* for, nothing at all concerning them can thereby be judged synthetically, nor can their application be determined theoretically, and hence no theoretical use of reason can be made of them at all, [while yet] all speculative cognition of reason properly consists in such use. Nonetheless, theoretical cognition, *not indeed of these objects* but of reason as such, has thereby been expanded insofar as through the practical postulates those ideas have after all been *given objects*, because a merely problematic thought has thereby for the first time acquired objective reality. This was, therefore, no expansion of the cognition *of given suprasensible objects*,[219] but still an expansion of theoretical reason and of its cognition with regard to the suprasensible as such,[220] insofar as theoretical reason was compelled to grant *that there are such objects*, even though it could not determine them more closely and hence could not itself expand this cognition of the

---

[216] [Cf. the beginning of the last paragraph at Ak. V, 133.]

[217] [*sich zum Objekte zu machen.*]

[218] [Actually, the concept of each of the *objects* of the three ideas.]

[219] [*Gegenstände* here and below, *Objekte* (or, in the singular, *Objekt*) earlier and later in this paragraph. Kant uses *Gegenstand* and *Objekt* interchangeably.]

[220] [Or 'in general': *überhaupt*. See above, Ak. V, 3 br. n. 3.]

objects (which have now been given to it on a practical basis and also only for practical use). Hence for this increase[221] pure theoretical reason, for which all those ideas are transcendent and without an object, is indebted solely to its[222] pure practical ability. Here these ideas become *immanent* and *constitutive* inasmuch as they are bases for the possibility of *making actual* the *necessary object* of pure practical reason (the highest good), while otherwise they are *transcendent* and are merely *regulative* principles of speculative reason,[223] which do not enjoin it to assume a new object beyond experience but enjoin it only to bring its use in experience closer to completeness. However, once reason is in possession of this increase, it will as speculative reason (and, in fact, only to secure its practical use) proceed *negatively* with these ideas, i.e., not expanding but purifying,[224] in order to forestall on the one hand *anthropomorphism* as the source of *superstition*, or the seeming expansion of those concepts through supposed experience, and on the other hand *fanaticism*,[225] which promises such expansion through suprasensible intuition[226] or through feelings of that sort.[227] All of these are obstacles to the practical use of pure reason; hence fending them off does indeed belong to the expansion of our cognition for a practical aim, while there is no contradiction in simultaneously admitting that for a speculative aim reason has gained nothing whatever by this.

136

For every use of reason in regard to an object, pure concepts of understanding (*categories*) are required; without them no object can be thought. These concepts can be applied to the theoretical use of reason, i.e., to cognition of that sort, only insofar as they are at the same time being based on intuition (which is always sensible), and hence merely in order to present through them an object of possible experience. Here, however, *ideas* of reason, which cannot be given in any experience at all, are what I would have to think through categories in order to cognize the object. On the other hand, the concern here is not with theoretical cognition of the objects of

---

[221] [In theoretical cognition.]

[222] [Actually, pure reason's.]

[223] [See the *Critique of Pure Reason*, A 642–68/B 670–96.]

[224] [*läuternd.*]

[225] [*Fanatizismus.*]

[226] [I.e., intellectual intuition. See above, Ak. V, 31 br. n. 77.]

[227] [Cf. the *Prolegomena*, Ak. IV, 363.]

these ideas, but only with these ideas' having objects at all. This reality[228] is provided by pure practical reason, and theoretical reason has nothing further to do in this than merely to *think* those objects through categories; this, as we have shown distinctly elsewhere, is entirely feasible without need of intuition (whether sensible or suprasensible), because the categories have their seat and origin, independently and prior to any intuition, in pure understanding solely as the power[229] to think, and they always signify only an object as such, *in whatever way it may be given to us*. Now insofar as the categories are to be applied to those ideas, it is indeed not possible to give to them an object in intuition. However, *that such an object is actual*—and that hence the category as a mere form of thought is here not empty but has signification—is sufficiently assured to them through an object that practical reason indubitably offers in the concept of the highest good, [viz.,] the *reality of the concepts* that are required for the possibility of the highest good, without however bringing about through this increase the slightest expansion of cognition according to theoretical principles.

If thereupon these ideas of God, of an intelligible world (the kingdom of God), and of immortality are determined through predicates taken from our own nature, then this determination must be regarded neither as a *making sensible*[230] of those pure ideas of reason ([i.e., as] anthropomorphisms) nor as an extravagant[231] cognition of *suprasensible* objects. For, these properties are no others than understanding and will, considered moreover as so related toward[232] each other as they must be thought in the moral law, hence only insofar as a pure practical use is made of them. One is then abstracting from everything else that attaches to these concepts psychologically, i.e., insofar as we observe these powers of ours empirically *in their exercise* (e.g., that the human being's understanding is discursive, that his presentations are therefore thoughts rather than intuitions, that these follow one another in time, that his will is always encumbered by a dependence of [its] satisfaction on the existence of its object, etc.—which cannot be so in the supreme being). Thus what remains of the concepts through which we

137

---

[228] [I.e., the applicability of the ideas to objects.]

[229] [Or 'ability': *Vermögen.*]

[230] [*Versinnlichung.*]

[231] [I.e., transcendent: *überschwenglich.*]

[232] [*gegen.*]

[then] think a pure being of the understanding[233] is nothing more than exactly what is required for the possibility of thinking a moral law. Hence there remains indeed a cognition of God, but only in a practical reference, so that, if we attempt to expand it to a theoretical cognition, we get an understanding of his that does not think but *intuits,*[234] a will that is directed to objects on whose existence its satisfaction does not in the least depend (I shall not even mention the transcendental predicates, such as, e.g., a magnitude of existence, i.e., duration, which however does not occur in time, although time is for us the only possible means of presenting existence as magnitude). All of these are properties of which we can frame no concept at all that would be suitable for *cognition* of the object; and this teaches us that they can never be used for a *theory* of suprasensible beings, and that hence on this [theoretical] side they cannot at all be the basis of a speculative cognition[235] but rather restrict their use solely to the carrying out of the moral law.

This latter [point][236] is so obvious and can be proved so clearly through the deed,[237] that one can confidently challenge all supposed *natural theologians*[238] (an odd name)[239] to mention (beyond the merely ontological pred-

138

---

[233] [I.e., a noumenon: *Verstandeswesen.* See the *Critique of Pure Reason,* B 306–07, and cf. A 562–63 = B 590–91.]

[234] [On an intuitive understanding (whose intuitions are thus intellectual), see above, Ak. 31 br. n. 77.]

[235] [See the *Critique of Pure Reason,* A 631–42 = B 659–70, A 685–702 = B 713–30.]

[236] [That the previously mentioned properties are not suitable for *cognition* of the object, thus can never be used for a *theory* of suprasensible beings, and hence cannot on the theoretical side be the basis of a speculative cognition.]

[237] [Or 'through action' (such as the action that Kant goes on to mention): *durch die Tat.* See above, Ak. V, 3 br. n. 11.]

[238] [Literally, 'scholars of God': *Gottesgelehrte.*]

[239] *Scholarship*[a] is, properly, only the sum[b] of *historical* sciences. Consequently only the teacher[c] of revealed theology[d] can be called a [*scholar of God* or] *theologian.*[e] But if one wanted to call even someone who is in possession of rational sciences (mathematics and philosophy) a scholar,[f] although this would conflict with the word's very meaning (which classes with scholarship only what one must definitely be *taught*[g] and hence cannot discover on one's own, through reason), then the philosopher with his cognition of God as positive science might indeed cut too poor a figure to allow himself to be called a *scholar* on that account.

138

   [a] [In the basic sense, as meaning 'learning': *Gelehrsamkeit.*]
   [b] [*Inbegriff.*]
   [c] [*Lehrer.*]

icates) even one property determining this object of theirs—say, that of the understanding or the will—of which one could not incontestably establish that, if everything anthropomorphic is separated from it, we are left only with the mere word, without being able to link therewith the least concept by which we might hope for an expansion of theoretical cognition. With regard to the practical, however, there nonetheless still remains to us, of the properties of understanding and will, the concept of a relation that the practical law (which a priori determines precisely this relation of the understanding to the will) provides with objective reality. Now, once this has occurred, reality is also given to the concept of the object of a morally determined will (to the concept of the highest good) and with it to the conditions of its[240] possibility, [i.e.,] to the ideas of God, freedom, and immortality, but always only in reference to the carrying out of the moral law (not on any speculative behalf).

After these reminders it is now also easy to find the answer to this important question: *whether the concept of God is one belonging to physics* (hence also to metaphysics, which only contains the pure a priori principles of physics in their universal signification) *or one belonging to morality.*[241] To *explain* arrangements of nature or the change in them, if in doing so[242] one resorts to God as the originator of all things, is at any rate not a physical explanation, and is definitely a confession that one has come to the end of one's philosophy, because one is compelled to assume something of which by itself one otherwise has no concept, in order to be able to frame a concept of the possibility of what one sees before one's eyes.[243] But to get, by means of metaphysics, from acquaintance with *this* world to the concept of God and to the proof of his existence *by safe inferences* is impossible; for

---

d [*Theologie.*]

e [*Gottesgelehrter.*]

f [I.e., 'learned person': *Gelehrter.*]

g [*gelehrt.*]

240 [I.e., this object's.]

241 [*Moral.*]

242 [Here 'in doing so' translates *da.*]

243 [For Kant's refutation of the teleological (physicotheological) proof (i.e., the argument from design), see the *Critique of Pure Reason,* A 620–30 = B 648–58, and above all the *Critique of Judgment,* Ak. V, 385–485, esp. 436–42, 461–66, and 476–85. See also *The Only Possible Basis of Proof for Demonstrating the Existence of God,* Ak. II, 116–37, and cf. 160–62.]

139

in order to say that this world was possible only through a *God* (as we must think this concept), we would have to cognize it as the most perfect whole possible and hence—in order to do so—cognize all possible worlds (so as to be able to compare them with this one), and hence would have to be omniscient.[244] However, to cognize the existence of this being altogether from mere concepts is absolutely impossible. For, any existential proposition—i.e., one that says, concerning a being of which I frame a concept, that it exists—is a synthetic proposition, i.e., one by which I go beyond that concept and say more concerning it than was thought in the concept: viz., that for this concept *in the understanding* there is posited correspondingly also an object *outside the understanding,* which it is manifestly impossible to make out[245] through any inference.[246] Thus there remains for reason only one single procedure by which to arrive at this cognition, viz., where as pure reason, starting from the supreme principle of its pure practical use (inasmuch as this principle is directed anyway merely to the *existence* of something as a consequence of reason), it determines its object. And there, in its unavoidable problem, namely that of the necessary directing of the will to the highest good, there manifests itself not only the necessity of assuming such an original being in reference to the possibility of this good in the world, but—what is most noteworthy—something that the advance of reason on the path of nature lacked entirely, viz., *a precisely determined concept of this original being.* Since we can be acquainted with this world only in small part, still less can compare it with all possible worlds, we can indeed from its order, purposiveness, and magnitude infer a *wise, benign, powerful,*[247] etc. originator of it, but not his *omniscience, omnibenevolence, omnipotence,*[248] and so on. It may also quite readily be granted that one is authorized[249] to compensate for that unavoidable lack by a permitted, entirely reasonable hypothesis, viz., that if in as many items[250] as offer themselves to our closer

---

[244] [For Kant's refutation of the cosmological proof, see the *Critique of Pure Reason,* A 603–14 = B 631–42; also the *Critique of Judgment,* 475–476, and cf. 473.]

[245] [*herausbringen.*]

[246] [For Kant's refutation of the ontological proof, see the *Critique of Pure Reason,* A 592–602 = B 620–30; also the *Critique of Judgment,* 475–476, and cf. 473.]

[247] [Respectively, *weise, gütig, mächtig* (literally, 'mighty').]

[248] [Respectively, *Allwissenheit, Allgütigkeit* (literally, 'omnibenignity'), *Allmacht.*]

[249] [*befugt.*]

[250] [Or 'components': *Stücke.*]

acquaintance [we find] wisdom, benignity, etc., shining forth, it will be the same in all the others, and that it is therefore reasonable to attribute all possible perfection to the originator of the world. However, these are not *inferences* through which we can pride[251] ourselves on our insight, but only authorized moves[252] that may be overlooked but that still require recommendation from elsewhere in order for us to use them. Therefore on the empirical path (of physics) the concept of God remains always a *concept*—of the perfection of the primary[253] being—*not determined precisely* [enough] to be considered adequate to the concept of a deity. (With metaphysics in its transcendental part, however, nothing at all can be accomplished.)

I now attempt to hold this concept up to the object of practical reason, and I then find that the moral principle admits this concept as possible only on the presupposition of an originator of the world who has the *highest perfection*. He must be *omniscient,* in order to cognize my conduct even to my innermost attitudes in all possible cases and throughout the future; *omnipotent,* in order to assign to this conduct the appropriate consequences; likewise *omnipresent, eternal,* etc. Hence the moral law, through the concept of the highest[254] good, determines the concept of the original being as *supreme being;* the physical (and, pursued higher, the metaphysical) and thus the entire speculative course of reason was unable to bring this about. Therefore the concept of God is one belonging originally not to physics, i.e., to speculative reason, but to morality,[255] and the same can also be said of the other concepts of reason with which we earlier dealt as postulates of reason in its practical use.

If in the history of Greek philosophy we find no distinct traces of a pure rational theology before[256] *Anaxagoras,* the reason[257] for this is not that the more ancient philosophers lacked the understanding and the insight to raise themselves to it by the path of speculation, at least with the aid of an entirely reasonable hypothesis; [for,] what could have been easier, what more natural, than the thought offering itself on its own to everyone, to assume—

140

---

[251] [*dünken.*]

[252] [*Befugnisse.*]

[253] [Or 'first': *erste.*]

[254] [*höchst,* translated as 'supreme' below.]

[255] [*Moral.*]

[256] [Literally, 'beyond': *über . . . hinaus.*]

[257] [*Grund.*]

instead of indeterminate degrees of perfection of various causes of the world—a single rational one having *all perfection?* But the bad things[258] in the world seemed to them to be objections far too important to consider themselves entitled to such a hypothesis. Hence those philosophers showed understanding and insight precisely in not permitting themselves this hypothesis and instead searching around among the natural causes [to see] if they could not find among them the characteristic[259] and abilities required for original beings. But once this acute people had advanced in its investigations so far as to treat philosophically even moral objects, about which other peoples had never done more than chatter, they first discovered a new need, namely a practical one, which did not fail to indicate to them determinately the concept of the original being.[260] In this, speculative reason could only look on; at most it still had the merit of adorning a concept not grown on its soil and of furthering—with a retinue of confirmations from the contemplation of nature that now for the first time came to the fore—not indeed the concept's authority[261] (which was already established), but instead only the pageantry of supposed theoretical insight of reason.

141

By these reminders the reader of the critique of pure speculative reason will completely convince himself how extremely necessary, how profitable for theology and morality, was that laborious *deduction* of the categories.[262] For if one posits the categories in pure understanding, only that deduction can keep one from considering them, with *Plato,*[263] to be innate and from basing on them extravagant pretensions of theories of the suprasensible—[theories] of which there is no end in sight—thus turning theology into a magic lantern of chimeras; or, on the other hand, if one considers the categories to be acquired, only the deduction can keep one from restricting, with *Epicurus,*[264] each and every use of them, even that for a practical aim, merely to objects and determining bases of the senses. As it is,[265] however,

[258] [*Übel.* See above, Ak. V, 59 br. n. 259.]

[259] [*Beschaffenheit.*]

[260] [Cf. the *Critique of Pure Reason,* A 452–53 = B 880–81.]

[261] [*Ansehen.*]

[262] [See the *Critique of Pure Reason,* A 95–130/B 124–69.]

[263] [Cf. ibid., A 313–20/B 370–77, A 853–54 = B 881–82.]

[264] [Cf. ibid., A 471–72 = B 500, A 853–54 = B 881–82.]

[265] [*Nun.*]

in that deduction the *Critique* proved, *first,* that the categories are not of empirical origin but have their seat and source a priori in pure understanding; and also, *second,* that since they are referred *to objects as such,*[266] independently of the intuition thereof, they indeed bring about *theoretical cognition* only when applied to *empirical* objects. But yet [we now see, this having been proved,] that when they are applied to an object given through pure practical reason, they also serve for [our] *determinate thinking* of the *suprasensible,* although only insofar as this [suprasensible] is being determined merely through such predicates as belong necessarily to the pure [and] a priori given *practical aim* and to the possibility thereof. Pure reason's speculative restriction and its practical expansion first bring reason into that *relation*[267] *of equality* in which reason can be used purposively at all;[268] and this example proves better than any other that the path to *wisdom,* if it is to become safe and not impassable or misleading, must for us human beings unavoidably pass through science; but that science leads to this goal—of this we can become convinced only after it is completed.

VIII
ON ASSENT[269] FROM A NEED OF PURE REASON

142

A *need* of pure reason in its speculative use leads only to *hypotheses;* but that of pure practical reason, to *postulates.* For in the first case I ascend from the derivative as high up in the series of bases *as I will,*[270] and need an original basis not in order to provide the derivative (e.g., the causal linkage of things and [of] changes in the world) with objective reality but only in order to satisfy my investigating reason completely with regard to it. Thus I see before me order and purposiveness in nature, and I do not need to proceed to speculation in order to assure myself of their *actuality,* but need only, in order *to explain* them, *to presuppose a deity* as their cause; and

---

[266] [Or 'in general': *überhaupt.* See above, Ak. V, 3 br. n. 3.]

[267] [Or 'proportion': *Verhältnis.*]

[268] [Or, possibly, 'in which reason as such can be used purposively': *worin Vernunft überhaupt zweckmäßig gebraucht werden kann.*]

[269] [Literally, 'considering-true': *Fürwahrhalten.* On this section, cf. On Opinion, Knowledge, and Faith, *Critique of Pure Reason,* A 820–31 = B 848–59.]

[270] [*wie ich will* (which can also mean 'as I want to'); cf. below, near the end of the paragraph.]

thus, because an inference from an effect to a determinate cause—above all to so precisely and so completely determined a cause as we have to think in [the case of] God—is always unsafe and precarious, such a presupposition cannot be brought further than to the degree of [being] for us human beings the most reasonable opinion of all.[271] By contrast, a need of pure *practical* reason is based on a *duty* to make something (the highest good) the object of my will in order to further it with all my powers; in doing so, however, I must presuppose the possibility of this [highest good], and hence also the conditions for this, viz., God, freedom, and immortality, because I cannot prove these—although also not refute them—by my speculative reason. This duty is based on a law that is indeed independent of these latter presuppositions and apodeictically certain, namely the moral law, and is to this extent not in need of any further support by a theoretical opinion concerning the intrinsic character[272] of things, the secret aim[273] of the world order, or a governor[274] presiding over it, in order to obligate us most perfectly to unconditionally lawful[275] actions.[276] But the subjective effect of this law, viz., the *attitude,* adequate to it and also necessary through it, to further the practically possible highest good, nonetheless presupposes at least that this good is *possible;* otherwise striving for the object[277]—of a concept that basically would be empty and without an object—would be impossible practically. Now, the above postulates pertain only to the physical or metaphysical conditions—in a word, those lying in the nature of things—for the

143

---

[271] But even here we could not plead a need *of reason*[a] if there did not lie before us a problematic but yet unavoidable concept of reason, viz., that of an absolutely necessary being. Now, this concept requires[b] to be determined, and this, when the urge toward expansion [of cognition] is added, is the objective basis of a need of speculative reason, viz., to determine more closely the concept of a necessary being that is to serve others as original basis, and thus to make this being recognizable through something. Without such prior necessary problems there are no *needs,* at least not of *pure reason,* the others being needs of *inclination.*

   [a] [*Bedürfnis der Vernunft.*]
   [b] [Literally, 'wants': *will.*]

[272] [*Beschaffenheit.*]

[273] [*Abzweckung.*]

[274] [Or 'ruler': *Regierer.*]

[275] [I.e., law-conforming: *gesetzmäßig.*]

[276] [See the *Metaphysics of Morals,* Ak. VI, 486–91.]

[277] [The object of the will, i.e., the highest good.]

possibility of the highest good, but for the sake not of a discretionary speculative aim but of a practically necessary purpose of the pure rational will.
Here this will does not *choose*,[278] but rather *obeys* an unremitting command
of reason. This command has its basis *objectively* in the character of things
as these must be judged[279] universally by pure reason, and is by no means
based on *inclination,* which is in no way entitled immediately to assume,
for the sake of what we *wish* on merely *subjective* bases, that the means to
it are possible, or perhaps even that the object is actual. This is, therefore, a
need for an absolutely necessary aim, and it justifies its presupposition not
merely as a permitted hypothesis, but as a postulate for a practical aim; and,
granted that the pure moral law unremittingly obligates everyone as a command (not as a rule of prudence), the righteous person may indeed say: I
will that there be a God, that my existence in this world be even apart from
the natural connection also an existence in a pure world of understanding,
and finally that my duration be endless; I abide by this, and shall not let this
faith be taken from me; for, this is the only [case] where my interest, because I *must* not[280] remit anything of it, unavoidably determines my judgment, without paying attention to subtle reasonings,[281] however little I may
be able to answer them or oppose them with more plausible ones.**[282]**

---

[278] [*wählen.*]

[279] [beurteilt. See above, Ak. V, 8 br. n. 78.]

[280] [*nicht . . . darf.*]

[281] [*Vernünfteleien.*]

[282] In the *Deutsches Museum,* February 1787, there is a treatise by a very fine and
bright mind,[a] the late *Wizenmann,*[b] whose early death is to be lamented, in which he
disputes [our] authority to make an inference from a need to the objective reality of
its object; and he elucidates his point[c] by the example of a *man in love,* who, having
become infatuated with an idea of beauty that is merely his [own] chimera, wanted
to infer that such an object actually exists somewhere. I grant that he is perfectly
right on this in all cases where the need is based on *inclination,* which cannot, even
for the one assailed by it, postulate necessarily the existence of its object, much less
contains a demand valid for everyone, and hence is a merely *subjective* basis of
wishes. Here, on the other hand, a *rational need*[d] arising from an *objective* determining basis of the will, namely from the moral law, is what necessarily obligates
every rational being and therefore entitles [us] a priori to presuppose the conditions
adequate to it in nature and makes these inseparable from the complete practical use
of reason. It is a duty to make the highest good actual to the utmost of our ability;
thus this good must, after all, also be possible, and hence for every rational being in

143

144   In order to prevent misinterpretation in the use of a concept still so unaccustomed as is that of a pure practical rational faith, I may be permitted to add a further comment. It might almost seem as if this rational faith is here itself proclaimed to be a *command,* viz., to assume the highest good to be possible. But a faith that is commanded is an absurdity. One must remember, however, the above discussion of what is required to be assumed in the concept of the highest good, and one will then become aware that assuming this possibility does not need[283] to be commanded at all and demands no practical attitudes to *grant* this possibility, but that practical reason must admit it without solicitation; for, surely no one can wish to maintain that a worthiness—commensurate to the moral law—of rational beings in the world to be happy, as combined with a possession of happiness proportionate to this worthiness, is in itself *impossible.* Now with regard to the first component[284] of the highest good, viz., as far as morality is concerned, the moral law gives us merely a command, and to doubt the possibility of this constituent[285] would be tantamount to casting doubt on the moral law itself. But as far as the second component of that object[286] is concerned, viz., the

---

the world it is also unavoidable to presuppose what is necessary for the objective possibility of this good. This presupposition is as necessary as the moral law, and is moreover valid only in reference to it.

ᵃ [*Kopf.*]

ᵇ [Thomas Wizenmann (1759–87), a close friend and ally of Friedrich Heinrich Jacobi in the latter's dispute with Mendelssohn (see above, Ak. V, 101 br. n. 509), joined the controversy with his *Die Resultate der Jacobi'schen und Mendelssohn'schen Philosophie, kritisch untersucht von einem Freywilligen* (*The Results of Jacobi's and Mendelssohn's Philosophy, Critically Investigated by a Volunteer*), published anonymously in Leipzig in 1786; reprinted, with an epilogue by Rainer Wild (Hildesheim: Gerstenberg, 1984). Kant, in commenting on the controversy in his treatise (*Berliner Monatsschrift,* in October 1786; and see Ak. VIII, 140–47) *Was heißt: Sich im Denken orientieren?* (*What Does It Mean: to Orient Oneself in* [*One's*] *Thought?*), referred to Wizenmann as the "acute author of the *Resultate.*" Wizenmann then responded in turn with the treatise (*Deutsches Museum,* February 1787) to which Kant here refers, viz., *An den Herrn Professor Kant von dem Verfasser der Resultate Jacobi'scher und Mendelssohn'scher Philosophie* (*To Professor Kant, from the Author of the Results of Jacobi's and Mendelssohn's Philosophy*).]

ᶜ [*Gegenstand.*]

ᵈ [*Vernunftbedürfnis.*]

283 [*nicht . . . dürfe.* Cf. 'not in need' later in this paragraph; and see above, Ak. V, 129 br. n. 170.]

284 [*Stück.*]

285 [Of the highest good: *Bestandstück.*]

286 [I.e., of the highest good.]

happiness commensurate to that worthiness, the granting of its possibility as such is indeed not in need of a command at all, since theoretical reason itself has nothing against it; only *the manner in which* we are to think such a harmony of the laws of nature with those of freedom has something about it in regard to which a choice[287] belongs to us, because concerning it theoretical reason decides nothing with apodeictic certainty, and with regard to this manner there can be a moral interest that turns the scale.

145

I had said above that according to a mere course of nature in the world [a] happiness precisely commensurate to the moral worth is not to be expected[288] and is to be considered impossible, and that therefore from this standpoint the possibility of the highest good can be granted only on the presupposition of a moral originator of the world. I deliberately delayed restricting this judgment to the *subjective* conditions of our reason so as first to make use of this [restriction] only when the manner of [reason's] assent[289] was to be determined more closely. In fact, the mentioned impossibility is *merely subjective,* i.e., our reason finds it *impossible for it* to make comprehensible to itself, according to a mere course of nature, a connection[290] so precisely commensurate and thoroughly purposive between two events of the world that occur according to such different laws, even though—as with everything else in nature that is purposive—it yet also cannot prove, i.e., establish sufficiently from objective bases, that this connection is impossible according to universal laws of nature.

Now, however, a basis of decision[291] of a different kind[292] comes into play in order to turn the scale in speculative reason's wavering. The command to further the highest good has an objective basis (in practical reason); this good's possibility as such likewise has an objective basis (in theoretical reason, which has nothing against it). But as to the manner in which we are to conceive this possibility, whether according to natural laws without a wise originator presiding over nature or only on the presupposition of such an originator, reason cannot decide this objectively. Now, here

---

[287] [*Wahl.*]

[288] [See above, Ak. V, 22–26, and cf. the *Grounding for the Metaphysics of Morals,* Ak. IV, 395–96.]

[289] [Literally, 'considering-true': *Fürwahrhalten.*]

[290] [Or 'coherence': *Zusammenhang.*]

[291] [*Entscheidungsgrund.*]

[292] [*Art,* also translated as 'manner' above and below.]

a *subjective* condition of reason enters, [viz.,] the only manner theoretically possible for reason, and at the same time conducive to morality (which is subject to an *objective* law of reason), of thinking the precise harmony of the kingdom[293] of nature with the kingdom of morals, as condition for the possibility of the highest good. Now, the furtherance of this good and therefore the presupposition of its possibility are *objectively* necessary (though only as a consequence of practical reason); but the manner as to how[294] we want to think it as possible rests within our choice, in which however a free interest of pure practical reason decides for the assumption of a wise originator of the world. [Therefore] the principle which determines our judgment in this is the basis—*subjectively* indeed as a need, but simultaneously also as a means of furthering what is *objectively* (practically) necessary— of a *maxim* of assent for a moral aim, i.e., a *pure practical rational faith*. This faith, therefore, is not commanded; rather, as a voluntary[295] determination of our judgment, conducive to the moral (commanded) aim and also accordant with the theoretical need of reason to assume that existence[296] and to base thereon the further use of reason, it has itself arisen from the moral attitude. Thus [we find] repeatedly [that] even in well-meaning[297] people this faith can sometimes fall into wavering, but never into lack of faith.[298]

146

IX
ON THE WISELY COMMENSURATE PROPORTION[299] OF THE HUMAN BEING'S COGNITIVE POWERS TO HIS PRACTICAL VOCATION

If human nature's vocation is[300] to strive toward the highest good, then the measure of its cognitive powers, above all their proportion[301] to one an-

---

[293] [Or 'realm': *Reich.* Likewise below.]

[294] [*die Art, auf welche Weise.*]

[295] [*freiwillig.*]

[296] [Of a wise originator of the world.]

[297] [*wohlgesinnt.*]

[298] [*Unglaube.*]

[299] [*Proportion.*]

[300] [Or 'determination is': *bestimmt ist.*]

[301] [Or 'relation': *Verhältnis.*]

other, must also be assumed to be fitting for this purpose. However, the critique of pure *speculative* reason proves this power's utmost inadequacy for solving, commensurately[302] with this purpose, the most important problems put before it. Even so, that critique does not fail to recognize this same reason's natural hints—not to be overlooked—as well as the great steps that this power can take in order to approach this great goal that is marked out for it. However, speculative reason can never reach this goal by itself, even with the aid of the greatest cognition of nature. Thus nature here seems to have provided for us only *in a stepmotherly way* with a power required for our purpose.

Supposing now that nature had here been compliant to our wish and had conferred on us that capacity for insight or that illumination[303] which we would like to possess or which some perhaps even *fancy* themselves actually possessing, what, presumably, would be the consequence of this, as far as one can tell? Unless our entire nature were at the same time transformed, the *inclinations,* which, after all, always have the first word, would first demand their satisfaction and, combined with reasonable deliberation, their greatest possible and lasting satisfaction under the name of *happiness;* thereafter the moral law would speak, in order to keep the inclinations within their fitting limits and even to subject them, one and all, to a higher purpose that takes no account of any inclination.[304] But instead of the conflict that the moral attitude now has to carry on with the inclinations, in which—after some defeats—moral fortitude of soul is yet gradually to be acquired, *God* and *eternity* with their *dreadful majesty* would lie unceasingly *before our eyes* (for, as regards certainty, what we can perfectly prove[305] counts[306] as much for us as what we assure ourselves of as manifest to the eye). Transgression of the law would indeed be avoided; what is commanded would be done.[307] However, the *attitude* from which actions ought to be done cannot likewise be instilled by any command, and the spur to activity is in this [case] immediately at hand and *external,* and thus reason does not first need to work itself up in order to gather strength to resist

147

---

[302] [Or 'adequately': *angemessen.*]

[303] [Or 'enlightenment' (the standard rendering for *Aufklärung*): *Erleuchtung.*]

[304] [Cf. the *Grounding for the Metaphysics of Morals,* Ak. IV, 395–96.]

[305] [Viz., God and (our) eternity.]

[306] [*gelten.*]

[307] [*getan* here, *geschehen* above.]

inclinations by vividly presenting the dignity of the law. Therefore most lawful[308] actions would be done from fear, only a few from hope, and none at all from duty; and a moral worth of actions—on which alone, after all, the worth of the person and even that of the world hinges in the eyes of the highest wisdom—would not exist at all. The conduct of human beings, as long as their nature remained as it is, would thus be converted into a mere mechanism, where, as in a puppet show,[309] everything would *gesticulate* well but there would still be *no life* in the figures. However,[310] it is[311] quite different with us. With all the endeavor of our reason we have only a very obscure and ambiguous outlook into the future; the governor of the world allows us only to conjecture his existence and splendor, not to behold them or clearly prove them. On the other hand, the moral law in us, without promising us anything with assurance, or threatening us,[312] demands of us respect devoid of self-interest;[313] but otherwise, when this respect has become active and prevalent,[314] only then and only thereby does this law grant us outlooks into the kingdom[315] of the suprasensible, and even this only with feeble glances. Thus there can be a truly moral attitude, dedicated directly to the moral law, and a rational creature can become worthy of that share in the highest good which is commensurate with the moral worth of his person and not merely with his actions. Thus what the study of nature and of the human being teaches us sufficiently elsewhere may well be correct here also, viz., that the inscrutable[316] wisdom through which we exist is not less worthy of veneration in what it has refused us than in what it has allotted us.

148

---

[308] [I.e., law-conforming: *gesetzmäßig.*]

[309] [*Marionettenspiel.* Cf. above, Ak. V, 101.]

[310] [*Nun.*]

[311] [*beschaffen ist.*]

[312] [I follow Natorp and the *Akademie* edition—rather than Vorländer and the *Philosophische Bibliothek* edition—in retaining the comma before *ohne zu drohen.* I do so in part because *drohen,* like 'threaten,' is intransitive, so that 'anything,' the object of *verheißen* ('promising'), cannot also be *its* object.]

[313] [*uneigennützige.*]

[314] [*herrschend.*]

[315] [Or 'realm': *Reich.*]

[316] [*unerforschlich.*]

PART II

DOCTRINE OF THE METHOD

OF

PURE PRACTICAL REASON

By the *doctrine of the method* of pure *practical* reason one cannot mean the   151
way of proceeding (in meditation[1] as well as in exposition[2]) with pure practical principles with a view to a *scientific* cognition of them; ordinarily this
alone is properly called method in the *theoretical* [sphere] (for, popular
cognition requires a *manner*;[3] but science requires a *method,* i.e., a procedure *according to principles* of reason, through which alone the manifold of
a cognition can become a system).[4] Rather, by this doctrine of method is
meant the way in which one can impart to the laws of pure practical reason
admittance to the human mind and *influence* on that mind's maxims, i.e.,
the way in which one can make objectively practical reason *subjectively*
practical as well.

Now, it is indeed clear that those determining bases of the will which
alone make maxims properly moral[5] and give them a moral worth—viz.,
direct[6] presentation of the law, and objectively necessary compliance with it
as duty—must be presented as the proper incentives to action, because
otherwise *legality* of actions would indeed be brought about, but not *morality* of attitudes.[7] But not so clear, and instead at first glance quite improba-
ble, must it seem to everyone that subjectively too this exhibition of pure
virtue can have *more power* over the human mind, and can provide a far
stronger incentive—to bring about even that legality of actions and to give
rise to more forceful decisions to prefer the law, from pure respect for it, to
any other concern[8]—than can ever be produced[9] by any enticements,[10]
those [arising] from pretenses of gratification and in general from every-

---

[1] [*Nachdenken.*]

[2] [*Vortrag.*]

[3] [*Manier.*]

[4] [Cf. the *Critique of Pure Reason,* A 707–08 = B 735–36.]

[5] [*moralisch* here, *sittlich* below.]

[6] [*unmittelbar.*]

[7] [See above, Ak. V, 72; cf. also the *Grounding for the Metaphysics of Morals,* Ak. IV, 411–12,
and the *Metaphysics of Morals,* Ak. VI, 219.]

[8] [*Rücksicht.*]

[9] [*wirken.*]

[10] [Cf. the *Grounding for the Metaphysics of Morals,* Ak. IV, 394–96.]

152

thing that may be classed with happiness, or for that matter produced by any threats of pain and bad things.[11] Yet this is actually the case, and if human nature were not so constituted, then no way of presenting the law through circuities[12] and commending means would ever give rise to morality of attitude either. Everything would be sheer hypocrisy; the law would be hated or perhaps even despised, although still complied with for the sake of one's own advantage. The letter of the law (legality) could be found in our actions, but the spirit of the law could not be found at all in our attitudes (morality); and since with all our endeavor we still could not entirely detach ourselves from reason in our judgment, we would unavoidably have to appear in our own eyes as worthless, depraved human beings. [We would so appear to ourselves] even if we sought to compensate ourselves for this mortification [suffered] before the inner tribunal by taking delight in the gratifications that, according to our delusion, a supposed natural or divine law had linked with the machinery[13] of its police—a police that is guided merely by what one does, without worrying about the motives from which one does it.

To be sure, it cannot be denied that in order to bring either a still unmolded[14] or a brutified[15] mind onto the track of the morally good in the first place, some preparatory guidance[16] is needed to entice it with its own advantage or scare it with harm. But as soon as this machinery, these leading strings, have had even some effect, the pure moral motive must definitely be applied to[17] the soul. This motive—not just because it is the only one that can be the basis of a character (a consistent practical way of thinking according to unchangeable maxims), but also because it teaches the human being to feel his own dignity—gives to his mind a power,[18] unexpected even by himself, to tear himself away from all sensible attachment insofar as this attachment wants to become dominant, and to find rich compensation for the sacrifices that he makes in the independence of his intelligible

[11] [*Übel*. See above, Ak. V, 59 br. n. 259.]

[12] [*Umschweife*.]

[13] [*Maschinenwesen* here, *Maschinenwerk* below.]

[14] [*ungebildet*.]

[15] [More literally, 'turned wild': *verwildert*.]

[16] [*Anleitungen*.]

[17] [*an . . . bringen;* likewise below.]

[18] [*Kraft*, also translated as 'force' below.]

nature and the greatness of soul to which he sees himself destined.[19] We shall therefore prove, by observations that anyone can perform, that this property of our mind, this receptivity to a pure moral interest and hence the motive force of the pure presentation of virtue, when it is duly applied to the human heart, is the most powerful[20] and—when a lasting and meticulous compliance with moral maxims is at issue—the only incentive to the good.[21] It must also be remembered here, however, that if these observations prove only the actuality of such a feeling but not any moral improvement brought about by it, this does not impair[22] the only method of making the objectively practical laws of pure reason subjectively practical merely through [one's] pure presentation of duty, just as if this method were an empty fantasy. For since this method has never yet been initiated,[23] experience also cannot yet show anything of its result; rather, one can demand only documentation[24] of the receptivity to such incentives; this I shall now briefly put forth, and shall then outline in a few words the method of founding and cultivating genuine moral attitudes.

153

If one attends to the course of conversations in mixed companies[25] that consist not merely of scholars and subtle reasoners[26] but also of business people or women, one notices that besides recounting[27] and jesting, another entertainment has its place in them, namely arguing;[28] for recounting, if it is to have novelty and with it interest, is soon exhausted, and jesting easily becomes insipid. Among all [kinds of] arguing, however, there is none that more arouses the participation[29] of persons who are otherwise soon bored with all subtle reasoning, and brings a certain liveliness into the company, than that about the *moral worth* of this or that action, by which

---

[19] [*bestimmen.*]

[20] [Or 'the mightiest': *die mächtigste.*]

[21] [Cf. the *Metaphysics of Morals,* Ak. VI, 377–78.]

[22] [*Abbruch tun.* See above, Ak. V, 25 br. n. 44.]

[23] [More literally, 'set in motion': *in Gang gebracht.*]

[24] [*Beweistümer.*]

[25] [Or 'parties': *Gesellschaften.*]

[26] [*Vernünftler.* Below, 'subtle reasoning' similarly renders *Vernünfteln.*]

[27] [*Erzählen.*]

[28] [Literally, 'reasoning': *Räsonnieren.*]

[29] [*Beitritt.*]

the character of some person is to be established. Those to whom otherwise everything subtle and meditative[30] in theoretical questions is dry and irksome will soon participate[31] when the issue is to establish the moral import[32] of a good or evil action that has been recounted; and they are then so precise, so meditative, so subtle in excogitating everything that could diminish or even just make suspect the purity of the intention—and hence the degree of virtue in it—as one does not otherwise expect of them in the case of any object of speculation. In these judgments[33] the character of the person himself who is judging others can often be seen shining forth. Some seem especially inclined, since they exercise their judicial office above all upon deceased persons, to defend the good that is recounted concerning this or that deed of the deceased persons against any mortifying objections of impurity,[34] and ultimately to defend the entire moral worth of the person against the reproach of dissimulation and secret malice.[35] Others, on the contrary, [incline] more to thinking up charges and accusations to challenge that worth. Yet one cannot always attribute to the latter the intention of trying to subtly reason virtue away entirely from all examples[36] of human beings in order thereby to turn virtue into an empty name. Rather, it is often only a well-meant strictness in determining genuine moral import according to an unforbearing law—[a law][37] through comparison with which, instead of with examples, self-conceit in the moral [sphere] sinks greatly and humility is by no means only taught but is, upon keen self-examination, felt by everyone. Nonetheless, one can usually see by the look[38] of those who defend the purity[39] of intention in given examples, that, where this purity has the presumption of righteousness on its side, they would like to

154

---

[30] [*alles Subtile und Grüblerische.*]

[31] [Or 'join in': *beitreten.*]

[32] [*Gehalt.*]

[33] [*Beurteilungen.* See above, Ak. V, 8 br. n. 78.]

[34] [*Unlauterkeit.* Ordinarily, including both earlier and later in this paragraph, I use 'purity' for *Reinigkeit.*]

[35] [*Bösartigkeit.*]

[36] [I.e., models: *Beispiele.*]

[37] [Cf. above, Ak. V, 37, 74, 78.]

[38] [*man kann es . . . ansehen.*]

[39] [*Reinigkeit* here, *Lauterkeit* below.]

wipe off it even the slightest blemish[40]—from the motive lest, if the truth-fulness of all examples were disputed and the purity of all human virtue denied, this virtue be in the end considered a mere chimera and thus all endeavor [directed] toward it be disdained as idle affectation and deceptive self-conceit.

I do not know why educators of the youth have not long since made use of this propensity of reason to enter with gratification upon even the sub-tlest examination when practical questions are raised; and why, after laying a solely moral catechism at the basis, they have not searched through the bi-ographies of ancient and modern times with the aim of having at hand, for the duties put forth, supporting instances[41] by[42] which to activate, above all through comparison of similar actions under different circumstances, their pupils' judgment[43] in noting the lesser or greater moral import of such ac-tions. [For] they will soon find even the early youth, which is otherwise not yet mature enough for any speculation, to be very sharp-sighted in this and also[44] not a little interested, because it feels the progress of its power of judgment; but, what is primary, they will be able to hope with assurance that repeated practice[45] in knowing[46] good conduct in all its purity and giv-ing it approbation while noting even the slightest deviation from it with re-gret or contempt—even though thus far this is carried on only as a game of the power of judgment in which children can compete with one another—will nonetheless leave behind a lasting impression of high esteem on the one side and of loathing on the other, which through a mere habit of repeat-edly looking upon such actions as worthy of approbation or censure would amount to a good foundation for righteousness in the future way of life. I only wish [educators] to spare the youth[47] examples of so-called *noble* (suprameritorious[48]) actions, which our sentimental writings bandy about

155

---

[40] [Literally, 'spot': *Fleck.*]

[41] ['supporting instances' translates *Belege.*]

[42] [*an.*]

[43] [*Beurteilung.* See above, Ak. V, 8 br. n. 78.]

[44] [*dabei.*]

[45] [*Übung.*]

[46] [*kennen.*]

[47] [Or perhaps 'the pupils': *sie.*]

[48] [*überverdienstlich.*]

so much, and to stake everything merely on duty and on the worth that a human being can and must give himself in his own eyes through the consciousness of not having transgressed it; for, what amounts to empty wishes and longings for unattainable[49] perfection produces nothing but heroes of novels who, while crediting themselves very much with their feeling for the extravagantly[50] great, absolve themselves in return from observing the common and prevalent obligation,[51] which then seems to them insignificantly small.[52]

But if one asks, what, then, properly, is *pure* morality,[53] by which as touchstone[54] one must test the moral[55] import of every action, then I must admit that only philosophers can make the decision of this question doubtful; for in common human reason this question is long since decided, not indeed by abstract general formulas, but yet by habitual[56] use—like the difference, as it were, between the right and the left hand. We shall, therefore, first show by an example the test mark[57] of pure virtue; and, conceiving it as having been put before, say, a ten-year-old boy for his judgment,

[49] [More literally, 'unscalable': *unersteiglich.*]

[50] [*überschwenglich.*]

[51] [*Schuldigkeit.* See above, Ak. V, 82 br. n. 385.]

[52] It is entirely advisable to praise actions from which a great, not self-interested,[a] compassionate attitude shines forth. However, one must here call attention not so much to the *elevation of the soul,* which is very fleeting and transitory, as rather to the *submission of the heart* to *duty,* from which a more lasting impression can be expected, because it carries principles with it (but the former, only bursts [of emotion]). One need reflect only a little, and one will always find some guilt[b]—with which one has burdened oneself by something or other in regard to humankind (even if it were only the guilt that, through the inequality of human beings in the civil constitution, one enjoys advantages on account of which others must all the more do without)—to keep the self-loving[c] imagining of the *meritorious* from displacing the thought of *duty.*
   [a] [*uneigennützig.*]
   [b] [*eine Schuld.*]
   [c] [*eigenliebig.*]

[53] [*Sittlichkeit.*]

[54] [Literally, 'proof metal': *Probemetall.*]

[55] [*moralisch.*]

[56] [Or 'ordinary': *gewöhnlich.*]

[57] [Or 'test characteristic': *Prüfungsmerkmal.*]

we shall see whether he must necessarily judge thus on his own as well, without having been instructed to do so by his teacher. Recount the story of an upright man whom some people[58] want to induce to join the defamers of an innocent but otherwise powerless person (such as, say, Anne Boleyn upon having been accused by Henry VIII of England). These people offer him gains, i.e., large gifts or high rank; he rejects them. This will effect mere approbation and approval[59] in the soul of the listener, because it is gain. Now they start to threaten him with loss. Among these defamers are his best friends, who now renounce their friendship; close relatives, who threaten to disinherit him (who has no assets); powerful people, who can pursue and hurt him in every place and situation; a prince, who threatens him with loss of freedom and indeed of life itself. But in order to make him feel, so that the measure of suffering may be full, even the pain that only a morally good heart can feel quite intimately, one may conceive his family, threatened by extreme plight and neediness, as *imploring* him *to yield,* and himself—although righteous, yet of course[60] not made of[61] solid organs of feeling that are insensitive to sympathy as well as to his own plight[62]—at a moment when he wishes that he had never seen the day that exposed him to such unspeakable pain, as nonetheless remaining faithful, without wavering or even doubting, to his resolve of uprightness. Then my youthful listener will be elevated gradually from mere approval to admiration, from there to amazement, and finally to the greatest veneration and a lively wish to be able himself to be such a man (although not, to be sure, in his situation); and yet virtue is here worth so much only because it costs so much, not because it yields a return.[63] The entire amazement and even striving toward similarity with this character here rests entirely on the moral principle's purity, which can be presented as quite obvious only by removing from the incentives of the action everything that human beings might class with happiness. Therefore morality must have the more power over[64] the human

156

---

[58] [*man;* similarly for 'These people,' below.]

[59] [*Beifall und Billigung.*]

[60] [*eben.*]

[61] ['made of' translates *von.*]

[62] [Literally, Kant says 'solid, insensitive organs of the feeling for sympathy as well as [the feeling] of his own plight.']

[63] [*etwas einbringen.*]

[64] [Literally, 'upon': *auf.*]

heart the more purely it is presented.[65] From this, then, it follows that if the law of morals, and [with it] the image of holiness and virtue, is to exert any influence at all on our soul, it[66] can do so only insofar as it is—as incentive—laid to heart pure, unmingled with intentions [directed] at one's well-being,[67] and this because it shows itself most splendidly in suffering. That, however, whose removal strengthens the effect of a motive force must have been an obstacle. Consequently any admixture of incentives that are taken from one's own happiness is an obstacle to providing the moral law with influence on the human heart. I maintain further that, even in that admired action, if the motive from which it was done was high esteem for one's duty, then it is precisely this respect for the law—and by no means a claim to the inner opinion[68] of [possessing] magnanimity and a noble, meritorious way of thinking—which has the greatest force directly on the spectator's mind; and that consequently duty, not merit, must have not only the most determinate but, when conceived[69] in the proper light of its inviolability, also the most penetrating influence on the mind.[70]

157

In our times, when people hope to accomplish more with tender, softhearted feelings or with highflying, puffed-up pretensions concerning the mind that sooner wither than strengthen the heart, than by the dry and earnest[71] presentation[72] of duty, which is more appropriate to human imperfection and to progress in [regard to] the good, we need to point to this method more than ever. To adduce—as a model—actions to children as being noble, magnanimous, meritorious, with the intent[73] of prepossessing the children in their favor by instilling an enthusiasm, is altogether contrapurposive. For since children are still so far behind in the observance of the

---

[65] [Or 'conceived': *vorgestellt;* likewise above.]

[66] [Reading, as Vorländer suggests, *es* for (the singular) *sie;* Kant may still have had in mind *Sittlichkeit* ('morality') from the preceding sentence.]

[67] [*Wohlbefinden.*]

[68] [*Meinung.*]

[69] [Or 'presented': *vorgestellt.*]

[70] [See above, Ak. V, 71–82.]

[71] [*ernsthaft.*]

[72] [Or 'conception': *Vorstellung.*]

[73] [*Meinung.*]

commonest duty and even in the correct judging[74] of it, this is tantamount to soon turning them into fantasists. But even with the more informed and experienced part of humankind, this supposed incentive has, if not a detrimental, then at least no genuine moral effect on the heart—which was, after all, what one wanted to bring about by means of it.

All *feelings,* above all those that are to give rise to unaccustomed endeavor, must produce[75] their effect at the moment of their intensity and before they subside; otherwise they do nothing, since the heart by nature returns to its natural, moderate vital motion and accordingly lapses into the languor that belonged to it before, because there was indeed applied to[76] it something that stimulated it, but nothing that strengthened it. *Principles* must be built on concepts; on any other foundation there can arise only bursts that can impart to the person no moral worth and indeed not even confidence in himself; yet without these the consciousness of one's moral attitude and of a character of that kind, the highest good in a human being, cannot occur at all. Now, these concepts, if they are to become subjectively practical, must not stay with the objective laws of morality, in order to admire these and highly esteem them in reference to humanity; rather, they must consider the presentation of these laws in relation to the human being and to the individual in him; and thus that law[77] appears in a guise that, although indeed supremely worthy of respect, is not so likable[78] as if the law belonged to the element to which he is naturally accustomed,[79] but [the law appears], rather, as it compels him to leave this element, often not without self-denial, and to betake himself into a higher element in which he can maintain himself only with effort and with unceasing worry about relapsing. In a word, the moral law demands compliance from duty, not from predilection, which one cannot and ought not to presuppose at all.[80]

158

Let us now see in an example whether the presentation of an action as a noble and magnanimous one contains more [of the] subjectively motive

---

[74] [*Beurteilung.* See above, Ak. V, 8 br. n. 78.]

[75] [Literally, 'do': *tun,* translated as 'do' below.]

[76] [*an . . . gebracht.*]

[77] [I.e., the moral law.]

[78] [*gefällig.*]

[79] [I.e., the element of feeling.]

[80] [See above, Ak. V, 80–88; and cf. the *Grounding for the Metaphysics of Morals,* Ak. IV, 397–403.]

force of an incentive than if the action is presented merely as duty in relation to the serious[81] moral law. The action where someone tries, at the greatest danger to his life, to rescue people from a shipwreck, if in doing so he himself ultimately loses his life, is indeed on the one hand credited to duty, but is on the other hand and for the most part also credited as a meritorious action;[82] but our high esteem for it is weakened very much by the concept of *duty toward oneself,*[83] a duty that here seems to suffer some impairment. More decisive is the magnanimous sacrifice of one's life for the preservation of one's country; and yet there remains some scruple as to whether it is indeed so perfectly a duty to dedicate oneself to this aim on one's own and without having been ordered to do so, and the action does not contain the full force of a model and impulse for imitation. But if something[84] is an irremissible duty, transgression of which violates the moral law in itself and without regard for human well-being and, as it were, tramples on this law's holiness (duties of this sort are usually called duties toward God,[85] because in him we think the ideal of holiness in substance[86]), then we dedicate to the compliance with it—compliance at the sacrifice of everything that might have any value[87] for the most fervent of all our inclinations—the maximally perfect deep respect, and we find our soul strengthened and elevated by such an example if we can convince ourselves through[88] it that human nature is capable of so great an elevation over everything that nature might, by way of incentives, bring forth as an opposite. *Juvenal* presents such an example in a climax that lets the reader vividly feel the force of the incentive hidden in the pure law of duty as duty:

> Esto bonus miles, tutor bonus, arbiter idem
> Integer; ambiguae si quando citabere testis

---

[81] [*ernst.*]

[82] [Cf. the *Metaphysics of Morals,* Ak. VI, 390–91.]

[83] [Cf. ibid., Ak. VI, 417–18.]

[84] [*es.*]

[85] [See above, Ak. V, 83–85.]

[86] [Cf. above, Ak. V, 41.]

[87] [*Wert.*]

[88] [*an.*]

Incertaeque rei, Phalaris licet imperet, ut sis
Falsus, et admoto dictet periuria tauro,
Summum crede nefas animam praeferre pudori
Et propter vitam vivendi perdere causas.[89]

If we can bring into our action anything flattering concerning the meritorious, then the incentive is already somewhat mixed with love for oneself and therefore has some assistance from the side of sensibility. But to put everything second to the holiness of duty alone and to become conscious that one *can* do this because our own reason acknowledges it as its command and says that one *ought* to do it—this is, as it were, to elevate oneself entirely above the world of sense, and is linked, as also an incentive of a power *that rules over sensibility,* with[90] that same consciousness of the law inseparably, even if not always with effect; yet this effect does also, through repeated occupation with this incentive and the initially slighter attempts at using it, give hope of being brought about [more frequently], so as to produce in us little by little the greatest but pure moral interest[91] therein.

The method therefore takes the following course. *At first* the concern is only to make the judging[92] according to moral laws a natural occupation accompanying all our own free actions as well as our observation of those of other people,[93] and to make it, as it were, a habit,[94] and to sharpen it by first asking whether the action objectively *conforms to the moral law,* and to which one; in doing this, one distinguishes attention to that law

[89] [The quote is from Juvenal, *Satires,* VIII, 79–84, and says: "Be a good soldier, a good guardian, or an impartial judge; if ever you are summoned as a witness in a dubious and uncertain case, though Phalaris himself should command you to be deceitful and, having brought his bull, should dictate perjury, count it the highest crime to prefer life to honor and to lose, for the sake of living, all that makes life worth living." (Cf., for parts of the same quote, the *Religion within the Bounds of Reason Alone,* Ak. VI, 49n, and the *Metaphysics of Morals,* Ak. VI, 334.) Phalaris (d. 554 B.C.), a tyrant of the Greek colony of Akragas (Roman Agrigentum, now Agrigento) in southwestern Sicily, is said to have had his enemies killed in a brass bull by having a fire lit under it.]

[90] [Reading *mit* for *in.* This slight adjustment seems preferable to Natorp's and Vorländer's proposals for dealing with this passage.]

[91] [See the *Grounding for the Metaphysics of Morals,* Ak. IV, 401n, 413n, 448–50, 460n, 461–63; also above, Ak. V, 79–81; and the *Metaphysics of Morals,* Ak. VI, 212–13.]

[92] [*Beurteilung.* See above, Ak. V, 8 br. n. 78.]

[93] [See *On Pedagogy* (*Über Pädagogik*), Ak. IX, 486–99.]

[94] [See the *Metaphysics of Morals,* Ak. VI, 479–80.]

which provides merely a *basis* for obligation[95] from the law which is in fact obligatory[96] (*leges obligandi a legibus obligantibus*)[97] (e.g., the law of what the *need* of human beings requires of me from what their *right* requires of me, the latter of which prescribes essential but the former only nonessential[98] duties), and thus one teaches how to distinguish different duties that come together in an action. The other point to which attention must be directed is the question as to whether the action was also done (subjectively) *for the sake of the moral law* and therefore has not only moral[99] correctness as a deed but also, according to its maxim, moral worth[100] as an attitude. Now, there is no doubt that this exercise[101] and the consciousness of a cultivation of our reason, arising therefrom, in making judgments merely about the practical must little by little produce a certain interest even in reason's law and hence in moral actions. For we finally become fond of that whose contemplation lets us feel the expanded use of our cognitive powers, a use that is furthered above all by that wherein we find moral correctness, because only in such an order of things can reason, with its ability to determine a priori according to principles what ought to occur, find itself good. After all, an observer of nature finally becomes fond of objects that initially offend his senses, when he discovers in them the great purposiveness of their organization[102] and thus feasts his reason on his contemplation of them; and Leibniz put an insect, which he had carefully examined through the microscope, gently back again onto its leaf, because he had found himself instructed by the sight of it and had, as it were, received from it a benefaction.

But this occupation of the power of judgment, which lets us feel our own cognitive powers, is not yet interest in the actions and in their morality itself. It merely brings about [the fact] that one gladly entertains oneself with

160

[95] [*Verbindlichkeit.*]

[96] [I.e., obligating: *verbindend.*]

[97] [Laws of obligation from obligating (or obligatory) laws. Cf. the *Metaphysics of Morals,* Ak. VI, 224.]

[98] [*außerwesentlich.*]

[99] [*sittlich* here; *moralisch* above.]

[100] [*Wert.*]

[101] [*Übung.*]

[102] [On organization and organized beings, cf. the *Critique of Judgment,* Ak. V, 193, 349, 375–76, 384, 420, and 426.]

such judging, and it gives to virtue or the way of thinking according to moral laws a form of beauty that is admired but not yet therefore sought (*laudatur et alget*),[103] [just] as everything the contemplation of which brings about subjectively a consciousness of the harmony of our powers of presentation,[104] and in which we feel our entire cognitive power[105] (understanding and imagination) strengthened, produces a liking[106] that can also be communicated to other people[107]—the existence of the object remaining nonetheless indifferent to us, inasmuch as it is regarded only as the prompting whereby we become aware of the predisposition of the talents in us, which is elevated above animality.[108] Now, however, the *second* exercise enters upon its task, namely to make the purity of the will discernible in the vivid exhibition of the moral attitude in examples, at first only as a negative perfection of the will insofar as in an action done from duty no incentives whatever of the inclinations influence the action as determining bases. By this the learner is at least kept attentive to the consciousness of his *freedom*,[109] and although this renunciation[110] arouses an initial sensation of pain, yet, because it withdraws that learner from the constraint of even true needs, there is proclaimed to him at the same time a liberation[111] from the manifold dissatisfaction in which all these needs entangle him, and the mind is made receptive to satisfaction from other sources. The heart is, after all, freed[112] and relieved of a burden—which always secretly weighs upon it—when in pure moral decisions, of which examples are put forth, there is uncovered to the human being an inner ability not quite familiar otherwise even to him, *the inner freedom* to detach himself from the vehement obtrusiveness of the inclinations to such an extent that none at all, not even the

161

---

[103] [*probitas laudatur et alget:* 'Uprightness is praised and [shivers with] cold.' Juvenal, *Satires,* I, 74.

[104] [*Vorstellungskräfte.*]

[105] [*Erkenntnisvermögen.*]

[106] [*Wohlgefallen.* On this kind of liking (a feeling of pleasure), cf. the *Critique of Judgment,* Ak V, 190, 191, 197, 216–19, 244, 289, 292, and 306.]

[107] [Cf. ibid., 217, 218, 221, 231, 238–39, 275, 293, 295, 306, and 433.]

[108] [See *On Pedagogy,* Ak. IX, 466–85.]

[109] [*Freiheit.*]

[110] [Of influence from incentives of the inclinations.]

[111] [*Befreiung.*]

[112] [Or 'liberated': *befreit.*]

one that we care about most, shall have[113] an influence on a decision for which we are now to employ our reason.[114] Consider a case where *only I alone* know that the wrong is on my side and where—although a free confession of this wrong and an offer of satisfaction find themselves strongly contradicted by vanity, self-interest,[115] and even an otherwise not illegitimate aversion to him whose right I have encroached upon—I can nonetheless brush aside all these qualms: such a case does, after all, contain a consciousness of an independence—from inclinations and from fortunate circumstances—and of the possibility of being sufficient to oneself, a consciousness that is salutary to me throughout for other aims as well. And now the law of duty, through the positive worth that compliance with this law lets us feel, finds readier admittance [to the human mind][116] through the *respect for ourselves* in the consciousness of our freedom. On this respect, if it is well-founded—if the human being dreads nothing more intensely than to find himself, in inner self-examination, inferior[117] and reprehensible in his own eyes—every good moral attitude can now be grafted, because this[118] is the best and indeed the only guard to prevent ignoble and corrupting impulses from penetrating into the mind.

With this [discussion] I wanted only to point to the most general[119] maxims of the doctrine of method for moral molding and exercise.[120] Since the manifoldness of duties would require, for each kind of duty, also particular determinations and would thus amount to a lengthy task,[121] I shall be considered excused if in a work like this, which is only a preparation, I settle for these basic features.

---

[113] ['shall have' translates (the subjunctive) *habe.*]

[114] [See above, Ak. V, 78–79.]

[115] [*Eigennutz.*]

[116] [Cf. above, Ak. V, 151.]

[117] [*geringschätzig.*]

[118] [One's self-respect's being thus well-founded: *dieses.*]

[119] [*allgemeinst.*]

[120] [*Bildung und Übung.*]

[121] [Kant undertook this task in the *Metaphysics of Morals,* which appeared in 1797, some nine years after the *Critique of Practical Reason.*]

Conclusion

Two things fill the mind with ever new and increasing admiration and reverence, the more frequently and persistently one's meditation deals with them: *the starry sky above me and the moral law within me*. Neither of them do I need to seek or merely suspect outside my purview, as veiled in obscurities or [as lying] in the extravagant:[122] I see them before me and connect them directly with the consciousness of my existence. The first thing starts from the place that I occupy in the external world of sense and expands the connection in which I stand into the immensely large, with worlds upon worlds and systems of systems, and also into boundless times of their periodic motion, the beginning[123] and continuance thereof. The second thing starts from my invisible self, my personality,[124] and exhibits me in a world that has true infinity but that is discernible[125] only to the understanding, and with that world (but thereby simultaneously also with all those visible worlds) I cognize myself not, as in the first case, in a merely contingent connection, but in a universal[126] and necessary one. The first sight,[127] of a countless multitude of worlds, annihilates, as it were, my importance as an *animal creature* that, after having for a short time been provided (one knows not how) with vital force, must give back again to the planet (a mere dot in the universe) the matter from which it came. The second sight, on the contrary, elevates infinitely my worth as that of an *intelligence* by my personality, in which the moral law reveals to me a life independent of animality and even of the entire world of sense, at least as far as can be gleaned from the purposive determination[128] of my existence by this law, a determination that is not restricted to conditions and boundaries of this life but proceeds to infinity.[129]

162

---

[122] [I.e., in the transcendent: *im Überschwenglichen.*]

[123] [Or 'start': *Anfang.*]

[124] [I.e., personhood: *Persönlichkeit;* likewise below.]

[125] [*spürbar.*]

[126] [*allgemein.*]

[127] [Or 'spectacle': *Anblick;* likewise below.]

[128] [*Bestimmung,* which also means 'vocation.']

[129] [Or *ad infinitum: ins Unendliche.*]

However, although admiration and respect can stimulate investigation, they cannot make up for the lack of it. What, then, is to be done in order to engage in investigation in a way that is useful and appropriate to the sublimity of the object? Examples may serve as a warning in this, but also for imitation. Contemplation of the world started from the most splendid spectacle[130] that could ever be put before human senses and that our understanding could ever bear to pursue in its vast range, and it ended—with astrology. Morals started with human nature's noblest property, whose development and cultivation point[131] to infinite benefit, and it ended—with fanaticism, or with superstition. So it is with all still crude attempts wherein the primary part of the task hinges on the use of reason, which, unlike the use of the feet, is not found on its own, by means of frequent exercise, above all if it concerns properties that cannot be exhibited so directly in common experience. But after there had come into vogue, although late, the maxim to deliberate carefully beforehand on all steps that reason proposes to take and not to let it enter upon its course except on the track of a method carefully reflected upon beforehand, the judging of the world edifice[132] acquired an entirely different direction and therewith also an incomparably happier outcome. The fall of a stone, the motion of a sling, resolved into their elements and into the forces manifesting themselves in these [actions] and treated mathematically, ultimately produced that clear insight—unchangeable throughout the future—into the world structure which, as observation proceeds, can hope to keep always expanding but need never fear having to regress.

163

Now, this example can counsel us to enter upon this same path in dealing with the moral predispositions of our nature and can give us hope for a similar good result. We do, after all, have at hand the examples of the morally judging reason. If we now dissect these examples but, lacking *mathematics,* take up in repeated experiments on common human understanding a procedure—similar to *chemistry*—of *separation* of the empirical from the rational that may be found in them, this can allow us to cognize[133] both of them *pure* and, with certainty, what each can accomplish by itself; thus it can forestall in part the straying of a still *crude,* unpracticed judging, and in part

[130] [Or 'sight': *Anblick.*]

[131] [*hinaussehen.*]

[132] [*Weltgebäude;* 'world structure,' below, translates *Weltbau.*]

[133] [*kennbar machen.*]

(what is needed far more) the *soarings of genius* through which—as usually happens with the adepts of the philosopher's stone[134]—without any methodical investigation and cognition[135] of nature, dreamed-up treasures are promised and true ones dissipated. In a word: science (critically sought and methodically initiated) is the narrow gate that leads to the *doctrine of wisdom,* if this is taken to mean not merely what one ought *to do* but what ought to serve *teachers* as a standard for preparing well and recognizably[136] the path to wisdom that everyone ought to walk, and to secure others against erroneous paths; [it is] a science of which philosophy must always remain the preserver, and although the public need not take an interest[137] in philosophy's subtle investigation, it must indeed take one in the *doctrines*[138] which, after such treatment, can for the first time be quite clearly evident to it.

---

[134] [Literally, 'stone of the wise': *Stein der Weisen.*]

[135] [*Kenntnis.*]

[136] [*kenntlich.*]

[137] [*Anteil.*]

[138] [Or 'teachings': *Lehren.*]

SELECTED BIBLIOGRAPHY

A. EDITIONS OF THE GERMAN TEXT

1. Original Editions

Critik der practischen Vernunft von Immanuel Kant. 1st ed. Riga: Johann Friedrich Hartknoch, 1788. Reprinted. Kant im Original, vol. 12. Erlangen: Fischer, 1984. Reprinted, with an introduction by Lewis White Beck. *Kant's Three Critiques.* New York: Routledge, 1993.

Critik der practischen Vernunft von Immanuel Kant. 2nd and 4th eds. Riga: Johann Friedrich Hartknoch, 1792, 1797. [There is no 3rd edition, perhaps because the 2nd was twice as large as the others.]

Critik der practischen Vernunft von Immanuel Kant. 5th and 6th eds. Leipzig: Johann Friedrich Hartknoch, 1818, 1827.

2. Nineteenth-Century Editions

Immanuel Kant's sämmtliche Werke. 14 vols. Ed. Karl Rosenkranz and Friedrich Wilhelm Schubert. Leipzig: Leopold Voss, 1838–42. Vol. 8. Ed. Karl Rosenkranz, 1838.

Immanuel Kant's Werke. Carefully revised complete edition in ten volumes. Edited, with a preface, by Gustav Hartenstein. Leipzig: Modes und Baumann, 1838–39. Vol. 4, 1838.

Immanuel Kant's sämmtliche Werke. 12 vols. Ed. Julius Hermann von Kirchmann. Philosophische Bibliothek. Vol. 7. Leipzig: Leopold Voss, 1838–42. 2nd ed. Berlin: L. Heimann, 1869. 3rd ed. Heidelberg: Weiss, 1882.

Immanuel Kant's sämmtliche Werke. 8 vols. In chronological order. Ed. Gustav Hartenstein. Leipzig: Leopold Voss, 1867–68. Vol. 5, 1867.

Kritik der praktischen Vernunft. Text of the 1788 ed. with consideration of the 2nd and 4th editions (1792, 1797). Ed. Karl Kehrbach. Reclams Universal-Bibliothek. Leipzig: Philipp Reclam Jr., 1878. Reprint. Ed. Raymund Schmidt. Reclams

206

Universal-Bibliothek. Leipzig: Philipp Reclam Jr., 1924. Reprint. Ed. Joachim Kopper. Reclams Universal-Bibliothek. Stuttgart: Reclam, 1961, 1989.

3. Contemporary Editions

Kants gesammelte Schriften. Königlich Preußische Akademie der Wissenschaften. Berlin: G. Reimer; Berlin and New York: Walter de Gruyter & Co. and Predecessors, 1902–. Vol. 5, ed., with introduction, variant readings, and factual elucidations, by Paul Natorp, 1908. Electronic edition according to vols. 1–13 of the Akademie-Textausgabe. Edited and electronically processed for Word-Cruncher for Windows by the Institut für Angewandte Kommunikations- und Sprachforschung (IKS) e.V. Version 12.02.98. Computer optical disc. Bonn: IKS, 1998.

Kants sämtliche Werke. 10 vols. Edited, in association with Otto Buek, Paul Gedan, Walter Kinkel, Friedrich Michael Schiele, and Theodor Valentiner, by Karl Vorländer. Philosophische Bibliothek. Leipzig: Felix Meiner, 1904–40. Vol. 2, with introduction and indexes by Karl Vorländer, 1906.

Immanuel Kants Werke in acht Büchern. 8 books in 2 vols. Selected, and provided with an introduction, by Hugo Renner. Berlin: Weichert, 1904, 1921. Vol. 2, book 5.

Immanuel Kants sämtliche Werke. 6 vols. Ed. Felix Gross. Großherzog Wilhelm-Ernst Ausgabe. Leipzig: Inselverlag, 1913, 1920–23. Vol. 5.

Immanuel Kants Werke. 11 vols. Ed. Ernst Cassirer, Hermann Cohen, Artur Buchenau, Otto Buek, Albert Görland, and Benzion Kellermann. Berlin: Bruno Cassirer, 1912–23. Vol. 5, ed. Benzion Kellermann, 1914.

Kritik der praktischen Vernunft als Prüfung der tätigen Vernunft (*Critique of Practical Reason as Test of Acting Reason*). Ed. Georg Deycke. Lübeck, Germany: Coleman, 1919. 3rd ed. Lübeck: Coleman, 1922.

Kritik der praktischen Vernunft. Nebst Grundlegung zur Metaphysik der Sitten. Ed. Heinrich Schmidt. Leipzig: Alfred Kroner, 1925.

Kritik der praktischen Vernunft. Ed. Karl Vorländer. Philosophische Bibliothek, vol. 38. 9th ed. Leipzig: Felix Meiner, 1929. 10th, expanded ed., with a bibliography by Heiner Klemme. Hamburg: Felix Meiner, 1990. Reprint. Hamburg: Felix Meiner, 1993.

Immanuel Kant. Werke. Theorie-Werkausgabe. 12 vols. Ed. Wilhelm Weischedel. Frankfurt-am-Main: Suhrkamp, 1968, 1977. Vol. 7. Previously issued as *Werke in zehn Bänden.* 10 vols. Darmstadt: Wissenschaftliche Buchgesellschaft, 1968, 1975, 1983. Vols. 6–7. Originally issued as *Werke in sechs Bänden.* 6 vols. Wiesbaden, Germany: Inselverlag; Darmstadt: Wissenschaftliche Buchgesellschaft: 1956–64, 1966–70. Vol 4.

Kritik der praktischen Vernunft; Grundlegung zur Metaphysik der Sitten. Suhrkamp Taschenbuch Wissenschaft, vol. 56. Frankfurt-am-Main: Suhrkamp, 1956, 1974.

Kritik der praktischen Vernunft. Ed. Raymund Schmidt. Unchanged reprint of the 1928 revision of the former Kehrbach edition. Wiesbaden, Germany: VMA-Verlag, 1982.

Immanuel Kant. Werke in sechs Bänden. 6 vols. Ed. Rolf Toman. Cologne: Könemann, 1995. Vol. 3.

Die drei Kritiken. Ed. Alexander Ulfig. 2 vols. Cologne: Parkland, 1999. Vol. 2.

B. PREVIOUS COMPLETE ENGLISH TRANSLATIONS

Kant's Critique of Practical Reason and Other Works on the Theory of Ethics. Trans. Thomas Kingsmill Abbott. "Being an enlarged edition of *Kant's Theory of Ethics.*" London: Longmans, Green, 1879. 3rd ed., revised and enlarged, with a memoir and portrait. London: Longmans, Green & Co., 1883. 5th ed., revised, with a memoir and two portraits. London: Longmans, Green & Co., 1898; Reprint, Chicago: Encyclopædia Britannica, 1952, 1955. 6th ed., revised, with a memoir and one portrait. London: Longmans, Green, 1909, 1927, 1967. The *Critique* by itself. Amherst, N.Y.: Prometheus Books, 1996.

Critique of Practical Reason, and Other Writings in Moral Philosophy. Translated and edited, with an introduction, by Lewis White Beck. Chicago: University of Chicago Press, 1949; The *Critique* by itself. New York: Liberal Arts Press, 1956. Indianapolis, Ind.: Bobbs-Merrill, 1956. New York: Garland, 1976. 3rd ed., with notes. New York: Macmillan; Toronto: Maxwell Macmillan Canada; New York: Maxwell Macmillan International, 1993; Upper Saddle River, N.J.: Prentice Hall, 1993.

Critique of Practical Reason. Translated and edited by Mary Gregor; with an introduction by Andrews Reath. Cambridge Texts in the History of Philosophy. Cambridge: Cambridge University Press, 1997. Also in Immanuel Kant, *Practical Philosophy.* Translated and edited by Mary J. Gregor; general introduction by Allen Wood. Cambridge: Cambridge University Press, 1996.

Critique of Practical Reason. Trans. Heinrich Walter Cassirer; ed. G. Heath King and Ronald Weitzman; with an introduction by D. M. MacKinnon. Marquette Studies in Philosophy, vol. 17. Milwaukee, Wisc.: Marquette University Press, 1998.

C. REFERENCE WORKS ON THE SECOND *CRITIQUE*

Materialien zu Kants 'Kritik der praktischen Vernunft.' Ed. Rüdiger Bittner and Konrad Cramer. Frankfurt-am-Main: Suhrkamp, 1975.

Stellenindex und Konkordanz zur "Kritik der praktischen Vernunft." Ed. Heinrich P. Delfosse and Michael Oberhausen, with the collaboration of Michael Albrecht, Elfriede Conrad, and Michael Trauth. 2 vols. Stuttgart–Bad Cannstatt: Frommann-Holzboog, 1995.

D. OTHER WORKS BY KANT CITED IN THIS TRANSLATION

Volume and page numbers refer to the original texts in the *Akademie* edition. The index lists these works under their English titles, as given here.

Anthropology from a Pragmatic Point of View (Anthropologie in pragmatischer Hinsicht). Vol. 7, 117–333.

Critique of Judgment (Kritik der Urteilskraft). Vol. 5, 165–485.

Critique of Pure Reason (Kritik der reinen Vernunft). Vol. 3; vol. 4, 1–252.

Dispute among the University's Schools (Streit der Fakultäten). Vol. 7, 1–116.

First Introduction to the *Critique of Judgment (Erste Einleitung zur Kritik der Urteilskraft)*. Vol. 20, 193–251.

Grounding for the Metaphysics of Morals (Grundlegung zur Metaphysik der Sitten). Vol. 4, 385–463.

Logic (Logik). Vol. 9, 1–150.

Metaphysical Foundations of Natural Science (Metaphysische Anfangsgründe der Naturwissenschaft). Vol. 4, 465–565.

Metaphysics of Morals (Metaphysik der Sitten). Vol. 6, 203–493.

On a Supposed Right to Lie out of Love of Humankind (Über ein vermeintes Recht, aus Menschenliebe zu lügen). Vol. 8, 427–30.

The Only Possible Basis of Proof for Demonstrating the Existence of God (Der einzig mögliche Beweisgrund zu einer Demonstration des Daseins Gottes). Vol. 2, 63–163.

On Pedagogy (Über Pädagogik). Vol. 9, 437–99.

Prolegomena to Any Future Metaphysics . . . (Prolegomena zu einer jeden künftigen Metaphysik . . .). Vol. 4, 253–383.

Religion within the Bounds of Reason Alone (Die Religion innerhalb der Grenzen der bloßen Vernunft). Vol. 6, 1–202.

What Does It Mean: To Orient Oneself in One's Thought? (Was heißt: Sich im Denken orientieren?) Vol. 8, 131–48.

E. SOURCES FROM OR CONCERNING THE ANCIENT BACKGROUND THAT ARE CITED IN THIS TRANSLATION

The Epicurus Reader: Selected Writings and Testimonia. Trans. Brad Inwood and Lloyd P. Gerson; introduction by D. S. Hutchinson. Indianapolis, Ind.: Hackett, 1994.

Horace. *Satires*. In *The Satires of Horace*. Ed. Niall Rudd. London: Cambridge University Press, 1966. Reprint. London: Bristol Classical Press, 1982, 1994.

Juvenal. *Satires*. In *The Satires of Juvenal Translated*. With explanatory and classical notes relating to the laws and customs of the Greeks and Romans. 1st AMS ed. Works. English and Latin. 1978. New York: AMS Press, 1978.

Plato. *The Republic*. Trans. G.M.A. Grube. Revised by C.D.C. Reeve. Indianapolis, Ind.: Hackett, 1992.

Plautus. *Persa*. In *Plautus*. With an English translation by Paul Nixon. The Loeb Classical Library. London: W. Heinemann; New York: G. P. Putnam's Sons, 1916.

F. Sources from or Concerning the Seventeenth- and Eighteenth-Century Background That Are Cited in This Translation

Baumgarten, Alexander Gottlieb. *Metaphysica (Metaphysics)*. Magdeburg: Hemmerde, 1739. Second reprint of the 7th edition of 1779. New York: G. Olms, 1982. Translation. *Die Vorreden zur Metaphysik*. Edited, translated, and commented upon by Ursula Niggli. Frankfurt-am-Main: Klostermann, 1999.

Beattie, James. *An Essay on the Nature and Immutability of Truth, in Opposition to Sophistry and Scepticism*. Edinburgh: A. Kincaid & J. Bell, 1770. Reprint. New York: Garland, 1983.

Cheseldon, William. Report of the reaction of one of his patients. In *Philosophical Transactions* XXXV 1728: 447.

Crusius, Christian August. *Entwurf der nothwendigen Vernunft-Wahrheiten, wiefern sie den zufälligen entgegen gesetzet werden (Outline of Necessary Truths Insofar as They Are Contrasted with Contingent Truths)*. Leipzig: Gleditsch, 1745. Reprint. Hildesheim, Germany: G. Olms, 1964.

—————. *Weg zur Gewissheit und Zuverlässigkeit der menschlichen Erkenntniss (Path to Certainty and Reliability of Human Cognition)*. Leipzig: Gleditsch, 1747. Reprint. Hildesheim, Germany: G. Olms, 1965.

Feder, Johann Georg Heinrich. *Über Raum und Caussalität, zur Prüfung der Kantischen Philosophie*. Göttingen: Johann Christian Dieterich, 1787. Reprint. Brussels: Culture et civilisation, 1968.

Flatt, Johann Friedrich. Review of the *Grounding for the Metaphysics of Morals* by Immanuel Kant. *Tübingische gelehrte Anzeigen (Tübingen Scholarly Announcements)*. February 16, 1786, item 14, 105–12.

Fontenelle, Bernard Le Bovier de. *Entretiens sur la pluralité des mondes (Conversations on the Plurality of Worlds)*. Paris: C. Blageart, 1686. Contemporary critical edition with (French) introduction and notes, by Alexandre Calame. Paris: Nizet, 1984. Trans. H. A. Hargreaves, with an introduction by Nina Rattner Gelbart. Berkeley: University of California Press, 1990.

Garve, Christian. Review of the *Critique of Pure Reason* by Immanuel Kant. *Zugaben (Supplement)* to the *Göttingische gelehrte Anzeigen (Göttingen Scholarly Announcements)*, January 19, 1782, item 3, 40–48. Reprinted as *Beilage (Attachment) II* in the *Philosophische Bibliothek* edition of Kant's *Prolegomena to Any Future Metaphysics*, vol. 40, 167–74. Kant's reply to that review is contained in the *Anhang (Appendix)* to the *Prolegomena*, Ak. IV, 371–83.

Hume, David. *Philosophical Essays Concerning Human Understanding*, later renamed *An Enquiry Concerning Human Understanding*. London: A. Millar, 1748. Contemporary edition. *An Enquiry Concerning Human Understanding; A Letter from a Gentleman to His Friend in Edinburgh; An Abstract of a Treatise of*

Human Nature. Edited and introduced by Eric Steinberg. 2nd ed. Indianapolis, Ind.: Hackett, 1993.

———. *A Treatise of Human Nature*. London: J. Noon, 1739–40. Contemporary edition. Edited, with an analytical index, by L. A. Selby-Bigge. 2nd ed. with text rev. and variant readings by P. H. Nidditch. Oxford: Clarendon Press; New York: Oxford University Press, 1978.

Hutcheson, Francis. *An Inquiry into the Original of Our Ideas of Beauty and Virtue; in Two Treatises, in Which the Principles of the Earl of Shaftesbury Are Explain'd and Defended Against the Author of The Fable of The Bees, and the Ideas of Moral Good and Evil are Establish'd According to the Sentiments of the Antient Moralists. With an Attempt to Introduce a Mathematical Calculation in Subjects of Morality*. London: J. Darby, 1725. 4th, corr., ed. London: for D. Medwinter, 1738. Reprint. Westmead, Farnborough, Haunts, U.K.: Gregg International, 1969.

Leibniz, Baron Gottfried Wilhelm von. *Principia philosophiae, more geometrico demonstrata* (*The Principles of Philosophy, Demonstrated in the Manner of Geometry*), 1714. Contemporary edition: *Monadology, and Other Philosophical Essays*. Trans. Paul Schrecker and Anne Martin Schrecker; with an introduction and notes by Paul Schrecker. Indianapolis, Ind.: Bobbs-Merrill, 1965.

Mandeville, Bernard. *The Fable of the Bees: or, Private Vices, Publick Benefits: Containing Several Discourses to Demonstrate That Human Frailties, During the Degeneracy of Mankind, May Be Turn'd to the Advantage of the Civil Society, and Made to Supply the Place of Moral Virtues*. London: J. Roberts, 1714. Edited, with an introduction, by E. J. Hundert. Indianapolis, Ind.: Hackett, 1997.

Mendelssohn, Moses. *Morgenstunden, oder Vorlesungen über das Dasein Gottes* (*Morning Hours, or Lectures on the Existence of God*). Berlin: C. F. Voss & Sohn, 1785. Recent edition, including the *Briefwechsel* (*Correspondence*) *Mendelssohn–Kant*. Ed. Dominique Bourel. Stuttgart: Reclam, 1979.

Montaigne, Michel Eyquem. "Apologie de Raymond Sebond." In the *Essais*. Bordeaux, France: S. Millanges, 1580. Translation. *An Apology for Raymond Sebond*. Translated and edited with an introduction and notes by M. A. Screech. London: Penguin Books, 1993.

Pistorius, Hermann Andreas. Anonymous review of the *Grounding for the Metaphysics of Morals* by Immanuel Kant. *Allgemeine deutsche Bibliothek*. Berlin: F. Nicolai. Vol. 66, part II, 447–63.

Priestley, Joseph. *The Doctrine of Philosophical Necessity Illustrated*. London: J. Johnson, 1777. Contemporary edition: *Disquisitions Relating to Matter and Spirit, and The Doctrine of Philosophical Necessity Illustrated*. New York: Garland, 1976.

Smith, Robert. *A Compleat System of Opticks in Four Books, viz. a Popular, a Mathematical, a Mechanical, and a Philosophical Treatise: To Which Are Added Remarks upon the Whole*. 2 vols. Cambridge: Printed for the author, sold by Cornelius Crownfield, 1738. Translated and adapted by Abraham Gotthelf Kästner as *Vollständiger Lehrbegriff der Optik*. Altenburg: Richterische Buchhandlung, 1755.

Spinoza, Baruch (Benedict). *Ethica ordine geometrico demonstrata* (*Ethics Demonstrated in Geometric Order*). Part of the *Opera posthuma* (*Posthumous Works*). Amsterdam: Rievwertsz, 1677. Contemporary edition of the *Ethica*. Ed. J. van Vloten and J.P.N. Land. The Hague: Nijhoff, 1914. English translation: *The Ethics: Treatise on the Emendation of the Intellect; Selected Letters*. Trans. Samuel Shirley; ed., with introduction, by Seymour Feldman. 2nd ed. Indianapolis, Ind.: Hackett, 1992.

The Stoics. Reprint of the Chatto & Windus edition of 1975. Indianapolis, Ind.: Hackett, 1994. Copublished in the U.K. by Gerald Duckworth & Company Ltd.

Tittel, Gottlob August. *Über Herrn Kants Moralreform* (*On Mr. Kant's Moral Reform*). Frankfurt and Leipzig: Gebrüder Pfähler, 1786. Reprint. Brussels: Culture et civilisation, 1969.

Wizenmann, Thomas. *An den Herrn Professor Kant von dem Verfasser der Resultate Jacobi'scher und Mendelssohn'scher Philosophie* (*To Professor Kant, from the Author of the Results of Jacobi's and Mendelssohn's Philosophy*). Deutsches Museum, February 1787.

———. *Die Resultate der Jacobi'schen und Mendelssohn'schen Philosophie, kritisch untersucht von einem Freywilligen* (*The Results of Jacobi's and Mendelssohn's Philosophy, Critically Investigated by a Volunteer*). Published anonymously. Leipzig, 1786. Reprinted, with an epilogue by Rainer Wild. Hildesheim, Germany: Gerstenberg, 1984.

Wolff, Baron Christian von. *Psychologia rationalis* (*Rational Psychology*). Frankfurt and Leipzig: Renger, 1734. Contemporary edition: *Psychologia rationalis Christiani Wolfii*. Critical edition with (French) introduction, notes, and index, by Jean École. Hildesheim, Germany: G. Olms, 1972.

G. Book-Length Secondary Sources in English and Some Foreign Languages

1. Studies of the Second Critique or of Kant's Practical Philosophy as a Whole

Beck, Lewis White. *A Commentary on Kant's Critique of Practical Reason*. Chicago: University of Chicago Press, 1996, 1960.

Delbos, Victor. *La Philosophie pratique de Kant*. 2nd ed. Paris: F. Alcan, 1926.

Hare, John E. *The Moral Gap: Kantian Ethics, Human Limits, and God's Assistance*. Oxford: Clarendon Press; New York: Oxford University Press, 1996.

Hartnack, Justus. *Immanuel Kant: An Explanation of His Theory of Knowledge and Moral Philosophy*. Atlantic Highlands, N.J.: Humanities Press, 1974.

Höffe, Otfried. *Immanuel Kant*. Trans. Marshall Farrier. Albany, N.Y.: State University of New York Press, 1994. Translation of *Immanuel Kant*. Munich: C. H. Beck, 1983. 5th, rev. ed. Munich: Beck, 2000.

Kirchmann, Julius Hermann von. *Erläuterungen zu Kant's Kritik der praktischen Vernunft.* Berlin: L. Heimann, 1869.

Klemme, Heiner F., and Manfred Kuehn, eds. *Immanuel Kant.* 2 vols. Aldershot, U.K.; Brookfield, Vt.: International Library of Critical Essays in the History of Philosophy. Aldershot, U.K.: Ashgate, 1999. Vol. 2.

Landucci, Sergio. *La "Critica della ragion pratica" di Kant: Introduzione alla lettura.* Rome: Nuova Italia scientifica, 1993.

Messer, August. *Kommentar zu Kants ethischen und religions-philosophischen Hauptschriften: Grundlegung zur Metaphysik der Sitten, Kritik der praktischen Vernunft, Religion innerhalb der Grenzen der blossen Vernunft.* Leipzig: F. Meiner, 1929.

Nelson, Leonard. *Gesammelte Schriften in neun Bänden.* Ed. Paul Bernays et al. 9 vols. Hamburg: F. Meiner (1970–74). Especially vol. 4.

O'Farrell, Frank. *Per leggere la Critica della ragione pratica di Kant: La "Critica della ragione pratica" pensata come risposte a domande.* Rome: Editrice Pontificia Università Gregoriana, 1990.

O'Neill, Onora. *Constructions of Reason: Explorations of Kant's Practical Philosophy.* Cambridge: Cambridge University Press, 1989.

Prauss, Gerold, ed. *Kant: Zur Deutung seiner Theorie von Erkennen und Handeln.* Cologne: Kiepenheuer und Witsch, 1973.

Walker, Ralph Charles Sutherland. *Kant.* London: Phoenix, 1997. Reprint. New York: Routledge, 1999.

Watson, John. *The Philosophy of Kant Explained.* Glasgow: J. Maclehose and Sons, 1908.

2.   Studies on Basic Topics in Moral Philosophy

Acton, Harry Burrows. *Kant's Moral Philosophy.* London: Macmillan; New York: St. Martin's Press, 1970.

Alquié, Ferdinand. *La Morale de Kant.* Paris: Centre de documentation universitaire, 1974.

Allison, Henry E. *Kant's Theory of Freedom.* Cambridge: Cambridge University Press, 1990.

Altmann, Amandus. *Freiheit im Spiegel des rationalen Gesetzes bei Kant.* Berlin: Duncker & Humblot, 1982.

Ameriks, Karl. *Kant and the Fate of Autonomy: Problems in the Appropriation of the Critical Philosophy.* Cambridge: Cambridge University Press, 2000.

Astrada, Carlos. *La ética formal y los valores.* La Plata, Argentina: Imprenta López, 1938.

Atwell, John E. *Ends and Principles in Kant's Moral Thought.* Dordrecht: M. Nijhoff; distributed in the U.S. by Kluwer Academic Publishers, 1986.

Aune, Bruce. *Kant's Theory of Morals.* Princeton, N.J.: Princeton University Press, 1979.

Auxter, Thomas. *Kant's Moral Teleology*. Macon, Ga.: Mercer University Press, 1982.

Balbir Singh. *Kant's Ethics of Practical Reason*. Jullundur City, India: S. Nagin, 1970.

Baron, Marcia W. *Kantian Ethics Almost without Apology*. Ithaca, N.Y.: Cornell University Press, 1995.

Bauch, Bruno. *Vom Prinzip der Moral bei Kant*. Halle/Saale, Germany: Hofbuchdruckerei von C. A. Kaemmerer & Co., 1903.

Beets, Muus Gerrit Jan. *Reality and Freedom: Reflections on Kant's Moral Philosophy*. Delft, The Netherlands: Eburon, 1988.

Böckerstette, Heinrich. *Aporien der Freiheit und ihre Aufklärung durch Kant*. Stuttgart-Bad Cannstatt: Frommann-Holzboog, 1982.

Boutroux, Émile. *La morale de Kant et le temps présent*. Paris: A. Colin, 1904.

Buchenau, Artur. *Kants Lehre vom kategorischen Imperativ: Eine Einführung in die Grundfragen der Kantischen Ethik*. 2nd, unchanged ed. Leipzig: F. Meiner, 1923 (1913).

Carnois, Bernard. *The Coherence of Kant's Doctrine of Freedom*. Trans. David Booth. Chicago: University of Chicago Press, 1987. Translation of *La cohérence de la doctrine kantienne de la liberté*. Paris: Seuil, 1973.

Carpi, Orlando. *E. Kant: Dalla critica alla metafisica della moralità*. Bologna, Italy: V.A.E.; Distribuzione EDS, 1988.

———. *Kant: L'etica della ragione*. Rimini, Italy: Panozzo, 1989.

Chadwick, Ruth F., ed. *Kant's Moral and Political Philosophy*. New York: Routledge, 1992.

Conrad, Judith. *Freiheit und Naturbeherrschung: Zur Problematik der Ethik Kants*. Würzburg, Germany: Königshausen & Neumann, 1992.

Cox, J. Gray. *The Will at the Crossroads: A Reconstruction of Kant's Moral Philosophy*. Lanham, Md.: University Press of America, 1984.

Cresson, André. *La morale de Kant: Étude critique*. 2nd, revised and expanded edition. Paris: F. Alcan, 1904.

Forschner, Maximilian. *Gesetz und Freiheit: Zum Problem der Autonomie bei I. Kant*. Munich: Pustet, 1974.

Goldman, Alan H. *Moral Knowledge*. New York: Routledge, 1988, 1990.

Guisán, Esperanza, coord. *Esplendor y miseria de la ética kantiana*. Contributions by José Luis L. Aranguren et al. Barcelona: Anthropos, 1988.

Gunkel, Andreas. *Spontaneität und moralische Autonomie: Kants Philosophie der Freiheit*. Bern: P. Haupt, 1989.

Guyer, Paul. *Kant on Freedom, Law, and Happiness*. Cambridge: Cambridge University Press, 2000.

Hägerström, Axel. *Kants Ethik im Verhältnis zu seinen erkenntnistheoretischen Grundgedanken, systematisch dargestellt*. Uppsala, Sweden: Almqvist & Wiksells; Leipzig: O. Harrassowitz, 1902.

Herman, Barbara. *Morality as Rationality: A Study of Kant's Ethics*. New York: Garland, 1990.

———. *The Practice of Moral Judgment*. Cambridge, Mass.: Harvard University Press, 1993.

Hochberg, Gary M. *Kant, Moral Legislation and Two Senses of 'Will.'* Washington, D.C.: University Press of America, 1982.

Hudson, Hud. *Kant's Compatibilism*. Ithaca, N.Y.: Cornell University Press, 1994.

Jones, William Thomas. *Morality and Freedom in the Philosophy of Immanuel Kant*. London: Oxford University Press, 1940.

Köhl, Harald. *Kants Gesinnungsethik*. Berlin: W. Gruyter, 1990.

Krüger, Gerhard. *Philosophie und Moral in der Kantischen Kritik*. Tübingen, Germany: Mohr, 1931. 2nd ed. Tübingen: J.C.B. Mohr (P. Siebeck), 1967.

Lambertino, Antonio. *Il rigorismo etico in Kant*. 2nd, revised and expanded ed. Parma, Italy: Maccari, 1970.

Landucci, Sergio. *Sull'etica di Kant*. Milan: Guerini, 1994.

Laupichler, Max. *Die Grundzüge der materialen Ethik Kants*. Berlin: Reuther & Reichard, 1931.

Liebert, Arthur. *Kants Ethik*. Berlin: Pan-Verlagsgesellschaft, 1931.

Lo, Ping-cheung. *Treating Persons as Ends: An Essay on Kant's Moral Philosophy*. Lanham, Md.: University Press of America, 1987.

Lorenzen, Max-Otto. *Metaphysik als Grenzgang: Die Idee der Aufklärung unter dem Primat der praktischen Vernunft in der Philosophie Immanuel Kants*. Hamburg: F. Meiner, 1991.

Manganaro, Paolo. *Libertà sotto leggi: La filosofia pratica di Kant*. Catania, Italy: C.U.E.C.M., 1989.

Marchi, Vittore. *La filosofia morale di Emanuele Kant*. Rome: Casa ed. "L'idealismo realistico," 1931.

Meiklejohn, Alexander. *Inclinations and Obligations*. Berkeley: University of California Press, 1948.

Messer, August. *Kants Ethik: Eine Einführung in ihre Hauptprobleme und Beiträge zu deren Lösung*. Leipzig: V. Veit, 1904.

Meyer, Herbert. *Kants transzendentale Freiheitslehre*. Freiburg, Germany: K. Alber, 1996.

Miller, Edmund Morris. *Moral Law and the Highest Good: A Study of Kant's Doctrine of the Highest Good*. Melbourne, Australia: Macmillan & Co. Ltd. in association with the Melbourne University Press, 1928.

Miller, Ronald Duncan. *An Interpretation of Kant's Moral Philosophy*. Harrogate, U.K.: Duchy Press, 1993.

Moritz, Manfred. *Studien zum Pflichtbegriff in Kants kritischer Ethik*. Lund, Sweden: C.W.K. Gleerup, 1951.

———. *Die subjektive Sittlichkeit und das Objektiv-Sittliche in der Ethik Kants*. Dortmund, Germany: H. Lucker, 1933.

Müller, Carl. *Die Methode einer reinen Ethik, insbesondere der Kantischen, dargestellt an einer Analyse des Begriffes eines "praktischen Gesetzes."* Berlin: Reuther & Reichard, 1908.

Murphy, Jeffrie G. *Character, Liberty, and Law: Kantian Essays in Theory and Practice.* Boston: Kluwer Academic Publishers, 1998.

Nabert, Jean. *L'expérience intérieure de la liberté et autres essais de philosophie morale.* Preface by Paul Ricoeur. Paris: Presses universitaires de France, 1994.

Nell, Onora. *Acting on Principle: An Essay on Kantian Ethics.* New York: Columbia University Press, 1975.

Nicolaci, Giuseppe. *Aporetica della conoscenza morale.* Palermo, Italy: Manfredi, 1979.

Nisters, Thomas. *Kants kategorischer Imperativ als Leitfaden humaner Praxis.* Freiburg, Germany: K. Alber, 1989.

Ortwein, Birger. *Kants problematische Freiheitslehre.* Bonn: Bouvier, 1983.

Paton, Herbert James. *The Categorical Imperative: A Study in Kant's Moral Philosophy.* London: Hutchinson's University Library, 1947; Chicago: University of Chicago Press, 1948; New York: Harper & Row, 1967.

Pelegrinēs, Theodosios N. *Kant's Conceptions of the Categorical Imperative and the Will.* London: Zeno, 1980.

Perreijn, Willem. *Kants ethiek tussen ervaring en a priori.* Tilburg, The Netherlands: Tilburg University Press, 1993.

Porter, Noah. *Kant's Ethics.* Chicago: S. C. Griggs & Company, 1886.

Poser, Hans, ed. *Philosophische Probleme der Handlungstheorie.* Contributions by Holger van den Boom et al. Freiburg, Germany: K. Alber, 1982.

Prauss, Gerold. *Kant über Freiheit als Autonomie.* Frankfurt-am-Main: V. Klostermann, 1983.

Quinn, Dennis P. *An Examination of Kant's Treatment of Transcendental Freedom.* Lanham, Md.: University Press of America, 1988.

Richli, Urs. *Transzendentale Reflexion und sittliche Entscheidung.* Bonn: Bouvier, 1967.

Rohden, Valério. *Interesse da razão e liberdade.* São Paulo, Brazil: Editora Atica, 1981.

Rossvær, Viggo. *Kant's Moral Philosophy: An Interpretation of the Categorical Imperative.* Oslo: Universitetsforlag; Oslo: Hestholms boktrykkeri, 1979.

Rotenstreich, Nathan. *Practice and Realization: Studies in Kant's Moral Philosophy.* The Hague: M. Nijhoff, 1979.

Sandermann, Edmund. *Die Moral der Vernunft: Transzendentale Handlungs- und Legitimationstheorie in der Philosophie Kants.* Freiburg, Germany: K. Alber, 1989.

Schefczyk, Michael. *Moral ohne Nutzen: Eine Apologie des kantischen Formalismus.* Sankt Augustin, Germany: Academia, 1995.

Schnoor, Christian. *Kants kategorischer Imperativ als Kriterium der Richtigkeit des Handelns.* Tübingen, Germany: J.C.B. Mohr, 1989.

Schopenhauer, Arthur. *On the Basis of Morality.* Translated by E.F.J. Payne; with an introduction by David E. Cartwright. Rev. ed. Providence, R.I.: Berghahn Books, 1995. Reprint. Indianapolis, Ind.: Hackett, 1998. Translation of *Über das Fundament der Moral.* In *Die beiden Grundprobleme der Ethik: Behandelt in zwei akademischen Preisschriften.* Frankfurt-am-Main: Hermann, 1841. Contemporary edition. Ed. Hans Ebeling. Philosophische Bibliothek. 2 vols. Hamburg: Meiner, 1978–79.

Sciacca, Giuseppe Maria. *L'idea della libertà: Fondamento della coscienza etico-politica in Kant.* Palermo, Italy: Palumbo, 1963.

Soloweiczik, Rafail. *Kants Bestimmung der Moralität.* Berlin: A. W. Hayn's Erben, 1901.

Sommerlath, Ernst. *Kants Lehre vom intelligiblen Charakter: Ein Beitrag zu seiner Freiheitslehre.* Leipzig: A. Deichert, 1917.

Sternberg, Kurt. *Beiträge Zur Interpretation der kritischen Ethik.* Berlin: Reuther & Reichard, 1912.

Stevens, Rex Patrick. *Kant on Moral Practice: A Study of Moral Success and Failure.* Macon, Ga.: Mercer University Press, 1981.

Stockhammer, Morris. *Kants Zurechnungsidee und Freiheitsantinomie.* Cologne: Kölner Universitäts-Verlag, 1961.

Strange, Carl. *Die Ethik Kants: Zur Einführung in die Kritik der praktischen Vernunft.* Leipzig: Dieterich'sche Verlagsbuchhandlung, 1920.

Stratton-Lake, Philip. *Kant, Duty, and Moral Worth.* New York: Routledge, 2000.

Strecker, Reinhard. *Kants Ethik: Eine offene Schrift an meinen verehrten Freund Herrn Professor Dr. A. Messer, Giessen.* Giessen, Germany: Emil Roth, 1909.

Sullivan, Roger J. *An Introduction to Kant's Ethics.* Cambridge: Cambridge University Press, 1994.

———. *Immanuel Kant's Moral Theory.* Cambridge: Cambridge University Press, 1989

Teale, A. E. *Kantian Ethics.* London: Oxford University Press, 1951. Reprint. Westport, Conn.: Greenwood Press, 1975.

Tognini, Giorgio, ed. *Introduzione alla morale di Kant: Guida alla critica.* Rome: La nuova Italia scientifica, 1993.

Travaglia, Sandro. *Metafisica ed etica in Kant. Dagli scritti precritici alla Critica della ragion pura.* Padua, Italy: CEDAM, 1972.

Velkley, Richard L. *Freedom and the End of Reason: On the Moral Foundation of Kant's Critical Philosophy.* Chicago: University of Chicago Press, 1989.

Verondini, Enrico. *La filosofia morale di Emanuele Kant.* Bologna, Italy: Cappelli Editore, 1966.

Vialatoux, Joseph. *La Morale de Kant.* 5th ed. Paris: Presses universitaires de France, 1968 (1956).

Ward, Keith. *The Development of Kant's View of Ethics.* Oxford: Blackwell, 1972; New York: Humanities Press, 1972.

Washington, William Morrow. *The Formal and Material Elements of Kant's Ethics.* New York: Macmillan, 1898.

Weeland, Horst. *Autonomie und Sinnprinzip: Zum Vorgang kantischen Philosophierens.* Bern: Peter Lang, 1987.

Willaschek, Marcus. *Praktische Vernunft: Handlungstheorie und Moralbegründung bei Kant.* Stuttgart: J. B. Metzler, 1992.

Williams, Terence Charles. *The Concept of the Categorical Imperative: A Study of the Place of the Categorical Imperative in Kant's Ethical Theory.* Oxford: Clarendon Press, 1968.

Wood, Allen W. *Kant's Ethical Thought.* Cambridge: Cambridge University Press, 1999.

3. Studies on Special Topics in Moral Philosophy

Anderson-Gold, Sharon. *Unnecessary Evil: History and Moral Progress in the Philosophy of Immanuel Kant.* Albany, N.Y.: State University of New York Press, 2001.

Aramayo, Roberto Rodríguez. *Crítica de la razón ucrónica: Estudios en torno a las aporías morales de Kant.* Foreword by Javier Muguerza. Madrid: Tecnos, 1992.

Axinn, Sidney. *A Moral Military.* Philadelphia: Temple University Press, 1989.

Bowie, Norman E. *Business Ethics: A Kantian Perspective.* Malden, Mass.: Blackwell Publishers, 1999.

Cattaneo, Mario A. *Dignità umana e pena nella filosofia di Kant.* Milan: A. Giuffrè, 1981.

Crowther, Paul. *The Kantian Sublime: From Morality to Art.* Oxford: Clarendon Press; New York: Oxford University Press, 1989

Cummiskey, David. *Kantian Consequentialism.* New York: Oxford University Press, 1996.

Denis, Lara. *Moral Self-Regard: Duties to Oneself in Kant's Moral Theory.* New York: Routledge, 2001.

Edelman, Bernard. *The House That Kant Built: A Moral Tale.* Trans. Graeme Hunter. Toronto: Canadian Philosophical Monographs for the Canadian Association for Publishing in Philosophy, 1987. Translation of *La Maison de Kant: Conte moral.* Paris: Payot, 1984.

Fairbanks, Sandra Jane. *Kantian Moral Theory and the Destruction of the Self.* Boulder, Colo.: Westview Press, 2000.

Firla-Forkl, Monika. *Untersuchungen zum Verhältnis von Anthropologie und Moralphilosophie bei Kant.* Bern: Peter Lang, 1981.

Goodreau, John R. *The Role of the Sublime in Kant's Moral Metaphysics.* Washington, D.C.: Council for Research in Values and Philosophy, 1998.

Gregor, Mary J. *Laws of Freedom: A Study of Kant's Method of Applying the Categorical Imperative in the Metaphysik der Sitten.* Oxford: Blackwell; New York: Barnes & Noble, 1963.

Guevara, Daniel. *Kant's Theory of Moral Motivation.* Boulder, Colo.: Westview Press, 2000.

Hansson, Mats G. *Human Dignity and Animal Well-Being: A Kantian Contribution to Biomedical Ethics.* Uppsala, Sweden: [Uppsala University]; distributed by Almqvist & Wiksell International, 1991.

Harper, William L., and Ralf Meerbote, eds. *Kant on Causality, Freedom, and Objectivity.* Minneapolis, Minn.: University of Minnesota Press, 1984.

Heinrichs, Jürgen. *Das Problem der Zeit in der praktischen Philosophie Kants.* Bonn: Bouvier, 1968.

Henrich, Dieter. *Aesthetic Judgment and the Moral Image of the World: Studies in Kant.* Stanford: Stanford University Press, 1992.

Hess, Heinz-Jürgen. *Die obersten Grundsätze Kantischer Ethik und ihre Konkretisierbarkeit.* Bonn: Bouvier, 1971.

Hill, Thomas E., Jr. *Dignity and Practical Reason in Kant's Moral Theory.* Ithaca, N.Y.: Cornell University Press, 1992.

———. *Respect, Pluralism, and Justice: Kantian Perspectives.* New York: Oxford University Press, 2000.

Homsi, Hikmat. *Vernunft und Realität in der Ethik Kants.* Bern: Peter Lang, 1975.

Hylkema, Govert Willem. *Homo duplex: Het geweten als kern der ethiek.* Haarlem, The Netherlands: Erven F. Bohn, 1963.

Kneller, Jane, and Sidney Axinn, eds. *Autonomy and Community: Readings in Contemporary Kantian Social Philosophy.* Albany, N.Y.: State University of New York Press, 1998.

Korsgaard, Christine Marion. *Creating the Kingdom of Ends.* Cambridge: Cambridge University Press, 1996.

Langthaler, Rudolf. *Kants Ethik als "System der Zwecke": Perspektiven einer modifizierten Idee der "moralischen Teleologie" und Ethikotheologie.* Berlin: Walter de Gruyter, 1991, 1990.

Louden, Robert B. *Kant's Impure Ethics: From Rational Beings to Human Beings.* New York: Oxford University Press, 2000.

Ludwig, Ralf. *Kategorischer Imperativ und Metaphysik der Sitten: Die Frage nach der Einheitlichkeit von Kants Ethik.* Bern: Peter Lang, 1992.

Méndez-Burguillos, Manuel. *Zweckmäßigkeit und Autonomie: Im Zusammenhang mit den Versuchen Kants, die Gültigkeit des moralischen Gesetzes zu begründen.* Bern: Peter Lang, 1996.

Michalson, Gordon E. *Fallen Freedom: Kant on Radical Evil and Moral Regeneration.* Cambridge: Cambridge University Press, 1990.

Miller, Edmund Morris. *Moral Action and Natural Law in Kant, and Some Developments.* Melbourne, Australia: G. Robertson & Company, 1911.

Moreau, Paul. *L'éducation morale chez Kant*. Paris: Cerf, 1988.

Müller, Peter. *Transzendentale Kritik und moralische Teleologie: Eine Auseinandersetzung mit den zeitgenössischen Transformationen der Transzendentalphilosophie im Hinblick auf Kant*. Würzburg, Germany: Königshausen & Neumann, 1983.

Müller, Wolfgang Hermann. *Ethik als Wissenschaft und Rechtsphilosophie nach Immanuel Kant*. Würzburg, Germany: Königshausen & Neumann, 1992.

Munzel, G. Felicitas. *Kant's Conception of Moral Character: The "Critical" Link of Morality, Anthropology, and Reflective Judgment*. Chicago: University of Chicago Press, 1999.

Nieschmidt, Gerd-Peter. *Praktische Vernunft und ewiger Friede: Eine Untersuchung zum Freiheitsbegriff in der Philosophie Kants*. Munich: F. Frank, 1965.

Pirillo, Nestore. *Morale e civiltà: Studi su Kant e la condotta di vita*. Naples: Loffredo, 1995.

Probst, Peter. *Kant: bestirnter Himmel und moralisches Gesetz: Zum geschichtlichen Horizont einer These Immanuel Kants*. Würzburg, Germany: Königshausen & Neumann, 1994.

Puder, Martin. *Kant, Stringenz und Ausdruck*. Freiburg, Germany: Rombach, 1974.

Ramos, Samuel. *Más allá de la moral de Kant: An Essay*. México, D.F.: Imprimió A. Chápero, 1938.

Renda, Antonio. *Conoscenza e moralità in Kant*. Palermo, Italy: G. B. Palumbo, 1944.

Rodríguez Aramayo, Roberto. *Immanuel Kant: La utopía moral como emancipación del azar*. Madrid: Edaf, 2001.

Rösler, Winfried. *Argumentation und moralisches Handeln: Zur Kantrekonstruktion in der konstruktiven Ethik*. Bern: Peter Lang, 1980.

Ruge, Arnold. *Die Deduction der practischen und der moralischen Freiheit aus den Prinzipien der kantischen Morallehre*. Tübingen, Germany: H. Laupp Jr., 1910.

Schmidt, Helmut. *Maximen politischen Handelns: Bemerkungen zu Moral, Pflicht und Verantwortung des Politikers*. Speech by the Federal Chancellor at the Kant Congress of the Friedrich Ebert Foundation on March 12, 1981. Bonn: Presse und Informationsamt der Bundesregierung, 1981.

Schmidt, Karl. *Beiträge zur Entwicklung der Kant'schen Ethik*. Marburg, Germany: J. Hamel, 1900.

Schmidt-Sauerhöfer, Paul. *Wahrhaftigkeit und Handeln aus Freiheit: Zum Theorie-Praxis-Problem der Ethik Immanuel Kants*. Bonn: Bouvier, 1978.

Schnädelbach, Herbert. *Zum Problem der Entscheidbarkeit in der Kantischen Ethik*. Frankfurt-am-Main: H. Heiderhoff, 1971.

Schroeter, François. *La critique kantienne de l'eudémonisme*. Bern: Peter Lang, 1992.

Schwaiger, Clemens. *Kategorische und andere Imperative: Zur Entwicklung von Kants praktischer Philosophie bis 1785*. Stuttgart–Bad Cannstatt: Frommann-Holzboog, 1999.

Schwemmer, Oswald. *Philosophie der Praxis: Versuch zur Grundlegung einer Lehre vom moralischen Argumentieren in Verbindung mit einer Interpretation der praktischen Philosophie Kants.* Frankfurt-am-Main: Suhrkamp, 1980 (1971).

Seidler, Victor J. *Kant, Respect and Injustice: The Limits of Liberal Moral Theory.* London: Routledge & Kegan Paul, 1986.

Sena, Michelantonio. *Etica e cosmopolitismo in Kant.* Reggio Calabria, Italy: Parallelo 38, 1976.

Seung, T. K. *Kant's Platonic Revolution in Moral and Political Philosophy.* Baltimore, Md.: Johns Hopkins University Press, 1994.

Shimizu, Daisuke. *Freiheit und Zweck: Kants Grundlegung der Ethik in zwei Phasen.* Vienna: WUV-Universitätsverlag, 1997.

Sussman, David G. *The Idea of Humanity: Anthropology and Anthroponomy in Kant's Ethics.* New York: Routledge, 2001.

Tenkku, Jussi. *Are Single Moral Rules Absolute in Kant's Ethics?* Jyväskylä, Finland: Jyväskylän Yliopisto, 1967.

Toyama, Yoshitaka. *Kants praktische Philosophie mit Rücksicht auf eine Theorie des Friedens.* Hamburg: H. Buske, 1973.

Tunick, Mark. *Practices and Principles: Approaches to Ethical and Legal Judgment.* Princeton, N.J.: Princeton University Press, 1998.

Van der Linden, Harry. *Kantian Ethics and Socialism.* Indianapolis, Ind.: Hackett, 1988.

Voeller, Carol W. *The Metaphysics of the Moral Law: Kant's Deduction of Freedom.* New York: Garland, 1999.

Wellmer, Albrecht. *Ethik und Dialog: Elemente des moralischen Urteils bei Kant und in der Diskursethik.* Frankfurt-am-Main: Suhrkamp, 1986.

Wike, Victoria S. *Kant on Happiness in Ethics.* Albany, N.Y.: State University of New York Press, 1994.

Witschen, Dieter. *Kant und die Idee einer christlichen Ethik: Ein Beitrag zur Diskussion über das Proprium einer christlichen Moral.* Düsseldorf, Germany: Patmos, 1984.

Zwingelberg, Hans Willi. *Kants Ethik und das Problem der Einheit von Freiheit und Gesetz.* Bonn: H. Bouvier, 1969.

4. Studies on Basic Topics in Philosophy of Religion

Bruch, Jean-Louis. *La Philosophie religieuse de Kant.* Aubier, France: Éditions Montaigne, 1968.

Cortina Orts, Adela. *Dios en la filosofía trascendental de Kant.* Salamanca, Spain: Universidad Pontifica, 1981.

Gómez Caffarena, José. *El teísmo moral de Kant.* Madrid: Ediciones Cristiandad, 1983.

Green, Ronald Michael. *Religious Reason: The Rational and Moral Basis of Religious Belief.* New York: Oxford University Press, 1978.

Hasenfuß, Josef. *Die Grundlagen der Religion bei Kant: dargestellt und kritisch gewürdigt.* Würzburg, Germany: C. J. Becker, 1927.

Lacorte, Carmelo. *Kant: ancora un episodio dell' alleanza di religione e filosofia.* Urbino, Italy: Argalìa, 1969.

Lamacchia, Ada. *La filosofia della religione in Kant.* Manduria, Italy: Lacaita, 1969.

Mancini, Italo. *Kant e la teologia.* Assisi, Italy: Cittadella editrice, 1975.

Mavrodes, George I., ed. *The Rationality of Belief in God.* Englewood Cliffs, N.J.: Prentice Hall, 1970.

Michalson, Gordon E. *Kant and the Problem of God.* Oxford: Blackwell Publishers, 1999.

Odero, José Miguel. *La fe en Kant.* Pamplona, Spain: Ediciones Universidad de Navarra, 1992.

Palmquist, Stephen. *Kant's Critical Religion.* Aldershot, U.K.: Ashgate, 2000.

Picht, Georg. *Kants Religionsphilosophie.* Stuttgart: Klett-Cotta, 1985.

Reardon, Bernard M. G. *Kant as Philosophical Theologian.* Totowa, N.J.: Barnes & Noble, 1988.

Rosenberg, Philipp. *Die Grundzüge der Kant'schen Religionsphilosophie in der "Kritik der praktischen Vernunft" und in der "Kritik der Urteilskraft."* Bazin, Hungary: Alfred Klein, 1904.

Rossi, Philip J., and Michael Wreen, eds. *Kant's Philosophy of Religion Reconsidered.* Bloomington, Ind.: Indiana University Press, 1991.

Sacken, Helene. *Zur Frage des Religionsbegriffs im System der Philosophie.* The problem of the philosophy of religion in the framework of Kant's critical system. Marburg, Germany: J. Hamel, 1919.

Sala, Giovanni B. *Kant über die menschliche Vernunft: Die Kritik der reinen Vernunft und die Erkennbarkeit Gottes durch die praktische Vernunft.* Weilheim-Bierbronnen, Germany: Gustav-Siewerth-Akademie, 1993.

Sänger, Ernst Adolf. *Kants Lehre vom Glauben.* Leipzig: Dürr, 1903.

Sasao, Kumetaro. *Prolegomena zur Bestimmung des Gottesbegriffes bei Kant.* Halle/Saale, Germany: E. Karras, 1900.

Schroll-Fleischer, Niels Otto. *Der Gottesgedanke in der Philosophie Kants.* Odense, Denmark: Odense University Press, 1981.

Schweitzer, Albert. *Die Religionsphilosophie Kants von der Kritik der reinen Vernunft bis zur Religion innerhalb der Grenzen der blossen Vernunft.* Freiburg, Germany: Mohr, 1899. Reprint. Hildesheim, Germany: G. Olms, 1974.

Thilo, Christfried Albert. *Kants Religionsphilosophie.* Langensalza, Germany: H. Beyer & Söhne, 1905.

Vos, Harmen de. *Kant als theoloog.* Baarn, The Netherlands: Het Wereldvenster, 1968.

Walsh, William Henry. *Kant's Moral Theology.* Oxford: Oxford University Press, 1963.

Webb, Clement Charles Julian. *Kant's Philosophy of Religion*. Oxford: Clarendon Press, 1926.

Wimmer, Reiner. *Kants kritische Religionsphilosophie*. Berlin: Walter de Gruyter, 1990.

Winter, Aloysius. *Der andere Kant: Zur philosophischen Theologie Immanuel Kants*. With a foreword by Norbert Hinske. Hildesheim, Germany: G. Olms, 2000.

Wood, Allen W. *Kant's Moral Religion*. Ithaca, N.Y.: Cornell University Press, 1970.

————. *Kant's Rational Theology*. Ithaca, N.Y.: Cornell University Press, 1978.

5.   Studies on Special Topics in Philosophy of Religion

Aviau de Ternay, Henri d'. *Traces bibliques dans la loi morale chez Kant*. Preface by François Marty. Paris: Beauchesne, 1986.

Baumbach, Rudolf. *Das Irrationale in Kants Religionsphilosophie*. Marburg, Germany: Euker, 1929.

Chang, Maria Hsüeh-Chu. *Die Einheit der Wirklichkeit: Kants Gotteslehre in metaphysischer Perspektive*. Bern: Peter Lang, 1996.

Crumbach, Karl-Heinz. *Theologie in kritischer Öffentlichkeit: Die Frage Kants an das kirchliche Christentum*. Munich: Kaiser; Mainz, Germany: Grünewald, 1977.

Davidovich, Adina. *Religion as a Province of Meaning: The Kantian Foundations of Modern Theology*. Minneapolis, Minn.: Augsburg Fortress, 1993.

Dell'Oro, Regina O. M. *From Existence to the Ideal: Continuity and Development in Kant's Theology*. New York: Peter Lang, 1994.

Eklund, Harald. *Die Würde der Menschheit: Über die erkenntnistheoretischen Voraussetzungen der Religionsphilosophie bei Kant*. Uppsala, Sweden: Lundequistaka Bokhandeln, 1947.

Elschazli, A. E. Abd Elhamid. *Kants kritische Philosophie und das Problem der Offenbarung*. Hamburg: Buske, 1970.

England, Frederick Ernest. *Kant's Conception of God: A Critical Exposition of Its Metaphysical Development Together with a Translation of the Nova dilucidatio*. With a foreword by G. Dawes Hicks. London: G. Allen & Unwin, 1929. Reprint. New York: Humanities Press, 1968, 1969.

Frankenberger, Horst. *Kant und die Frage nach der göttlichen Allgenugsamkeit: Zur transzendentalen Wende in der philosophischen Gotteslehre*. Bern: Peter Lang, 1984.

Galbraith, Elizabeth Cameron. *Kant and Theology: Was Kant a Closet Theologian?* San Francisco: International Scholars Publications, 1996.

Geisler, Ralf. *Kants moralischer Gottesbeweis im protestantischen Positivismus*. Göttingen, Germany: Vandenhoeck & Ruprecht, 1992.

Guttmann, Julius. *Kants Gottesbegriff in seiner positiven Entwicklung*. Berlin: Reuther & Reichard, 1906.

Habichler, Alfred. *Reich Gottes als Thema des Denkens bei Kant: Entwicklungs-geschichtliche und systematische Studie zur kantischen Reich-Gottes-Idee.* Mainz, Germany: M.-Grünewald, 1991.

Hauser, Linus. *Religion als Prinzip und Faktum: Das Verhältnis von konkreter Subjektivität und Prinzipientheorie in Kants Religions- und Geschichtsphilosophie.* Bern: Peter Lang, 1983.

Heimsoeth, Heinz. *Astronomisches und Theologisches in Kants Weltverständnis.* Mainz, Germany: Akademie der Wissenschaften und der Literatur; in Kommission bei F. Steiner, Wiesbaden, 1963.

Jansen, Bernhard. *Die Religionsphilosophie Kants. Geschichtlich dargestellt und kritisch-systematisch gewürdigt.* Berlin: F. Dümmlers, 1929.

Kielkopf, Charles F. *A Kantian Condemnation of Atheistic Despair: A Declaration of Dependence.* New York: Peter Lang, 1997.

Lazzarini, Renato. *Dalla religione naturale prekantiana alla religione morale di Kant.* Rome: Perrella, 1942.

Lötzsch, Frieder. *Vernunft und Religion im Denken Kants: Lutherisches Erbe bei Immanuel Kant.* Cologne: Böhlau, 1976.

Michalson, Gordon E. *The Historical Dimensions of a Rational Faith: The Role of History in Kant's Religious Thought.* Washington, D.C.: University Press of America, 1977.

Noti, Odilo. *Kant, Publikum und Gelehrter: Theologische Erinnerung an einen abgebrochenen Diskurs zum Theorie-Praxis-Problem.* Fribourg, Switzerland: Universitätsverlag, 1994.

Scholz, Heinrich. *Die Religionsphilosophie des Als-ob: Eine Nachprüfung Kants und des idealistischen Positivismus.* Leipzig: F. Meiner, 1921.

Waldau, Knut. *Das Problem der Denkmöglichkeit der notwendigen Existenz Gottes bei Immanuel Kant.* Neuried, Germany: Ars Una, 1997.

6.   Studies on Other Special Topics

Albrecht, Michael. *Kants Antinomie der praktischen Vernunft.* Hildesheim, Germany: G. Olms, 1978.

Allison, Henry E. *Idealism and Freedom: Essays on Kant's Theoretical and Practical Philosophy.* Cambridge: Cambridge University Press, 1996.

Attisani, Adelchi. *Metodo attivo e metodo speculativo nella Metodica della ragion pratica di E. Kant.* Messina, Italy: A. Sessa, 1951.

Bache, Kurt. *Kants Prinzip der Autonomie im Verhältnis zur Idee des Reiches der Zwecke.* Berlin: Reuther & Reichard, 1909.

Baum, Hermann Alois. *Kant: Moral und Religion.* Sankt Augustin, Germany: Academia, 1998.

Benton, Robert J. *Kant's Second Critique and the Problem of Transcendental Arguments.* The Hague: M. Nijhoff, 1977.

Chadwick, Ruth F., ed. *Immanuel Kant: Critical Assessments*. 4 vols. New York: Routledge, 1992.

Council for Philosophical Studies. *Kantian Ethical Thought: A Curricular Report and Annotated Bibliography Based on an NEH Summer Institute Exploring the Moral, Political, and Religious Views of Immanuel Kant*. Tallahassee, Fla.: Florida State University, 1984.

Dünnhaupt, Rudolf. *Sittlichkeit, Staat und Recht bei Kant. Autonomie und Heteronomie in der Kantischen Ethik*. Dessau, Germany: C. Dünnhaupt, 1926.

Ertl, Wolfgang. *Kants Auflösung der "dritten Antinomie": Zur Bedeutung des Schöpfungskonzepts für die Freiheitslehre*. Freiburg, Germany: K. Alber, 1998.

Gaziaux, Éric. *L'autonomie en morale: Au croisement de la philosophie et de la théologie*. Leuven, Belgium: Leuven University Press; Uitgeverij Peeters, 1998.

Goldschmidt, Ludwig. *Kant über Freiheit, Unsterblichkeit, Gott*. Gotha, Germany: E. F. Thienemann, 1904.

Guyer, Paul. *Kant and the Experience of Freedom: Essays on Aesthetics and Morality*. Cambridge: Cambridge University Press, 1993.

Kawamura, Katsutoshi. *Spontaneität und Willkür: Der Freiheitsbegriff in Kants Antinomienlehre und seine historischen Wurzeln*. Stuttgart–Bad Cannstatt: Frommann-Holzboog, 1996.

Kinker, Johannes. *Le dualisme de la raison humaine; ou, Le criticisme de Emmanuel Kant, amélioré sous le rapport de la Raison pure, et rendu complet sous celui de la Raison pratique*. Published under the care and auspices of, and with notes by, J. D. Cocheret de la Morinière. 2 vols. Amsterdam: Weytingh & Van der Haart, 1850–52.

Nobile, Emilia. *Concetto e funzione della dialettica nella linea di svolgimento del pensiero di Kant: introduzione allo studio della dialettica della Ragion pura-pratica*. Naples: L. Loffredo, 1940.

Ouden, Bernard den, ed. *New Essays on Kant*. New York: Peter Lang, 1987.

Pascher, Manfred. *Einführung in den Neukantianismus: Kontext, Grundpositionen, praktische Philosophie*. Munich: Fink, 1997.

Pirni, Alberto. *Il regno dei fini in Kant: Morale, religione e politica in collegamento sistematico*. Genoa, Italy: Il Melangolo, 2000.

Pleines, Jürgen-Eckardt, ed. *Kant und die Pädagogik: Pädagogik und praktische Philosophie*. Würzburg, Germany: Königshausen & Neumann, 1985.

———. *Praxis und Vernunft: zum Begriff praktischer Urteilskraft*. Würzburg, Germany: Königshausen & Neumann; Amsterdam: Rodopi, 1983.

Raschke, Carl A. *Moral Action, God, and History in the Thought of Immanuel Kant*. [Tallahassee]: American Academy of Religion; Missoula, Mont.: distributed by Scholars Press, 1975.

Strangas, Iōannēs S. *Kritik der kantischen Rechtsphilosophie: Ein Beitrag zur Herstellung der Einheit der praktischen Philosophie*. Cologne: Böhlau, 1988.

Teichner, Wilhelm. *Die intelligible Welt. Ein Problem der theoretischen und prakti-schen Philosophie I. Kants.* Meisenheim-am-Glan, Germany: Hain, 1967.

Vaihinger, Hans. *The Philosophy of 'As If': A System of the Theoretical, Practical and Religious Fictions of Mankind.* Trans. C. K. Ogden. London: K. Paul, Trench, Trubner & Co., Ltd.; New York: Harcourt, Brace & Co., 1924, 1925. 2nd ed., reprinted. London: Routledge & Kegan Paul, 1965. Translation of *Die Philoso-phie des Als Ob: System der theoretischen, praktischen und religiösen Fiktionen der Menschheit auf Grund eines idealistischen Positivismus.* Ed. Raymund Schmidt. 7th and 8th eds. Leipzig: F. Meiner, 1922.

Venturelli, Domenico. *Etica e fede filosofica: Studi sulla filosofia di Kant.* Naples: Morano, 1989.

Yovel, Yirmiyahu, ed. *Kant's Practical Philosophy Reconsidered.* Papers Presented at the Seventh Jerusalem Philosophical Encounter, December 1986. Boston: Kluwer Academic, 1989.

7.   Comparative Studies

Abdullah, M. Amin. *Kant and Ghazali: The Idea of Universality of Ethical Norms.* Frankfurt-am-Main: Landeck, 2000.

Adam, Armin. *Despotie der Vernunft?: Hobbes, Rousseau, Kant, Hegel.* Freiburg, Germany: K. Alber, 1999.

Anderson, Pamela Sue. *Ricoeur and Kant: Philosophy of the Will.* Atlanta: Scholars Press, 1993.

Appelmann, Anton Hermann. *Der Unterschied in der Auffassung der Ethik bei Schiller und Kant.* With source documentation. New York: G. E. Stechert and Company, 1917.

Attfield, Robin. *God and the Secular: A Philosophical Assessment of Secular Rea-soning from Bacon to Kant.* Cardiff, Wales: University College Cardiff Press, 1978.

Baake, Wilhelm. *Kants Ethik bei den englischen Moralphilosophen des 19. Jahr-hunderts.* Leipzig: Fock, 1911.

Bailey, William H. *The Ethics of Kant and Brunner: An Existential Blend.* New York: Peter Lang, 1998.

Balbir Singh. *A Comparative Study of the Ethical Teachings of Kant and the Bha-gavadgita.* Hoshiarpur, India: Vishveshvaranand Book Agency, 1958.

————. *The Concept of Perfection in the Teachings of Kant and the Gita.* Delhi, India: M. Banarsidass, 1967.

Baron, Marcia W., ed. *Three Methods of Ethics: A Debate.* Essays presented at a conference by the Department of Philosophy, Monash University, June 1995. Malden, Mass.: Blackwell, 1997.

Baumann-Hölzle, Ruth. *Autonomie und Freiheit in der Medizin-Ethik: Immanuel Kant und Karl Barth.* Freiburg, Germany: K. Alber, 1999.

Bernstein, John Andrew. *Shaftesbury, Rousseau, and Kant: An Introduction to the Conflict between Aesthetic and Moral Values in Modern Thought.* Rutherford, N.J.: Fairleigh Dickinson University Press, 1980.

Besse, Guy. *La morale selon Kant et selon Marx.* Paris: Centre d'études et de recherches marxistes, 1963.

Blosser, Philip. *Scheler's Critique of Kant's Ethics.* Athens, Oh.: Ohio University Press, 1995.

Bockow, Jörg. *Erziehung zur Sittlichkeit: Zum Verhältnis von praktischer Philosophie und Pädagogik bei Jean-Jacques Rousseau und Immanuel Kant.* Bern: Peter Lang, 1984.

Brady, Jules M. *New Approaches to God: Based on Proofs by Anselm, Aquinas, and Kant.* With an introduction by Joseph Bobik. North Andover, Mass.: Genesis Pub., 1996.

Brezina, Friedrich F. *Die Achtung: Ethik und Moral der Achtung und Unterwerfung bei Immanuel Kant, Ernst Tugendhat, Ursula Wolf und Peter Singer.* Bern: Peter Lang, 1999.

Bueb, Bernhard. *Nietzsches Kritik der praktischen Vernunft.* Stuttgart: E. Klett, 1970.

Carus, Paul. *Kant and Spencer: A Study of the Fallacies of Agnosticism.* Chicago: Open Court, 1899.

Chalier, Catherine. *Pour une morale au-delà du savoir: Kant et Levinas.* Paris: A. Michel, 1998.

Colebrook, Claire. *Ethics and Representation: From Kant to Post-Structuralism.* Edinburgh: Edinburgh University Press, 1999.

Cook, Webster. *The Ethics of Bishop Butler and Immanuel Kant.* Ann Arbor, Mich.: Andrews & Company, 1888.

Dorschel, Andreas. *Die idealistische Kritik des Willens: Versuch über die Theorie der praktischen Subjektivität bei Kant und Hegel.* Hamburg: F. Meiner, 1992.

Engstrom, Stephen, and Jennifer Whiting, eds. *Aristotle, Kant, and the Stoics: Rethinking Happiness and Duty.* Essays originally prepared for a conference entitled "Duty, Interest, and Practical Reason: Aristotle, Kant, and the Stoics," held at the University of Pittsburg in March 1994. Cambridge: Cambridge University Press, 1996.

Field, Guy Cromwell. *Moral Theory: An Introduction to Ethics.* With a new introduction by Stephan Körner. 2nd ed. Reprint. London: Methuen, 1966.

Fleischacker, Samuel. *A Third Concept of Liberty: Judgment and Freedom in Kant and Adam Smith.* Princeton, N.J.: Princeton University Press, 1999.

Gracanin, G. *La personnalité morale d'après Kant: Son exposé, sa critique à la lumière du thomisme.* Preface by Jacques Maritain. Paris: Mignard, 1929.

Greene, Theodore Meyer. *Moral, Aesthetic, and Religious Insight.* New Brunswick, N.J.: Rutgers University Press, 1957.

Harris, George W. *Agent-Centered Morality: An Aristotelian Alternative to Kantian Internalism.* Berkeley: University of California Press, 1999.

Heizmann, Winfried. *Kants Kritik spekulativer Theologie und Begriff moralischen Vernunftglaubens im katholischen Denken der späten Aufklärung: Ein religionsphilosophischer Vergleich.* Göttingen, Germany: Vandenhoeck & Ruprecht, 1976.

Hepfer, Karl. *Motivation und Bewertung: Eine Studie zur praktischen Philosophie Humes und Kants.* Göttingen, Germany: Vandenhoeck & Ruprecht, 1997.

Horstmann, Rolf-Peter. *Die Grenzen der Vernunft: Eine Untersuchung zu Zielen und Motiven des deutschen Idealismus.* Frankfurt-am-Main: A. Hain, 1991.

Jackson, William Taylor. *Seneca and Kant.* Dayton, Oh.: United Brethren Publishing House, 1881.

Jacobs, Wilhelm G. *Trieb als sittliches Phänomen: Eine Untersuchung zur Grundlegung der Philosophie nach Kant und Fichte.* Bonn: H. Bouvier, 1967.

Jaffro, Laurent, coordinator. *Le Sens moral: Une histoire de la philosophie morale de Locke à Kant.* Paris: Presses universitaires de France, 2000.

Kelly, Michael. *Kant's Ethics and Schopenhauer's Criticism.* London: Swan Sonnenschein, 1910.

Kerner, George C. *Three Philosophical Moralists: Mill, Kant, and Sartre: An Introduction to Ethics.* Oxford: Clarendon Press; New York: Oxford University Press, 1990.

Kim, Chin. *Kants Postulatenlehre: Ihre Rezeption durch Ernst Bloch und ihre mögliche Anwendung zur Interpretation des Buddhismus: Zur Unterscheidung zwischen postulatorischer Struktur und Postulats-Inhalten bei der Auflösung der Dialektik des praktischen Vernunftgebrauchs.* Bern: Peter Lang, 1988.

Kittmann, Siegfried. *Kant und Nietzsche: Darstellung und Vergleich ihrer Ethik und Moral.* Bern: Peter Lang, 1984.

Kleinhans, Bernd. *Der "Philosoph" in der neueren Geschichte der Philosophie: "eigentlicher Philosoph" und "vollendeter Gelehrter": Konkretionen des praktischen Philosophen bei Kant und Fichte.* Würzburg, Germany: Königshausen & Neumann, 1999.

Kleppel, Erich. *Autonomie und Anerkennung: Eine Untersuchung des Verhältnisses der Grundlagen der Südwestdeutschen Kantschule zum Sittlichkeitsbegriffe Kants.* Bern: Peter Lang, 1978.

López Thode, Mario A. *Tres sistemas morales: Jesús, Kant, Marx.* Mercedes, Uruguay: distributed by J. Bastreri, 1970.

Martin, Werner. *Bestimmung und Abgrenzung von Ethik und Religion: Ein Beitrag zur Diskussion über das christliche Proprium in der Ethik unter besonderer Berücksichtigung der Philosophie Kants.* Pfaffenweiler, Germany: Centaurus-Verlagsgesellschaft, 1990.

Mathieu, V. et al., eds. *A partire da Kant: L'eredità della "Critica della ragion practica."* Introduction by S. Marcucci. Proceedings of the national convention of the Società filosofica italiana held in Lucca on May 19–21, 1988. Milan: F. Angeli, 1989.

Mazzantini, Carlo. *L'etica di Kant e di Schopenhauer*. Turin, Italy: Editrice tirrenia, 1965.

Muguerza, Javier, and Roberto Rodríguez Aramayo, eds. *Kant después de Kant: En el bicentenario de la Crítica de la razón práctica*. Instituto de Filosofía del C.S.I.C. Madrid: Tecnos, 1989.

Novak, David. *Suicide and Morality: The Theories of Plato, Aquinas, and Kant and Their Relevance for Suicidology*. New York: Scholars Studies Press, 1975.

Olson, Phillip. *The Discipline of Freedom: A Kantian View of the Role of Moral Precepts in Zen Practice*. Albany, N.Y.: State University of New York Press, 1993.

Osongo-Lukadi, Antoine-Dover. *La philosophie pratique à l'époque de l'ontologie fondamentale: Le dialogue de Heidegger avec Kant*. Prefaces by Gilbert Gérard and V. Y. Mudimbe. Paris: Harmattan, 2000.

Otto, Rudolf. *The Philosophy of Religion, Based on Kant and Fries*. Translated by E. B. Dicker, with a foreword by W. Tudor Jones. London: Williams & Norgate Ltd., 1931. Translation of *Kantisch-Fries'sche Religionsphilosophie und ihre Anwendung auf die Theologie: zur Einleitung in die Glaubenslehre für Studenten der Theologie*. Tübingen, Germany: J.C.B. Mohr, 1909.

Park, Chan-Goo. *Das moralische Gefühl in der britischen moral-sense-Schule und bei Kant*. Tübingen, Germany: [s.n.], 1995.

Pasquali, Antonio. *Fundamentos gnoseológicos para una ciencia de la moral: Ensayo sobre la formación de una teoría especial del conocimiento moral en las filosofías de Kant, Lequier, Renouvier y Bergson*. Caracas: Universidad Central de Venezuela, 1963.

Phillips, D. Z., and Timothy Tessin, eds. *Kant and Kierkegaard on Religion*. Basingstoke, U.K.: Macmillan; New York: St. Martin's Press, 2000.

Pioletti, Antje Ehrhardt. *Die Realität des moralischen Handelns: Mou Zongsans Darstellung des Neokonfuzianismus als Vollendung der praktischen Philosophie Kants*. Bern: Peter Lang, 1997.

Pleines, Jürgen-Eckardt. *Eudaimonia zwischen Kant und Aristoteles: Glückseligkeit als höchstes Gut menschlichen Handelns*. Würzburg, Germany: Königshausen & Neumann, 1984.

Reich, Klaus. *Kant und die Ethik der Griechen*. Tübingen, Germany: J.C.B. Mohr (P. Siebeck), 1935.

Reiner, Hans. *Duty and Inclination: The Fundamentals of Morality Discussed and Redefined with Special Regard to Kant and Schiller*. The Hague: Nijhoff; distributed by Kluwer, 1983. Translation, accompanied by four previously published essays, of the first four chapters of *Die Grundlagen der Sittlichkeit*. Meisenheim-am-Glan, Germany: Hain, 1974.

Schalow, Frank. *Imagination and Existence: Heidegger's Retrieval of the Kantian Ethic*. Lanham, Md.: University Press of America, 1986.

Scheler, Max Ferdinand. *Formalism in Ethics and Non-Formal Ethics of Values: A*

New Attempt toward the Foundation of an Ethical Personalism. [5th, rev. ed.] Trans. Manfred S. Frings and Roger L. Funk. Evanston, Ill.: Northwestern University Press, 1973. 6th, rev. ed. Bern: Francke, 1980. Translation of *Der Formalismus in der Ethik und die materiale Wertethik; neuer Versuch der Grundlegung eines ethischen Personalismus*. 3rd, unchanged edition, supplemented by a comprehensive subject index. Halle/Saale, Germany: M. Niemeyer, 1927.

Schmitt-Wendel, Karl. *Kants Einfluss auf die englische Ethik*. Berlin: Reuther & Reichard, 1912.

Schneewind, Jerome B. *The Invention of Autonomy: A History of Modern Moral Philosophy*. Cambridge: Cambridge University Press, 1998.

Schneewind, Jerome B., ed. *Moral Philosophy from Montaigne to Kant: An Anthology*. 2 vols. Cambridge: Cambridge University Press, 1990.

Schröer, Christian. *Naturbegriff und Moralbegründung: Die Grundlegung der Ethik bei Christian Wolff und deren Kritik durch Immanuel Kant*. Stuttgart: W. Kohlhammer, 1988.

Sherman, Nancy. *Making a Necessity of Virtue: Aristotle and Kant on Virtue*. Cambridge: Cambridge University Press, 1997.

Slote, Michael A. *From Morality to Virtue*. New York: Oxford University Press, 1992.

Swabey, William Curtis. *Ethical Theory: From Hobbes to Kant*. New York: Philosophical Library, 1961. Reprint. New York: Greenwood Press, 1969.

Verma, Krishna Murari Prasad. *Kant and the Gita*. New Delhi: Classical Publishing Co., 1980.

Vincenti, Luc. *Pratique et réalité: Dans les philosophies de Kant et de Fichte*. Preface by Bernard Bourgeois. Paris: Kimé, 1997.

Zenkert, Georg. *Konturen praktischer Rationalität: Die Rekonstruktion praktischer Vernunft bei Kant und Hegels Begriff vernünftiger Praxis*. Würzburg, Germany: Königshausen & Neumann, 1989.

Zupancic, Alenka. *Ethics of the Real: Kant, Lacan*. London: Verso, 2000.

8.   Studies from the Eighteenth and Nineteenth Centuries

Abicht, Johann Heinrich. *Kritische Briefe über die Möglichkeit einer wahren wissenschaftlichen Moral, Theologie, Rechtslehre, empirischen Psychologie und Geschmackslehre mit prüfender Hinsicht auf die Kantische Begründung dieser Lehre*. Nürnberg: Felseker, 1793.

Barni, Jules Romain. *Philosophie de Kant: Examen des fondements de la métaphysique des moeurs et de la Critique de la raison pratique*. Paris: Ladrange, 1851.

Bauernfeind, Gotthold. *Wie verhält sich in Kants Religionslehre das theoretische Element zum praktischen?* Rostock, Germany: C. Boldt, 1875.

Bernhardi, Ambrosius Bethmann. *Gemeinfassliche Darstellung der Kantischen Lehren über Sittlichkeit, Freyheit, Gottheit und Unsterblichkeit.* Freyberg: Craz, 1796–97. Reprint. Brussels: Culture et civilisation, 1968.

Brandt, Samuel. *Kant's Lehre von der Freiheit: ein kritischer Versuch.* Bonn: C. Georgi, 1872.

Brastberger, Gebhard Ulrich. *Untersuchungen über Kants Kritik der practischen Vernunft.* Tübingen: J. G. Cotta, 1792. Reprint. Brussels: Culture et civilisation, 1968.

Bridel, Philippe. *La philosophie de la religion de Immanuel Kant: Étude présentée à la Faculté de théologie de l'église libre du canton de Vaud.* Lausanne, Switzerland: G. Bridel, 1876.

Caird, Edward. *The Critical Philosophy of Immanuel Kant.* 2nd ed. 2 vols. Glasgow: J. Maclehose & Sons, 1909, 1889. Reprint. 2 vols. Amsterdam: Rodopi, 1969.

Cohen, Hermann. *Kants Begründung der Ethik.* Berlin: F. Dümmler, 1877.

Colani, Timothée. *Exposé critique de la philosophie de la religion de Kant.* Strasbourg: Berger-Levrault, 1845.

Edmunds, James. *Kant's Ethics: The Clavis to an Index.* Including extracts from several oriental sacred scriptures, and from certain Greek and Roman philosophical writings. Louisville, Ky.: Louisville Courier-Journal, 1877, 1884.

Frederichs, Friedrich. *Über Kant's Princip der Ethik.* Berlin: Bahlke, 1875.

Grillo, Friedrich. *Aphoristische Darstellung der Religion, innerhalb der Gränzen der blossen Vernunft des Herrn Immanuel Kant.* Rostock: Karl Christoph Stiller, 1794. Reprint. Brussels: Culture et civilisation, 1968.

Hegler, Alfred. *Die Psychologie in Kants Ethik.* Freiburg, Germany: J.C.B. Mohr (P. Siebeck), 1891.

Hoffbauer, Johann Christoph. *Anfangsgründe der Moralphilosophie und insbesondere der Sittenlehre nebst einer allgemeinen Geschichte derselben.* Halle: C. A. Kümmel, 1798.

Immanuel: Ein Buch für Christen und Juden. Oder: die völlige Vernichtung der natürlichen Religion durch die kritische Philosophie. Ein neuer Beweis für die Nothwendigkeit und Wünschenswürdigkeit der in der Bibel wirklich enthaltenen Offenbarung. Berlin: F. Nicolai, 1805. [No editor.] Reprint. Brussels: Culture et civilisation, 1968.

Jenisch, Daniel. *Ueber Grund und Werth der Entdeckungen des Herrn Professor Kant in der Metaphysik, Moral und Aesthetik. Nebst einem Sendschreiben des Verfassers an Herrn Professor Kant über die bisherigen günstigen und ungünstigen Einflüsse der kritischen Philosophie.* Berlin: Friedrich Vieweg dem Älteren, 1796. Reprint. Brussels: Culture et civilisation, 1973.

Koppelmann, Wilhelm. *Immanuel Kant und die Grundlagen der christlichen Religion.* Gütersloh: C. Bertelsmann, 1890.

Kügelgen, Constantin von. *Immanuel Kants Auffassung von der Bibel und seine Auslegung derselben: Ein Kompendium Kantscher Theologie.* Leipzig: A. Deichert, 1896.

Mayer, Emil Hugo Walter. *Das Verhältniss der Kantischen Religions-Philosophie zu dem Ganzen des Kantischen Systems.* Halle: [s.n.], 1879; Berlin: Kayssler & Co.: [s.d.].

Mengel, Wilhelm. *Kants Begründung der Religion. Ein kritischer Versuch.* Leipzig: W. Englemann, 1899.

Obereit, Jacob Hermann. *Finale Vernunftkritik für das grade Herz.* Nürnberg: A. Schneider und Weigel, 1796.

Porter, Noah. *Kant's Ethics: A Critical Exposition.* 2nd ed. Chicago: S. C. Griggs, 1886.

Promnitz, Charlotte Friederike von. *Antischrift zur Vertheidigung der Vernunft und Religion, wider die Critik des Herrn Kant, in fünf Abhandlungen.* Berlin: [s.n.], 1796.

Reiner, Gregor Leonhard. *Kant's Theorie der reinmoralischen Religion mit Rücksicht auf das reine Christenthum kurz dargestellt.* Riga: J. F. Hartknoch, 1796.

Romundt, Heinrich. *Kants philosophische Religionslehre: Eine Frucht der gesamten Vernunftkritik.* Gotha, Germany: E. F. Thienemann, 1902.

Schrempf, Christoph. *Die christliche Weltanschauung und Kant's sittlicher Glaube: Eine religiöse Untersuchung.* Göttingen, Germany: Vandenhoeck & Ruprecht, 1891.

Storr, Gottlob Christian. *Bemerkungen über Kant's philosophische Religionslehre.* Trans. Friedrich Gottlieb Süskind. Tübingen: J. G. Cotta, 1794. Reprint. Brussels: Culture et civilisation, 1968. Translation of *Annotationes quaedam theologicae ad philosophicam Kantii de religione doctrinam.* Tübingen, Germany: [s.n.], 1793.

Treutmann, Max. *Darstellung und Beurteilung des Kantschen Pflichtbegriffs.* Marienburg: L. Giesow, 1888.

Zwanziger, Johann Christian. *Commentar über Herrn Professor Kants Kritik der praktischen Vernunft; nebst einem Sendschreiben an den gelehrten Herrn Censor in Rücksicht der dem Verfasser des Commentars in den gelehrten Gothaischen Zeitungen mitgetheilten kritischen Anmerkungen.* Leipzig: C. G. Hilscher, 1794. Reprint. Brussels: Culture et civilisation, 1968.

GLOSSARY

The German terms are usually given not as they appear in the original text, but in their modern spelling, so that they can be found more easily in a modern German dictionary. For translations from English to German, please see the Index.

A

Abbruch (tun)	impairment (to impair)
Aberglaube	superstition
Ableitung	derivation
Abscheu	loathing
Absicht	aim, intention, respect, view
abwürdigen	to degrade
Achtung	respect
allgemein	universal, general
allmächtig	omnipotent
allwissend	omniscient
Änderung	change
anerkennen	to acknowledge
angemessen	appropriate, adequate, commensurate
angenehm	agreeable
Anlage	predisposition
Anleitung	guidance
Anlockung	enticement
anmaßen (sich)	to presume, to (lay) claim
annehmen	to assume, to suppose, to take, to accept
Anschauung	intuition
Anspruch	claim, pretension
Anstrengung	endeavor
Antrieb	impulse
Art	kind, way, manner, mode
auferlegen	to impose, to enjoin
Aufführung	behavior
Aufgabe	problem, task, assignment
aufheben	to annul
auflösen	to solve, to resolve
Aufmerksamkeit	attentiveness, attention
Aufopferung	sacrifice
Aufrichtigkeit	sincerity
aufstellen	to put forth, to adduce, to pose, to list
aufzeigen	to show
Augenblick	moment, instant
augenscheinlich	obvious
ausmachen	to amount to, to establish, to decide
äußer	external, outer

233

ausüben	to exercise, to per-	Bestimmungsgrund	determining basis
	form, to carry	Bestrafung	punishment
	out, to exert	Bestrebung	endeavor, striving
Autonomie	autonomy	bestreiten	to dispute
		betrachten	to consider, to
			regard, to
B			examine
		Betrachtung	contemplation,
bedeuten	to signify, to		consideration
	mean	Betragen	behavior
Bedingung	condition	Bewegungsgrund	motive
bedürfen	to need, to require	Bewegursache	motivating cause
befolgen	to comply with, to	Beweis	proof
	follow	beweisen	to prove
befriedigen	to satisfy	Bewunderung	admiration
Befugnis	authority	Bewußtsein	consciousness
Begebenheit	event	bezeichnen	to designate
begehen	to commit, to	Beziehung	reference, rela-
	perpetrate		tion, regard
Begehrung, Begierde	desire	bezweifeln	to doubt
begreifen	to comprehend	billigen	to approve
Begriff	concept	Blendwerk	deception,
Beharrlichkeit	perseverance,		illusion
	permanence	Bösartigkeit	malice
behaupten	to assert, to main-	böse	evil
	tain, to claim,	Bosheit	villainy
	to affirm	Brauchbarkeit	usefulness
Beistimmung	assent		
bekannt	familiar		
Bemühung	endeavor	**C**	
Benennung	designation		
Beobachtung	observation,	Charakter	character
	observance		
berechtigen	to entitle		
Beschaffenheit	character(istic),	**D**	
	constitution		
beschränkt	limited	darlegen	to set forth, to
Beschuldigung	accusation		display
besonder	particular, special	darstellen	to exhibit
bestätigen	to confirm	Darstellung	exhibition
bestehen	to consist, to	dartun	to establish
	subsist	Dasein	existence
Bestimmung	determination,	Dauer	duration
	vocation,	dauerhaft	lasting
	attribute	Demut	humility

denken	to think	Empfindung	sensation
Denkungs-	of thinking, of thought	Endabsicht	final aim
		Endzweck	final purpose
deutlich	distinct	entdecken	to discover, to un-
dienlich	useful		cover, to reveal
Ding	thing	entscheiden	to decide
Ding an sich (selbst)	thing in itself	erdulden	to endure
durchgängig	thoroughgoing, throughout, thoroughly	Erfahrung(s)	experience (experiential, of experience)
		Ergötzung	delight
		ergründen	to fathom
	E	erhaben	sublime, exalted
		erheben	to elevate, to raise
echt	genuine	erkennen	to cognize, to
edel	noble		recognize
Ehre	honor, glory	Erkenntnis(-)	cognition (cognitive, of cognition)
Ehrfurcht	reverence		
Eigendünkel	self-conceit, conceit for oneself	erklären	to explicate, to explain, to declare
Eigenliebe	love for oneself		
Eigennutz	self-interest	Erlassung	remission
Eigenschaft	property	erlauben	to allow, to per-
Einbildung	imagination, imagining, conceit		mit, to grant
		erläutern	to elucidate
Einheit	unity	erreichen	to attain, to
einhellig	accordant		achieve
Einhelligkeit	agreement	Erscheinung	appearance
einleuchtend	evident, plausible	Erstaunen	amazement
einräumen	to grant, to concede, to admit	erweitern (sich)	to expand
		Evidenz	(self-)evidence
Einschränkung	restriction, limitation	ewig	eternal
		Existenz	existence
einsehen	to have (gain) insight into, to see		
Einsicht	insight		**F**
Einstimmung	agreement, accordance, harmony		
		Fähigkeit	capacity
		falsch	false
Einwurf	objection	fassen	to grasp
einzeln	individual	Fehler	mistake, error
eitel	vain	Feld	realm
empfänglich	susceptible, receptive	festsetzen	to establish
		feststehen	to be established

Folge	consequence	gesetzwidrig	unlawful
Folgerung	inference	Gesinnung	attitude
fordern	to demand, to require	gewiß	certain
		Gewissen	conscience
fördern	to further	Gewohnheit	habit, custom
forschen	to investigate, to search	Glaube	faith
		glauben	to believe
Freiheit	freedom	gleichartig	homogeneous
freiwillig	voluntary	Gleichheit	equality
fühlen	to feel	gleichgültig	indifferent
Fürwahrhalten	assent	Gleisnerei	hypocrisy
		Glück	fortune
		glücklich	happy, fortunate, favorable

G

		Glückseligkeit	happiness
Gang	progression, course, path	Gott(heit)	God (deity)
		Grenzen	bounds, boundaries
Ganzes	whole		
Gebot	command	Größe	magnitude
Gedanke	thought	Großmut	magnanimity
Gefühl	feeling, touch	Grund	basis, ground, reason
Gegenstand	object		
Gegenteil	opposite, contrast	Grundlage	foundation
Gehalt	import	Grundsatz	principle
gehorchen	to obey	gültig	valid
Geist	spirit, intellect	Güte	benignity
Gelegenheit	occasion, opportunity		
Gelehrsamkeit	scholarship		

H

gelten	to hold, to count		
gemäßigt	moderate	Handlung	action
gemein(sam)	common	Hang	propensity
Gemüt(s-)	mind (mental)	heilig	holy, sacred
genau	exact, accurate	herabsetzen	to downgrade, to degrade
Genuß	enjoyment		
Gerechtigkeit	justice	heucheln	to be hypocritical
Geschäft	task, business, occupation	hinreichend	sufficient
		Hirngespinst	chimera
Geschöpf	creature		
Gesetz	law		
gesetzgebend	legislative, legislating	**I**	
gesetzlich	legal	Imperativ	imperative
gesetzmäßig	lawful	Individuum	individual

inne	aware	Mäßigung	moderation
inner	inner, internal, intrinsic	Maßregel (-stab)	guideline (standard)
Irrtum	error	Maxime	maxim
		meinen	to mean, to deem, to suppose, to think

K

kategorisch	categorical	Meinung	opinion, intent, intention
kennen	to be acquainted (familiar) with, to cognize, to know	Mensch(heit)	human being (humanity)
Kenntnis(se)	acquaintance, knowledge, cognition(s)	Merkmal	characteristic, mark
		mißbilligen	to disapprove
klar	clear, evident	Mitleid	sympathy
klug	prudent	mitteilen	to communicate
konsequent	consistent	Mittel	means
Kraft	power, force, strength	mittelbar	indirect
		möglich	possible
Kritik	critique	Moral(ität)	morality
kritisch	critical	moralisch	moral
		Moralist	moralist
		Muster	model
		Mut	courage, mettle

L

N

Lassen	refraining	Nachahmung	imitation, imitating
Laster	vice		
Lauterkeit	purity	nachdenken	to meditate
Lehre	doctrine, science, teaching	Nachforschung	investigation
		Nachsicht	forbearance
Lehrsatz	theorem	nachsinnen	to reflect
letzt	ultimate	Neigung	inclination
leugnen	to deny	nichtig	null, void
locken	to entice	nichtswürdig	worthless
Lust	pleasure	nötig	needed
		nötigen	to compel

M

		Nötigung	necessitation
mannigfaltig	manifold, ample	notwendig	necessary
Maß	measure, extent, degree	Nutzen	benefit, utility

O

oberst	supreme
Objekt	object
objektiv	objective
Obliegenheit	obligation
offenbar	manifest, obvious
Opfer	sacrifice
Ordnung	order

P

parteiisch	partial
Persönlichkeit	personality
Pflicht	duty
pflichtmäßig	conforming to (in conformity with) duty
pflichtwidrig	contrary to duty
Philosophie	philosophy
praktisch	practical
preisen	to praise
Primat	primacy
Prinzip	principle
Probe	test
Probierstein	touchstone
prüfen	to test
Prüfung	examination

Q

Quelle	source

R

rational	rational
real	real
recht	proper, right, quite
Recht	right
rechtfertigen	to justify

rechtmäßig	legitimate
rechtschaffen	righteous
Regel	rule
Reich	kingdom
Reihe	series
rein	pure
reizen	to stimulate
Reue	repentance
richtig	correct
Richtmaß, -schnur	standard, guidance

S

Sache	thing, matter, business
Satz	proposition, principle
schätzen	to esteem
Schein	illusion
scheinbar	seeming, specious, plausible
schicklich	fitting
Schlechte, das	the bad
schlechterdings, schlechthin	absolutely, simply
schließen	to conclude, to infer, to make (an) inference(s)
Schluß	inference
Schmerz	pain
Schöpfung	creation
Schranke	limit
Schuld	guilt
schuldfrei	innocent
Schwäche	weakness
Schwanken	wavering
schwärmen	to rove
Schwärmerei	fanaticism
Seele	soul
Selbstliebe	self-love
Selbstsucht	selfishness

Seligkeit	bliss	tugendhaft	virtuous
setzen	to place, to put, to set, to suppose, to posit	Tun	doing
		tunlich	feasible
		Tunlichkeit	practicability
sicher	secure, safe, sure		
Sinn	sense, mind		
sinnlich	sensible	**U**	
Sitten	morals		
sittlich	moral	übel	bad
Sittlichkeit	morality	überall	at all, throughout, everywhere
sollen	ought, to be to, should		
		überdenken	to reflect upon
Stärke	strength, fortitude	Übereinstimmung	agreement, harmony
Stolz	pride		
Strafe	punishment	überhaupt	as such, in general, at all
streben	to strive		
Streit	conflict	überlegen	to deliberate
streiten	to dispute	überschwenglich	extravagant
Streitigkeit	controversy	übersinnlich	suprasensible
streng	strict, severe, stern	übertreten	to transgress
		überwinden	to overcome
Stück	component, item, point	überzeugen	to convince
		umändern	to transform
Subjekt	subject	unablässig	unceasingly
subjektiv	subjective	unaufhörlich	incessantly, unceasing
		unausbleiblich	unfailingly
T		unbedingt	unconditioned, unconditional
Tadel	censure, blemish	unbezweifelt	indubitable
tadeln	to rebuke	Unding	absurdity
Tat	deed	unecht	spurious
Tätigkeit	activity	unempfindlich	insensitive
tauglich	suitable	unendlich	infinite
Täuschung	delusion, illusion	unentbehrlich	indispensable
teilnehmend	compassionate	unerläßlich	irremissible
theoretisch	theoretical	unfehlbar	unfailing
Tier(heit)	animal(ity)	ungereimt	absurd
transzendent	transcendent	ungezweifelt	indubitable
transzendental	transcendental	Unglaube	lack of faith
treu	faithful	ungleichartig	different in kind, heterogeneous
Triebfeder	incentive		
trüglich	deceptive	Unlust	displeasure
Tugend	virtue	unmittelbar	direct

unnachläßlich	unremittingly	Verbrechen	crime
unrecht	wrong	verdienen	to deserve
unschuldig	innocent	Verdienst	merit
Unsterblichkeit	immortality	Verehrung	veneration
unterlassen	to omit, to abstain	vereinigen	to unite, to
unterscheiden,	to distinguish		reconcile
Unterschied	distinction,	Verfahren	procedure
	difference	vergeblich	futile, vain
untersuchen	to investigate	Vergehung	offense
ununterbrochen	uninterrupted	Vergnügen	gratification
unverletzlich	inviolable	Verhalten	conduct, behaving
unvermeidlich	unavoidable,	Verhältnis	relation, propor-
	inevitable		tion
unwandelbar	immutable	verheißen	to promise
unwidersprechlich	incontestable	verhindern	to prevent
Unwissenheit	ignorance	verhüten	to prevent, to
Urbild	archetype		keep from, to
Urgrund	original basis		help
Urheber	originator	verkennen	to fail to
Ursache	cause, reason		recognize
Ursprung	origin	Verknüpfung	connection
Urteil(s)	judgment (of	verlangen	to demand, to
	judgment)		require
urteilen	to judge, to make	Verlegenheit	perplexity
	(a) judgment(s)	verletzen	to violate
Urwesen	original being	Verleugnung	denial
		Verleumder	defamer
		vermeiden	to avoid
V		Vermögen	power, ability,
			assets
verabscheuen	to loathe	Vermutung	presumption
verachten	to despise	vernichten	to annihilate
Verachtung	contempt	Vernunft	reason
Veränderung	change	Vernunft-	rational, of rea-
veranlassen	to prompt, to		son, reason's
	occasion	Vernünfteln	subtle reasoning
verantwortlich	responsible	vernünftig	reasonable,
verbieten	to forbid		rational
verbinden	to combine, to	Vernunftschluß	syllogism, infer-
	link, to oblige,		ence of reason
	to obligate	verraten	to betray
verbindend	obligatory	verrichten	to perform, to
Verbindlichkeit	obligation		accomplish

versäumen	to neglect
verschieden	different, various
Verstand	understanding, meaning, mind
verstehen	to understand, to mean
verstoßen	to offend
Versuch	attempt, experiment
Versuchung	temptation
verteidigen	to defend
verträglich	compatible
verwandeln	to transform, to convert
verweigern	to refuse
verwerflich	reprehensible
Verwirrung	confusion
Vollendung	perfection, completion
vollkommen	perfect, complete
vollständig	complete
voraussetzen	to presuppose
Vorbedacht, mit	deliberately
vorgeben	to allege, to profess
Vorsatz	project, resolve
vorsätzlich	deliberate
vorschreiben	to prescribe
Vorschrift	precept
vorstellen (sich)	to present, to conceive, to represent
Vorstellung	presentation, presenting, conception
Vorteil	advantage
Vortrag	exposition
vortragen	to set forth, to propound
Vorzug	superiority, advantage, pre-eminence, merit

W

wählen	to select, to choose
Wahn(sinn)	delusion (madness)
wahr(haftig)	true (truly)
wahrnehmen	to perceive
wechselseitig	reciprocal
Weg	path, way
weigern (sich)	to refuse
weihen	to dedicate, to devote
Weisheit	wisdom
Weite	distance
Werk	work
Wert	worth, value
Wesen	being, essence
wesentlich	essential
wichtig	important
widerlegen	to refute
widersinnisch	paradoxical
widersprechend	contradictory
Widerstand	resistance
widerstehen	to oppose
Widerstrebung	resistance
Widerstreit	conflict
widmen	to devote, to dedicate
Wille	will
Willkür	power of choice
willkürlich	chosen, by choice
wirklich	actual
wirksam	efficient, active
Wirkung	effect, action
Wissen	knowledge
Wissenschaft	science
Wohl(befinden), Wohlsein	well-being
Wohlgefallen	liking, fondness
Wohltat	benefaction
Wohlwollen	benevolence
Würde	dignity

würdig	worthy	zureichend	sufficient
		Zusammenhang	coherence, connection
Z		zusammenhängen	to be linked
		zusammenstimmen	to agree, to har-
zeigen	to show, to		monize, to be
	manifest		harmonious
Zeit	time	zuschreiben	to ascribe
Zeitalter	age	Zustand	state, situation
zergliedern	to dissect	zuträglich	conducive,
Ziel	goal		beneficial
Zucht	discipline	Zutrauen	trust
zufällig	contingent	Zuversicht	confidence
Zufriedenheit	satisfaction	zuwider	contrary, opposed
zugleich	at the same time,	Zwang	constraint
	simultaneous,	Zweck	purpose
	also, as well	zweckmäßig	purposive
zulangen	to be sufficient	zweideutig	ambiguous
Zulänglichkeit	adequacy	Zweifel	doubt
zuletzt	ultimately, finally	Zweifellehre	skepticism
zumuten	to require, to demand		

INDEX

All references are to the numbers in the margin of the text, which follow the pagination of the *Akademie* edition on which this translation is based. Headings are arranged alphabetically, but subheadings are ordered by affinity of topics. The sequence of the individual references follows the arrangement of the text in this volume, except that indirect references (introduced by 'cf.') follow direct references as a group. References to Kant's own notes are marked by 'n.' or the plural 'ns.' References to the translator's bracketed notes are marked by 'br. n.' or 'br. ns.' (Notes identified by lower-case letters are notes to other notes; see the Translator's Preface for further details.) Works by Kant are listed by their English titles, with the original titles given in parentheses. Other authors are listed here only by their names; their works, insofar as these are cited in this translation, are listed in the Selected Bibliography.

Abel, Jacob Friedrich von, 12 br. n. 95

Ability (*Vermögen*), 3 br. n. 7, 9 br. n. 90c, 12, 13, 20, 23, 32 br. n. 80, 33 br. n. 91, 37, 57 incl. br. n. 243, 58, 94, 109, 113, 121, 127 incl. br. n. 151m, 129, 132, 135, 136 br. n. 229, 143 n. 282, 160, 161, *see also* Power, Capacity, Inability

Absolute(ly) (*absolut* [*schlechthin, schlechterdings*]), 3 incl. br. ns. 2 and 15, 14, 20, 28, 31, 43, 48, 58, 59 br. n. 259, 60, 62, 64, 70, 74, 81, 90, 97, 99, 107 incl. br. n. 3, 111, 113, 114, 134, 139, 142 n. 271, 143

Abstract(ed) *or* abstractly (*abstrakt, abstrahiert, abziehen* [*abgezogen*]), 10 br. n. 91, 21, 49, 51, 109, 134, 137, 155, see also *Abstracto: in*

Abstracto: in, 67, *see also* Abstract, *Concreto: in*

Absurd(ity) (*ungereimt* [*Unding*]), 37, 56, 98, 102, 144

Accidents (*Akzidenzen*), 102, *see also* Contingent

Accordance *or* accordant (*Einstimmigung, einhellig*), 20, 24, 26, 28, 46, 54, 87, 105, 110, 112, 120, 131, 146, cf. 7 br. n. 73, *see also* Agree

Acquaintance *or* be acquainted with (*Kenntnis, kennen*), 8, 10, 35 br. n. 120, 36, 55, 56, 81 br. n. 377a, 99, 113, 138, 139, *see also* Familiarity, Cognition, Knowledge, Expert, Unacquainted

Action *or* act (*Handlung, Wirkung, handeln, wirken*), 3 br. n. 11, 8 br. ns. 78

243

Mysticism *or* mystic (*Mystizismus, Mystiker*), 70, 71 incl. br. n. 310, 120

Natorp, Paul, 5 br. n. 57, 7 br. n. 73, 8 br. n. 83a, 9 br. n. 90*l*, 34 br. ns. 98 and 106, 56 br. n. 233, 57 br. n. 240, 62 br. n. 273, 63 br. n. 276, 64 br. n. 279, 70 br. n. 304, 71 br. n. 308, 73 br. n. 333, 75 br. n. 345, 80 br. n. 372, 117 br. n. 66, 147 br. n. 312, 159 br. n. 90

Natural (*Natur*[-], *natürlich*), order as such, 128; law, *see* Law; connection (linkage), 69, 100, 119, 143; causes, 140; mechanism, 6 n. 64, 102; possibility, 67 incl. br. n. 293; necessity, 34, 49, 94–99, 114; conditions, 66; consequence, 37, 98; hints, 146; science, 26 n. 52 and br. n. 52a, 51, 53; occupation, 159; ability (powers), 94, 127 n. 151; human reason, 91; idea, 87; thought, 140; point of view, 99; need, 108; gratification, 34; moderate vital motion of the heart, 157; basis, determining an action, 96; aversion, 86; punishment, 38; constitution of the minds of young villains, 99–100; dialectic, 108; illusion, 108; member in the chain of purposes, 120 br. n. 93; perfection, 123 n. 125; simplicity, prudence, wisdom, and holiness, 127 n. 151; theologians, 137; *see also* Nature, Physical, Supranatural

Nature (*Natur*), in the most general meaning, 43; as such, 97; concepts of, 68; categories (pure form of understanding) of, 65, 70; of the world of sense, 70; constitution of, 44 incl. br. n. 183; as a whole (whole of), 44, 125; arrangements of, 138; path (course) of, 139, 145; steady chain of, 95; (possible) order of, 44, 45; law of, *see* Law (natural); mechanism of (all of), 29, 30, 87, 97, 100, 114; events in, 28; objects of, 69; contemplation

(investigation, study, observer) of, 141, 148, 160, 163; cognition of, 19, 45, 55, 146; our (human, animal), 8 incl. br. n. 87, 61, 74, 82, 87, 127 n. 151, 137, 146, 152, 158, 162, 163; (our) finite, 25; pathologically affected, 88; of human cognition, 10; of the (our) soul, 94, 133; moral vocation of (our), 122, cf. 87, 146; sublimity of our, 87, 117; possible, 46; actual(ity of), 44, 45, cf. 46; sensible, 43, 47, 71; suprasensible, 43, 45, 47, cf. 44; intelligible, 70, 152; archetypal and ectypal, 43 incl. br. n. 174; and freedom, 67 br. n. 293, 97; and morals, 128, 145, *see also* Morals; purposiveness in, 142, 145; final purpose beyond, 120 br. n. 93; basis of, 125; (supreme) cause of, 124, 125; (intelligible, wise) originator of (presiding over), 115, 145; *see also* Natural, World

Necessary (*notwendig, nötig*), 4, 5, 7–9 incl. n. 90, 11 n. 93, 13, 25, 29, 32, 34–36, 42, 46, 48, 50–53 incl. br. n. 221, 56, 58, 63 72, 74, 84, 90–92, 94–96, 98, 100, 101, 104–06, 111, 113–17, 119–22, 124, 125, 128, 129, 130 br. n. 174, 132–35, 139, 141, 142 n. 271, 143 incl. n. 282, 145, 146, 151, 155, 162; object, law, aim, *see these headings;* subjectively, objectively, practically, morally, *see* Subjective, Objective, Practical, Moral; determination (object) of the will, *see* Will; *see also* Needed, Necessity, Necessitation, Unnecessary

Necessitation (*Nötigung*), 20, 32, 80–84, 96, 117, cf. 20 br. n. 17; practical, *see* Practical; moral, *see* Moral; *see also* Necessary, Will

Necessity (*Notwendigkeit*), 4 incl. br. n. 38, 11 n. 93, 12–14 incl. br. n. 98, 20, 22, 26, 30, 32, 34, 42, 49, 51–54, 57,